رحيم

قدم الى اخينا واختنا العزيزية

السيد الفاضل خبير والسيدة المكرمة

احسان

من هذا الفقير الى ربه

سيد حسين نصر

والحمد لله وحده

In Search of the Sacred

Selected Works by Seyyed Hossein Nasr in English

The Essential Seyyed Hossein Nasr (2007; ed. W. Chittick)
The Garden of Truth (2008)
The Heart of Islam (2004)
Ideals and Realities of Islam (2001)
An Introduction to Islamic Cosmological Doctrines (1993)
Islam: Religion, History, and Civilization (2003)
Islam and the Plight of Modern Man (2002)
Islamic Art and Spirituality (1987)
The Islamic Intellectual Tradition in Persia (1996)
Islamic Life and Thought (2001)
Islamic Philosophy from Its Origin to the Present (2006)
Islamic Science: An Illustrated Study (1995)
Islam, Science, Muslims, and Technology (2007)
Knowledge and the Sacred (1989)
Man and Nature: The Spiritual Crisis of Modern Man (1997)
Muhammad: Man of God (1988)
The Need for Sacred Science (1993)
The Pilgrimage of Life and the Wisdom of Rumi (2007)
Poems of the Way (1999)
Religion and the Order of Nature (1996)
Ṣadr al-Dīn Shīrazī (1997)
Science and Civilization in Islam (1997)
Sufi Essays (1991)
Three Muslim Sages (1986)
Traditional Islam in the Modern World (1990)
A Young Muslim's Guide to the Modern World (1993)

In Search of the Sacred

A Conversation with Seyyed Hossein Nasr on His Life and Thought

Seyyed Hossein Nasr with Ramin Jahanbegloo

Introduction by Terry Moore

AN IMPRINT OF ABC-CLIO, LLC
Santa Barbara, California • Denver, Colorado • Oxford, England

Library of Congress Cataloging-in-Publication Data

Nasr, Seyyed Hossein.
In search of the sacred : a conversation with Seyyed Hossein Nasr on his life and thought / Seyyed Hossein Nasr with Ramin Jahanbegloo ; introduction by Terry Moore.
p. cm.
Includes index.
ISBN 978-0-313-38324-3 (hard copy : alk. paper)—ISBN 978-0-313-38325-0 (ebook)
1. Nasr, Seyyed Hossein—Interviews. 2. Muslim philosophers—Interviews. 3. Muslim philosophers—Biography. 4. Islamic philosophy. I. Jahanbegloo, Ramin. II. Title.
B5074.N374A3 2010
181′.5—dc22 2010002983

ISBN: 978-0-313-38324-3
EISBN: 978-0-313-38325-0

14 13 12 11 10 1 2 3 4 5

This book is also available on the World Wide Web as an eBook.
Visit www.abc-clio.com for details.

Praeger
An Imprint of ABC-CLIO, LLC

ABC-CLIO, LLC
130 Cremona Drive, P.O. Box 1911
Santa Barbara, California 93116-1911

This book is printed on acid-free paper ∞

Manufactured in the United States of America

Contents

Introduction

The Spiritual and Intellectual Journey of Seyyed Hossein Nasr

G. K. Chesterton wrote: "There are two main moral necessities for the work of a great man: the first is that he should believe in the truth of his message; the second is that he should believe in the acceptability of his message." Seyyed Hossein Nasr has both. An Islamic philosopher of rare exemplarity, he has also been all through his life a man of dialogue with different faiths and diverse cultures. Not only has Nasr heralded a renaissance of Islamic sciences, but he has also been the agent and mediator through whom, in our day, the perennial philosophy has found a second birth. An unrelenting opponent of religious fundamentalism in all its forms throughout his career, Nasr presents his critique of modernity as a vision rooted in a traditional Muslim understanding of the world that respects both nature and human dignity.

For Nasr, the traditional world was based on an overwhelming sense of the Sacred and the Absolute, whereas the invention of modernity involved precisely the dissolution of that awareness, resulting in what Max Weber would call the "disenchantment of the world." Nasr's critique of modernity, while being a severe condemnation of secularism, is not a call for regression. Like his inspirers of the Perennialist School—René Guénon, Amanda K. Coomaraswamy, and Frithjof Schuon—Seyyed Hossein Nasr provides his reader with a rigorous definition of what he understands by the term *tradition*. Nasr considers tradition as the principal milestone for spiritual authenticity and an infinite source of grace. Tradition, as described by Nasr, is the whole structure of thought that articulates the concepts embodied in the world of myth and symbols. This is why, according to Nasr, there has always been in the history of mankind, before the rise of modernity, an esoteric aspect to all traditions that reached to God and understood all things in God. Since the secularization of the Christian tradition and the techno-scientific domination of the world by the Western world in the last few hundred years, however, all traditions have been undergoing secularization.

Actually, Nasr's critique of secularization in the modern world is far from being an obscurantist attempt to idealize tradition. On the contrary, his attempt to reestablish the esoteric tradition has created new grounds for a genuine comparative study of religions. One begins to see here how much of Nasr's work has to do with tradition as something alive and a ceaselessly renewed insight. Nasr would himself be the first to recognize that tradition is an ever renewed vision of life. He is in a sense himself a remarkable product of the living traditions of Iran and Islam. In fact, unlike his traditionalist and perennialist predecessors, he identifies closely with a unique religious tradition that is Islam, while being an active member of the Iranian society in the years before the 1979 Iranian Revolution. Still, Nasr has subscribed all his life to Meister Eckhart's formula: "If you want the kernel, you need to break the husk." Unlike his teacher Frithjof Schuon, Nasr's point of departure has been Islam and not Advaita Vedanta. However, like Schuon, he believes in the multileveled structure of Reality and the Divine Will. Esoterism is for Nasr nothing less than the most comprehensive grammar of the Self. Nasr's understanding of Schuon's notion of "quintessential esoterism" finds its true universalist perspective in the former's reading of famous Sufi thinkers such as Ibn 'Arabī or Rūmī. In his *Tarjumān al-ashwāq*, Ibn 'Arabī sings:

My heart is open to all forms;
It is a pasture for gazelles
And a home for Christian monks,
A temple for idols,
The Black Stone of the Ka'bah,
The tablet of the Torah
And the book of the Quran.
Wherever God's caravans turn,
The religion of love shall be my religion
And my faith.

Following the paths of Ibn 'Arabī, Meister Eckhart, Rūmī and others, Nasr's opus is a quest for the "essential elements of communiality" among religions and a demonstration of the "transcendent unity of religions" based on an interfaith dialogue. His philosophical work includes indeed both a metaphysical and an erudite demonstration of such communiality at the summit of the great religious traditions and contains a strong response to the predominant relativism in today's world.

Another relevant aspect of Nasr's outlook is his spiritual journey toward sacred art. Very few authors have actually covered, in the manner and style of Seyyed Hossein Nasr, the highlighted themes of traditional art, architecture, calligraphy, music, poetry, and prose literature in Islamic lands. Nasr treats Islamic art as a manifestation of the unity of Islam. As in the case of Islamic sciences, Islamic art, according to Nasr, came into being from a wedding between the spirit that issued from the Quranic revelation and the artistic techniques that Islamic civilization inherited from the civilizations that preceded it, especially the Persian and the Byzantine. For him, both the arts and the sciences in Islam are based on the idea of unity, which is the heart of the Islamic revelation. To understand the Islamic arts and sciences in their essence, therefore, requires an understanding of some of the principles of Islam itself.

Nasr demonstrates in his work that it is necessary and also reasonable to see Islam in a positive light despite the recent atrocities committed in its name, as is also the case with other religions. Also, like all other religions, Islam has contributed numerous positive elements to humanity. Nasr is certainly aware of the deviations and corruptions of certain currents within Islam and other religions in the modern world. However, he places the greatest emphasis on the application of spiritual principles of traditions in solving the crisis of the modern world.

Each tradition, Nasr affirms, has a wealth of principial knowledge. The resuscitation of this knowledge, he argues, would allow religions all over the globe to enrich one another and cooperate together to heal the wounds of the present-day secularized world.

In his work, Nasr traces the historical process through which Western civilization moved away from the idea of nature as sacred and embraced a worldview that sees human beings as alienated from nature and nature itself as a machine to be dominated and manipulated by them. Thus he argues that the devastation of our world has been exacerbated, if not actually caused, by the reductionist view of nature that has been advanced by modern secular science. Consequently, his goal is to negate the totalitarian claims of modern science and to reopen the way to the religious view of the order of nature, developed over centuries in the cosmologies and sacred sciences of the great traditions.

In addition to his natural sensibility to the beauty and majesty of nature, Nasr provides a knowledge that invites his readers to reexamine traditional ideas and values in order to be able to tackle the contemporary predicament of the environmental crisis. In other words, one cannot analyze Nasr's contribution to the world of the spirit without taking into account his contribution to a new ecological vision. Nasr's work is, therefore, an organic whole that covers a plurality of dimensions such as science, metaphysics, art, religion, and so forth.

A prolific writer and a gnostic thinker, Nasr remains above all an encyclopedic mind who combines in a masterly manner his own Islamic tradition with that of the East and the West. To put it another way, Seyyed Hossein Nasr has inherited his Islamic scholarship and also perennial and comparative spiritual identity from a long and prestigious line of remarkable thinkers and wise men who provided him with a coherent and cohesive religious and civilizational framework. Through them he learned that having a real religious dialogue depends on acquiring an open mind and an open heart. Dialogue is, therefore, for Nasr, not only a pursuit of truth, but also a challenge to spiritual responsibility in a secular world heading for a forced uniformity imposed by a single set of secularized values. Nasr is quite aware of the fact that the world of the 21st century is standing at the edge of a precipice. Civilization to him, as to Gandhi, Tagore, and many other sage figures of the 20th century, is not equivalent to progress in science, technology, and industry. For Nasr, a civilization is like a living organism: it grows and changes and adapts itself to the ever-changing environments; and yet in this process, the central core and the roots of a civilization are capable of resisting historical changes, and at the same time producing new manifestations in conformity with this essential reality. This is how, in its own unique way, it offers its members paths of self-transcendence.

A true dialogue among religious traditions and civilizations must be based on a universalist outlook that enables people of different faiths to transcend their differences and arrive at unity. But Nasr is quite aware of the fact that dialogue among religions is not an easy task. He is even more concerned with the difficulty of "unlearning intolerance." "It is very easy to learn intolerance and unlearn tolerance, but difficult to unlearn intolerance," he declared at a seminar on December 7, 2004, at the United Nations Headquarters in New York. It goes without saying that for Nasr the fear of religions by many people goes hand in hand with the lack of authentic knowledge about religious traditions. In his point of view, despite the modest gains made through dialogue in promoting better understanding between believers of different religions, dialogue has become increasingly vulnerable to popular mistrust in the eyes of many in the Western, but also in the non-Western, worlds. And yet, dialogue is not perceived by Nasr as an attempt to undermine one's own faith in order to preserve interfaith harmony and to promote peaceful coexistence at the expense of the destruction of the sacred traditions of various religions. Nasr has another vision for interfaith dialogue, where the goal is not to solve immediate political problems but to reach the "transcendental unity of religions." The unity claimed here is "transcendental" in the sense that it lies within the religions of the world without denying their forms.

Nasr's approach seems to hold out hope for a genuine dialogue between the Oriental and the Occidental cultures at their most profound level. According to Nasr, "the Sufi is one who seeks to transcend the world of forms, to journey from multiplicity to unity, from the particular to the Universal. It is this supreme doctrine of Unity . . . that the Sufis call the 'religion of love.' This love is not merely sentiment or emotions; it is the realized aspect of gnosis. It is a transcendental knowledge that reveals the inner unity of religions." There are two elements essential for Nasr in the making of traditional civilizations and also in the mutual understanding among them. One is knowledge (*'ilm*) and the other instruction (*ta'līm*). As Nasr explains, in Islam, the training of the mind was never separated from that of the soul. Islamic education is, therefore, concerned not only with the instruction and training of the mind and the transmission of knowledge (*'ilm*), but also with the education of the whole being of men and women (*ta'līm* combined with *tarbiyah*). The teacher is, therefore, not only a transmitter of knowledge (*mu'allim*), but also a trainer of souls and personalities (*murabbī*).

For fifty years, Seyyed Hossein Nasr has been a man in quest of truth, wisdom, and the sacred, but he has also served as a mentor to several generations of scholars in Islamic, religious, and philosophical studies. Through his writings and teachings, Nasr has been able to resuscitate the Islamic traditions of philosophy, science, and Sufism. His spiritual journey through different sacred scriptures and quest for wisdom has also been a quest for a knowledge that enables man to understand the essence of life, a wisdom that "liberates and delivers him from the fetters and limitations of earthly existence."

Today, at age 74, Nasr leads an extremely prolific intellectual life, with many future projects in hand, added to his present extraordinary corpus of books and articles in different languages, and an intense program of lectures and meetings around the world. His work has been a significant contribution to comparative religious studies with insights from a variety of disciplines. Today, from the immensely creative pen of Seyyed Hossein Nasr comes to us answers to the pressing issues of our fractured world.

These answers appear in this book of conversations with Nasr. What began as a dialogue between two close family members and two Iranian philosophers grew into a series of conversations (recorded in Washington, D.C. in 2000–2001), comprising a sort of intellectual memoir. They retrace Nasr's life and thoughts through a journey of self-discovery. This book recounts his childhood in Iran and later his formative years as an adolescent and a young student in America. It also focuses on the stages of his career around the world (with special emphasis upon his forced exile from Iran since the Islamic Revolution of 1979). It is hoped that these conversations will provide a thorough introduction to Nasr's thoughts on Islam, Sufism, and Persian art, tradition, and modernism, but also a fitting history of the ideas of individuals who shaped Seyyed Hossein Nasr's thought in one way or another. This book demonstrates that not only is Nasr a skillful writer covering fascinating topics of the history of Islamic thought and Sufism, and so forth, but that he is also best at engaging in a stimulating and educating intellectual conversation. As the book's title suggests, this is the biography of the intellectual and spiritual journey of Seyyed Hossein Nasr that focuses most strongly on his quest of the sacred and his search for truth.

In closing, I would like to express my thanks to the Radius Foundation for its help in producing the English edition of this book, and to Abigail Tardiff for her invaluable editorial and technical assistance.

Ramin Jahanbegloo

Who Is Seyyed Hossein Nasr?

As the famous American philosopher of religion Huston Smith has noted, it is rare indeed for both the highest accolade in philosophy and the highest accolade in theology to be bestowed upon the same individual.

The greatest honor the academic world grants to a living philosopher is the dedication of a volume of *The Library of Living Philosophers* to his work and thought; and the most prestigious recognition a thinker can receive in the field of natural theology is an invitation to deliver the annual Gifford Lectures at the University of Edinburgh. In the year 2000, the twenty-eighth volume of *The Library of Living Philosophers* was devoted to the philosophy of Seyyed Hossein Nasr, placing him in the company of Einstein, Sartre, Russell, Whitehead, and other luminaries of 20th-century intellectual life. Fourteen years previously, Nasr had delivered the Gifford Lectures, and the text of these lectures became his magnum opus, *Knowledge and the Sacred.*

Who is Seyyed Hossein Nasr, and what makes his work worthy of such international recognition? What does he have to offer our times that is so distinctive as to earn him such honors? For those who may not be familiar with his work, this brief introduction is my attempt to provide an overview of Nasr's accomplishments.

Nasr's life's work has been to expound and defend Tradition. At first glance, the prominence he gives to Tradition may puzzle the reader, because the modern ear hears *tradition* as *nostalgia.* We assume that the worldview of the past is false simply because it is outdated. But lurking behind this view is the assumption that our own vision is not subject to any kind of blindness peculiar to our times.

What makes Nasr a revolutionary thinker is his ability to throw into relief, in light of perennial truths, the false, yet unstated, cultural constructs that frame our vision of the world. Our metaphysical assumptions about the cosmos, which constrain the way we see the world around us, are so pervasive that we do not realize they exist at all. We believe, perhaps only half consciously, that other times looked at the cosmos through the filter of their own cultural biases, but that we moderns have no such filter. We think we simply see the world as it really is.

Nasr offers not only an exposure of our own false ideas, but a restoration of an unfragmented vision of reality, including the cosmos, that is rooted in something more stable than the styles of thought peculiar to any specific age or culture. Nasr makes a sharp and crucial distinction between tradition in the accustomed sense of the word, something like *folkways,* which indeed simply means customs that have been passed down from generation to generation, whose value lies in their power to unify us with our ancestors; and Tradition with a capital "T," which is our link with the Sacred, for which Nasr offers this definition: "the Sacred is the Eternal Absolute Truth as It manifests Itself in our world. It is the appearance of the Eternal in time, the Center in the periphery, of the Divine in the world of space and time. The Sacred is present in Itself and in Its manifestations." It is this connection with the Sacred that anchors Nasr's worldview.

The reader who believes in a religion whose claim to truth he accepts will understand the distinction between these two meanings of *tradition*. Religions claim not to be merely human inventions, but to have their source in revelation—a gift given directly by God to man. Now, if revelation is given at a certain point in time, but is intended to enlighten future generations as well, then there must be some means of transmitting its content through the ages. Nasr locates this vehicle of transmission in not only the doctrines, but also the rites and sacred art of what he terms "true religions." Thus the value of the past is not derived from its temporal distance from us, but from the connection it gives us, through revelation, to the Sacred here and now. For this reason, it is *only* through Tradition that we can be fully liberated from the biases of whatever cultural atmosphere we have been breathing all our lives. The value of Tradition is not that it is our path back to the past, but that it is our means of transcending our congenitally faulty vision, whose defects, without the timeless touch points of Tradition, we may not even be able to perceive.

Moreover, Nasr powerfully and brilliantly sets forth the urgency, for both man and society, of rebuilding this understanding of Tradition, lest both man and society lose all sense of purpose and descend into chaos. To see the wholeness of the worldview Nasr proposes, one must first of all be aware of the deficiencies of our own worldview, the narrowness of our culture's own pervasive myths. By throwing light on both the poverty of the modernistic vision of the cosmos and the truth of the Traditional understanding of the world, he sets forth a clear and compelling path for the seeker of Truth.

What is this impoverished worldview of modernity that Nasr seeks to expose and replace? Many of us have already accepted the idea that one of the prime ideologies of modernism we must reject is materialism, the belief that only matter exists. By rejecting materialism, we believe we transcend one of the cosmological biases peculiar to our culture. But Nasr takes us much further. Even those who are not materialists often speak as if we dwell in two separate worlds: the world of fact and matter and science, on the one hand, and the world of meaning and spirit and religion on the other. Most of us live our daily lives in the first world, and, if we strive to be what is vaguely termed "spiritual" people, we try to visit the second world as much as possible. Those who embrace a particular religion practice its rites, which are designed to raise the mind and heart to that which transcends the everyday world. Those who do not practice a religion may endeavor to be mindful of the beauty of nature or art, and to live selflessly.

But even those who recognize the existence of these two spheres—the realm of fact and the realm of meaning—have trouble integrating them. Those of us who believe, but have our footing mainly in the world of science, feel a little uncomfortable about theology, as if it were a friend with whom we would be embarrassed to be seen when people we respect are around. Or, if we orient ourselves more by our theology, we feel slightly distrustful of science—we remain always a little wary of it, in case it might reveal some fact that undermines our understanding of God. When thinkers who live mostly in the world of science add a bit of theology, it has an *ad hoc* artificial flavor to it; and when theologians speak of science, their remarks usually come across as the same kind of afterthought.

Nasr solves the problem of this bifurcation of the world by bringing Tradition into "now." He explains how the timeless truths of Tradition are not disconnected from our own times and issues. He brings the wisdom of the ages to bear on answering questions about the nature of the world and our place in it. And he lets this wisdom inform us about ourselves and about our relationships with the natural world, with the World of Spirit, and with each other. His ability to situate our world and thought within the perspective of Tradition and perennial wisdom is unequalled by any other living thinker.

In the present work and elsewhere, Seyyed Hossein Nasr contrasts today's understanding of what it means to be human with the traditional concept of man. Modern Western man understands himself according to the paradigm of Prometheus, a creature of Earth who has rebelled against Heaven. But traditional man does not reject Heaven in order to become purely a creature of Earth; instead, he sees himself as an intermediary between Earth and Heaven, standing simultaneously on both shores of existence. Traditional man understands himself not as a rebel, but as a bridge, a *pontifex*.

When one examines the life and work of Seyyed Hossein Nasr, this image of a bridge emerges again and again. There are good grounds for seeing Nasr himself as a modern example of a Pontifical Man, for he bridges many shores between which there had formerly been little commerce.

A bridge cannot allow communication between two lands unless it has an equally firm foundation in each one. It is these dual foundations on many divergent pairs of shores that account for Nasr's unique contributions to our times. He enables true discourse, for example, between traditional sacred science and modern Western science; between Islamic tradition and the Western world; between Tradition and contemporary language and art; between the perennial philosophy and mainstream

Western thought; and between perennialist and modern philosophies of nature. He offers a critique of Western modernity not only from the viewpoint of Tradition, but at the same time through the eyes of one who lives within the modern West and knows this world intimately.

Philosophy and Metaphysics

One of the distinguishing bridge-making features of Nasr's work has been his ability to present the pure metaphysics of the traditional authors and classical texts in a contemporary language. In doing so, he has made this abstruse and complex discipline more accessible to the large sector of people who are attracted to "the supreme science" but who otherwise would not have encountered these ideas or understood their relevance to modern times and to themselves.

His contribution in this way to the revival of metaphysics has been twofold. First, concerning Islamic philosophy, his works have been instrumental in resuscitating the Islamic philosophical tradition and in bringing out the significance, to the English-speaking world, of the works of neglected classical Islamic philosophers such as Mullā Ṣadrā and Suhrawardī. Within the discipline of Islamic philosophy there is really no other work like Nasr's, which issues from the belly, or bosom, of the living Islamic philosophical tradition, but is presented to the English-speaking world as an intrinsic part of the intellectual life of both Islamic civilization and today's world. Nasr's explication of Islamic philosophy treats it not as a "history of ideas," but as living philosophy—his work seeks understanding not merely of the society of a particular period of history, but of the truth itself. Much of this resuscitation of the Islamic intellectual tradition and its presentation to the English-speaking world has come about through the production of several key works, from *Three Muslim Sages*, texts of lectures given at Harvard University in 1962, which first revealed this new methodology of the study of Islamic philosophy, to his most recent book, *Islamic Philosophy from Its Origin to the Present: Philosophy in the Land of Prophecy*, which is a bird's-eye view of the whole tradition of Islamic philosophy, especially the later period, examined not for the light it might throw on social or intellectual history, but as authentic philosophy.

Second, in the field of Western philosophy, Nasr has synthesized and expanded the critique of the modern world that has already been carried out by Guénon, Coomaraswamy, Schuon, Burckhardt, and others, and he has furthermore been able to present this critique in an academic language that is of sufficient rigor to be acceptable to those trained in Western academic philosophy and the Western philosophical tradition, especially Cartesianism. This accomplishment is to be seen especially in his *Knowledge and the Sacred.* The creation of a kind of nexus or link between the perennial philosophy and mainstream Western philosophy and thought is perhaps his greatest legacy in this field, and his work has had extensive influence in many circles, far beyond those interested in the more strict sense of the definition of Tradition.

Fifty years ago, when scholars in the academic world in the West spoke about philosophy, the place of the perennial philosophy was not properly recognized; and when they spoke about Islamic philosophy, they spoke about only one period of Islamic philosophy, and that only insofar as it influenced the West. Today, scholars acknowledge the continuous and long Islamic philosophical tradition in its own right. This change is greatly a result of Nasr's work, though certainly Nasr was not alone in bringing this change—the works of such scholars as Corbin, Izutsu, and others have also been instrumental. But Nasr's influence has been immense, and it is also worth noting that it was Nasr's personal influence on Izutsu that turned Izutsu's attention toward the study of Islamic philosophy and resulted in the remarkable works that he then produced. Especially notable in this part of Nasr's legacy has been his work's influence on a number of Christian theologians and philosophers of religion. His key works in this area are *Knowledge and the Sacred* and *The History of Islamic Philosophy*, of which he was the chief editor. This latter work has influenced a whole younger generation of scholars in this field and will probably remain of the greatest influence for the next generation to come.

Perennialism and Tradition

Nasr is perhaps most often thought of as a philosopher of perennialism and tradition and is, indeed, this movement's greatest living spokesman and contributor. Part of his achievement, Nasr would say, is to have remained, since his twenties, faithful to the purely traditional perspective, and not to have been swayed by the modernist ideas that are so prevalent in our times. It is this authenticity that has allowed his work not only to reformulate and reflect the ideas of the founders of traditionalism such as Guénon, Coomaraswamy, and Schuon and bring these ideas into Western academic circles, but also to apply them to domains that these earlier writers did not sufficiently address, especially cosmology and the natural environment. Nasr's application of the perennial philosophy is unique within the traditionalist corpus of works, as we will see later with regard, for example, to his work in building a philosophical foundation for the environmentalist movement.

Not only has Nasr been a conduit for integral Islamic philosophy to come to the modern West, but he has also turned the attention of much of modern Islamic academia back to the wealth of the Islamic philosophical tradition. His work has furthermore introduced perennialism to many non-Western countries, especially in the Islamic world. In a sense, he is the first traditionalist to have an extensive impact upon the Islamic world, especially Iran, his own country, but also Pakistan, Turkey, Malaysia, Indonesia, Bosnia, and India—principally Muslim India, but also to a large extent Hindu India. But perhaps his most enduring legacy in both Islamic philosophy and in perennial philosophy has been the training of students. He has trained several generations of students, starting with his earliest period of teaching in Iran and followed by nearly thirty years in the United States. Many of his students have themselves understood the traditional perspective and made it their own, and have become famous scholars and writers in countries all over the world. The result of this influence has been nothing short of the establishment of a new intelligentsia in the Islamic world, which is neither the traditional *'ulama'*, who know nothing at all about the West, nor modernized Muslims who know practically nothing about their own intellectual tradition or Tradition in general. And so primarily because of Nasr's influence over the last fifty years, there now exists a new group of intellectuals of the highest order who are both strictly speaking traditionalists, and also very well acquainted with the modern world. This impact has been primarily within the Islamic world and India, but this impact has also been felt in the West, as he has also trained many Western students.

Environmentalism

In the 1960s, two books appeared warning us of the impending ecological crisis: Rachel Carson's *Silent Spring* (1962) and Seyyed Hossein Nasr's *The Encounter of Man and Nature* (1968). These two works can be considered the beginning of the "environmental movement." In the decades that have followed, Nasr has worked tirelessly in his books and lectures to expose the depths and dimensions of the ecological crisis and to explain its underlying causes.

Nasr's firm footing in both Tradition and the modern West has enabled him to hold a unique place in the environmentalist movement and particularly in its philosophical aspects. Nasr predicted today's environmental crisis years before its existence came to the attention of the media, and before it was accepted by mainstream society, precisely because he understands both the traditional view of nature and that of the modern West so well. His 1968 book *Man and Nature* identifies the crisis according to its spiritual roots, and not just its physical manifestations, by revealing the progressive loss in the West of an understanding of the sacred meaning of nature. Nasr predicts and explains the outward effects of this transformation, and shows—this is the crucial point the modern world still needs to learn from Nasr—that the only solution to the crisis is the recovery of the traditional understanding of nature as sacred. As long as this vision of nature is lacking, no improvements in engineering and technology can heal the damage we have caused and are causing to the environment.

Thirty years after his seminal *Man and Nature*, Nasr made another unique and vital contribution to the environmentalist movement. His Cadbury Lectures, published as the book *Religion and the Order of Nature*, are a key philosophical work in ecology. This work draws on all the major world religions to bring out the perennial and universal theology of nature, whose loss is the source of the devastation we see around us. Nasr writes not just as a representative of one particular religion, but as the spokesman for the perennial wisdom to be found in every traditional culture. His voice is thus the call for a restoration of the traditional understanding of the meaning of nature in a universal context transcending any particular culture or society.

Islam and the West

Nasr's contribution to the environmentalist movement is only one example of the unifying power of the perennial philosophy that he brings both to the Islamic world and to the West. By relating the traditional philosophy of the Islamic world and of the West to the perennial philosophy, he has served as the representative of perennialism at the highest level of discourse in both worlds. His deep knowledge of and respect for religious traditions other than Islam have made him an especially effective lecturer, because he speaks to the heart of all traditions. His audiences are thus able to listen to his critiques of the modern West because it is so clear that he understands and appreciates the Christian tradition as well as his own. Since his critique is always a call for a return to the core of one's own tradition, he never comes across as an "outsider" to the people he is addressing, and he has been invited to lecture for a wide spectrum of audiences, from Catholic universities, which appreciate his emphasis on Tradition and the Sacred, to a Navajo college, which recognized him as a thinker who understands the importance of traditional knowledge and especially cosmology.

For these reasons, Nasr has been able to achieve distinction both in his critique of the West and as a peacemaker between the East and the West. Because his voice is both respectful and uncompromising, he has been an invaluable spokesman for Islam to the Western world. The media often seek him out to respond to or explain some event in the news. HarperOne commissioned him to write *The Heart of Islam: Enduring Values for Humanity* to be published on the first anniversary of the tragic events of September 11, 2001; he also gave the keynote address to the United Nations conference on Islamophobia in 2004.

At the same time, Nasr has been constantly active in academic circles, advancing traditionalist and perennialist teachings as well as Islamic studies. He edited *The Essential Writings of Frithjof Schuon*, and continues to direct the activities of the Foundation for Traditional Studies, including its journal *Sophia*. Throughout this work he has dedicated himself to elucidating the perennial philosophy within the academy and philosophical circles. He has also worked to bring this thinking to the public and nonacademic audiences. In this endeavor he has represented the voice of Islam, especially the mystical traditions and teachings of Sufism, and he has stressed their importance to both the perennialist movement and to the West at large.

Revival of Traditional Islam and Its Intellectual Tradition

Frithjof Schuon, one of the chief representatives of traditionalism, insists that all true religions are revealed by God as paths for mankind to Him, and that believers must practice their religion not only by learning its spiritual teachings, but also by performing the duties and rituals it prescribes. Nasr embraces and teaches this tenet of perennialism, but he does this as a Muslim and his own commitment to Islam is complete. He has served as an advocate for the revival of traditional Islam in two ways. First, he addresses himself to Muslims living in America and Europe, and the special problem of how to practice Islam amidst the culture of the modern West. To this end, he has written books and articles, notably *Traditional Islam in the Modern World* and *A Young Muslim's*

Guide to the Modern World, and has lectured to enthusiastic Muslim audiences in mosques and Islamic centers around the world. His own rich experience of being at home in the West, but recommitting himself as a young man to the practice of Islam—of appreciating the "good things" of the West, but recognizing at the same time the dangers of the rejection of the Sacred in the modern West—makes him a compelling speaker with a universal voice.

In this way he has been an advocate of the revival of the practice of traditional Islam in the lives of Muslims in America and around the world, but he has also concentrated on the revival of the Islamic intellectual tradition, not only in the Western world, but in the Islamic world itself. At Tehran University, he redirected the attention of the University, which had come to concentrate on French and European philosophy, back toward Islamic and Eastern philosophies. He brought a whole generation of scholars back to the richness of their own tradition, contributing monumental scholarly works toward this end, such as his *Anthology of Philosophy in Persia* (edited with M. Aminrazavi), his *Science and Civilization in Islam*, and two volumes on Islamic Spirituality for the *World Spirituality* series. His work *Three Muslim Sages* opened the door to a new understanding of the philosophical and intellectual tradition in Islam. Even before immigrating to the United States, he worked with American universities, contributing to the planning and expansion of Islamic and Iranian studies at Harvard, Princeton, the University of Utah, and the University of Southern California.

One aspect in particular of the Islamic intellectual tradition that Nasr has almost single-handedly brought back into academia has been traditional Islamic cosmology. His book *Introduction to Islamic Cosmological Doctrines*, written over fifty years ago, is still taught today all over the world. Because Nasr is trained in modern Western science, he has dedicated much of his life to building a bridge between traditional and modern science, offering modernity a way to understand the value of traditional cosmologies, not as a merely outdated and false understanding of the universe, but as a symbolic understanding of the cosmos that speaks more than ever to our times. His book *The Need for a Sacred Science* explains what the West has lost: he exposes the false dichotomy that even some who acknowledge the importance of Tradition have unwittingly accepted, that science is the great achievement of the West, while spirituality is the great achievement of the East. It is precisely this banishment of spirituality from science—and science from spirituality—that Nasr seeks to rectify.

Religion and Science

Ever since the rise of modern science in the 17th century, there has been great interest in the dialogue between science and religion. Throughout his career, in both his teaching and his scholarly works, Nasr has focused on this dialogue. As usual, Nasr brings to the discussion a firm foundation in both worlds. His degrees in physics and mathematics from M.I.T. and in geology and the history of science and philosophy from Harvard make him well qualified to examine Western scientific principles and theories. His course "Science and Religion," which he began teaching after taking the position of University Professor at The George Washington University in 1984, won the John Templeton award in 1997 for the best course in America in science and religion. Prior to the advent of Nasr's course, the religious side of the dialogue was limited to Christian religious concepts; for example, Christianity's reaction to Darwinism is different from that of Islam, but often the dialogue between Darwinism and religion is cast solely in terms of Christianity's viewpoint. Nasr's course was, and perhaps still is, the only course in America that explores the relationship between religion and science not only in the West but also in other great traditions as well. In doing so, Nasr examines the relationship between science and religion from the perspectives of both Western and non-Western cultures. He includes discussion of religion and science from the perspectives of the ancient Egyptian and Greek traditions, as well as the living civilizations of Asia and the Far East, all in light of their own traditional sciences.

This global perspective that Nasr brings to the table, not only through his teaching but also through many academic papers and conferences, has added a whole new dimension to the debate. The broadness of Nasr's perspective allows him to defend not simply a particular religion, such as Islam or Christianity, but religion itself. And in his defense of traditional religion, he insists that the discourse between religion and science be carried out with both sides on an equal footing, for all too often science dictates the premises and religion tries to change itself to conform to what science proclaims. Nasr's work combats this "inferiority complex" on the part of religion, both by insisting that religion preserve its own intellectual status and the authenticity of its understanding of the cosmos and by exposing the falsity of many of science's claims, using modern science's own methods, which are taken to be empirically proven but which are actually open to considerable doubt.

Nasr has similarly been one of the severest critics of scientism within the Islamic world. His book *Islam, Science, Muslims and Technology* is a distillation of a lifetime's meditation on this topic. Nasr has devoted considerable energy to combating the view, prevalent in parts of the Islamic world, that the Islamic world's adoption of modern science and technology is a great glory of Islam. In light of Nasr's insistence that one must understand science not only for what it accomplishes, but also for its limitations, thinkers in Islam and other traditions can engage modern science without renouncing their own inner teachings. Before Nasr's contributions, contemporary scholarship had no access to an understanding of the nature and depth of Islamic science in its own right, not only in relation to modern Western science. Nasr's work reveals the underpinning of Islamic metaphysics, cosmologies, and philosophy not only to the West, but to Muslim scholars as well, and it provides an Islamically authentic methodology for the study of Islamic science, especially his books *Science and Civilization in Islam* and *Islamic Science: An Illustrated Study*.

To appreciate the full importance of this work, one must understand the context in which it first appeared. Before Nasr's scholarship, the academic fields of the history and philosophy of science were characterized by a lack of understanding of what traditional Islamic science had been. The scope of Nasr's achievement cannot be overestimated, for it has done nothing short of demonstrating that there is another form of science besides the modern West's definition. With this understanding, he calls for the world's religious and spiritual philosophies to reclaim their contribution to science in a broader sense, a systematized knowledge of the universe. Traditional cosmological and natural sciences have much to contribute, and Nasr's perspective has been acknowledged with the inclusion of his essay on the topic in *The Oxford Handbook of Religion and Science*. The editors' selection of his essay shows that certain barriers in this discourse are finally being removed.

Islamic Art

Nasr's reintroduction of the contributions of Tradition has also been especially influential in the area of traditional Islamic art, the theoretical and metaphysical foundation of which he has presented and expanded to both the Islamic world itself and to Western audiences. Nasr's work fills a void, because although others have since followed Nasr's example, when he began to write on this topic more than forty years ago, the

Islamic world had practically no explication of the religious and philosophical foundations of the theory of sacred art. At that time, the works of Burckhardt and Coomaraswamy had not become known in the Islamic world to any appreciable degree. In the West, the writings of Burckhardt and a few others had addressed the meaning and symbolism of sacred Islamic art; but in the Islamic world, although artisans practiced the traditional arts, there was very little exposition of the principles of sacred art for the younger generation who would have to apply these principles for themselves. It is for this reason that Nasr's work has been most influential among practicing artists, architects, calligraphers, designers, and craftsmen in many parts of the Islamic world, and largely through his influence, Burckhardt also gained appreciation there. His 1987 book *Islamic Art and Spirituality* became a bible for the study of Islamic art in Iran. Further, in Iran, the newly established Academy of the Arts grew directly out of Nasr's writings and inspiration.

Before Nasr's influence, there were essentially two classes of people trained in the arts in the Islamic world: the traditional artists and craftsmen, who were highly competent in the tradition of Islamic art but who could not express the principles behind their work in a contemporary language; and the modernist architects and painters who studied in the West or were influenced by modern Western art and whose work had a destructive effect on the traditional arts within the Islamic world. Nasr's articulation, in a contemporary language, of the meaning, symbolism, and sacred geometry in Islamic art has helped to preserve the traditional arts of the Islamic world, and his work has been maintained and furthered by his many students among the contributing artists in the Arab world, Pakistan, Turkey, and, of course, Iran. It is in large part because of Nasr's work that the modern influences of the West have not succeeded in completely supplanting traditional Islamic art and design.

Nasr has also been deeply involved in the practical defense of traditional Islamic art. In Iran in the 1960s and 1970s, with the support of the Shah and Empress of Iran, his work contributed to the preservation of the traditional structure of many Iranian towns and cities, and within them, many individual buildings. In the 1970s, Nasr organized the first conference ever held on traditional Islamic art and architecture in Iran. This conference brought significant traditional artisans and architects such as Hasan Fathi to the fore. One must also note Nasr's major role in the creation of the School of Traditional Arts of the Prince of Wales in London. This school has been greatly instrumental in the survival, growth, and dissemination of the traditional arts, and Nasr has lectured there many times to the young architects, artists, and craftsmen, as he has in other schools in Pakistan, Morocco, Egypt, Turkey, Jordan, Malaysia, and Iran. Nasr also played a major role in the first and second Festival of the World of Islam in London. It was Nasr who introduced Titus Burckhardt to the project. For the second festival, he organized an exhibition of Islamic science at the Science Museum in London, the first of its kind, and wrote the introduction to Burckhardt's book *The Art of Islam*, which was published in conjunction with the exhibition of Islamic art at the Hayward Gallery in London that was inaugurated by Queen Elizabeth.

On an even more directly practical level, Nasr practices the principles of traditional art in his own poetry, in both English and Persian, which is an expression of his philosophical and spiritual teaching that traditional knowledge is not simply a geographic, ethnic, or historical phenomenon, but a living spiritual reality.

Sufism

Like his work in the field of Islamic art, Nasr's contribution to the study of Sufism has both a scholarly or academic side and a practical or applied side, for although many volumes have been written about Sufism through the centuries, Sufism is, principally, an applied discipline whose aim is the perfection of the soul and the purification of the heart. Therefore, it is necessary to discuss not only Nasr's work as a scholar of and spokesman for Sufism, but also his role as a Sufi teacher and spiritual guide.

Without a doubt, one of Nasr's greatest scholarly achievements has been to introduce authentic Sufism to the academic world in the West. Prior to Nasr's work in this field, there were almost no other works in Western languages that expounded Sufism in a completely scholarly language and were at the same time written from within the Sufi tradition. The works of Louis Massignon and Henry Corbin came closest, but although their work certainly had empathy for Sufism and an appreciation for the necessity of participation and practice, neither scholar was a Sufi in a tenable sense of the term. Nasr's voice is both authentically Sufi and rooted in the classical sources of Sufism in both Arabic and Persian.

Nasr's initial work on the subject, *Sufi Essays*, was the first authentically Sufi work to be accepted in the mainstream academia of the West. Numerous other books followed this seminal work, and, in its wake, Nasr has trained several generations of Western students in Sufism. Nasr's work is unique in that it presents authentic Sufism as a contemporary reality and not simply as a medieval phenomenon expressed by

Rūmī, Ibn 'Arabī, and other such classical Sufis—that is, Nasr's studies are not merely historical. Nevertheless, before Nasr's *Three Muslim Sages*, Ibn 'Arabī was hardly known in the English-speaking world, and the tremendous interest in him that has grown over the last forty years is to some extent due to Nasr's early work. Nasr's voluminous writings and lectures on Sufism have also given rise to a new generation of scholars who have taken on Nasr's mantle, including William Chittick, who is the foremost authority on Ibn 'Arabī today in America.

Equally important has been Nasr's exposition and defense of Sufism within the Islamic world, a task made necessary by the currents of modernist, fundamentalist, exclusivist, and exoteric points of view. Nasr answers these views with his exposition of the innate value of Sufism for contemporary humanity. It is this work for which Nasr's writings have become especially known within the Islamic world itself. Nasr's contribution here has been not only to present Sufism in a scholarly way, free from "new age" and fundamentalist interpretations, but also as a living practice and reality. This undertaking, in concert with the other great advocates of traditional Sufism such as Schuon, Burckhardt, Guénon, and Martin Lings, has brought significant changes to the lives of many young Muslims studying in the West, and also of Westerners who have sought a door into the spiritual world outside of modern Western culture. Within the Islamic world itself, in such places as contemporary Iran, Pakistan, and Turkey, many have been led to the serious study of Sufism through Nasr's writings.

Nasr's work in both the Islamic and Western worlds has corrected two common errors about Sufism. First, it has refuted the claim that Sufism is not Islamic in origin. Nasr, along with Massignon and Annemarie Schimmel, has argued strongly against this assertion, completely settling the argument, at least in academia. The second error that Nasr has helped to correct is the idea that Sufism is a purely philosophical or metaphysical discipline and not a spiritual path. Nasr has demonstrated beyond question that Sufism's objective is spiritual realization and that its application is not simply conceptual or historical but existential, current, and immediate. In light of Nasr's work, one can live in and understand the modern world perfectly well, and at the same time espouse and practice traditional Sufism without destroying its authenticity. For example, Nasr was the very first person to write on the significance of Sufism for the environmental crisis, in an essay that is the text of a talk given in Japan in 1970, and which appears in his *Sufi Essays*. In this context, two of Nasr's works deserve particular attention: *Knowledge and the*

Sacred, which explicates the philosophical and metaphysical basis of Sufism and, indeed, of spiritual knowledge per se; and *The Garden of Truth*, which is not simply about Sufism, but is an authentic Sufi work written in the English language.

Since Sufism is not simply a philosophical discipline, but a living reality, it can only be known "from the inside" or, as the Sufis say, "by tasting." Nasr is, by nature, a teacher, and he has never shrunk from the responsibilities of teaching the practical as well as theoretical dimensions of Sufism. This task requires a number of important, and sometimes contradictory, gifts, since neither personal virtue nor doctrinal knowledge alone is sufficient for one to be an efficacious spiritual guide. The gifts required are those of orthodoxy, of understanding and accuracy of transmission; the ability not only to expound the truth, but to reach within the soul of the disciple; the ability to tailor and apply universal truths to particular cases and individual situations; the ability to be a doctor of the human soul, and a healer of the heart; and the ability to affirm and encourage the growth of the soul and manage its direction until it flows into the ocean of divine beatitude.

An authentic spiritual guide must also have the confirmation of Heaven, or *ta'yīd*, as it is known in Sufism. For Nasr the authority of this function has grown over the decades, and his purpose as a spiritual guide continues to be the central reality of his life. It is this rare combination of skills that includes both scholarly knowledge and practical experience that makes Nasr unique. Indeed, the ability to guide others on this journey requires knowledge that is both factual and existential, or doctrinal and practical, for the vocation of a spiritual guide calls for the application of the "science of the soul," which is both objective and subjective.

Relations between Religions

One of the most important contributions Nasr has made in his lengthy career is his contribution to the study of relations between religions. His achievement in this field is not the devising of a new theory or vision of the relation between religions, for the transcendent unity of religions (to use Frithjof Schuon's elegant phrase) was already expounded in a magisterial way by Schuon, and in another cadre by René Guénon. Nasr's own achievement has been to take this doctrine of the inner unity of religions and elucidate it for the first time in an academic way, so as to bring it to the attention of those who study religion in the West. His work has taken such concepts as universalism and the transcendent unity of religion out of the realm of "popular" or "new age" literature and exposed their traditional depth and meaning with full academic rigor.

One of Nasr's key works in helping to introduce the perennialist perspective is his essay "The Perennial Philosophy and the Study of Religion," which was written for a *Festschrift* for Wilfred Cantwell Smith, at that time perhaps the most perspicacious of North American scholars of religion. Smith was a close friend of Nasr's and a colleague at Harvard, although he did not share completely the idea of the perennial philosophy. That essay also appears in Nasr's book *The Need for a Sacred Science* and was seminal in introducing many to this field. One can see the change that has been wrought through Nasr's influence by comparing the present-day place of the perspective of the perennial philosophy concerning the plurality of religions with its place forty years ago. The introduction of the perennialist perspective, along with its influence on the mainstream academic community in this field, continues to be one of Nasr's most important and enduring contributions.

This voice of perennialism in the academic study of religion was completely missing when Nasr arrived upon the scene. Prior to his arrival, most scholars of religion in universities studied religion solely against a linguistic, historical, and cultural background—the discussion was largely about who influenced whom, and the question of truth was not addressed at all. Now there is a wide discussion of the claim that there is a perennial and eternal truth that is neither purely historical, nor determined by temporal flow, nor simply a phenomenon without reference to truth. This change has made it possible to study the various religions in a way that is religiously, theologically, and metaphysically significant, rather than studying religion by removing from it that which is religious—a method that had characterized most of the study of religion in academic circles since World War II, when this field began to be popular in the general programs of Western universities and not only in divinity schools and seminaries.

Nasr's work in this domain has had a tremendous influence on scholars in the West, particularly younger scholars who are studying religion, whether they are from Christian, Jewish, Muslim, or other traditions. Most notably it has influenced a number of Muslim scholars who are now faced for the first time with taking religious pluralism seriously. The more traditional societies become diluted through the influence of modernism, the more they evidence a cognizance of the presence of other religions that have to be taken into consideration. Here Nasr's seminal influence is clearly seen among Turkish, Persian, Indian, Pakistani, Malaysian, Indonesian, and Arabic writers and scholars. In the current of contemporary dialogue, for example in Iran and Turkey, where this issue is perhaps more hotly debated than in other countries, the name of Nasr is at the very center of all these debates.

This change of bringing the idea of truth to the academic study of religion—the perennialist perspective—is perhaps Nasr's greatest legacy in this field, and it is a change of enduring importance, intellectually and spiritually speaking, because it has provided the way for many a student in the field of religion to take religion seriously—and to be religious—without closing his or her mind to the reality of other religions or being unscholarly. Nasr and Huston Smith, whom Nasr brought to this perspective, have probably influenced the landscape of religious studies more than any other two people by demonstrating that one is not compelled to choose between either absolutizing one's own religion and rejecting everything else, or relativizing one's own religion by taking it as only a historical event or an interesting phenomenon without intrinsic meaning. Nasr has brought to us the perspective that the study of religion cannot be accomplished without understanding the presence of revelation and the penetration of a divine message into the human order. This mission continues to occupy Nasr's life and work.

Nasr's books continue to be so widely read and translated into so many languages that they greatly exceed the impact of any other traditional writer, with the exception perhaps of Guénon in his native France. But even in the West, Nasr's works are much better known in the United States than those of Guénon or Schuon. Nasr's body of writings now includes over 500 articles and 50 books written and edited, many of which have been translated into many languages. This corpus is certainly one of Nasr's most important legacies. But, as already mentioned, one must also look to the great number of students he has trained who themselves have produced a large number of works and trained many of their own students: scholars like William Chittick, Osman Bakar, and others who are first-rate scholars globally. Their works and the students they have trained are perhaps among the most enduring parts of Nasr's legacy.

The present work is a long interview with Nasr, consisting of two main parts: the story of his life, which is captivating in its own right, for the events that shaped him have been dramatic; and an intellectual autobiography exploring the different themes of his life's work. This book will serve well as an introduction to Seyyed Hossein Nasr for those who are encountering his work for the first time; but also for those who are already well acquainted with his work, this book is a journey into the mind behind it, revealing the unity of the different facets of his thought. What Nasr offers us is indeed nothing new; rather he has given back to us that which we already possessed but which had slipped from our awareness. The wisdom that shines through the work of Seyyed Hossein Nasr from his more than fifty books and five hundred articles is not his own; it is timeless and eternal. It shines forth from its Source and is reflected and refracted by those precious individuals who know its nature and who come in every age and time to show us its light. One of these great lenses, in our day and age, is Seyyed Hossein Nasr.

Terry Moore

Part One

Childhood

R.J.: Thank you for having accepted this interview, and I would like to start this book with a series of biographical questions about your family life and your childhood years. You were born into a family of scholars and physicians in 1933. Can we start with the memories of your childhood?

Ancestors

S.H.N.: In the Name of God, the Infinitely Good, the All-Merciful.

Yes of course, with pleasure. I will be glad to say something about my childhood. I have very vivid memories of my childhood, and they have left a permanent mark upon me not only emotionally, but also intellectually. As you said, I was born into a family of scholars. From my mother's side, my grandfather and great-grandfather were famous religious scholars. My great-grandfather was one of the foremost religious scholars during the Constitutional Revolution of 1906. Shaykh Faḍl Allāh Nūrī,[1] my mother's grandfather, was put to death at that time, and this event left a deep imprint upon my mother's family, a kind of psychological impact from which many of them suffered. Many of them remained, of course, pious, but at the same time a number of the people in the family turned against Islam, including the head of the Iranian Communist party, Nūr al-Dīn Kianouri, who was a first cousin of my mother and a grandson of Shaykh Faḍl Allāh Nūrī. So there was both a religious inheritance, a very strong one, and also a psychological trauma which I felt from the side of my mother's family concerning religious matters. Nevertheless, the dimension of religious concern was always very much present.

As far as my father's side is concerned, he was a physician—so was his father—but my father was also a great scholar of the Persian language and a philosopher. He was the only person, I think, in the history of modern Iran who had been dean of the Medical School, Law School, and the Faculty of Arts of Tehran University as well as being the chancellor of the Teacher's College of Iran. He was also involved in politics. He was a member of the first parliament when it was established after the Constitutional Revolution and had a hand in writing the Constitution. For that very reason his closest friends were the leading dignitaries in Iran from a political point of view, men such as Muḥammad 'Alī Forughi[2] and Muḥtashim al-Ṣalṭanah Isfandiyārī.[3]

My childhood was marked by a combination of an intense religious and cultural upbringing and also an awareness of the political situation of the country through contact with the political elites, many of whom were well-read scholars. Not only were my mother and father very literate in the Persian language, but my father was an authority in Persian literature and my mother was also very well versed in classical Persian poetry.

Early Memories

From this early period of my life I have vivid memories of several things. First of all, nights spent, from the time that I remember, when I was three, four years old, in the reading of the Persian classics of poetry and prose, especially Sa'dī, Ḥāfiẓ, Rūmī, and Firdawsī.[4] I started with these four, and later on I studied Niẓāmī.[5] When I was just a few years old, probably eight or nine years old, one day the late Muḥammad 'Alī Forughi came to our house, and my father said: "Mr. Forughi, why do you not compete with Hossein in exchange of verses of poetry (*mushā'irah*)," and Foroughi put me on his lap and the exchange of verses began. Finally, I beat him in the competition because I knew so many poems by heart. I knew thousands of poems at that time, including verses of other poets such as 'Aṭṭār, and that left a very important impression upon my mind later in life. In those days in Iran the old tradition of combining the social gathering of men with scholarly discussions was still alive. My father had a few close friends who were very great scholars such as Hādī Ḥā'irī,[6] who was probably the greatest master of the *Mathnawī* of his day, and even people such as Foruzanfar[7] would go and ask him questions when they had difficulties with the *Mathnawī*, and Sayyid Muḥammad Kāẓim 'Aṣṣār.[8] I came to know them well at that time. My father also had other friends who were likewise, as I said, "men of letters" and at the same time political figures like Forughi. My father used to have these "literary" sessions about once a week with them, and Shukūh al-Mulk, who was then the head of Reza Shah's[9] special bureau, came to these sessions. He was also a very close friend of my father, and we lived on the same street. My father used to take me to these sessions in which they would spend hours reading just a few verses of poetry and commenting on them and discussing them. This experience permeated deeply my mind and soul. It is an important impression of my childhood that I will always remember.

The second memory of my childhood is the combination of piety and interest in Sufism that surrounded me. My father and his father and grandfather all belonged to the Sufi tradition and espoused what is usually called the idea of "tolerance" (I use this term here even if I do not like to use the word *tolerance* because it is too weak and also inadequate a word when used in relation to other religions and worldviews), but the presence of the universality of Sufism was part of my upbringing, which was both religious and universally oriented.

The third memory concerns philosophy. I was interested in philosophical questions from the earliest age, when I was seven or eight years old. I would sit down at the feet of my father and ask him, for example, if there were to be no earth and no sky, where would we be? What would be the end of time and space? You know, questions like these. Really metaphysical questions haunted me. My mother would force me to go and play some football or something like that because I used to keep sitting at my father's feet and ask him such questions. I remember that when I was about ten years old, I read Persian translations of Maurice Maeterlinck[10] which had just appeared at that time and also some passages from Pascal[11] and Descartes.[12] It is interesting that this early philosophical interest I had was also related to Western philosophy, because my father had an excellent library of French as well as Persian books which I gave to the central library of Tehran University when I returned to Iran in the late 1950s. I could not read French at the time, although I was studying French with a tutor, but there were a lot of translations, and my father also discussed these matters with me. So when I was ten years old, I knew who Pascal was and especially I knew that the Catholic philosophers in France contrasted with the skeptical philosophers who came later on. At least I had heard of many of the French philosophers' names, and so a part of the recollection of my childhood is also intense philosophical interest.

My last memory of that period is the very rigorous mental and also moral training that I was put through by the discipline placed upon me by my father and mother, but especially my father, who taught me how to be very precise in intellectual matters and how to be a good student. A lot of care was taken over my education, so that I became first among all students in Iran in the sixth-grade national exam, and I was always an outstanding student at school. It was ingrained in my mind that I should always be a very good student and also an upright person, and that, of course, has been the basis of all the intellectual and moral discipline I have had throughout my life.

Nasr's Father

R.J.: We will get to that part later. Let us talk for the moment about the book written by your father which is called *Dānish wa Akhlāq* ("Knowledge and Ethics").[13] Both the questions of knowledge and ethics are important concepts in your thought. I am interested to know more about this book of your father's and in which way it influenced you.

S.H.N.: First of all, my father wrote a large number of books, most of which were never published. They are still in manuscript form, and I am very sad that I gave a big iron box with the manuscripts of my father in it to Dr. Rezvani, professor of history at Tehran University, who was working on the history of the Qajar period and was going to write a book on my father. I gave him the box the year before the Revolution, and I never discovered what has happened to it. Now Dr. Rezvani is no more among us, and I do not know what has happened to those manuscripts. When I came back to Iran in 1958, I was very unhappy that my father had written so much and so little of his writings had been published. So it is I who took the manuscript of many essays, put the chapters together and gave it the title of *Dānish wa Akhlāq,* two subjects about which my father had always spoken. At that time I asked my oldest still living paternal uncle, Seyyed Ali Nasr, who was a famous writer and one of the fathers of the modern Iranian theater and who had been very close to my father, "What title do you think my father would have liked for this book?" My uncle told me that my father always emphasized these two elements of knowledge and ethics. This is why I thought that the title *Knowledge and Ethics* would be a very appropriate title.

These were the two poles, in fact, of what I remember of my father's own personality and what he cultivated in me. First of all, he was a highly ethical person. Two years before his death he was hit by a bicycle when he was walking back home, while we were at my maternal grandfather's house for lunch. He left earlier by himself, and somebody hit him with a bicycle while driving on the sidewalk, as a result of which my father fell into a ravine, and that fall broke his pelvis bone. He should have been helped immediately, but he told the person who hit him to go away. He said because of who he was, if the authorities discovered the identity of that person, they would imprison him and cause problems for him. Therefore, he should go away. He forced this man to go away and no one ever found out who he was. After we had discovered what happened and brought my father home, the prime minister came to our house and asked my father about the accident. "We will have the whole government chase him down," said the prime minister. But my father smiled and said, "No, no. It happened as an accident." And until he died, from the consequences of that accident, he never revealed his name. He was a man of great character.

So the questions of ethics and knowledge were very important elements of my education. My father was sort of a perennial student seeking knowledge to the end of his life. He studied every night. He was in his early sixties when I was born, since he married late. He was already very prominent both culturally and politically and did not have to study, but every night he would read for hours, and so he always tried to instill in me love for knowledge.

A Pneumatic Child

But there is something more profound which I need to mention now that I have spent years and years as a philosopher thinking about the question of human types. There are several human types to which the ancient Greeks also alluded. There are people who are somatic, who are satisfied by bodily pleasures; that is what they seek in life. There are those who are *psychoi*, as it is said in Greek: these are people who are satisfied with emotional responses to states belonging to the psychic realm. And then there are people who are pneumatic: these are people whose nature is to seek knowledge because that is what makes them happy. Even if spiritual knowledge is not available to them, they go into the field of theoretical physics or philosophy and logic, although the truly pneumatic type always seeks *sophia*. That type of mind seeks knowledge and is drawn by nature to knowledge even if it not be always what Plotinus or other traditional philosophers had in mind when they spoke of knowledge. In my case, the love of knowledge was always primary even when I was a child. Even when I was a young boy, nothing really made me as happy as knowing something. My parents would buy me a new football or a new suit.

You know how little boys are. I did not say that I did not like these things. I liked them, but I was always happier to have a book. So in my case there was a kind of congruence between this nature in me and my father's ability to actualize it. Throughout my life I think I have always been after the quest of knowledge, and that goes back to my childhood days.

R.J.: That is interesting. You said that from your mother's side and father's side both your grandfathers were religious people and religious scholars, and it is interesting to see that your father had a modernist education. He gave a great deal of importance to modern education even if his father had a religious background. How do you explain this phenomenon?

Traditional and Modern Education: A Synthesis

S.H.N.: This is a very good question, a very profound question, which I have never fully discussed anywhere. Many people consider my father to be the founder of the modern educational system in Iran, and this is certainly true. People such as Dr. Ṣadīqa'lam[14] and Dr. A. Siyāsī [15] worked at the beginning of their careers under the direction of my father. He did not want to become the minister of education, although for a while he had to accept the title of the acting minister of education because the ministers changed all the time during the reign of Reza Shah, and my father wanted to preserve stability in the new educational system and that began during the Qajar period when my father was the head of the whole educational system of the country. My father ran the Iranian educational system into and through the reign of Reza Shah; so he was, in a sense, the "Father of Modern Education in Iran." What he wanted to do, however, was to integrate the modern ideas of education and also modern learning into the more traditional Islamic pattern, because he himself had had both a traditional and a modern education. There was, in my father's vision, the goal of integration of our own traditional patterns of education and modern ideas that were coming from the West, and he therefore always encouraged me to learn modern science, modern ideas in addition to Persian classics. But he did not want to have the kind of dichotomy that our culture has in fact faced since the Qajar period, as we also see in all Middle Eastern and Asian cultures, a dichotomy between tradition and modernity, which is the core problem of the 20th and now 21st centuries for Muslim countries and has not been solved by any means. And yet, the very attitude of my father towards these matters caused me a great deal of intellectual questioning later on in life, because I was not simply a young man brought up in a purely traditional family, let us say, learning only the Quranic sciences and the ritual aspects of the religion; because while there was piety in our house, there were also modern ideas. I will not call it free thinking, but there were doors opened towards the West.

Besides the Persian classics, I read the translations of Shakespeare when I was very young. I remember the first time I read *The Merchant of Venice*, when I was ten or eleven years old. Also at that time my father gave me a book of Victor Hugo. Another of my paternal uncles had translated some works of French literature into Persian in the late Qajar and early Pahlavi periods, and this is part of our family heritage. I was reading everything written by Alexandre Dumas *père* and Alexandre Dumas *fils* that I could find in Persian, and, of course, my orientation, as far as the West was concerned, was completely towards the French world rather than the English world. My father, in a sense, had created a synthesis within himself between the sapiential and metaphysical aspects of the Islamic heritage, which he received through Sufism, Islamic philosophy and medicine, and Western sciences and ideas whose philosophical foundations he did not necessarily accept, because he was not a positivist, nor an agnostic, just the other way around. But he had solved the problem of the dichotomy between tradition and modernism through a metaphysical vision, as we see in one of his essays in his book *Dānish wa Akhlāq* in which he talks about darkness as a very profound symbol.

My father did not live long enough and I was not old enough for him to transfer to me this synthesis which he had created within himself. I had to search for this myself. But what he did leave with me was three things: first of all, love of knowledge for our own Persian culture, our religious, literary, philosophical tradition; secondly, an avid interest in what was going on in the West in the realm of science and philosophy, literature and everything else; thirdly, a sense of serenity that he had within himself and which I observed constantly. He always had an incredible angelic smile on his face, because he was a very serene man and one could tell there were no inner tensions and conflicts within him as we see in so many of our contemporaries whose soul is in a sense torn by the different worldviews of tradition and modernism; he was not like that.

Leaving Iran

I left Iran at the age of twelve and a half; I was then not even thirteen years old. The date was the fall of 1945, shortly after the end of the

Second World War. Precisely because of my closeness to my father, my mother, in order for me not to be present at the moment of his death, decided against the will of the members of my larger family to send me to the United States, where our uncle, Emad Kia, was then the Iranian consul in New York. He did not have any children, and he liked me very much. He always wanted a boy and so insisted that I should be sent there, promising that he would become my guardian and take care of me. But the reason they sent me so early to America was precisely because of the remarkable closeness that I had to my father. When I left I had learnt a great deal, more than what an ordinary twelve-year-old child would have learnt from his father; most of all he had taught me the means of gaining knowledge of a lot of things at that tender age. I knew many verses of poetry and had an in-depth command of Persian, I had read a lot of philosophy and things like that, and so when I left Iran, from the intellectual point of view it was as if I were sixteen or seventeen years old.

Nasr's Mother and Her Family

R.J.: Can you also say a word about your mother and your mother's family because your mother, my aunt, was from a religious background and yet she was very modern.
S.H.N.: That is right. I always found my mother had two aspects to her. On the one hand, she was a remarkably learned person among the women of her day. She wrote well and even had a beautiful handwriting and she continued to do so almost until her death. She knew a lot of poetry. On one level, she was very conservative. On another level, however, she was very rebellious as far as the status of women in her days was concerned, and she had been the first woman in her family to cut her long hair. Her own aunts, that is, the daughters of Shaykh Faḍl Allāh Nūrī, and people like that, would not speak to her for a very long time because of this act. She had both of these aspects in her, that is, being at once very conservative and modernist. For example, ethically she was very conservative and so was she in her love for Islam and Persian culture. She played an important role in my early education, but she had certain modernist ideas against which I turned later on, and we oftentimes had cultural and intellectual conflicts. By the time my father had died, I was very close to her and yet even at that time in disagreement with her over certain matters. Of course I mean in intellectual matters and in the domain of ideas and not in human relations.

R.J.: Which ideas were these?

S.H.N.: The ideas we were in agreement about were the defense of the Persian language, of classical Persian literature, of traditional ethics, of respect for Islam, all of these things. Where we did not agree was her kind of rebellious, modernistic nature, a kind of "feminist" attitude toward which I became ever more opposed as I grew older. Later on when we returned to Iran, I prevented her from becoming a member of the parliament, to which she was invited to run by the Pahlavi regime, because I did not want her to become entangled in politics. And even when she was in Boston, sometimes I did not like her excessive assertion of certain "feminist" themes with students and matters like that. There was also some tension between us not as a result of who I was but as a result of what had happened to her family, the consequence of which was in fact to be seen in many of her family members. I mean the result of the fact that the family patriarch, who was a very powerful man, was suddenly hanged. This blow was felt by all of her relatives. I can understand the trauma. I can understand perfectly well our own grandfather, Aqa Ziyaoddin Kia, who had studied the religious sciences like his father, having profound problems with the consequences of the event of his father's hanging.

R.J.: He decided to go into exile with his children.

S.H.N.: Not exactly. For a while, he tried to replace his father as a religious authority, but some people would throw stones at him in public. So finally he took off the traditional garb of a religious scholar and became a very respectable judge, but also that affected him psychologically. When I was a child and until I reached the age of ten when my grandfather died, I remember that we used to go to our grandfather's house, that is, my mother's father's house, every Friday. We would go there and spend the whole afternoon, eat dinner, and then come back at night. They lived on one side of town and for most of that period we lived on the other side. I remember fully the kinds of debates that would be carried out between my grandfather and my father on religious questions. My grandfather had become much more of a modernist than my father on religious matters. My grandfather was a distinguished jurist, and my father was one of the leading figures in the country. It was therefore of great interest to watch the intense religious debates that were carried out between them. I still remember some of those debates.

Also as a reaction to what had happened in my mother's family, we saw two extremes in that family. That left a great deal of impact upon me as a child, and I felt this sense of conflict within Iranian culture at that time, the conflict between tradition and modernism. My interest in this issue throughout my life goes back to this time.

R.J.: It was present in your family?
S.H.N.: Yes, this debate and conflict was present in my family.

Nasr Family Friends and Connections

R.J.: Were your parents in close relationship with Reza Shah's entourage? As you said, your father was a close friend of Forughi, who was the prime minister.
S.H.N.: Let me tell you as far as the entourage is concerned. My father did not want to go back into politics at all after what happened to the first parliament of which he was a member at the end of the Qajar period, but he was very close to a number of the most important political figures during the time of Reza Shah. As I told you, Forughi was like my uncle. Another close friend of my father, Muḥtashim al-Ṣalṭanah Isfandiyārī, was the head of the parliament, as was also Ṭabāṭabā'ī,[16] who was moreover a relative of my mother. Then, of course, many of the ministers such as Ali Akbar Davar[17] and especially Ali Asghar Khan Hekmat[18] and Esmail Mer'at,[19] were close friends of my father. Hekmat and Mer'at would come to our house often especially when my father was sick. I would say some 70 percent of the prime ministers such as Qawam al-Saltaneh[20] and Mansur al-Mulk[21] and ministers of the various cabinets were his close friends. I do not want to go over all their names.

R.J.: Who were the traditional figures, the religious scholars for example, who frequented your house?
S.H.N.: One of the closest persons to my father was Sayyid Muḥammad Kāẓim 'Aṣṣār, who was also, later on, one of my main teachers in Islamic philosophy; also Sayyid Muḥammad Abduh,[22] who was a great expert on law and as you know one of the founders of modern civil law in Iran; and Hādī Ḥā'irī who was not a member of the clergy but was a very eminent Sufi figure. There was a triumvirate consisting of my father, Ḥā'irī, and 'Aṣṣār. They were very close spiritually and intellectually. At the time of the reforms of Reza Shah, many of my father's friends had to take off their long robes and turbans and wear Western dress. My father did not have too much contact with the *'ulamā'*[23] at Qom, although he had known Ayatollah Ḥā'irī Yazdī,[24] but he never came to our house as far as I remember. Mudarris,[25] however, did come to our house from time

to time, and my father knew him quite well. Of course he also knew the Imam Jum‘ah of Tehran and also a number of the traditional scholars of Iran who were the great masters of traditional learning and literature at that time, such as Fāḍil-i Tūnī,[26] Malik al-Shu‘arā‘ Bahār,[27] Foruzanfar, Humā‘ī,[28] Naf īsī,[29] and Bahmayār.[30] They would all come to our house, and I came to know all these people well.

They were one group, but there was also another group of a very different kind consisting mostly of close friends of my cousins who had studied in France, and these people were mostly leftists. It was not only Kianouri[31] who would come every week to our own house and debate about Karl Marx with my father, but also people such as Eskandari[32] and Keshavarz.[33] My father did not want my cousins to take me to their houses because of the presence of such people, but often times they would, and so I had the experience of all these three different worlds, all the way from the traditional ‘*ulamā*’, to the eminent professors of the Tehran University, to those leftists who were just coming back from France or Switzerland.

The Debate between Modernity and Tradition

R.J.: So actually you grew up with this debate between modernity and tradition.
S.H.N.: Exactly.

R.J.: Which still follows you until today?
S.H.N.: Of course, but it does not follow me in the sense of being an unresolved question.

R.J.: How is it so?
S.H.N.: It became resolved for me before I was twenty years old when I was at M.I.T., but of course the issue remains central to the concerns of every serious intellectual from the East or even from the West. This issue is therefore always with me; I have written many pages about it,[34] and I have come back to it again and again.

Religious Practices

R.J.: Were your parents religious people? Did they practice the Islamic faith?
S.H.N.: That is a very good question. I shall be very frank with you. My father, when he had been younger, had never missed his fasting and

daily prayers. When I was born, he did not fast any longer, but he used to pray inwardly, although I never saw him perform a prayer in a mosque. My mother had ceased to say her prayers. She was not praying the daily canonical prayers (*namāẓ*),[35] but she was nevertheless pious. She would often go on pilgrimage to holy sites such as Haḍrat-i 'Abad al-'Aẓīm and Qom,[36] and she would often take me with her. I remember those trips very clearly, being there in the sanctuary sometimes at two o'clock in the morning when that time coincided with the beginning of the Persian New Year (Norouz). Being a child, I would be half asleep just lying down on the floor and listening to her supplications and that of the many other pilgrims. But she started performing the canonical prayers again when she saw me pray in America. When I started praying regularly the daily prayers I was twenty years old, and she did not think that this was possible after my long stay in a non-Islamic ambience in America.

R.J.: She was impressed?
S.H.N.: Yes, she was very impressed, and one day she said to me, "Hossein, it is impossible for me to be your mother and to see you praying every day and not doing so myself." So during the last some fifty years she had not missed any canonical prayers.

R.J.: So when was your first contact with religion, I mean before you went to the United States?
S.H.N.: During my childhood, as I said, I used to be taken to pilgrimage sites and to holy places, often with your grandmother. Our father would not come, and I was mostly with the women of the family. The women would also take me as a child to Muḥarram processions. Moreover, there was a little mosque behind our house when I lived in the area of Shahabad, and I used to visit it often.

R.J.: Did these events affect you?
S.H.N.: Very much so. I felt myself very deeply Muslim from the beginning without any kind of fanaticism. There is a fact that I will mention to you; it is a very personal point but, nevertheless, I shall mention it to you. Through all the cultural and intellectual ups and downs I have experienced in my life, I have always loved God. The first memory I have of my childhood is of loving God, and that has lasted until now. This relation has never ceased, and I never went through a period of religious doubt as have so many people, including the great St. Augustine.

Relationship with God

R.J.: How did you imagine God at that age?
S.H.N.: That is a pertinent question. I had two or three very important dreams which appeared very early in my life. I do not even know when it was. Maybe I was two or three years old. Among my very first memories is that I was falling from a great height and I was saved by the angels. The angels were very beautiful beings, very large, luminous beings. They picked me up in the middle of the air and told me that they would never let me fall, and, in fact, I have never had a really bad dream since, never had a terrible nightmare. I have also had several dreams of being in the Presence of God. I did not see God as a big, bearded man sitting on a throne or something like that, but it was always a sort of luminous Presence. I would use these two words, light and presence, in relation to these experiences. I have also had an intense personal relationship with God. It has always been a strong direct relationship from the moment of childhood. I have always prayed to God, and I have felt that He always hears me and is always very close. I have never, however, had an anthropomorphic image of Him with two ears or two eyes. It has never been like that.

Muslim Practices

R.J.: Did you try to imitate some Muslim practices when you were a child?
S.H.N.: I learned some of the verses of the Quran, but the daily prayers were not compulsory for me at that time. I had not reached the age of puberty when I left Iran. As a child, therefore, I did not perform the daily prayers, but I used to imitate the maids and servants by fasting half a day at least during Ramadan. In those days in so many households of Iran's upper classes only the maids and servants fasted, and the lady and the man of the house did not. Our maids and servants also all fasted, and that always used to fascinate me, and I would try to imitate them. I had a great deal of joy in doing so, and also the chanting of the Quran always attracted me. I was very attracted to music from the time I was a little child, and traditional music has played an important role in my life. Perhaps we will come back to this issue later, but I need to mention here that I consider the chanting of the Quran as the highest form of sacred music. We do not call it *music* in Persian or Arabic, but it is a very melodious music, and that always attracted me very much.

R.J.: You said that you learned some of the verses of the Quran. Who taught you the Quran?
S.H.N.: I learned it both at school and at home. I learned it like Persian poetry, by memorizing it.

Memories of Tehran

R.J.: Let us talk about your education, but before that I would like you to talk a little bit more about the Tehran of your childhood. Was it a typical traditional city or a modern city? What are your memories of Tehran in those days?
S.H.N.: During the first seven years of my childhood, we lived on Sheibani Street near Shahabad Avenue. Our house was in a narrow street, and the structure was very much like a medieval, either Persian or Arabic, city or even a medieval European town. Furthermore, we had a traditional house with an exterior and an interior. At the exterior section of the house, my father held his medical clinic for his patients and received his own male guests. We also had a big and very beautiful courtyard in the interior section where we lived. So, the ambience of my early childhood was, in a sense, like that of the medieval period. At least that was the case until we came into a modern quarter of Tehran. I have to tell you more about my old neighborhood. It had a famous *saqqā-khānah*[37] (a water fountain), which was very impressive because it was covered with tiles and small mirrors, and the people who came there were very pious. Of course, they all knew my father very well. When my father walked down the street, he was like a king coming through. Everyone was just so polite towards him. I must tell you an episode which will tell you something about what kind of person he was. Once when I was a child we were walking on the street, and there was a man who was a shopkeeper who greeted us. My father was always very warm with simple people. So he replied with his own warm greetings and conversed with him. Then about a hundred yards farther the prime minister was passing by. When he got close to us he smiled and my father tipped his hat and said a simple hello to him. So my mother asked my father, "This was your friend the prime minister. Why did you just say a few words to him while you spent all that time with the shopkeeper?" My father replied: "Because he was the shopkeeper."

I remember the main avenues with all the shops, for example, Naderi Avenue with the Armenian stores and also small shops where those Russian exiles would sell *pirashkis*[38] and things like that from Russia, which were exciting for a small boy like me. My father would often take me for a walk there, and my mother would always buy things for me from the shops in streets such as Lalehzar. So that was a sort of shopping center for us. From Shahabad Avenue to Naderi was really the spine of the city for me, but there was also the bazaar area, which was always of great interest to me. We did not go there very often, yet as a child I used to love the bazaar area, and I have wonderful recollections of it. There was also the Sepahsalar Mosque[39] and the avenue going all the way down to Sarcheshmeh. That area was close to our house, and sometimes my mother would shop for food in that area of the city. I know those areas extremely well, from our house all the way to Sarcheshmeh. Also we would go from time to time to Āqā-yi ʻAṣṣār's house and also the homes of some relatives who were living in the ʻAyn al-Dawlah area, which was close to Shahabad. This was really my area of the city. Shah Avenue and those places were sort of far away, but coming from Naderi all the way to Sarcheshmeh and Shahabad, that was really what I experienced most and remember most vividly from my earliest childhood.

What was beautiful in Tehran at that time was, first of all, the number of gardens. Everything was green, and some modernized Iranians would come back from Europe and say: "Oh, we are embarrassed. Tehran is just a big garden. Why are there not more buildings; look at Paris, there are relatively few trees and there are plenty of buildings in the streets." You can consider such comments a sign of the stupidity of this modernist mentality of Orientals, whether Persian or otherwise, who came back from the West and destroyed their traditional cities.

At that time the air was extremely fresh and clear in Tehran. Every morning you could see Mount Damavand, which I loved. In fact, during the summers we used to go to the town of Damavand, to a garden that belonged to my mother's aunts. These are the things that really impressed me deeply in a positive way, although it was a hectic time in Iran. The Allied Forces had invaded our country in 1941 and we had deprivations of all kinds, especially until 1944. I was born eight years before this event, and these eight years were really sort of the most settled and rooted part of my life in Iran.

Because of my mother's insistence, we moved in 1940 to the new quarter of the city. At that time they had just torn down, I still remember, the ditch (*khandaq*) which was north of Tehran. I still recall that the municipality had just torn down the gates in the northern part of Tehran, and they had built the Shahreza Avenue area to which many people were moving, but my father did not want to move out of our house in Shahabad. He had been there for decades. Shahabad was the old family quarters of the Nasr family. My aunts had lived there for forty, fifty years. Anyway, due to the insistence of my mother we built a house off Shahreza Avenue, a house designed by Kianouri, the later general secretary of the Iranian Communist Party. It was a beautifully designed house that took a lot of time to construct. During the war there was little brick available, and all the responsibility for supervising the project was on my mother's shoulders.

In any case, a short time before the Allied Forces invaded Iran, we moved from Shahabad to Shahreza Avenue. That was a big change for me, a very big change in the sense that we moved out of the heart of traditional Tehran and our own quarter of the city. Things became more anonymous. We had no longer this intimacy with the shopkeepers, with the neighbors. It was already a more modern ambience because you had wider avenues like Shahreza Avenue, which was a very fashionable part of Tehran at that time. But as it would happen, as it was in the hands of destiny, from that period onward during the next several years, we did not stay very long in any single house. I do not know why my mother and father rented out our house and moved near the Czech embassy off Shah Avenue, where I cut my leg and I was bedridden for a while when my father was already sick after having had his accident. Then we moved from there to a house next to our grandfather's. I think it was my mother who mostly wanted to be there because of her attachment to her father. She was very close to him. He even gave her his own name, Zia (Ḍiā'), so she came to be called Zia Ashraf. It was from that house that I came to America; so it was the last place I occupied before leaving Iran.

Primary Schools

R.J.: You went to a Zoroastrian school.
S.H.N.: Yes, for the fourth grade. I did not study the first grade at school; because of all my home education they put me in the third grade when I was five years old, but then brought me back to the second grade because the pressure of work was considered to be too much for a boy of my age. For the second and third grades I was at a school near Shahabad Avenue right near the parliament. I think that school is still there. And then I came to the Jamshid Jam Zoroastrian school. Then we moved to the house near Café Shahrdari, and I went to the

Manouchehri and then Firouzkouhi schools. That is where I finished the sixth grade. The school is still there. At least it was there until 1979.

R.J.: Can we talk briefly about your primary school? Do you have any recollections of the teachers or the students from that time?
S.H.N.: Since I went to three different schools in three years, there was not time for me to develop many good friends. There was one person, Kouros Faraḥ, who was one of my closest friends, as was Davar Ansari, whose house was next to ours, and whose parents were good friends of my parents. Then in Firouzkouhi there were Jamshid Behnam, Houchang Nahavandi, and Rokn al-Din Sadat Tehrani, although they are somewhat older than I. I still know them quite well, especially Sadat Tehrani, whom I saw often and we played with each other before I left Iran. They all became eminent personalities in the later stage of the Pahlavi regime. For the most part, however, I sort of kept to myself. I was not very garrulous and wanted to have time to read. Yet, I would not say I was a complete introvert.

R.J.: Solitary?
S.H.N.: Yes, I liked solitude. My mother always used to push me to participate in sports, especially group sports, and to be with other boys, but I did not want that very much. I preferred to be alone to read or even play by myself or spend time with my father. I was not a student who was difficult to handle. I tried to be polite and to be always on time in class. My father made me to undergo so much discipline and practice always the traditional Persian courtesy that we call *adab*. For secondary school, I had just begun to go to Firouz Bahram where I completed seventh grade, but I was supposed to go to America soon, although my trip was somewhat delayed. So I began to go to Sharaf High School just for a couple of months in 1945 for the eighth grade before I left Iran in October of that year. After that I did not keep up my friendship with my schoolmates from Iran, since I was sent to a boarding school in America. Most of my good friends are from a later period, although friendship with some of those childhood friends was renewed when I returned to Iran in 1958.

R.J.: Were you a shy person? Did you spend a lot of time at home?
S.H.N.: No, I was not shy because I was inquisitive and a good speaker even as a child. When I went to kindergarten, I was only three years old. There was only one kindergarten in Iran at that time to which the children of the upper classes, including even some of those

of the king, were sent, and your mother also went there with me. We were supposed to perform a play in which I had a very important role. I had to tell the famous story of the fox and the crow by Lafontaine. The crow has a piece of cheese in its beak; so the fox says, "How beautiful you are," and appeals to the pride of the crow. Consequently the crow opens its mouth, the cheese falls down, and the fox picks it up and runs away. The lesson we learn from the story is that we should not be fooled by people, which in Persian is "*gūl-i mardum rā nakhurdan*," but I could not pronounce the "*gāf*" and I pronounced it as "*dāl*." You know what that would mean in Persian.[40] So, everyone who was there, even the prime minister, laughed and clapped, and I was on the first page of an Iranian journal at the age of three. As you see, I was not shy because I could speak well as a child, but I liked to be by myself. I liked solitude and I was not unhappy with myself. I was a very happy child, an extremely happy child. I liked to be very active and was often naughty, "*shayṭān*," as we say in Persian, but I also liked to read books and journals and to be in the bosom of nature away from people.

New Technology

R.J.: Did you listen to the radio? I suppose all the instrumental elements of modernity were finding their ways into Iran at that time.

S.H.N.: I remember them all. I remember the very first night when electricity came to Tehran. My mother told me that electricity is going to come through the bulbs and wiring that were installed in our house already. Then one day they said that the electricity was going to be turned on. Until then we always used to use kerosene lamps. One cannot imagine these things now, but one could live nicely with the beautiful light of oil lamps. I remember when these electric lights were suddenly turned on; I must have been around five years old. It was really quite an experience, which I have never forgotten, and soon after that, they brought one of these big radios, a French radio, into our house.

One of the things that I always recall is this curiosity that I had to see how things worked. One day, when my parents were not at home, I took the plug out of the wall, opened up the back of the big radio in our house, and took out all the bulbs and everything else. When they came home, they saw that all the entrails were on the floor. My mother said, "Oh, my God." I was going to get a spanking. So I said, "Please wait. Let me put it back together." Everybody said, "How are you going to put them back?" But I did put everything back and the radio worked.

So everyone thought I was going to be a great engineer when I grew up. But as I recollected later on, my love for engineering was not the reason for this curiosity. Rather, I wanted to know the nature of things. It was really my philosophical nature to try to understand the way things worked. I have now an innate aversion to modern technological gadgets, and I can hardly turn on the DVD player after years at M.I.T. But that element of seeking to discover the nature of things was there from the beginning—an intense curiosity to see how things worked, which was really a philosophical urge and not at all interest in modern technology and engineering.

Cars

R.J.: Not just instrumental.
S.H.N.: No not just instrumental. Anyway, these technological innovations came one after another at that time to Iran. For example, when I was a small child, there were some cars in Tehran, but they were rare. I mean every ten to twenty minutes a car would pass in Shah Avenue and practically nothing in other streets. It was the horse-drawn carriage or *doroshkeh* that was dominant, but gradually cars began to come and then we ourselves had a car.

R.J.: What kind of car?
S.H.N.: A Mercedes Benz, which the government bought for my father, and we had a driver, Ali Akbar, who drove us around. Then our grandfather bought a Russian car—you had to push it all the time for it to start. My father used to say "*Āqā,* why did you go and buy a Russian car? The Russians are good for other things, but not cars." About this Russian car there was quite a story. Your grandmother even learned how to drive, but she would get stuck on the road all the time. We had all kinds of fun in our childhood with the car and her driving. I remember that cars gradually began to become more common after 1941. Gradually, more members of the family began to buy Shckodas, a Czech car, during the war, for it was very difficult to buy American cars. In our family, only our uncle, Emad Kia, had one. I do not know why, but it seems that he had some kind of relation with Americans so that he used to have the latest style fancy American cars even during the war, and he used to change them practically every year. Once in a while he would take me for a drive in them. We drove on Shahreza Avenue, and everyone would look at the car, because there was nothing like it around. So, all of these things, cars, radio, electricity, et cetera, came step by step into our lives.

Movies

R.J.: Did you go to the movies also?
S.H.N.: Yes. That is another matter of interest for the understanding of the cultural life of modern Tehran at that time. Of course, the cinema had been in Iran before I was born. All of the cinemas during my childhood were on the Lalezar Avenue area, but it was sort of considered below the dignity of good families to go to the movies often. It was not like today. It was seen as a kind of frivolity, but, nevertheless, my father permitted my mother or my aunt, his sister, Marziyyeh Khanum, the mother of, among others, Mohsen Nasr,[41] to take me to the movies. She was one of the people who took us to the movies regularly, and we usually saw films such as *Tarzan* or *Laurel and Hardy.* Then, when I became a little bit older, a few times, my father and mother would come to the movies and take me with them. That was when some major film such as *Gone with the Wind* or something like that was showing. I remember vividly when we went to see this film. It was so long and I was bored stiff. In general, however, I liked movies. When I became older, most movie houses were then right around Islambol, Naderi, and Lalezar Avenues, and it was a great pleasure for me to go with my cousin, Mostafa Nasr, who was a little bit older than I and who died of a heart attack some years ago, to the movies by ourselves. I was about ten or eleven; he was thirteen or fourteen, so they trusted me in his hands. At that time the films were not dubbed but were in English with subtitles.

R.J.: Which were you favorite movies? I mean, everyone has some memories of . . .
S.H.N.: I liked very much the *Tarzan* films when I was a young child.

R.J.: Johnny Weissmuller.
S.H.N.: Yes, that kind of thing, and later on action films in general, especially if they involved the East, such as *Ali Baba and the Forty Thieves* and Rudolph Valentino in *The Sheik.* Of course romantic movies did not interest me at all at that time. What attracted me were action films, especially with Oriental themes.

R.J.: Did you like Westerns?
S.H.N.: Yes, Westerns, but not all of them because I was always on the side of the Indians, who usually lost. Also I liked films with sword buckling such as *The Three Musketeers* with Douglas Fairbanks.

Heroes

R.J.: Did you have heroes when you were a kid? I mean, any kind of heroes, spiritual heroes, or were there popular heroes or artistic heroes?

S.H.N.: Well, first of all, religious heroes, yes.

R.J.: People you admired the most.
S.H.N.: Yes, religiously, the personage of the Prophet, Imam 'Alī and Imam Ḥusayn. Those were very important figures before my eyes and, of course, they remain so to this day. Then there was Rostam because I had read the *Shāh-nāmah*[42] completely before I was ten years old. My father forced me to read the whole of the book with the help of my mother and of himself, and so I knew all the stories, especially the story of Rostam and Sohrab[43] that is the greatest tragedy of this work. Rostam, who epitomized valor and chivalry, was a great epic and literary hero for me. He was, in fact, my greatest literary hero in the world at that time.

Politically, there was a kind of infatuation with the Germans in Iran when I was a child, because the Persians had been defeated by the Russians and the British in the 19th century. So everyone in school was pro-German, but that feeling was nebulous. For example, Field Marshal Rommel was a great hero for Iranians because he was a genius in battle and was a great general with a kind of traditional chivalry, but people like Roosevelt and Churchill, although admired, were not seen as great heroes. I shared in this general pervasive outlook among my friends and peers at school. Personally, I used to have a lot of respect for Reza Shah, whom I would see strangely enough often as a child, the reason being that he had ordered to have a program called *Parwarish-i afkār*, which was held once a week. I would translate this term into English as "The development of mind."

Reza Shah

R.J.: The Intellect.
S.H.N.: Let us say "mental or intellectual development." Anyway, in the winter sessions were held in Dar al-Fonoun, in the summers in Bagh-i Ferdaws. Very often, I would not say every time, my father would speak, and sometimes other people. Most of the time when my father would speak, Reza Shah would come himself. It was relatively informal. The king of the country was there to encourage such gatherings, and of course many of the dignitaries of the country were there, along with many interesting intellectuals and scholars—such people as Forughi, Hekmat, Golsha'iyan,[44] Isfandiyārī, Rahnima.[45] I remember the Shah used to sit in the front row, and my father, who often took me there, would sit right behind Reza Shah with me at his side. I remember the back of the head of Reza Shah to this day because I would sit behind him hour after hour about a meter and a half or so away. At the end, the dignitaries would stand and he would bid them farewell, and so he

would shake hands with my father with me standing by my father. I also remember his face very well. Of course, he would never talk to me, but sometimes he would just look at me with a very sharp glance.

R.J.: You felt his authority?

S.H.N.: Oh, absolutely. He was a charismatic figure, a person of incredible authority, and everybody was afraid of him—everybody except my father, because my father did not want anything from him. This takes us away from our discussion, but I want to tell you a story, which is interesting because it left a deep impression on my attitudes towards politics. Its result was that when I was in Iran and several opportunities arose, I avoided becoming a minister and things like that, although just before the Revolution I entered the political domain on the highest level as a result of the exceptional situation prevailing at that time. Before that date, my aim was to remain in the academic world, which I succeeded in doing.

In any case, toward the end of his rule Reza Shah began to confiscate the land of many people in Mazandaran,[46] and there were certain political elements who pushed him in that direction. They wanted to make him like themselves, in a sense corrupting him.

And he loved Mazandaran because he came from the town of Nour in that province. Perhaps an element of greed or love of possessing land took possession of him. I do not know the real cause and do not want to make any kind of definitive assertion; I just know the result. Many people, of course, were not happy, including our own family, because we lost much of our land in the north, but it was not a personal matter. My father was very disturbed by this turn of events not because of the interest of his family but because of its effect on society at large. I shall never forget that in one of these sessions of *Parwarish-i Afkār* the late king was sitting right in front. My father was speaking and I was sitting right behind his royal seat waiting for my father to come back to his place. My father spoke about the vice of greed (*ṭama'*) and gave a beautiful talk, at the end of which he read this poem of Sa'dī:

Dast-e ṭama' be mal-e ra'iyyat koni derāẕ
Pol baste'ī ke bogẕarī aẕ āberū-ye khwīsh[47]

He extended his arm towards Reza Shah when the words about creating a bridge came up. Reza Shah's face turned red and everyone thought that my father's head would roll. At the end we stood at the door and Reza Shah came forward as usual. As he was passing by us he said, "*Valiollāh Khān khūb mārā tanbīh kardīd.*"[48] That is all he said without any later repercussions.

I also remember that once Foroughi came to our house before Ali Aṣghar Khan Hekmat became minister of education. Reza Shah had insisted very much at that time that my father become minister of education. My father had said before, "Ministers come and go, Your Majesty. Just allow me to run the Ministry of Education as general secretary (there was no deputy minister [*mu'āwin*] at that time). The Shah accepted, although my father did act for some time as acting minister. Then one day Hekmat got into trouble and Forughi came to our house and said, "Valiollah Khan, His Majesty has said that this time it is absolutely essential that you become minister. There is nobody else and you must accept." My father said, "Please tell His Majesty that I cannot." He said, "I cannot do that; you go and tell him yourself." So, my father went to the court and we were waiting to see what happened. He came back very happy. Forughi also came to our house and asked what had happened. He said, "His Majesty accepted that I would not have to accept this post." Forughi said, "How in the world did you do it? He insisted that you must accept this post." My father said, "I told him 'Your Majesty, I have spent my lifetime studying the Persian language. Does Your Majesty know where the word *wazīr* (minister) comes from?' He said, 'Of course not, I am a soldier.' I said, 'It comes from the root *wizr* (in Arabic), which means 'to become debased or humiliated.' 'Please allow me not to be humiliated.'" Apparently Reza Shah laughed and accepted my father's request. My father was not afraid of the king and for that very reason I never felt those negative aspects of Reza Shah that other people talked about.

Reza Shah was a kind of hero to me as he was to many of the young people at that time. It is very interesting that Iranians who had some experience of Iran before 1941 (1320) had a kind of deep patriotism different from most of those who came later during the time of Mohammad Reza Shah.[49] There were also patriotic people among the latter group, but that experience of the prewar years was something else. There was a strong attachment to Iran. Of course some things were exaggerated; I think that the policies towards the removal of the veil were too harsh and abrupt and therefore caused strong reactions some four decades later. The situation in Iran should have been like Egypt where people were left alone to choose what they wanted to wear. Reza Shah was too much influenced by Ataturk, who carried out policies catastrophic for Islam in Turkey. And then there was this question of land grabbing. But as young boys we looked upon him as a hero for the nation, and his positive qualities outweighed the negative ones. Besides him I had no contemporary political heroes in my early life.

Gandhi

Later on, I was very much attracted to the personality of Gandhi, Mahatma Gandhi, but as a young boy I had just heard about him from my father, who always spoke very highly of him. One day he showed me a picture of him in the newspaper and said, "Hossein, look, look at this man. This is how one should be. I want you to not be avaricious. I want you to not be greedy. One should not seek power." All these ideas were put into my head by him. So I knew something of Gandhi even in my early years, but it was later in America that I realized his true significance. While in Iran I was too young to know the significance of Gandhi's politico-religious movement, and he had not even become as yet the "Father of India," because there was no independent India at that time. That period coincided with the middle of his campaign of civil strikes and civil disobedience. In any case, he made an indelible mark upon me even at that time.

Invasion of Allied Forces

R.J.: So, we approach the invasion of Iran by the Allied Forces. What was the impact of this invasion on your family and on yourself?
S.H.N.: As for my family, the invasion had no major external impact except that one of our servants died of typhus and we were all worried about the epidemic that was everywhere. We had to wear camphor in a little box around our neck because apparently that was the best protection against the insect which carried the germ, but that was the only major external result. As far as food and other provisions were concerned, the occupation did not affect us to any degree that I would notice, but the invasion did affect me very much on the psychological plane.

I shall never forget that one early morning, I was walking downstairs from my bedroom in our house on Shahreza Avenue when our servant said, "Hossein, did you hear what happened?" I said, "No." He said, "Iran had been invaded." So I came downstairs where my mother and father were sitting down for breakfast and I began to cry. My father was very worried as to what would happen, because for a few days nobody knew what awaited Iran. Reza Shah went to Isfahan and was then forced to leave the country and go into exile, and we did not know that Mohammad Reza Shah was to become king. We were especially afraid that the Russians were going to invade, take over the country and make it communist. Although I was only nine years old when the invasion occurred, it was for me a moment of trepidation for the future of the country and also a terrible humiliation. I remember the day when the Russian soldiers marched in Shahreza Avenue. We all went to see the parade. It was a terrible sight. We had lived in Iran before that event with a great deal of pride, and then to see the Iranian army crushed so rapidly, and then these Russian soldiers marching in our streets was truly sad. Also a few bombs were dropped on Tehran. I remember that we were given instructions concerning how to go hide in the basement in case of general bombardment. That left a lot of psychological effect upon me, a fear of being bombed. But that fear wore off soon. We knew that a few bombs were dropped on sites of *ājurpazī* (brick-making factories) and their chimneys toppled, but it did not kill anybody in our area and the bombing was not continued. In any case, this idea of being run over by the Allies was very difficult to bear.

This reality touched home more directly when our young aunt Badri became sick with meningitis while she was living in our house. My father and our family tried everything possible to get some penicillin from the American base, everything that they could, but the American authorities would not provide it, and so she died in our house. I remember my mother and everybody discussing the tragedy. The whole episode left a terrible effect on me. But despite all these things, at that time the Iranians liked the Americans much more than the British and the Russians. Nobody was afraid of the Americans, while everybody except the Iranian communists was afraid of the Russians. Therefore, people treated the Americans well. I remember that despite this tragic incident, which was very sad, we did not entail any bitter feelings towards the United States in my family. I was brought up to always be suspicious of the Russians and the British, the two colonial powers that had dominated over Iran for so long. In any case, the occupation was psychologically difficult. We lost that sense of confidence which we had in our country. Important changes began to take place, and the new generation became cut off from the cultural and psychological climate of the Reza Shah era.

Part Two

Going to America

R.J.: So you were saying you left Iran. You left Iran in what year was it, 1948?
S.H.N.: 1945.

R.J.: 1945, yes, and in those days I suppose traveling to America was not a very easy task. Actually, it took you two months to get to New York.
S.H.N.: That is right. It was a very difficult and adventurous journey, and it is amazing that I was able to carry it out so well. I was not in any way afraid, and for some reason I was very happy to be able to go to America. I began to study English in the British Council language school in Shemiran that summer before my departure. I learned just a few rudimentary sentences, but my French was still better because I had studied it for several years. In any case, the family decided to send me abroad, and I felt that I was going on a great adventure. Although I was not afraid, the journey was very difficult because the Second World War had just ended, and most of the ships that were going to America were being used for taking the American armed forces back to their country. Furthermore, there was no direct flight like today from Tehran to London or other European cities. So I flew with a little plane with only one propeller carrying only four people from Tehran to Kermanshah.[1] At that time the Mehrabad airport was just a dusty field and nothing else.

One of the most bitter experiences of my life was when I said goodbye to my father at home before going to the airport. He said, "I will never see you again, but wherever you are, I will always be watching over you." Those were our last words in a very difficult departure. Then my mother, aunts and uncles, cousins, and so forth including your grandmother took me to the airport. I had never been in a plane before in my life; it was both exhilarating and extremely scary, since the small airplane took off almost immediately and did not need a long runway. As it took off, all these people from my family who were standing by the plane became smaller and smaller, and suddenly they disappeared from sight. We went to Kermanshah and from there to Baghdad where I spent a few memorable days. Our ambassador to Baghdad, to Iraq, Aqa-ye Ra'is,[2] was also a relative of ours, and so he gave me a royal treatment, but I did not stay with him. One of my mother's aunts was married to Aqa-ye Hakim[3] who was one of the greatest dignitaries of Iraq. I stayed with him in his immense medieval-looking house with many rooms and courtyards. He was a venerable *'ālim* with a turban and a long beard, and his immense house, or rather series of interlocking houses with gardens and pools of water, was unbelievably beautiful and like the *Thousand and One Nights.* They took me to Kaḍimayn for pilgrimage (*ziyārat*) and to different mosques as well as to the banks of the Tigris and the Euphrates rivers. After three or four very pleasant days, they obtained a reservation for me on a special bus service the British had created to go through the desert between Baghdad and Damascus. This service was run by the Nern Company. Because of the tremendous dust in the desert, not every bus could make this journey very easily. So we took this special bus in which we spent the whole night, arriving the next morning in Damascus.

In Damascus also there was a Persian whom my family had known. I do not remember his name, but I think he was a military officer. Anyway, he took me to his home and I had my first view of Damascus. It was a very beautiful and romantic city at that time as was Baghdad, both cities still reflecting their deeply Islamic character. Then the most difficult part of the journey began, because we had to cross Palestine. At that time Palestine had not been partitioned. There was some fighting between the Jewish side and the British side, but the country was still ruled by the British. We took a taxi, a big car which carried several people, from Damascus. One of them was a Persian, Isa Malek,[4] whose father was a family friend and relative. He was five or six years older than I. The two of us got into this car with the other passengers, who were Arabs, and we drove from Damascus to Haifa. All the way across Palestine I was very impressed by the greenery of all the orchards. The landscape seemed greener than the rest of the Middle East that was mostly dry, much of it desert. Our path did not, however, take us to Jerusalem. Then we took the train from Haifa along the coast to Cairo.

Cairo

My stay in Cairo marked in many ways my first experience of the West, because at that time, although it was called the "Bride of the East" and was a very beautiful city, it also had large Western-style areas and many modern elements. It was there that for the first time I saw a department store, an escalator, and all kinds of things like that. I stayed at the old Shepheard's Hotel, which was burned down later on during the Revolution of Gamal Abd al-Nasser. The film *The English Patient*, which has now become very famous and in which the atmosphere of the old hotel has been recreated, has brought back for me the memory of that time and place. Even now when I go back to Cairo, I always stay at the new Shepheard's Hotel.

Anyway, I had to spend several weeks there because there were no reservations available for ships going to America. Our ambassador to Cairo was Aqa-yi Jam,[5] who had been the prime minister of Iran. He was one of the good friends of my father, one whom I forgot to mention earlier, a person whom we used to see all the time in Tehran. His son, General Jam, became a major military figure during the reign of Mohammad Reza Shah. Aqa-yi Jam was very kind to me. He gave a dinner for me at the embassy and assigned somebody who knew Persian to take care of me, but this person could not find a ticket for me to go to America. And so I continued to stay at the Shepheard's Hotel, which was in a sense out of this world, especially for a young person from Tehran. King Faruq used to come there every Thursday evening and have dinner and then occupy himself with worldly matters, including drinking and gambling. The next morning, however, he would go to Friday prayers, his carriage passing by the hotel. I will never forget those sights and their contrasts. This period was in fact witness to the beginning of the riots that led later to the Revolution, and we were able to see a couple riots in Cairo from our hotel.

One day, when I was sitting in the hotel restaurant, eating by myself, a very distinguished Egyptian gentleman who was intrigued to see a young boy eating by himself came and asked me, "Who are you?" We could hardly converse together. I knew very little English and with a few sentences of French I told him that I was a Persian on my way to America. He was totally astounded and said, "Look, here you are my son." He took me to the pyramids and other sights of antiquity as well as to Islamic Cairo, and he obtained a ticket for me to America before many other Persians waiting there, including some dignitaries like the family of our general consul in New York, could do so.

Aboard the *Gripsholm*

In any case, thanks to this Egyptian friend, I was able to leave ahead of all of them. I came to Alexandria by train and boarded the Swedish ship *Gripsholm* there. We crossed the Mediterranean in a zig-zagging fashion, going to Thessalonica, Naples, and Marseilles, and then through the Gibraltar Strait into the Atlantic. We were always under the danger of mines. There were alarms and evacuation exercises, which were scary for me, since it was the first time I had been on a big ship in the middle of the ocean during the wintery season.

We finally arrived in New York. It was now December, over two months since I had left Iran. So, yes, it was a very difficult passage, but thank God I had a lot of self-confidence. One day on the ship, during drills when we would put on our life jackets, someone made a joke and said, "Now you have to jump into the sea to practice." With the ship being up there so high and the sea so far below, I was very scared, but otherwise I had a lot of self-confidence, and fortunately I did not become seasick often. Of course the food was Swedish, mostly bland fish, and I was not used to that type of cuisine. All of it was strange to me, but I was able to manage things very well, and on December 17, 1945, finally reached my destination. This journey was a very adventurous one and left an indelible effect upon me, especially in increasing my self-confidence and teaching me to rely more on myself and less on others.

R.J.: And you felt the impact of the Second World War in all these places to which you went?
S.H.N.: Oh yes, very much. The fear of mines was always there, because many other ships had been mined and some of them had sunk, and although the *Gripsholm* was a very big and beautiful Swedish ship, the danger was still there. This fear of mines was in a sense the continuation of the fear of being bombed in Tehran after the Allied invasion of Persia. But also this was, of course, a period full of excitement. There was also a kind of tension in feeling between seeing all these things new and the nostalgia of being cut off from my family. So it was a difficult period indeed.

New York

When I arrived in New York, both our uncle[6] and Dr. Taqī Nasr,[7] my cousin, and Bibi, his wife, who also was my first cousin, were waiting for me there at the pier. I had the first glimpse of New York when we got up in the morning on the last day of our journey. Before us stood all these skyscrapers, which at first seemed unbelievable, because I had never seen anything like them. At that time skyscrapers were very rare, and no other city in the world looked like New York. All these very tall buildings presented a unique sight, which looked both scary and exciting. I spent a few weeks in New York, during which time my Uncle Emad Kia found a preparatory school for me.

R.J.: Can you talk a little bit about New York and your first impression of America coming from the Middle East?
S.H.N.: Yes, as I said, I was very excited as well as frightened when I saw New York. It was a very large city. It was not as hectic as it is now but, nevertheless, hectic with many cars and people and very tall buildings. My uncle took me to the top of the Empire State Building, the Chrysler Building, and the Rockefeller Center Tower, where his own office was located. These were the three tallest buildings in New York at that time, and I was impressed with a sort of awe at the power that this city possessed and exuded. At first I came to like New York. Later on, however, I reacted to its chaotic pace, and for years I would not go to New York when I lived in Boston. In the beginning, since I liked New York and visited it often, I learned my way around the city quickly, and I felt very much at home there. I should mention that for all my holidays during the four-and-a-half years that I was at the Peddie School, I would come to New York for holidays to the house of my uncle or that of my cousins, and for one summer to the house of Dr. Osanlu, who was a famous plastic surgeon then residing in New York. So I came to know the city quite well, especially of course Manhattan.

The Peddie School Years

R.J.: So you went to New Jersey to the Peddie School. Was it difficult because you did not speak too much English?
S.H.N.: At the beginning it was very difficult. Let us not forget that Peddie (located in Hightstown, New Jersey) is one of the best secondary schools in this country. There was an Iranian psychologist named Mehdi Jalali who later on became a professor at Tehran University. At that time he was at Columbia University and a friend of my uncle Emad Kia. So my uncle asked him if he could find an American educator who could advise us concerning my schooling. Fortunately, Dr. Jalali knew

Dr. Hutchinson, who was the president of Lafayette College, which is a fine liberal arts college in Pennsylvania. Dr. Hutchinson came to Manhattan and we met at the Harvard-Yale University Club in Manhattan. Dr. Hutchinson took a liking to me, and he said that the best place to send me was the Peddie School, which is only fifty miles from New York. He told my uncle, "You can visit him very easily."

Of course, it was very difficult to get into the school, because the first term had finished already. Nevertheless, Peddie accepted me in the eighth grade where I was in the Sharaf School when I left Tehran in the fall of 1945, although I had missed most of the term. They accepted me, however, only provisionally to see how I would do. It was a very daunting task at first because of my lack of knowledge of English, and also because some of the American students, including my roommate, bullied me around a great deal. But I learned English very rapidly and was able to pass my courses. I will never forget that at the end of the first year when I finished the eighth grade, I received very good grades in mathematics and other subjects, but in English I received a seventy, which was just passing. One of the teachers came and stood at the door of my room and said, "Hossein, I want to ask you: would you accept to repeat the eighth grade again so that your English can improve?" I began to cry and responded, "No, please do not force me to repeat the class. I promise you that I will do much better next year." Later on when I became the valedictorian of the Peddie School, the same teacher said to me, "My God, if I had held you back one more year what would have happened?" The eighth grade was an uphill battle, but by the time I started the ninth grade my English had improved quite a bit, and courses became easy. I owe to Peddie several things, especially my mastery of the English language, resulting from the fact that they had a very good program in English. Peddie was a private secondary school where a lot of personal attention was paid to the students, for which I am grateful.

Loss of and Reacquaintance with Persian Culture

During those years, because I was cut off from Persia, I forgot a lot of the Persian poetry that I had memorized. I still know a lot of poetry by heart, but it is not like my childhood years. Also my Persian during this period became weakened. The years beginning with 1946 and extending to 1950 when I went to M.I.T. constituted the period when I was most removed from the Persian language and the Persian cultural ambience. Although later on when I was going to M.I.T. and Harvard, I was still in the United States, my mother was there with me, and we had decided to establish a Persian household where I would live rather than my boarding at M.I.T. My brother, Mehran, came also over to America with my mother and went to high school in Arlington outside of Boston, where we lived. Also some of my cousins and your own uncle stayed for some time with us. My mother fortunately insisted that in the house everyone had to speak Persian. So my Persian improved and I began to reemphasize Persian and even reread the classics. By the time I was twenty, my Persian was quite good again. I must add here that had it not been for the tremendous emphasis placed by my father upon my Persian education and the learning of the Persian language and Persian classics in my early years in Iran, it would have been very difficult for me after those years at Peddie to gain a mastery of writing Persian to the extent that I am a well-known writer in the Persian language today.

These days I do not write much in Persian, perhaps a couple articles a year, but when I was in Iran, I wrote many books and articles in my mother tongue, and my prose style was appreciated by many people. For some years also I was the dean in charge of running the Faculty of Letters of Tehran University, which was the most important center of Persian language and culture in Iran. I would not have been able to be dean of that faculty without the two following factors in my life: first of all, the early training given to me in Persian, and secondly, my mother coming to Boston, where we lived during all my years at M.I.T. and Harvard and where I was able to live in a completely Persian ambience. Our house in Arlington was completely Persian, the curtains, the rugs, the music heard, the cuisine, everything, but also Persian was spoken constantly.

Athletics

Those Peddie years were, in contrast, the period of my total immersion in the English language and in an American ambience culturally and in practically every other way. In this totally American ambience, I was able to accommodate myself to the circumstances easily, despite my cultural uprooting. I was an honor student in the ninth grade, and from then on, I was always at the very top of my class at Peddie and had an outstanding academic record. I was also good in sports. I played on several school teams, including the soccer, squash, and tennis squads, where I was able to play at the varsity level. I owe this developing into a good sportsman to Peddie because, as I said, in Tehran, I never wanted to do sports. I always wanted to read or be with my father and his friends, who were seventy or eighty years old. But even in Tehran I was physically fit; therefore, I developed quickly into a good sportsman when the opportunity arose at Peddie. I was on varsity teams not only at Peddie but also at M.I.T. I was the captain of the squash team at M.I.T. and considered a good squash and also tennis player. I still play tennis regularly and well enough to enjoy it, thanks to the physical training which was so emphasized when I went to the Peddie School.

Intellectual Development

The second debt that I owe to Peddie is related to the very rigorous program they had at that time. This helped me to develop myself intellectually. At that time everybody thought that I should become a scientist because, first of all, not only in mathematics but also in physics and chemistry I would receive the highest grades in the class. Especially in mathematics, people thought I was a "genius" because I constantly received unbelievable grades both at school and also on various national tests that were given for mathematical aptitude. Hence I decided to go to M.I.T. I applied to only three universities: M.I.T., Cal Tech, and Cornell University, and I was accepted at all three, since I was the valedictorian in one of the best schools in America. But I decided on M.I.T. where I wanted to study physics because I wanted to discover the nature of things in a philosophical sense.

Isolation

Anyway, the Peddie years were memorable for me in many ways. Psychologically, it was a period of isolation, as I said, from things Persian. My father died a few months after I came to Peddie, and it was decided by the family not to give me the news during the school year. But there was a spiritual and psychological link between us. At the time of his death in Iran, I had out-of-body and other strange experiences while I was a vast distance away at Peddie. Then, I became very much attached to my uncle Emad Kia, who played the role of a father for me. Later on in 1948, he was sent by the Iranian government to California to establish an Iranian consulate in Los Angeles, and he wanted to take me there to continue my studies. Fortunately, however, the government changed its mind and sent him back to New York. After spending the summer of 1948 in California, we therefore returned to the East, and thank God,

I was able to continue at Peddie. For some reason I did not want to study in California.

Contacts with Christianity

R.J.: Peddie was a Baptist school. Did you have to attend Sunday church services?

S.H.N.: That is an important question, because it refers to a significant part of my Peddie life. There were only two Muslims at Peddie, myself and an Afghan prince. I remember that later a third Afghan came there to join us. There were, however, no Arabs there at that time. It was required by school regulations that everyone had to attend church. The Catholic students were given the dispensation to go to a Catholic church. All others had to go to the Protestant (Baptist) Sunday service. So for four and a half years I went during the school year to church every Sunday and also to vespers on Sunday evenings, when hymns were sung.

As you know, I have worked a great deal during my life in the field of comparative religion and especially Muslim-Christian relations. My contact with Christianity came from two different sources: one, Christian metaphysics, theology, and philosophy and works of such figures as Saint Thomas Aquinas,[8] Saint Bonaventure,[9] and authorities like them; and the other from the practical experience of attending church service, which was Protestant, whereas my intellectual interest in Christianity has been more in the Catholic and Orthodox traditions. I have not been as much attracted to Protestant theology, although I have known well such Protestant theologians as Paul Tillich[10] and John Hick[11] who have been good friends of mine. I have kept friendships with many other Protestant theologians and scholars, but the study that I have made of Christian thought has been mostly Catholic. On the practical level, however, it was this attendance regularly every week of the school year at the Baptist church that left a notable impression upon me.

For both myself and the Afghan students, to one of whom I spoke all the time about our religious situation, attending church service was difficult, and we had to make adjustments to the situation. I used to be much more open to Christianity than he was. I used to say to him that Christ is one of our prophets, Sayyidunā ʿĪsā, and we should be very respectful in church, where I did not experience any tension within myself. I did not feel for one moment that I was going to become a Christian, but because of my childhood background and that emphasis upon the inner unity of religions contained in the poetry of Ḥāfiẓ[12] and others, it was easy for me to remain a Muslim and respect Christianity. You probably know some of the poems Ḥāfiẓ has written referring to Christ such as *samā'-e zohreh be raqs āvarad masīḥārā*.[13]

I had a great love for Christ even before coming to America, a spiritual love which many Sufis have had, and that love has developed over the decades within me within the framework of the Muḥammadan universe that is my religious abode. I did not feel any contradiction between being Muslim and having respect for Christ and Christianity. I think, of course, that those Baptists at Peddie would have liked to convert us to Christianity, but there was no question whatsoever of that desire becoming realized. My Islamic identity remained very strong, and at the same time this experience at Peddie brought me closer to understanding of what the Christians were saying. We heard the New Testament all the time in the beautiful King James Version, and I memorized many of its verses. I also learned many Protestant hymns, and observed and learned much about Christian ethics and ritual in a practical way.

R.J.: But how did you practice your Islamic faith at that time?
S.H.N.: I did not practice any rituals except for individual prayer to God.

R.J.: You did not practice the canonical prayers (*namāz*) at that time.
S.H.N.: I made individual prayers, *du'ā* but not *namāz* or *ṣalāh*.[14] In fact, I began to perform the *namāz* when I was at M.I.T.

R.J.: But you introduced yourself as a Muslim when they asked you?
S.H.N.: Yes. Definitely.

The M.I.T. Years

R.J.: Your interest in science and mathematics brought you to M.I.T. in 1950, and you had to go to Cambridge at that time; so the surroundings were quite different at M.I.T. and in Cambridge in comparison with Peddie.
S.H.N.: Yes, in many ways. First of all, physically Peddie was then located in a small town near Princeton University in a beautiful part of New Jersey. Now, there are a lot of strip malls around there, and they have destroyed much of the farmland that surrounded Hightstown during my Peddie years. At that time it was a very rural place, and the campus itself was very beautiful. The rural community around it was

relaxed, and there was much peace in the countryside around Hightstown, where Peddie was located. M.I.T. was just the reverse. Behind it, even more than now, there were all kinds of ugly industrial units, from soap factories to rubber mills. You could tell which way the wind was blowing each morning depending on whether you smelled soap, chocolate, or rubber in the air. Behind M.I.T. the cityscape was terribly ugly. It was the worst industrial part of Cambridge. Now they have built that technology square around Kendall Square in what used to be the worst kind of industrial wasteland you can imagine.

Physically, Boston itself had beautiful parts, much more beautiful than now, because there were no high buildings then, just the John Hancock Building, and then there were all these pleasant old streets on Beacon Hill as well as Beacon Street, Marlborough Street, et cetera, whose character has still been kept, fortunately. But in downtown, you now have all those crowded big buildings. At that time Boston was much more quiet with smaller buildings. You came down from Beacon Hill into the old Italian areas of the city, which were very charming. Where M.I.T. was located was, however, physically very challenging, because everything was so ugly. In my life I have always been very sensitive to beauty, not only artistic beauty, but all forms of beauty, including, of course, the beauty of nature. That is why I have written so much about the subject of beauty. I suppose that I am an aesthetician in the Platonic sense of the term. Beauty and truth are inseparable, and so it was a shock for me to see so much physical ugliness in Cambridge.

In addition to that, M.I.T. was a place that was austere, and the academic and intellectual life was very rigorous. There was little breathing space. I registered in the physics department, which had the most brilliant students and was the heart of the university. Physics is the queen of the modern sciences, and that department was seen to be, along with the department of mathematics, the heart of the school. All the engineering departments were involved in applied physics or chemistry in one way or another. We had ninety-six or ninety-seven students in our department, almost all of whom had been either first or second in their class from the very best schools in the country, there having been unbelievable competition for entry. Now, out of that chosen group, about half dropped out and only about 50 percent of us graduated. Can you imagine what the pressure was if you had a bad cold for two weeks? That would probably be the end of one's student career in the physics department because of those long laboratory hours, unbelievable preparations that had to be made, tests all the time, et cetera, which were very difficult to make up.

There was therefore tremendous pressure on all of us. But the discipline that was imparted to me going back to my childhood, and the fact that back in Peddie I had been such a good student, helped me to overcome all obstacles. I am a disciplined person and have a disciplined mind. I was, therefore, able to go through M.I.T. easily.

During the first year at M.I.T., I continued most of the extracurricular activities in which I had participated at Peddie. I did not want to become just a bookworm. Again, I was on the M.I.T. freshman team in both tennis and squash and also in soccer until I hurt my knee, and they carried me off the field. After that incident I never played soccer again, but I continued to play tennis and squash, as I already said, and later on I became the captain of the squash team. I was one of the best squash players in the Boston area when I was about twenty years old. So, I did not give up sports by any means. Furthermore, I developed a great interest in Western classical music. I was also much interested in the humanities and took more courses than necessary in that field. To be seen as an "M.I.T. nerd," as Americans would say, was anathema to me. During the first year, although I spent much time on sports and various other extracurricular activities, I received high honors in the physics department. I had a 4.9 cumulative out of 5, and so everybody thought I was going to be the next great physicist, but it was also at M.I.T. that the most important intellectual crisis of my life set in.

Intellectual Crisis: Physics or Metaphysics?

R.J.: How did that happen?

S.H.N.: Now, many years later I realize why I had gone to M.I.T. You know that Parmenides,[15] the famous Greek philosopher, has said that he was a *physicos* in the sense of one who understands the nature of the world.[16] Now, without knowing it at that time, that is what I really wanted to be when I went to M.I.T., that is, a *physicos* in the Parmenidean sense, but not the modern sense of a physicist studying in the department of modern physics. So here I was studying classical physics, Galileo, Newton, et cetera. But I felt that there was something really missing in my education. I was too philosophically minded not to notice this missing dimension, the fact that what I was studying was not really leading me to the understanding in the ontological sense of the nature of physical reality. Rather, it was teaching me mathematical structures related to the purely quantitative realm. Therefore, I began to study philosophy, including the philosophy of science.

Georgio De Santillana

There were also two seminal events that took place at M.I.T. in my freshman and sophomore years that really determined everything for me. The first was the meeting with the famous Italian philosopher Georgio De Santillana,[17] who was then a professor at M.I.T., a brilliant man, who not only knew most European languages including Latin and Greek, but also knew Western philosophy and the history of science like the palm of his hand. Moreover, he was also a thinker of the deepest kind, a perceptive thinker attracted to traditional thought and critical of most of modern Western philosophy. He did not just teach you Kant; he criticized him in depth. It was the meeting with him that opened my eyes to Western metaphysics. One day he said, "Hossein, why do you not just become an engineer and stop worrying about these philosophical problems?" I said, "Look, Georgio!" (I used to call him by his first name because we became close immediately; he later wrote the introduction to my book *Science and Civilization in Islam*[18] to some extent against my will in order to criticize me in that introduction.) "I am a physics major." He said, "You know, I found a niche for myself in the history of science in order not to have to deal with the crisis in the philosophy of science, which is a dangerous activity. But since you are studying physics, I understand why you are troubled by basic philosophical questions."

He realized the intellectual crisis that modern scientistic thought had brought about, as few people had done in the West at that time. He then introduced me to a much deeper understanding of Western thought. My first introduction to Western philosophy was through his eyes. It was he who introduced me to Descartes, Galileo,[19] Kant,[20] Hegel,[21] and also Greek philosophy, but always with a vision other than the ordinary. He taught me a lot of things about what you might call in the words of Corbin,[22] "the anti-history of anti-philosophy in the West." I think that you understand perfectly what I am talking about.

R.J.: Yes.
S.H.N.: De Santillana criticized the mainstream interpretations of Western thought from the point of view based on long familiarity with traditional thought, and this became intellectually very exciting for me. Consequently, I began to doubt more and more about my intention to continue to study physics with the goal of becoming a physicist.

R.J.: Was this part of your courses?
S.H.N.: We had to take one course in the humanities every term, but I took a lot more because I was so interested in the various branches of

this field. You could take as many courses as you wanted at that time at M.I.T. So I took advantage of this situation. As a result of these courses and my own studies, I began to doubt the validity of what I was doing, but there was an element of pride there within myself against which I had to fight. I speak in all honesty with you when I refer to this hidden sense of pride. Here I was the valedictorian of the Peddie School. Everybody expected me to go to Princeton. I was even taken there to see Einstein and the School of Advanced Studies. But I skipped over Princeton to go to M.I.T., the number one scientific institution in the world, in order to become a great scientist, and all my professors thought I was going to be outstanding in the field of physics. Now I had to deflate my ego and leave the field of physics in order to be honest with myself. It was really a spiritual and not only an intellectual question as I began to feel more and more that physics was not for me.

Bertrand Russell

Then another event related to De Santillana occurred which, as I have written in my autobiography in the Library of Living Philosophers[23] that you have read, that one might say was "the straw that broke the camel's back." That came when I met Bertrand Russell,[24] the famous English philosopher, some of whose works I had already read. He came to M.I.T. and gave a major public lecture. He was a very good and famous speaker and so attracted a large audience. After his lecture, De Santillana invited a few of us, who were outstanding students, to spend a couple of hours with Russell in a small gathering. So the six of seven of us sat in a room discussing philosophical issues about science, when Russell said openly and categorically that modern physics has nothing to do with the discovery of the nature of things; rather, it has to do with mathematical structures. He was an anti-realist in this respect and was speaking *à la* Poincaré[25] and similar figures who believed that what physics does is to provide mathematical structures to save appearances, which are tested by experimentation, and does not deal with the nature of things in themselves.

De Santillana himself had been a friend and collaborator of Émile Meyerson and opposed Poincaré in the famous debates that were carried on in the early part of the 20th century in France.[26] De Santillana did not therefore accept Russell's position and believed that physics was, or rather, should be concerned with all aspects of physical reality. Anyway, to cut this story short, I do not want to get into a deep philosophical discussion of this issue here, but to point to the impact of what

Bertrand Russell said had upon me even if he might have been just saying it "off the cuff." Here he was, perhaps the most famous philosopher in the Anglo-Saxon world, and look what he was saying. I asked myself, "Why am I wasting my time studying physics? Why do I want to study physics if it is not concerned with the nature of things? I want to understand not only how but also why things are as they are. What is the nature of the world? What is reality?" I was a metaphysician looking for metaphysics in physics in the modern sense.

Soul-Searching

Consequently, I faced a major intellectual crisis. I never lost my religious faith. My faith in God continued. But intellectually my "worldview" was turned inside out. Sometimes I would stay awake all night. There was in me an existential *angst* which was not just academic and concerned merely with books; it was an anxiety about my understanding of the nature of reality, which touched me existentially. As a young man, I had had the best education and was first in my class, having everything in the world before me. From the worldly point of view I was considered handsome and attractive to the opposite sex. I was good at sports and had a good family. None of these things, however, really satisfied me in what I was looking for. As a result, I went through several months of very painful soul-searching. What was I to do? Where should I turn? What is the nature of reality? What is the Truth? Is there Truth in the absolute sense? Who am I and what am I doing here? These questions came up over and over again in my mind and exhausted my mental energy and tormented my soul.

René Guénon

At that time another major event to which I alluded above took place. All of these events took place within a period of a year. This new event occurred when De Santillana himself introduced us to Oriental doctrines. I say "us" because I and three or four other physics students who were sort of "philosopher-physicists" like myself were discussing "Oriental philosophy" together. We asked him to teach us a course on Indian philosophy. This was the beginning of the Fifties, with early signs of interest in the West for non-Western philosophies. Now it is very common, but at that time this interest was just beginning. We were sort of at the frontier as pioneers, some of the most gifted students in the university always looking for the ideas "over the horizon." In response to our request, De Santillana said,

"All right. I will do that, provided that you accept to hear Indian philosophy from the 'horse's mouth.'" We said fine. He said, "We will read the books of René Guénon"[27]—something which would have never occurred in a university in France where his work was shunned in academic circles. At that time no one knew of the books of Guénon in America, but the *Introduction to Study of the Hindu Doctrines*[28] and *Man and His Becoming According to the Vedanta,*[29] published originally in 1921 and 1925, had been translated from the French into English shortly after the Second World War by Marco Pallis[30] and others in England. So De Santillana said, "Order these books from Luzac in London." We ordered the books and we studied Hinduism with De Santillana through the works of Guénon.

Can you imagine that at M.I.T.? Here was a group consisting of a few people studying traditional doctrines at M.I.T. in a seminar that was in fact held in the evenings. As soon as I read these works, the whole world shook under my feet, and very soon I realized that these teachings were what I was looking for. To me what Guénon was saying was the truth, and his criticisms of modern philosophy and of the modern world were absolutely true.

Leaving Physics

So during the sophomore year, when I was only eighteen or nineteen years old (I do not remember the month), I went to the physics department and told my professors, especially my main professor and advisor, that I was going to leave the field of physics. I remember that he was sitting in a big office behind his desk, writing something. He said, "Yes, Hossein!" without lifting his head. I said, "I want to leave the field of physics." He suddenly lifted his head and looked up sharply towards me and said, "You would have been a great physicist, but the world needs good people in other fields as well. Good luck to you." At that time, many of my physics professors were people who had worked with Robert Oppenheimer and Enrico Fermi, making the atomic bomb during the Second World War. Several of them died later of cancer, but at that time they did not know about the medical consequences of their work on the bomb. Many of them died in their forties. Oftentimes I also saw Oppenheimer, who always had a sense of melancholy about him and was a terribly tormented person.

R.J.: He used to come to M.I.T.
S.H.N.: Oh, yes.

R.J.: He was influenced by Indian philosophy also . . .
S.H.N.: Exactly, and he would often refer to Indian themes in the lectures that he would give, but he remained a tormented soul because . . .

R.J.: Of the atomic bomb.
S.H.N.: Yes, the atomic bomb and the resulting crisis of conscience that had not been solved within him despite his interest in Indian philosophy and the consolation its teachings provided. I knew that I did not want to become like Oppenheimer, but also that the consideration of a negative condition was not enough. I had to discover in a positive manner what I wanted to become.

Discovering the Traditionalists (Coomaraswamy and Schuon)

Anyway, the writing of Guénon led me by what would appear as an accident to a couple of people who had known Ananda Coomaraswamy[31] who had died a few years before in Boston. They introduced me to Mrs. Coomaraswamy, his widow, who had an apartment in Cambridge right between Harvard and M.I.T., and the Coomaraswamy Library was there. I went to meet her, and we became friends immediately. I spent the next four or five years in the richest traditionalist library in the Western world with totally open access to all the books. In exchange, I catalogued upon her request, and for the first time, the complete writings of the doctor before all these later catalogs saw the light of day. I also read Coomaraswamy's works avidly and later on even introduced his name and works in Iran at a time when no one had heard of him as yet. I remember the first time I talked to your mother about him. She was very excited and later on even wrote something about him, but nobody knew about him in 1958 when I returned home.

In any case, the writings of Guénon, Coomaraswamy, and later on Frithjof Schuon,[32] these three great traditionalist writers, all became known to me, and I studied them avidly and in depth. Already in my junior year at M.I.T., thanks to them, my intellectual crisis was settled through the discovery of traditional doctrines. I had discovered a worldview about which I felt complete certitude (*yaqīn*). I felt that this was the truth that satisfied me intellectually and accorded with my life existentially. It was in harmony with the faith that I had. It was universalist in its metaphysical perspective and also critical of Western philosophy and science in a manner that spoke directly to my concerns. I began to be myself again.

I decided at first that I would leave the West, that I would discontinue my formal education and go to some island in the Pacific or somewhere like that to spend the rest of my life away from the din of the modern world. I thought of that possibility seriously. What prevented me from doing so was the discipline that my father had given me when I was very young, a discipline that stipulated that one must finish what one has started. I really pray for his soul, and I am so glad that I did not take the step of leaving M.I.T. but decided to "stick it out." I said to myself that I would finish my degree in physics at M.I.T. no matter what, and that is exactly what I did.

Courses at Harvard

R.J.: Even if you were not interested any longer?
S.H.N.: Even though I was not interested, but instead of having the 4.9 cumulative, my grades "fell" to 4.5. I still graduated with honors, but I did not remain at the very top of my class with a 4.9 cumulative average. I did not care much about that and in fact I was spending much of my time from 1953 onward taking humanities courses at Harvard in addition to courses at M.I.T. I began to study the history of Western art and Oriental art with Benjamin Rowland[33] at Harvard. He had been a student of Coomaraswamy and was still active at that time. I used to take the Massachusetts Avenue bus; that avenue used to be two ways at that time, not one way as it is now. So I used to take the bus between classes, go to Harvard, and then come back with the Mass. Ave. bus to M.I.T.

R.J.: Did you register at Harvard at the same time?
S.H.N.: I did not have to, because I was not taking these classes for credit, but for my own knowledge. I, therefore, did not have to register formally in them. It was for my own intellectual gratification. There were also other interesting lecturers at Harvard during these years such as D. T. Suzuki.[34] I would attend as many of his lectures on Zen Buddhism as possible. At the same time I continued to take physics courses and also a lot of courses in the humanities at M.I.T., the latter especially with De Santillana. I also took a lot of mathematics courses, enough to have had a double major. If I had wanted to, I could have received a degree in mathematics as well as in physics, but I did not need it.

The Harvard Years

Upon graduation from M.I.T., I decided to study the more descriptive natural sciences, but I did not as yet know what I wanted to do and how I wanted to make a living after finishing school. But I said to myself that I should study natural sciences which are descriptive, so that if I were to decide to make a critique of Western science, people could not say, "You do not know what you are talking about, because you have a degree in physics and mathematics, but do not know the descriptive sciences." I decided to study geology and geophysics and even thought of perhaps becoming a professional geologist, since geology was more "neutral" than physics, intellectually speaking. So I went to Harvard, because there I could also pursue my other interests more easily. M.I.T. had made an offer of a wonderful fellowship to me, which I turned down, going instead to Harvard where I registered in the department of geology and geophysics for the doctoral program. Of course, besides geology I also took courses in paleontology and similar subjects. The way these subjects were taught aggravated me because whenever one asked deeper questions about the lack of evidence in the paleontological record for evolution and matters like that, the teacher would say, "We do not discuss these matters any more." The teachers were not at all interested in the philosophical discussions of the subject they were treating. Nevertheless, I said to myself that it was better to complete at least the master's program. Meanwhile, I decided definitely to leave the pure sciences and go into the field of the history of science and philosophy, and, therefore, even then while I was in the geology department, I began to take courses in the history of science and continued my study of philosophy, taking courses on Aristotle and Plato. Then finally in 1956, upon receiving my master's degree in geology and geophysics, I shifted officially to the history of science department. I did not want to enter the philosophy department at that time because it had become totally positivistic.

R.J.: Yeah, Quine?

S.H.N.: Yes, he and many others. The department was no longer the department of Emerson[35] and James[36] or for that matter Whitehead[37] and Hocking.[38] Such figures as Quine[39] and Aiken[40] had come to exercise great influence. Since it was dominated by logical positivism, the department did not interest me at all, although I took many courses in it. One of our professors, by the name of Williams, who was teaching a course in Aristotle, said that, "Philosophy begins with Kant, and there is no philosophy before him," an assertion which I considered to be nonsense. The one key person for me who was both in the philosophy department and independent of it was Harry Wolfson,[41] the famous scholar of Jewish and Islamic theology and philosophy. I am sure that you have heard of his name.

R.J.: Yes, sure.
S.H.N.: He was justly a very famous man and I am glad to have been the first to introduce his writings to Iran. Now he has been translated into Persian. I studied with him but, first of all, I began to study with Sarton,[42] who was the outstanding authority on the history of Islamic science. I was hoping to study primarily with him the general history of science, the history of various Islamic sciences, philosophy, and other branches of Islamic studies, and to bring everything together in a synthesis as far as my formal education was concerned. But Sarton died of a heart attack and Cohen[43] took over the Department of the History of Science. He taught me a great deal in the general history of science, but he did not know much about Islamic science. I did learn, however, a great deal from him from the point of view of methodologies of the discipline. Even then I was very critical of how the history of Islamic science was being studied, because the positivism of Sarton and Mach[44] had penetrated into the whole discipline of the history of science, and the influence of Duhem,[45] who was against positivistic trends, had been marginalized, although he was one of the three founders, along with Mach and Sarton, of this discipline. As a result of all this, I was mostly on my own and tried to devise a genuine method for the study of Islamic science, which I finally succeed in doing, at least to my own satisfaction, in my Ph.D. thesis and also in the book *Science and Civilization in Islam*,[46] most of which I wrote in 1958 along with my thesis.

Anyway, Sir Hamilton Gibb[47] was also at that time at Harvard, having just come from Oxford after the Suez Canal War, which he had opposed. He had resigned from his post in England and became a university professor of Islamic studies at Harvard. It was these three men, namely, Gibb, Wolfson, and I. B. Cohen, with whom I did my doctoral studies and who were my thesis advisors.

Islamic Studies

R.J.: So you knew you wanted to study Islam, or was it Gibb who interested you again?
S.H.N.: No, it was I, myself, who had decided to do so, and I approached Gibb, who took a great liking to me. We became good friends. Once he made the greatest compliment to me by saying, "You are the most brilliant student I have ever had," which is embarrassing praise coming from Gibb. He was very kind to me and liked the way I approached the subject of Islamic studies. I came into the whole

discipline with a mind that my professors called "razor sharp" after all these years of studying science and logic and especially mathematics with its intellectual rigor. Gibb appreciated these qualities greatly. I began to study Arabic again, which I had not done since childhood. I began on a fairly elementary level and proceeded all the way to advanced Arabic. My knowledge of Arabic consists of three phases: first of all, rudimentary Arabic, which I learned as a child in Iran; second, at Harvard; and third, when I came back to Iran, where I continued to learn Arabic, this time with traditional masters.

Languages

Language-wise, while at Peddie I had continued my study of French, and by the time I came to M.I.T., my reading knowledge of French was good. I read the books of Guénon in French and my French improved because of the writings of Guénon, Schuon, and others. I also would go to France and French Switzerland from time to time and had a lot of contact with the French intellectual world. All of these contacts facilitated my lecturing and speaking in French as well as reading and writing it.

R.J.: That is interesting.
S.H.N.: Yes. Then at M.I.T. I began to study German intensively and also some Italian; later I learned some Greek and Latin, but just on a rudimentary level, enough to be able to understand the roots of philosophical terms. That is what interested me as far as Greek and Latin were concerned, but Italian and Spanish, I just wanted to have a reading knowledge of them. German for me was much more than that. I was always very much interested in the German language, and I had to pass for my Ph.D. exams in both German and French; and also since Hegel was one of my fields for the Ph.D. exam, I had to know his writings in German. So, I was pretty good in German in the old days, but it became rusty when I went back to Iran. My knowledge of German has continued to deteriorate, because in contrast to French and English, I do not use it except when reading a German text from time to time.

Thesis

R.J.: How is it that you did not do your thesis on somebody like Guénon or Coomaraswamy or the *Sophia Perennis*?

S.H.N.: That is a very good question. First of all, that would not have been possible at that time at Harvard, because such figures were still too contemporary, and not enough time had passed to allow them to be seen "historically," and be thereby permitted by my thesis committee to become subjects of a doctoral thesis. Also, what I wanted to do was to apply the traditional teachings to something grandiose, which I usually advise my own Ph.D. students not to do. I really wanted to change the field of the study of Islamic science and go to the very heart of the question of the nature of Islamic scientific thought. That is what my thesis was about; one should always be humble, but this is a historical fact. My thesis came out almost unchanged as the book *An Introduction to Islamic Cosmological Doctrines.*[48] Almost fifty years have passed, and that is still the only book of its kind in the field, and it has had considerable influence on many people in their whole way of thinking about traditional cosmologies. This is true for not only Islamic scholars, but also for people in Japan, India, and elsewhere who have been inspired by that approach to try to study their own cosmological teachings, not from the point of view of the positivistic Western sciences, but from their own point of view. Perhaps undertaking this project was also a kind of ambition or hubris of a young scholar, but I did not see it as a way of self-aggrandizement. Rather, I thought that this was the occasion when I could produce a major work that would apply the ideas of Guénon, Coomaraswamy, and Schuon, which had now become my own, combined with rigorous scholarship to the field of Islamic science and philosophy.

R.J.: Who was your advisor, Gibb?
S.H.N.: Yes, but not only Gibb. As I have already mentioned, I had three advisors: Wolfson, Gibb, and Cohen. A. D. Nock,[49] the famous Harvard professor of Greek, who as you know worked with Festugière on the edition of Hermetic texts, which they published in four volumes in France (*La Révélation d'Hermès Trismégiste*)[50] was also a person with whom I worked a great deal, but he was not my direct advisor. My main advisors are those three cited above.

Harvard's Widener Library

R.J.: Yes, and can you talk a little bit about Harvard at that time? I mean people who impressed you . . .
S.H.N.: Harvard in those days was a very exciting place, and at the same time much more relaxed than M.I.T. as far as the intellectual ambience

was concerned; but, of course, what I loved most about Harvard was the Widener Library, which I believe is the number one library in the world for research, although it does not have as many books as the Library of Congress. Widener is quite an amazing place, and I knew the sections of the library that had to do with my interests all the way from Pythagoras to Ibn Sīnā, from Iran to India, from Western philosophy to Islamic thought, and so forth, like the palm of my hand. I spent much time in the Widener Library, and a great deal of the research that I did later is related to what I learned there during my Harvard years. Even many years later when I wrote my *Knowledge and the Sacred*,[51] I was living in Boston at that time, and almost all of the research for that book was done at the Widener Library. Therefore, the first thing that really impressed me at Harvard was the Widener Library and then, of course, the Fogg Museum, the inside of which was very beautiful and where I took all of those art courses with Benjamin Rowland.[52] It had a lot of wonderful Persian miniatures, as well as Indian, Chinese, and Japanese works. It was a sort of antidote to the ugly ambience of the laboratories of M.I.T., and it was also a kind of psychological and spiritual refuge for me.

Influences and Encounters at Harvard

Professors

As far as the professors at Harvard, whom I knew and who impressed me in the sciences, were concerned, there were two people in the geology department, Professor Birch[53] and Professor Billings,[54] who were among the leading geologists and geophysicists of the day. One was a geophysicist, one a geologist. I was Professor Birch's assistant for a couple of years. Both men were fine scientists and human beings. Also, Billings was a New England geologist very close to nature and helped to inculcate in me the love for the hills and mountains of New England that we visited on many field trips. One of the important aspects of my experiences in America of nature going back to Peddie was extensive trips taken in the national parks in the most beautiful areas of the United States, where I would spend a great deal of time. This experience extended into my years at Harvard. During the period when I studied geology, this experience was, in a sense, augmented by the fact that we had to take all those field trips, for example, in the granite country in New Hampshire in all those beautiful hills away from the cities.

In the general intellectual domain, in the field of thought, the people with whom I had contact and who impressed me a great deal were the following: First of all, there was Benjamin Rowland whom I have already mentioned. He was an art historian, but also a very perspicacious person with a philosophical mind, an incredible scholar, who had a completely traditional understanding of Oriental art. Although he did not teach Islamic art, he did teach Chinese and Indian art. But he knew something about Persian art as well, especially of the Islamic period. Not only did I take my courses with him, but we became good friends, and he even visited me later in Iran.

At that time, Jaeger,[55] the famous scholar of Greek who wrote the book *Paedeia* was still at Harvard. I liked him very much, and he impressed me by the catholicity of his interests and his knowledge. In contrast to Jaeger, Nock was an eccentric but also had tremendous knowledge of the Hellenistic world in all of its aspects. While I was at Harvard, for the first time a Catholic historian, Dawson,[56] was brought there, and I had a lot of contact with him. In fact, I sat in on one of his courses. I was, at that time, very interested in medieval European studies, not only philosophy, which was part of my field, but also medieval art and institutions. Also Taylor[57] taught a whole year's course on the Middle Ages, which I took, and we became friends. I learned much from him about medieval European civilization. When I was at M.I.T., as well as Harvard, Maritain[58] would come there from time to time, although he did not live in the area. I had met and spoken to him. It was also at Harvard that I met Gilson,[59] although he was not there permanently. It was a joy to make his acquaintance, and we remained friends to the end of his life; he always showed interest in my ideas and later works. Of course these figures are in addition to Sarton, Gibb, Cohen, and Wolfson, whom I have already mentioned.

R.J.: How was . . .
S.H.N.: Let me first finish with Harvard and say something about Frye,[60] who was professor of Iranian studies. I was his teaching assistant for some time. I knew him very well, like a member of the family, because he used to come to our house all the time. I was not influenced as much by his scholarship as I was by Gibb's, but I was very impressed by Frye's love of Iran and also his knowledge of Iranian languages, which was quite good. In the philosophy department, I had some attraction to the courses of Professor Williams, but the others did not really attract me.

Paul Tillich

There was also Tillich[61] who at that time was at Harvard and had become very famous as a Christian theologian. He was a very impressive person, deeply interested in religious dialogue. I was happy to deliver the Tillich Memorial Lecture at Harvard in 2000 on the theme of crossing religious frontiers.

R.J.: You went to his lectures?
S.H.N.: Yes. I went to some of his lectures, and later on in 1962, when he was still a professor at Harvard and I was a visiting professor there, we spent more time together. We had long conversations together because he had become very interested in comparative religion and wanted to discuss Christian-Islamic dialogue with me.

R.J.: So what was his point of view about traditional metaphysics and people like Coomaraswamy or Guénon?
S.H.N.: At first, he had very little knowledge of them, and their teachings had just passed him by; but I brought up their subject. I think that he just had read a few things by Coomaraswamy, becoming aware of him through Mircea Eliade,[62] who had been very deeply influenced by Coomaraswamy and Guénon. Tillich did not want to say much more about these figures and does not refer to them in his writings as far as I know. In any case, Eliade and Tillich had become friends, and I think that Tillich had discovered the writings of Coomaraswamy through Eliade, but the traditional doctrines had passed him by. As you know, Tillich had been brought up in the German School of philosophy and theology, and he had known and was especially attracted to Schelling[63] and 19th-century romantic philosophy. Tillich was a real philosopher and not only a theologian. He was in a sense a Platonist, a serious philosopher and thinker and at the same time a man of faith who had read a great deal about the various aspects of the modern experience, and knew modern thought well.

What he came to discover at the end of his life was what I talked about in my Tillich Lecture, namely two "others" which Christianity has had to face: one, secularism in all of its different modes; and the second, the other religions of the world which are not secularist and yet other than Christianity. It is this reality that Tillich had come to discover late in life, and it was on the basis of that reality that we had discussions together. In 1962, he had just come back from Japan after long discussions with Sin'ichi Hisumatsu, the famous Zen master. After his participation in Christian-Buddhist dialogue, he was just becoming interested in dialogue between Islam and Christianity, and we talked about the whole significance of comparative religion. He was then moving in that direction, away from this idea of Christianity as "crisis" of which Barth[64] spoke and his opposition to even comparing on a religious footing Christianity and other religions, Barth refusing even to call Christianity a religion like other religions. This view was of course anathema to people like myself interested in traditional metaphysics and the multiplicity of religions. I think Tillich was much more open to other religions than the other major Protestant theologians of his day. Also, something in Tillich that interested me was that Tillich had been deeply influenced, I think, by the mystical tradition of Meister Eckhart[65] and Angelus Silesius.[66] Tillich always spoke about the Ground of Being, the Absolute, which provided us with a common ground for metaphysical discourse.

Authors

R.J.: Yes. Did you start reading these at that time, I mean Meister Eckhart?
S.H.N.: Meister Eckhart, yes. I read him from cover to cover, but not Tillich. At that time, you know, I was such a purist. I wanted to learn first of all the basic sources. So I read and knew Meister Eckhart fairly well. I had read the Pfeiffer translation; I even read some of Eckhart in German, an archaic German difficult to understand.

R.J.: Who were the authors, I mean, the books you read, except traditional metaphysicians?
S.H.N.: They were the most important, but besides them and authors of works on Islam, I read most of the works of the important Catholic French intellectuals such as Gilson and Maritain and even writers such as Paul Claudel and François Mauriac, and then those Catholic theologians who were also Islamicists such as Gardet[67] and Anawati,[68] who was also Catholic but more of an Islamicist than a theologian. I also read the classics of Western philosophy, the books of Descartes, Leibniz, Spinoza, Kant, Hegel, et cetera in addition to classical works of Western mysticism. Moreover, I read texts of scholars who were at Harvard and in whom I was most interested. It is interesting to note that because of my relation with the French intellectual world, I was not reading much German Catholic thought, people such as Karl Rahner[69] and von Balthasar.[70] I had heard about them, but it was mostly the French,

Catholic intellectual circle and also some Italians such as Sciacca[71] and Rosmini[72] (whom I read mostly later) in whom I was interested. I did not pay much attention to Protestant theology (with the exception of Tillich) except when it was concerned with the relation between religion and science or Islamic theology.

R.J.: Who were then the philosophers who interested you most and to whom you devoted yourself to reading? Was it Pascal? Was it Hegel?
S.H.N.: Before we get to that question, I would like to mention a few more names of people who were writing on Western intellectual life and whom I read extensively. One such person was Koyré,[73] who would come to M.I.T. often, being a friend of De Santillana, and also to Harvard. I had read practically all of his works, and I knew his thought very well. I was attracted also to these medievalists who were trying to reappraise European medieval civilization, such as Christopher Dawson. I would read these medieval historians quite a bit. As for people writing about the East is concerned, besides Coomaraswamy, Guénon, and Schuon, who were of course my main conduits to the study of Indian thought, I read the main works of Dasgupta,[74] Murty,[75] Radhakrishnan,[76] and the like. As for the Far East, I read the standard works, such as the classical books in French by Marcel Granet,[77] *La Pensée chinoise*, on classical Chinese thought, and also in English the works of Needham, especially his *Science and Civilization in China*.[78] Although I disagreed with his point of view, which was Marxist, he included a lot of valuable documentation concerning the sciences in Chinese civilization. In fact, I named my first book on Islamic Science, *Science and Civilization in Islam*,[79] as a response to him, although I was working single-handedly, a twenty-five-year-old scholar, and he had a whole group working with him at Cambridge. I also studied Fung Yu-lan's famous history of Chinese philosophy.[80]

Greek Philosophers

Now, to come back to your question. As for the Western philosophers who attracted me the most, first of all, let me say I do not consider Greek philosophy to be just Western philosophy as it is considered to be so in standard histories of Western philosophy such as that of Bertrand Russell or other books in German, French, or other European languages. In such works one starts with Thales and other Greeks such as Plato and ends up with let us say Heidegger[81] as a seamless tradition.

But of course Greek philosophy is as much a part of Islamic philosophy as it is of Western philosophy. Greek thought belonged to the Eastern Mediterranean world, and two different civilizations made use of it, the Islamic and the Western, not to speak of the Byzantines, represented by such a figure as Plethon.[82] So let me start with the Greek philosophers. As far as Greek thought is concerned, I was and remain very much interested mostly in early Greek thought up to Aristotle, and of course including Pythagoreanism, Platonism, and the later schools of Neopythagoreanism and Neoplatonism.

It was only later in life that I became interested in Stoic thought and especially Stoic physics, thanks to the works of Sambursky, the famous Israeli scholar of German origin who wrote *Physics of the Stoics.*[83] I studied that subject, and in my book *Religion and the Order of Nature,*[84] a whole section is devoted to Stoic physics, which is very significant to the history of science, but metaphysically the Stoics were not that interesting to me. That is why I paid less attention to Marcus Aurelius, Chrysippus, and people like that. Then there are the "worldly" Greek philosophical schools such as Epicurianism, the New Academy, et cetera, which never really interested me. My attention was always centered on the pre-Socratics, Plato, Aristotle, and Plotinus, especially his *Enneads*, which I read in the MacKenna translation[85] in my twenties along with the Platonic dialogues, which I read in many different translations. My Greek was not unfortunately good enough to read the original Greek, but I could check the main Greek philosophical terms by going back to the original texts. I also read the works of Aristotle and his school extensively, and in fact when I was at Tehran University I taught regularly a course on Aristotle, whom I think I know well. I studied nearly all of his works in both European languages and also many in Arabic. This fact is important because the Arabic translations of Aristotle incorporate the oral tradition going back to Aristotle himself.

Among these figures of Greek philosophy I was especially attracted to Pythagoras and his philosophy of mathematics. As I have said, I have studied mathematics and poetry, which meet in my own being, and here we have Pythagoras as the only major figure known to the West who was both a major mathematician and a poet. It is very interesting that the Islamic world, especially Persia, has produced many figures who were both poets and mathematicians, but the West has not produced any major figures of this kind except Pythagoras. The meeting place between mathematics and poetry was always of great interest to me. So I read *The Golden Verses* and, of course, *The Pythagorean Sourcebook*, which was then extremely rare but has now just been made available again, containing all the later Pythagorean writings. I also studied closely the remarkable commentary of Fabre d'Olivet on *The Golden Verses.*[86] Everything Pythagorean on which I could lay my hands was of much interest to me.

Medieval Western Philosophy

As for medieval Western philosophy where specifically Western philosophy begins, let us start with Saint Augustine and Boethius. I read much of Saint Augustine, and he always attracted me a great deal before I discovered our own *ishrāqī* (illuminationist) tradition, which I believe to be even more metaphysically complete than Augustinian illuminationism. It was the book of Gilson that attracted me first to Saint Augustine. Furthermore, even at M.I.T. we had to read some of Saint Augustine's essays such as *Faith, Hope, and Charity,*[87] and in the course we had to take on masterpieces of Western civilization we also had to read his *Confessions*[88] and *The City of God.*[89] Besides his *Confessions,* I also read many of his theological treatises. *The City of God,* I read many times. As for Boethius, his *Consolation of Philosophy*[90] always spoke to me a great deal. I had a love for the thought of Boethius and still do. As for the Middle Ages proper, Johannes Scotus Erigena attracted me like a magnet, but the *De Divisionae Naturae,*[91] which is his major work, was not easily available in English at that time. There were only the Latin and Greek versions, and I had to struggle through the Latin text, with which I had a lot of trouble. Later, I finally found the English translation of it, and I have studied it many times over the years. As for the golden age of medieval European thought, it was the two figures of Saint Thomas and Saint Bonaventure who particularly attracted me, and not so much Duns Scotus, although he was influenced by my friend Avicenna (Ibn Sīnā).[92] The nominalists in the later Middle Ages did not interest me at all, because I was always interested in metaphysics, and you know the views of Ockham, William of Auvergne, and people like that. I read them and I had to learn their ideas, but not because of personal interest.

R.J.: But you are not interested in them.
S.H.N.: No, not as serious philosophical works.

Renaissance Philosophers

R.J.: What about the Renaissance?
S.H.N.: In the Renaissance period, what was of most interest to me was Ficino[93] and the revival of Platonism in the Florentine Academy. I

was also interested in Renaissance Hermeticism and alchemy. I had also read some of the works of Agrippa,[94] Paracelsus,[95] and even Montaigne[96] and several other philosophers of the Renaissance, but Ficino remained the one person to whom I was deeply attracted and remain so to this day. Of course, I read also works of the Italian cosmologist Giordano Bruno,[97] who was an enigmatic figure.

R.J.: Mystical.
S.H.N.: Yes, mystical but still a strange figure. At that time in my life, I was reading a lot of these figures such as him, John Dee,[98] Paracelsus, and Agrippa, this mystical, esoteric, and occult philosophy that was popular during the Renaissance. As you know there was at that time what Frances Yates has called the Rosicrucian Enlightenment[99] and much interest in Hermeticism, the Kabbala, Neo-Pythagoreanism, et cetera, to whose study I devoted some time. Of course the rise of modern philosophy and rationalism with Descartes marks a period of severe opposition to such currents, which were gradually relegated to the category of the occult.

Modern Western Philosophers

R.J.: And modern philosophy?
S.H.N.: Although I had to study them, most of the major modern Western philosophers did not attract me, and I have been critical of most of them; but there are two or three whom I like and whom I consider to be important philosophers in the traditional sense of the term. One is Pascal and the other Leibniz,[100] some aspects of whose works attracted me a great deal. It was De Santillana who introduced me to the work of Leibniz and said, "This is the most important metaphysical work of the 17th century. If you are interested in serious metaphysics, you should read Leibniz more than Spinoza and Descartes." But I also used to like Spinoza[101] until I discovered certain real flaws in his metaphysical views. As for the later period, major figures such as Hume[102] and Kant[103] I read, but without any personal attraction. Hegel was of greater interest to me for some time, but then I realized that his philosophy was a kind of temporalization of the metaphysical Absolute, metaphysically speaking. There are interesting elements in Hegel, but there are also major problems from the traditional point of view. Nevertheless, I chose his philosophy as one of my fields for the doctoral exam at Harvard. I was, however, much more interested in the German

Romantic philosophers, especially Schelling[104] and also later on Franz von Baader,[105] who is one of my favorite German philosophers. I have discovered more and more figures who are of great philosophical interest but who are never mentioned in general histories of Western philosophy. We have not talked about Corbin, but I must say that I owe something to Corbin in arousing my interest in some of these lesser-known figures, especially of the Renaissance, such as Tersteegen[106] and Hamann[107] about whom he wrote.[108]

R.J.: Counter-Enlightenmentists?
S.H.N.: Yes, I suppose so, although I do not like the word *Counter-Enlightenment* because that is putting the reaction in a kind of negative light; but in a sense, yes, they (those who came after the 18th century and in whom I was interested) were people who were definitely against the Enlightenment. However, I did also read a lot of Rousseau[109] and Voltaire.[110] Voltaire I had heard about as a child, and I read him over and over in the original French later in my life. Furthermore, I read many of the works of the French encyclopedists such as Didérot and Condorcet.[111]

R.J.: In the 18th century . . .
S.H.N.: Yes, as you know, the Encyclopedists who were rationalists, the Enlightenment philosophers, as they are usually known.

R.J.: You were never too much attracted by rationalists, no?
S.H.N.: No, never. As you know, I have a rational mind, and I never thought that I was any less rational than they were. However, I did not appreciate their narrowing the focus and vision of reason by cutting it off from the intellect. I am sure that we are going to get to that matter later on. A fundamental pillar of my whole intellectual vision is the relation between reason and intellect, which the rationalist philosophers collapsed into one single reality by reducing intellect to reason. I oppose such an act, but I have never been anti-rational at all. Rather, I am anti-rationalism, which is quite something else.

As for later philosophies, the positivism of the Vienna circle and its aftermath never held any attraction for me whatsoever. I had trouble even getting myself to study these things. Nor did Wittgenstein.[112] Of course you have the later Wittgenstein, who goes into "silence" and turns into a "mystical philosopher"; but the way he criticized metaphysics was something against my attitude and my interests. Edmund Husserl[113] and Max Scheler[114] were of some interest to me, as was the whole school around them, but I was never much attracted to Heidegger.

Heidegger

R.J.: You weren't?
S.H.N.: No.

R.J.: Why?
S.H.N.: Because I think Heidegger tried to take a "jump" towards Being without really getting there. Like Husserl, he wanted to reach Being without God and did not succeed. There is a story in connection with this question that is worth recounting. One day in 1966, on the occasion of the conference on Shiʿism held at the University of Strasbourg in France, Corbin and I were standing at the sanctuary of Saint Odil near Strasbourg on top of a hill from which one can look down on the Black Forest in Germany. Corbin put his arm around my shoulder and said, "My dear friend. You know, when I was a young man I walked down right on this path to Germany to go and meet Martin Heidegger, but ever since I discovered the Persian philosophy of Mullā Ṣadrā, Suhrawardī and the like, I do not need to do that anymore, because with Heidegger the end of being is death, but he who discovers real Being, at the end of his existence stands Pure Being."

Long before I made a study of Heidegger, I had an intuition of that truth. I did not become interested in Heidegger while I was at Harvard, but came to him primarily through Corbin and later on certain other people. By that time I had already immersed myself in the philosophy of Mullā Ṣadrā and our own philosophy of being, which is an *Existenz Philosophie* that I believe is much more profound than the version of Heidegger. So, he never attracted me as a thinker who could influence me. I was, however, attracted to his critique of technology, to his writing on poetry, and matters like that. No doubt he is an important thinker, and I am sad that for political reasons, he is somewhat cast aside these days in America. But each matter should be put in its own place, and a scholar should be objective and not allow his own ideology to color his study of a particular philosophy.

In any case, none of these philosophers attracted me as did those who followed the perennial philosophy, and I looked upon the former from that point of view. As I said, I consider Heidegger to be an important European philosopher who brought up some important philosophical issues. I believe that unfortunately he never understood what *Sein* is in itself in the Ṣadrian sense of the term, although Corbin believed that he did so in his heart. Heidegger was too much enmeshed in modern European philosophy to understand what *Sein* or *wujūd* means metaphysically. He did, however, realize the poverty of modern philosophy, and like Richard Rorty,[115] who spoke from another point of view, declared the end of Western philosophy as it is practiced today. Certainly I agree with that appraisal. I realized that truth already when I was at M.I.T. and came to know intuitively that this philosophy was going to reach an impasse. I do not, of course, believe that this marks the end of philosophy as such. Rather, I believe that it is the end of the process which began in the Renaissance. Heidegger takes the misunderstanding of Being back to Aristotle.

I do not agree philosophically with the whole development of mainstream modern Western philosophy, which from the 17th century onward turned to rationalism, and then ontology became gradually reduced to epistemology, epistemology to logic, and logic to irrationality. Finally, we are just left with shallow concepts, and modern philosophy has lost its vision. If there is any contribution that I have made to Western thought, it is precisely to speak about the importance of opening the door again to authentic philosophic vision. There is more to philosophy than the play of mental concepts. To summarize, Heidegger and similar philosophies did not really influence me, in contrast to my friend Dariush Shayegan,[116] who was for a while like my own student and protégé and shared the traditional worldview of perennial philosophy with me, and then became interested in Heidegger, and henceforth rejected the tradition perspective in order to follow to a large extent the Heideggerian worldview.

R.J.: This is a general question, but I am interested to know, if you had, if somebody asked you, "Who are the philosophers that influenced you the most in your life?" and you had to pick one or two, who would these be?

Greatest Influences

S.H.N.: I would like to put my answer in two categories, because my philosophical world is a kind of synthesis between the perennial philosophy, which I espouse and represent, and the Islamic philosophical tradition, which I have tried to revive and to which I also belong. And so I would say that for the first category, there are Guénon and Schuon; if I had to name a third person, then Coomaraswamy; and for the second category, Ibn Sīnā, Suhrawardī, Ibn ʿArabī, and Mullā Ṣadrā.[117] These two different traditions come together in my thought, and it would therefore not be possible to name one or two persons in general.

Part Three

Return to Iran

R.J.: Now, we are going to continue about your return to Iran after Harvard. So, in the summer of 1958, you left Harvard and returned to Iran, where you began your duties as associate professor of philosophy at Tehran University. My question is, why did you not continue teaching and doing research in America and have the desire to go back to Iran?
S.H.N.: The desire for me to go back to Iran was very, very strong. I never thought I would remain permanently in the United States, although as you know, golden opportunities arose for me to do so. I could have become a junior fellow at Harvard for three years if I had waited a year. That would have been a wonderful opportunity, because for three years I could have done research and nothing else and then begin a formal teaching career. Also, M.I.T. wanted to employ me as an assistant professor in the history of science as soon as I received my Ph.D., but I also turned that down. So there was no idea in my mind that I would stay in America. I wanted to go back to Iran and felt that that was where I belonged. This feeling became even stronger after the rediscovery of the traditional world and my own intellectual and spiritual heritage. In 1958, there was not even a debate in my mind whether I wanted to stay in America or go back to Iran.

R.J.: In which way did you find the return to Iran a challenging one?
S.H.N.: It was not at all challenging in the way that it is for many people who have lived for many years in the West, as I had spent nearly thirteen years in America at the time of my return. The challenge came more on a practical level; you know, finding housing and things like that, and I also did not want to indulge too much in social activity, but coming from a large family, my mother would require me to go here and there nearly every night. But I did not want to spend every night going

to family gatherings, meetings, and reunions. I was too much immersed in the inner life for such a program, which was simply difficult for me to follow. As I told you, I always cherished privacy and solitude and sought to be alone when that was possible. And, of course, I had an intense intellectual life going on at that time, and I needed the freedom to write and to do research. But other than that, I settled down fairly quickly and married very rapidly. One of the reasons why I married so quickly was in fact precisely that I wanted to gain my independence family-wise and not to have to go to family gatherings all the time. Wanting to be more independent from the larger extended family and my mother, I became married in just a few months after I returned to Iran. I then had my own house. My mother lived with us for a while, but then she began to live independently on her own, and my socially independent life began.

An early problem that was somewhat difficult was the question of the military draft. I thought serving in the army would be a waste of my life after all that I had studied; so I tried to avoid spending two years in military service. Since I was the oldest son of the family and my father had died, there was actually a provision for me to receive a deferment as provider for my mother. After much administrative struggle, I was finally given the deferment and was immediately employed by Tehran University as associate professor of philosophy and the history of science.

Outside of these challenges, other matters were easy. Becoming reintegrated into Persian society was easy for me, because I was not at all Westernized (*farangī ma'āb*) and could get along without any difficulty with ordinary people. It was very easy for me to sit down and talk to a beet seller in front of the bazaar or a shopkeeper (*dokkāndār*). Once a Westernized colleague said to me, "What do you have to say to these people?" I said, "I have more to say to them than I have to you, because they represent still the traditional Persian culture, which is also mine." Some Western-educated Iranians were in the clouds, only speaking to people who used English or French words in every sentence and spoke only of Western culture.

Of course I also had some trouble trying to establish myself financially, because I had promised myself not to do any kind of work outside the university. I therefore taught nightly courses for some time to complement my low salary as a professor. But gradually matters improved, and we became firmly established financially, especially when my books appeared. But of course I never sought to engage in any economic or administrative activity, and all my energy was devoted to scholarly, academic, and cultural pursuits.

R.J.: Actually, you became like your father, you were saying . . .
S.H.N.: Exactly. Yes, in fact, I always thought of that point. During the years when I held important positions in Iran, a person in my position would not usually walk in the bazaar and stay and talk to ordinary people, but I would do that all the time. I remember when I was president of Aryamehr University, I used to visit Isfahan nearly every week, because we were building an immense campus there, a task which was one of the major achievements in my life as far as the creation of a new educational entity was concerned. While in Isfahan, when I had a little time to myself, I would tell my driver to let me off at the mouth of the great bazaar in Meydan-i Jahan, and then I would just go into the bazaar and lose myself there in a space in which I could preserve my privacy, because in the main streets many people knew me and I had to greet everybody. In those streets, I was never left alone, but there in the bazaar I could lose myself in the crowd and talk to ordinary people. It was very enjoyable for me.

Architecture and Sacred Space[1]

R.J.: Do you actually like the Oriental space more than modern Western space?
S.H.N.: Oh, very much so. Of course there are Western medieval spaces such as in Carcassonne in France or something like that or even Île St. Louis in Paris, which I appreciate greatly, but the traditional spaces in which something of traditional life still survives, I appreciate even more, especially those of our own civilization.

R.J.: Why? What did you find in such a space? Is it more spiritual or more exotic?
S.H.N.: Architecture, you know, is not accidental. It always reflects a philosophy of space, of movement, of individual and social life, of presence, of light, and it has an effect upon one's soul. It is not as some people think like a machine to live in; it always affects us inwardly. Even if it be considered a machine to live in, it still affects our soul, except in a negative way. The traditional spaces of urban settings and individual buildings, however, convey a spiritual presence and have a symbolism that speaks to me very profoundly. Therein I find a sense of peace and

serenity. I am sure that you know many secular people or even atheists in France who feel a sense of calm and serenity when they go to one of the medieval French towns. That is not at all accidental. In traditional architecture, the space that is created is related to the world of the spirit. In fact, a conference was held at the World Bank recently in which I spoke about "Cities of the Spirit" and dealt with this very issue. I have always been sensitive to the effect of sacred spaces and have written about it. Also I worked very hard in Iran during the twenty-one years when I was there to try to protect the traditional architectural network (*bāft-e shahr*) and structure of our traditional cities, as well as individual buildings, from the demolition that was taking place by a new generation of people totally impervious and indifferent to the significance of traditional architecture and city planning.

R.J.: Yes, it has been unfortunate, because most of these cities are getting destroyed all over the world.
S.H.N.: Yes, all over the world; that is one of the great tragedies of modern life. You see, in the old days, because the tradition was living, when let us say a Seljuq city was destroyed and a Timurid city took its place, just to cite an example from our own country Iran, the replacement was just as beautiful; there was continuity and not the sense of loss. Today, if you destroy even a narrow street or building of the Qajar period, what is it replaced by? A big boulevard with dirty trucks coming and going and air pollution infecting every street, along with great heat during the summer, in contrast to the narrow streets which protected the cool air of the night during the day.

There were, in fact, incredible architectural inventions, especially in our own country, Iran, that in a sense took the place of modern air-conditioning facilities. Those energy-saving and environmentally friendly creations are now being destroyed just when we are facing the crisis of global warming. It is sad to observe this phenomenon, which is taking place all over the world. Fortunately, matters are somewhat better in the Islamic world than they were thirty or forty years ago. In some places like the city of San'a in Yemen, the city of Fez in Morocco, and in some of our own cities such as Yazd and Kashan, a lot of renovation of old houses and old streets and quarters have taken place, but still the bulldozer remains one of the greatest enemies of the human spirit.

R.J.: Can we say, maybe, because people used to feel more responsibility towards space because space was sacred for them . . .

S.H.N.: Of course.

R.J.: And it has been desacralized today?

S.H.N.: Yes, both space and human life itself, life which functions in this world in space and time. What happened in the modern world is that, first of all, thought and then life was secularized, followed by the secularization of space and time. Consequently, modern man does not even think about the significance of sacred space. Of course, I do not say that there are no exceptions and that no contemporary architect thinks of it. There are individual architects here and there who try to swim against the current, but by and large the loss of the source of the sacred had as its consequence the secularization of the world including, of course, space. Modern man has even tried to destroy the sacred space of virgin nature. And so we go about cutting the trees and destroying the forests with complete impunity. What remains of virgin nature, however, gives the lie to our illusion of space being purely quantitative. That is also why for so many people, the more the natural world is destroyed, the more do they realize how precious it is, not only from the point of supporting our biological life through the preservation of the biosphere, but also spiritually. When one journeys into primordial forests and what is called "old growth" here in America, old-growth forests being those which were not planted by man, one experiences being in another world, in another space. Outwardly, the space is the same, the oxygen is the same, the sun shines on the same soil, and from the point of view of physics nothing has changed. But in reality, everything has changed because, precisely there, we experience a space that is still sacred. It is created by the Hands of God, and it is very different from the space of a mall built primarily for greed. In the old days, in all traditional civilizations, architecture emulated the principles of nature, not its outward aspects, but created sacred spaces that corresponded to the inner reality of nature and our own inner reality while transcending nature in its outward dimension.

Traditional architecture did create sacred space, but the modes were different in various traditions. The gothic cathedral in Christianity creates a space that moves upward towards Heaven. As for the mosque, it creates a space that reposes upon itself and recreates the peace of virgin nature. It is in fact a recapitulation of the space of virgin nature. There one feels as if one were in the middle of a desert, or on a mountain, or even in a forest. This type of architecture enabled people to live in a city and yet allow their soul to experience the peace and repose beyond agitation of city life. It is this sense of space that has been lost in modern architecture.

Tehran University

R.J.: Yes. So going back to Iran with this new spiritual identity that you had acquired in America by reading Guénon, Coomaraswamy, and Schuon and others, after finishing your dissertation and going back to your roots in Iran, did you find things changed, or was it difficult for you, I mean, in relation with the architecture of the city, the people?

S.H.N.: It was more than a question of the architecture of the city. I had to carry out a major intellectual and spiritual *jihād*, you might say, in at least two domains. First of all, in my working ambience at Tehran University, and secondly, within my own family and circle of friends and people who like me had come back from the West but were very different from me. My own family had become more modernized than when I had left Iran, but with them one could always find a *modus vivendi*; that was not a major problem. The major struggle was at Tehran University, and that was really quite an experience. Had I not been a graduate of M.I.T. and Harvard, had I not had mastery of not only English, but also French, and known some other European languages as well as Arabic, and had my scholarship not been at a level where it could not be easily criticized, I would have been crushed, because the Faculty of Letters of Tehran University at that time, which was the heart of Persian culture and thought, was dominated by modern, Western ideas. The Faculties of Letters of Tabriz and Mashhad Universities were established more recently, but at that time 95 percent of all of the famous writers and thinkers of Iran were at Tehran University, if one were to put aside the *'ulamā'*. Putting traditional circles of learning aside, the Faculty of Letters of Tehran University was really the major intellectual center in Iran, and it was dominated in its philosophy department, psychology department, and sociology department by positivism, a kind of Comptean[2] positivism, not the modern Anglo-Saxon one. It was 19th-century French positivism, and such eminent scholars as the late Drs. Sadighi, Siassi, and Mahdavi, my very good friends, all of whom had studied in France, were dominant figures. I had the best human rapport with these people. Dr. Siassi had been the head of the bureau of my father in the Ministry of Education when I was a young man, and he had great love and respect for me, but none of these men liked everything that I was saying. In the very first article that I wrote in Persian after returning to Iran, I quoted the verse of Rūmī:

har kasī kū dūr mānd az aṣl-e khīsh,
Bāz jūyad rūzegār-e vaṣl-e khīsh.[3]

One day in the philosophy department office where the professors would meet between classes, before all the important professors who were there, Dr. Sadighi, who was a professor of sociology but also taught philosophy, came in and looked at the wall but not at me. Then he said, "There is a young man who quotes verses from Jalāl al-Dīn Rūmī about returning to one's roots in a way that is critical of us."

You cannot imagine the battle I had on my hands to try to turn things around in my own field of philosophy and in the philosophy department, which was the heart of the field of human sciences and humanities and exercised influence everywhere. This was a department that was dominated by French positivism to which I was strongly opposed, and I was trying to turn matters around in several ways. First of all, I wanted to reintroduce Islamic philosophy more seriously. To this end, I began to teach a new course myself, which I then taught for some twenty years at Tehran University for undergraduates and which became a required course for all students in the Faculty of Letters, and was even emulated later in other schools of higher learning in Iran. I called it "*falsafah va ma'ārif-e eslāmī*" using *ma'ārif* itself in a traditional sense of intellectual sciences including not only philosophy but also *'erfān* (gnosis) and disciplines like that. This was an introduction to the field. In addition, we had a course on Islamic philosophy taught first by Muḥammad Kāẓim 'Aṣṣār and after him by Abū'l-Ḥasan Sha'rānī, but it had been separated from everything else in the philosophical curriculum, whereas I tried to make it more central to the educational experience of the students of philosophy. I wanted to introduce this subject as the matrix for what was being taught. In addition, for about two decades I taught a doctoral seminar with Corbin, which dealt with comparative philosophy with emphasis on Islamic philosophy from the perspective of Corbin as well as myself.

Secondly, in addition to these courses, I tried to introduce other philosophical schools and Western perspectives, to balance out and ameliorate the impact of the French academic view. This included introducing Anglo-Saxon analytical philosophy that had been absent until that time. We brought Manuchehr Bozorgmehr there to teach philosophies which were not at all metaphysical but nevertheless would open up the mental horizon of the students. To this end, I also fought for teaching Oriental philosophies. That is why I asked that Dariush Shayegan be brought in. I encouraged him to finish his Ph.D. in Indian Studies, which he did at the Sorbonne, and proposed to make him a teacher in the department to teach different schools of Indian philosophy.

Anyway, I tried to expand the horizon for the study of philosophy and had a real *jihād* on my hands, made more difficult by the fact that I was a completely lonely voice, when especially in 1337 (1958), as a young man I had come back to Iran to begin my career at Tehran University, I was therefore very active on all these fronts. One day, I think it was L. Sūratgar, the famous poet and literary figure who was a professor of English at our Faculty, who asked me, "Why are you working so hard? Are you *jūyā-yi nām*?" (seeking to find a name). And then Hossein Khatibi, another celebrated professor in the department of Persian literature, who was present, said, "the *nām* has been already left for him by his father." I need to add that many of these men had been my father's students and had the greatest reverence for him. So it was a very strange situation, and as I said, I had to work very hard to attain the goals that I was seeking.

I began to write extensively, especially in Persian, in those days. I published things occasionally in Arabic and French, but I wrote mostly in Persian and English. I tried a politically expedient plan, which was very important at that time. It was to try to keep neutral in the battle that was then being fought between the Francophone and Anglophone parties within the Faculty, and Americanization versus Europeanization. I thought that if we struck a balance between the two, the two would to some extent neutralize each other, and therefore the Persian element, which was most important to me, would survive and become even strengthened and would not be crushed by either side. I was the only person there who knew both languages, that is, English and French, well enough not to be criticized by people saying, "Oh, you are taking one side or you are taking the other side because of your lack of knowledge." These were all factors that were instrumental in my being elected and also selected as dean. At the age of thirty, I was the youngest person in the history of Tehran University ever to become a full professor. At the age of thirty-five, I was the youngest person ever to have become the dean of the Faculty, succeeding Dr. Siassi and Dr. Zabihollah Safa, both of whom were a whole generation or two older than I.

I belonged to a new generation and was able to exercise much influence not only at Tehran University but also in the cultural and educational life of the country as a whole since I was a member of all the important national councils in those fields, Shorā-ye 'Ālī-ye Farang (Supreme Cultural Council), Shorā-ye 'Ālī-ye Amūzish (Supreme Council of Education), et cetera. So there was a really formidable *jihād* on my hands to try to turn things around and to make Iranian society more aware of its own heritage. I tried to create a bridge between the traditional and the modern elements of our society.

To finish answering the question that you posed, when I came back to Iran, I consciously sought out contact with the traditional elements of the society, and, of course, it was with them that I had a great deal of rapport, although they did not understand all aspects of my educational background, what I knew about the Western world and also about the Oriental world east of Iran. Nevertheless, on a philosophical/metaphysical level, there was a great deal of rapport on my part with the traditional circles of learning to which I am sure we shall turn later on.

Famous Students

R.J.: Yes. Let me just ask you about your students. Who were your students? I suppose some of them are now active in the Islamic Republic of Iran. Name the famous ones.

S.H.N.: First of all, I have trained several generations of students. I have been teaching for some fifty years, three years as an instructor at Harvard, twenty-one years in Iran, and now some thirty years in America, with interim years also at the American University of Beirut and Harvard when I was in Iran. I trained, first of all, a number of notable students during my first few years when I was at Tehran University. Dr. Mahdavi, Dr. Khonsari, and I were then the three main professors who directed the doctoral program in philosophy, and all the people who later on became well-known professors of philosophy in Iran and also went to other universities were graduates of our university, which had then the only program in Iran offering a Ph.D. degree in philosophy. Among these students I can mention Dr. Purhosayni,[4] who died some years ago and who was a fine scholar; Dr. Reza Davari,[5] who is a well-known thinker in Iran today; Dr. Dawudi,[6] a professor of philosophy who was most likely killed at the beginning of the Revolution; and Dr. Mujtabavi,[7] who died recently and who became the Dean of the Faculty of Letters for many years after the Revolution. These were all products of those early years. They were both my students and Dr. Mahdavi's students, and they worked with the two of us together. There were also a number of other students who came somewhat later, such as Mohsen Jahangiri[8] who is a fine scholar of Ibn 'Arabī. He worked mostly with me during his student days. There was a whole group of about ten or twelve of that kind of students who worked with me during the second decade of my stay at the Faculty of Letters and who later became well-known scholars.

Then there came the period during which I trained a number of younger scholars, ten to fifteen years younger than those mentioned above, and this list included a number of foreigners such as Arabs and Pakistanis as well as Persians. I trained a few fine Arab scholars, including the Moroccan 'Abd dal-Latif Sa'dani,[9] for whom a chair of Persian studies was established for the first time in Morocco, as well as Victor Alkik[10] and al-Sisi[11] from Lebanon. For the first ten years at Tehran University, I was the head of the doctoral program for foreign students before I became dean, at which time I relinquished the post.

For those ten years, I was both the head of the library and of this program besides being professor. I was therefore also very much engaged in the whole question of libraries in Iran. I helped bring Iraj Afshar[12] to Tehran University and made him professor in the history department. I was left in charge of establishing the Central Library of the university of which he soon became director. But that is a story for another day.

As for the foreign students, besides those already mentioned, there were many from India and Pakistan and some, besides the Arab world, from Turkey and Bosnia—a number of whom became famous scholars in the field of Persian studies. They all graduated from Tehran University and studied with me, people such as Ikram Shah[13] from Pakistan and L. Peerwani, who became a well-known Ismā'īlī scholar. Many of the present-day professors of Persian in Pakistan and India were my students and under my tutelage, although they did not all work only with me. Besides those from the Islamic world, India and Japan, there were also students from the West such as Jean During,[14] now a famous expert on Persian music. William Chittick[15] was the most outstanding among them. But I must also mention Sachiko Murata[16] from Japan. These two are among the most outstanding scholars of Islamic studies and also comparative studies in America today.

Among the Persians there was Nasrollah Pourjavadi[17] who is now a very well-known scholar in Iran, and Gholamreza A'vani,[18] my best Persian student in both philosophy and doctrinal Sufism, who is well known as a scholar in both fields today. Another student close to me in the field of philosophy was Gholam-Reza Haddad Adel,[19] who became the head of the Iranian Academy of Letters. I trained him mostly in the philosophy of Islamic science, in which he became a notable scholar. I must also mention Mozaffar Bakhtiar,[20] who was a professor of Persian literature and who now is working on Chinese-Persian cultural relations, because he was professor of Persian in China for several years. He was also very close to me and collaborated with me in the Persian edition of *Persia, Bridge of Turquoise.*[21] I consider him to be one of the most gifted of the present-day scholars of Persian literature. He was not in the philosophy department as were the other people noted above. But he was attracted very much to my presentation of Persian culture, philosophy, and thought. Dr. Mohammad Faghfoory,[22] a historian who is here in the United States, should also be mentioned among those students who were not in the philosophy department but who studied with me.

Quite a few people, about thirty or forty, were trained at that time by me in two phases. In the first few years, the students were older. Many of them, such as Purhosayni, were in fact older than myself or were of my age. They were followed by a second group that was much younger, including many students from Pakistan and India. I will not name them all, but many have become scholars who have made a name for themselves in scholarship.

The second phase of training students began when I came to America, and there again there are two periods. The first belongs to the five years from 1979 to 1984 when I was at Temple University in Philadelphia. We had the largest Ph.D. program of religious studies in America, larger than Chicago and Harvard. Ismāʿīl al-Fārūqī,[23] who was a very famous Arab scholar, and I were there as the main professors of Islamic studies. We had a large department with over twenty professors. Since both Ismāʿīl and I were there, many Ph.D. students in Islamic studies came to Temple from all over the world and especially from Islamic countries, and I trained a number of very fine students there. For the first time, I began to have students from Southeast Asia, specially from Malaysia, and some of my best students belonged to this group, including Osman Bakar,[24] who is today one of the greatest scholars in Malaysia and the Malay world. Like Haddad Adel, he also studied mostly the Islamic philosophy of science along with Sufism with me. Along with Chittick, Pourjavadi, Aʿvani, and Haddad Adel, I consider him among my best students in the field of Islamic thought. Anyway, Osman Bakar has done even more work in the field of Islamic science than Haddad Adel, because after the advent of the Islamic Revolution of 1979 Haddad Adel became deputy minister of the ministry of *Irshād* and then head of The Academy of Letters (*Fahangestān-e Adab*), followed by speakership of the parliament, and has not done as much work until now in the field of the Islamic philosophy of science as well as philosophy in general as I had hoped he would, although he has made important contributions in other fields. Like myself, he began in physics and then shifted to philosophy. He was a physics student at Pahlavi University in Shiraz when I gave a lecture on Mullā Ṣadrā there. That event changed his life, and he decided to devote himself completely to the study of philosophy, especially Islamic philosophy. Along with him, there was also a friend of his, Ahmad Jalali,[25] who was the Iranian Ambassador to UNESCO until recently. He also became my student for many years and then went from Iran to Oxford. These men belonged to that period of my training of students.

To come back to my Malay students, I must mention Zailan Moris,[26] who did her Ph.D. thesis on Mullā Ṣadrā with me here in Washington. She is, as far as I know, the only distinguished woman philosopher of the Malaysian world in the field of Islamic philosophy and also comparative philosophy. There is also Baharuddin Ahmad,[27] now a well-known scholar of comparative mysticism in Kuala Lumpur, and Saleh Yaapar, who later became dean of humanities at the University of Penang and who is one of the leading literary figures of the Malay world, and his wife Fatimah.[28] Both of them did their Ph.D. work with me. I also wish to mention Ali Abd al-Aziz,[29] who did his thesis on Islamic law under me and Fārūqī. There are many other Malay and Indonesian students whom I shall not mention here. But I need to refer to two students, Sulayman and Khadijah, who studied with me but did not do their Ph.D. under my care. They were both interested in Islamic art and both are today among the leading figures in the art world of Malaysia. So after 1979, I had for the first time a whole group of students from that part of the world, whom I had not had in Iran. Now they have become distinguished scholars and leaders in their countries.

During the Temple years, I also trained a number of students from other countries such as Mohsin Ibrahim from South Africa, who is now the leading Muslim scholar in the world today on Islamic bioethics. He is well known everywhere as a Muslim authority in the whole field of bioengineering, transplants, and similar subjects, which are now occupying so much the minds of Western theologians and philosophers. There are very few people in the Islamic world who are thinking about these issues today, and he is one of the most important among them. Another foreign student at this time at Temple was Hafiz Khan,[30] who studied Islamic philosophy and Sufism with me. Of course I also had a number of American students, among whom some have become known scholars. One is Gisella Webb,[31] who studied mysticism with me and wrote her Ph.D. thesis on Ibn 'Arabī and Suhrawardī. She is now a professor at Seton Hall. Another is Nikky Singh,[32] who is a Sikh woman who is now a well-known professor of comparative religion in this country. Then there is Grace Braeme,[33] who is a Christian theologian and a professor of Christian spirituality. She is among a number of women students of mine who are now well-known scholars in the field of religious studies. Another Christian woman student of Filipino origin, but now resident in America, is Vivienne Angeles,[34] who also worked directly under me.

Furthermore, at Temple I had a couple of Persian doctoral students. The most important was Mehdi Aminrazavi,[35] who came from Washington University and spent years studying with me, writing his Ph.D. thesis under my direction on Suhrawardī. He is now a well-established scholar with a number of works including a book on Suhrawardī. He is also cooperating with me on the five-volume *Anthology of Philosophy in Persia.* Parviz Dehghani,[36] another scholar who had been at Fordham, also came to Temple and finished his Ph.D. with me, writing his thesis on Afḍal al-Dīn Kāshānī.

I came to The George Washington University in 1984 and began the current phase of my life. I have not had many distinguished Persian students here, although many Persians have come and taken a few courses here with me, and a number of well-known Persian scholars have come from Persia to study with me more informally. But there are others who are now working or have worked on their Ph.D. thesis with me in Washington, such as Hejazi, who completed his thesis on a comparative study of the ethics of Malebranche, Mullā Muḥsin Fayḍ Kāshānī, and Hosseini, who did his doctoral thesis with me on religious pluralism.[37]

I have, moreover, trained since coming to Washington a number of advanced students from other countries, including Turks, Malays, Americans, and one or two Europeans. These students are still young, so they have not made a name for themselves yet, but they will do so soon. This last group of people comprises about a dozen students who are now just finishing or have finished their Ph.D. What I do usually here at The George Washington University is to have them complete their master's degree with me. Then I send them to places such as Princeton, Yale, the University of Chicago, or Temple after they are formed intellectually by me. I do this because I want them to have experience of another university, and also because it is good for their later employment. Nevertheless, they continue to consult or did consult with me on their thesis. There are also some who have completed their Ph.D. here at The George Washington University. All of these students are going to make an impact, I think, on religious and Islamic studies in this country. Among the best advanced students in the field of religious studies who have studied with me, I have to mention Ibrahim Kalin, David Dakake, Joseph Lumbard, Caner Dagli, Walid al-Ansari, 'Alī Aḥmad, Fu'ad Naeem, Tarik Quader, Faris Casewit, Zaynab Kot, Leena Danani, Yusuf Casewit, and Zachary Markwith.[38]

Teaching

R.J.: By the long list of your students, I understand that you like teaching, and you think that education has an important place in life, but you have not written much about education . . .
S.H.N.: I have written some . . .

R.J.: I mean some books.
S.H.N.: I have not written books devoted solely to education, but I have written at least half a dozen essays on education[39] and also chapters in some of my books.[40]

R.J.: I am sure for you, education is a very important part in life.
S.H.N.: Absolutely. First of all, I believe that a person who becomes a teacher should have a vocation for this task. It is like somebody becoming a violinist. It is not just something one should force oneself to do. My father was really a teacher, and I think that I inherited that art from him. I do not know the reason, but I never thought of myself being anything else but a teacher. I could have easily gone into politics in Iran, and many opportunities arose for me to do so when I was still young, but I never accepted the opportunities that arose. If I did accept administrative responsibilities, it was not in the government but in university administration. Even those tasks were accepted by me because in countries such as Iran, it was impossible for a person like myself to have avoided every nonscholarly duty. Therefore, I continued in the field of education, including its administrative aspect, and did not go into politics until just before the Revolution, and that was for special reasons, at a critical point in the history of our country.

I have always liked teaching, and students have always appreciated my teaching. I have also always had very close rapport with my students. Now that I have taught for over fifty years, I would be happy to teach less, but probably have to continue to teach a few more years for practical reasons. I do consider myself to be primarily a teacher in addition to a writer. Of course, since I have written so extensively and also lectured so much in addition to teaching all my mature life, my task has been a very heavy one. A lot of responsibility has rested on my shoulders, but I have never thought, as some professors do, that once one becomes famous in one's own field, one can delegate most of the teaching to assistants and devote oneself primarily to one's own research. I do not believe that that is the correct philosophy. One of the criticisms I have made of Harvard, not so much in my own days but especially in later years, is that the famous professors there are often away, especially for undergraduate courses, leaving some young teaching assistant to do the teaching. Of course it is important for the teaching assistants to teach once in a while so that they can be trained as teachers. I always do that with my assistants so as to give them an opportunity to teach, but I do not do that all the time.

I think that the teacher who has had years of experience, of deliberation, of thinking, could do a lot more, especially for undergraduates, than a young instructor. I have said jokingly that when you are a freshman, you ask profound questions about the nature of reality, but by the time you are a graduate student you ask, "By the way, according to this footnote, did Rousseau write this text in 1732 or 1733?" or something like that. Graduate students often become interested in details but no longer in the great questions. If you are a person who is philosophically minded like myself, it is very important to address the major questions for younger students. Consequently I have always enjoyed teaching in the way that a violinist enjoys playing the violin. That does not mean that it is not hard work. It definitely is hard work, but God has given me this gift for teaching, and I am happy and grateful to Him that I have been able to devote my life to what has been really my *dharma*, as you might say in a Hindu or Buddhist context. I have been very fortunate that my *dharma* has been my *karma*, if you understand what I mean.

Theory of Education

R.J.: Yes, yes, it seems you talked about the Indians and about *dharma* and *karma*. You remind me of what Gandhi and Tagore used to say about education, that education is actually a way of experiencing life and not just reading books. I suppose that for you education is more than just asking people to read books.

S.H.N.: You know, education has to be of the whole being of the student. Unfortunately in the modern world, education has become too cerebral and too mental, while physical education, emphasized more in

America than in Europe, is totally separated and not integrated with mental and emotional training, as one sees in Tai Ch'i or Yoga. As for spiritual education, it is practically absent from ordinary schools. You take a course on, let us say, the history of the 18th century in the morning, and then you go and play basketball in the afternoon. They have nothing to do with each other, and you do not have an integrated program of training. Even on the intellectual level, education is dispersed today, without an integrated vision, and then education does not include the emotional and spiritual elements of the human being. So the different aspects of the human being are segmented and compartmentalized.

I have always been in favor of an integral educational system. I have therefore championed the revival of the traditional Islamic educational system, which, like all traditional systems, has been based on all of the elements of the human microcosm being taken together. In that system, the student would have a very close human relationship with the teacher. The teacher has been like his or her father (or in some cases mother), and education would include the training of the soul as well as the mind. It would include moral and even physical elements as well as intellectual ones. Today modern education has become totally amoral, and we wonder why children are shooting each other in the streets and even at schools. These disturbing phenomena are in fact just the tip of the iceberg, because we have been still living the heritage of the time when education was not amoral. Just imagine what will happen when that heritage is exhausted. When that legacy comes to an end, we will really face much more acute problems, especially since the Western educational system cannot agree on a moral system, and so puts this aspect aside and hopes that the parents deal with it.

Many parents, however, do not deal with that part of education either, and so the moral fiber of society begins to fall apart. There is no integrated vision in the modern world, whereas in, let us say, in India which you mentioned, in traditional Hindu India, even now, if you go to Benares and want to study the Vedas with pundits, it is not just a question of learning Sanskrit. Education is also a certain way of living, a certain way of acting, has certain moral and spiritual characteristics. If the student is a thief, he is not going to be taught the Vedas in Sanskrit. The traditional pundit does not say, "Well, this is not my department; let the police take care of that. I am just a Sanskrit teacher." This way of thinking is catastrophic and has already wreaked havoc. We have a science on which most modern education is based that leaves morality completely aside. There are great scientists who are capitalists, great scientists who are communist, great scientists who are devout Christians, and great scientists who are atheists. The scientist's spiritual and moral character does not really matter as far as his or her science is concerned. Consequently, the application of modern science is left completely in the hands of people of totally different "values" from those of scientists, often people with a thirst for greater power, selfishness, and greed. This amorality has had catastrophic consequences upon us such as we see in modern technological warfare, new diseases, pollution, the environmental crisis, et cetera that cover the earth.

R.J.: Yes. People used to go, I mean, today's students, they go to university, get a diploma and start working and gaining money, but in the 15th century people who went to university would go to learn because they wanted to have knowledge of the world and of life.

S.H.N.: Exactly. What has been forgotten is the dimension of wisdom, that is, knowledge that makes one perfected and concerns the whole of one's being. It is the fulfillment of the possibilities of human beings on all levels that has been forgotten. What little remains of respect for knowledge is expressed in what some scientists claim when they assert, "We are interested only in science for the sake of science. We do not care about what happens to its applications"; but that is a very dangerous thing, because other people come along and create the nuclear bomb, means of biological warfare, et cetera. All these and many other dangerous things are invented, these inventions being made possible by the work of humble and gentle scientists sitting in some laboratory in some university. But look at what happened to the result of their work. That wisdom about which the traditional educational system spoke was not an assertion of art for art's sake and science for science's sake. Knowledge was for wisdom's sake, for the perfection of the human being, which of necessity includes ethics.

In a sense, all education had a use, but not in the modern sense of utilitarianism; rather, in the sense that it helped to perfect some aspect of the human being. In traditional education it was not even the question of the juxtaposition we have in the West between utility and a pure, objective view of studying science. In the present context, I am always on the side of the purely objective aspect of knowledge rather than its utility, because utility has been reduced to only the material level. De Santillana used to say, "Science starts where utility stops," with which I agree in the modern context. But, nevertheless, that is not sufficient. When you have wisdom in the deep sense of the term, education becomes then *paedeia* in the Greek sense of culture. Everything really is then part of education. Everything you do in life is education, and education should concern all aspects of one's being and is therefore useful in the deepest meaning of that term.

In my own life, as you probably know, I was very instrumental in the organization of the World Congress of Islamic Education held in Makkah in 1977. It was the most important conference of its kind ever held, which resulted in the creation of several Islamic universities in Pakistan, Malaysia, Africa, and other places, in the composition of many textbooks, and so on, but its goals were never fully realized. I was part of that historic event and the process that led to it. I need to mention this fact because many people have made claims to be the originator of one of the most important intellectual exercises that is taking place in the Islamic world today and which they call the "Islamization of knowledge," the effort to incorporate Western knowledge into the Islamic framework. I have never liked the usage of this term, but the fact is that I spoke about this integration in 1957/58 when I wrote my book *Science and Civilization in Islam* parallel with my Ph.D. thesis, although this book was not published until a few years later. It was then 1957, at least ten, fifteen years before other people such as Ismāʿīl al-Fārūqī and Naquib al-Attas, who are now known for this project, came to the fore that I wrote about the integration of all knowledge into the Islamic worldview.

I have always been concerned with the integral vision of education and been a critic of compartmentalized education imported from the West into our country, Iran, or other Islamic countries and even into other Oriental countries such as India or Burma, which are Hindu and Buddhist, respectively. It does not make a difference where you look. There is everywhere ever greater segmentation in the curricula of educational systems most of all in the West, but now to an ever greater degree in the rest of the world. For example, in Iran, we have the *ṭullāb* (students) in the religious schools, and then we have the students in modern universities based on completely different philosophies, completely different educational theories. And so for some time one can see in countries such as Pakistan, Iran, Egypt, or Turkey two types of people whose color of skin is similar, who actually speak the same language, have the same nationality, possess the same kinds of names, but who live practically on two different planets and who cannot understand each other. This is a major problem that prevents integration of such societies; rather, it causes tensions within them. So while the West has educational problems, we have now inherited those problems plus another set of problems of our own.

Although I have not written a separate book on education, I have devoted a great deal of my life to ideas that are important for education. That is why they have been used a great deal by many in the Islamic world devoted to the study of education. For example, in the *Muslim Educational Quarterly*, which used to come out in Cambridge, England, and now comes out in Malaysia, many of the writers who are specialists in education have made use of those ideas, and my ideas are very well known among Muslim educationalists. One of the main reasons I have never written a book directly on education is that in the United States, a whole academic discipline was created called "education," which I always believed to be in its foundation intellectually rather flimsy and substanceless, and of course we also followed suit in Iran, where we established a faculty called the Faculty of Education at Tehran University. I was never attracted to that idea because I felt that there is little use in studying the methods of education when you do not have sufficient knowledge of any subject that is to be taught. Here in America, if you want to even teach in high school and have a Ph.D. in physics from M.I.T., you cannot do so unless you have a teacher's certificate from a teacher's college. The whole educational philosophy here has been dominated by the philosophy of John Dewey.[41] I have always been opposed to that philosophy, and that way of looking at education has never attracted me.[42] I have always considered education to be part and parcel of integral knowledge itself. That is why I have never written a book separately on education but have dealt with education in the context of knowledge in general.

Education as understood traditionally is extremely important; it is really life itself. The whole of life, as Pythagoras said, is education. Education is not an element added to life even if we have to have special institutions for it; I also believe that what is called continuous education today already existed a thousand years ago. Education is really from the cradle to the grave; as the Prophet of Islam said: "Seek knowledge from the cradle to the grave." The Persian verse *ze gahvāreh tā gūr dānesh bejūy* is actually a poem that translates literally the *ḥadīth* of the Prophet in Arabic into Persian. This saying should not be understood only metaphorically. From the moment a little child is taught "da da" and "ba ba," a few words like that, and even before that, until he or she dies, the soul of that person has to grow through education. To be fully human you have to grow to a greater and greater perfection, and that occurs through education on all levels. In the old days in our cities, let us say five hundred years ago in a city such as Isfahan, you had the *madrasahs* and *ṭalabahs* like you and I when we were students going to school, but you also had merchants who would come in and sit in a class in the *madrasah* and then go back to their work. Ordinary people would come in and go out of these schools. You can still see that in a university such as al-Azhar in Cairo. Islamic *madrasahs* were open to everybody. A person might have been fifty-five years old, but if he was interested in learning about *tafsīr* (Quranic commentary) or something about law or something about God knows what, he could participate in the appropriate classes. He could sit in a class and learn to his heart's desire. That is real continuous education in which I believe. To segment, to separate education from the rest of the activities of society itself is very dangerous for society as a whole.

R.J.: That is why, to get back to Iran, that is why when you went back to Iran yourself, giving so much importance to education, you went and you studied with traditional philosophers and masters such as Ṭabāṭabā'ī[43] and 'Aṣṣār.[44]
S.H.N.: Yes. That is a very important period of my life. It was not only because of education in the abstract; it was because it concerned directly *my* education.

Studies with Traditional Masters

'Aṣṣār

R.J.: For your education, I understand . . .
S.H.N.: Yes. Let me tell you this story because this period of study is one of the most important phases of my life. When I was at Harvard, I began to study Islamic philosophical texts for my doctoral studies. I was studying Arabic and Persian texts of the Ikhwān al-Ṣafā', Ibn Sīnā, and others with the background that I described already for you, that is traditional metaphysics as expressed by Guénon, Schuon, and others and with full awareness of the works of historians of philosophy such as Wolfson and the writings of the Catholic scholars trying to revive Catholic thought in the 20th century going back to DeWulf[45] and Gilson. I saw that all the Islamic philosophy that I had learned from the greatest teachers of the West, such as Wolfson and Gilson, was not really complete and sufficient. I had to learn the techniques of Western scholarship, which were important, but this was not the whole of the story. Furthermore, already at Harvard I had read the books of Corbin, whom

I did not meet until I came back to Iran in 1958. I had especially concentrated on his book *Avicenne et le récit visionnaire*,[46] which had also come out in English, and also his writings on Suhrawardī. These works had already pointed to what I had intuited concerning the significance of later philosophical thought in Iran. And so when I came to Iran, I wanted very much to seek out the traditional teachers I had already heard about at Harvard, where I corresponded with Ḥujjat Allāh Bālaghī and one or two other people who were among the *'ulamā'* from whom I received books about later Islamic thought. I just could not accept that Islamic philosophy came to an end with Averroes and that nothing had happened in philosophy in the Islamic world during the last eight hundred years. That thesis was not intellectually acceptable.

So soon after I came back to Iran, I went to the house of Sayyid Muḥammad Kāẓim 'Aṣṣār, who was like my uncle from the old days. He told me one afternoon, "I want to take you to a special place." I said, "Fine." He took me to the house of Zho'l-Majd Tabataba'i[47] who was a well-known lawyer from Qom. His cousin was also the member of parliament from Qom. There, in the home of Zho'l-Majd, I discovered a beautiful garden located in Khiyaban-e Bahar north of Shahreza where Āqā-ye 'Aṣṣār taught traditional texts. I immediately became friends with Tabataba'i and after asking the master's permission, asked Tabataba'i if I could participate in those lessons and he said, "Of course. We would be glad to have you with us." Those lessons took place three afternoons a week, each session taking two or three hours, that is, practically the whole afternoon. The lessons, therefore, took a good part of my time, but for a very good purpose.

In addition to that, I asked 'Aṣṣār if I could go to his morning classes in Madrasa-ye Sepahsalar, where he was teaching Islamic philosophy and jurisprudence (*fiqh*). He would teach an hour of *fiqh* followed by an hour of philosophy. I was not interested too much in the *fiqh* class, but I was very much interested in philosophy. And so I would drive all the way from Tehran University—at that time the traffic was not as bad as now, but it was even then difficult—driving very fast with the little Volkswagen I had then, small enough to park almost anywhere. I would drive to the front of Sepahsalar Mosque and go to the one-hour philosophy class and that would be from eleven to twelve. And so my study with traditional masters began. We studied the *Sharḥ-i manẓūmah* of Sabziwārī[48] in the morning, and in the afternoon sessions Āqā-ye 'Aṣṣār had just begun teaching the Sufi (*'irfānī*) text, the *Ashi''at al-lama'āt* of Jāmī[49] (*Rays upon the Gleams*), which was a commentary upon the *Lama'āt* (*Gleams*) of Fakhr al-Dīn 'Irāqī,[50] one of the major texts of Persian literature. 'Aṣṣār was faithful to traditional teachings, and this was like a revelation to me. It confirmed everything that I had believed, since his teachings involved an oral tradition. In 'Aṣṣār's hands these texts spoke to me in a different way than when I was reading them in a library or some place else by myself. It was a marvelous, really marvelous experience also combined with the presence of a spiritual and intellectual teacher who was a remarkable person. What I was looking for was like seeking water in the middle of the desert, and here I had found that water.

'Allāmah Ṭabāṭabā'ī

A short time passed and one day Zho'l-Majd Tabataba'i said, "Look, I want to introduce you to one of the great luminaries of Iran, who comes here during the weekends, and we have a session of lessons with him." That person was 'Allāmah Ṭabāṭabā'ī (not a relative of Zho'l-Majd, but with the same last name). So in the fall of 1958 (1337), soon after my return to Iran, I met this remarkable man, and of course immediately I felt great respect and love for him. He also showed much love for me, and we became very close quickly. So, in addition to 'Aṣṣār's courses during the week, I pursued 'Allāmah Ṭabāṭabā'ī's courses over the weekends. He would come every other week on Thursdays from Qom and would leave Friday afternoon back to Qom. So every other week we met with him, in a small group including Zho'l-Majd himself, one of his friends, Karrubi, Motahhari,[51] and Manaqebi, who was the son-in-law of 'Allāmah Ṭabāṭabā'ī, and who was then a famous preacher. Motahhari, the famous Motahhari, now also well known in the West, became like my brother and very close friend. He was also one of the best-known students of 'Allāmah Ṭabāṭabā'ī. These sessions had also included Corbin during the Fall and before 1958 Isa Sepahbodi[52] had been the translator. When I joined the sessions, I became the main translator and later on Shayegan[53] shared this task. That is how he met 'Allāmah Ṭabāṭabā'ī. I introduced him to both 'Allāmah Ṭabāṭabā'ī and to Corbin. There were also a few other scholars who would come specially when Corbin was present.

R.J.: When did you meet Corbin?
S.H.N.: It was in the fall of 1958 when I first met Corbin. Shayegan was still a student in Geneva. He had not as yet come back, but as soon as he returned to Iran I introduced him to our sessions and to Corbin. Occasionally, Foruzanfar[54] would also come to them. Also until 1960

(1339), before he went to Mashhad, Sayyid Jalal al-Din Ashtiyani[55] would be present. These meetings were very important in the intellectual history of 20th-century Iran and more generally in the meeting between Islam and the West on the highest intellectual level. They were remarkable gatherings. When we were with 'Allāmah Ṭabāṭabā'ī without Corbin, over the years we would study many different texts including the *Asfār*[56] of Mullā Ṣadrā, and more and more we delved into discussions of comparative philosophy. Shayegan and I once translated the *Tao Te-Ching* into Persian in order to study the text with 'Allāmah Ṭabāṭabā'ī. We also discussed *Sirr-i akbar*, the Persian translation of the Upanishads,[57] which had been published by Na'ini and Tara Chand. Occasionally, we read the Gospels and 'Allāmah would make commentaries upon them from the Islamic point of view. It was a very rich experience, one that was really unique.

When Corbin was present, the themes for discussion were chosen by him. I have always said that the discourse which took place was on a level that had not taken place since the Middle Ages. When Corbin would leave, our sessions would of course continue. It was not confined to the fall, but was carried out for two decades throughout the academic year and occasionally during the summer. We would also go sometimes with 'Allāmah Ṭabāṭabā'ī outside of Tehran to Damavand and places like that for a few days, and we would study with him in the bosom of virgin nature, sometimes discussing chapters of the Quran. He was then writing his great commentary on the Quran.[58] One of my remarkable experiences, which was really unique, occurred during one of those summers when he would come to Darekah, a village north of Tehran, which at that time was much less crowded than now. He lived amidst a beautiful garden with a stream in the middle of it. There alone, just myself and him, I studied with him for the whole summer the *Dīwān* of Ḥāfiẓ. You just cannot imagine the depth of meaning that he would expound, meanings compared to which ordinary interpretations were like gravel. It was as if the walls were speaking with him. He was not only a philosopher and commentator on the Quran, but also a gnostic and mystic of a very high order, as was Āqā-yi 'Aṣṣār. And so my studies with 'Allāmah Ṭabāṭabā'ī continued for twenty years and with Āqā-yi 'Aṣṣār until his death. With 'Allāmah Ṭabāṭabā'ī, I continued my studies through the fall of 1978 (1357).

R.J.: Did you introduce the perennial philosophy to 'Allāmah Ṭabāṭabā'ī? What was his view of it?

S.H.N.: Oh, absolutely. He was of course very much interested in this matter. I do not know whether you remember or not, but a book came out in Ḥusayniyya-yi Irshād[59] about the Prophet of Islam and there was an article by me on Islam and the religions of the world in it,[60] a long article in Persian, which caused a lot of reaction at that time in Iran. It was in that essay that I spoke openly in Persian about the perennial philosophy in relation to the inner unity of religions. After reading it, 'Allāmah Ṭabāṭabā'ī told me, "This is wonderful. What you have written is wonderful, but I wish that now you would write about the other side of it also." What he meant was that there, I was talking about other religions of the world in relation to Islam and not very much about Islam itself; so he added, "Now, you should write about Islam in relation to other religions of the world"; but he was appreciative of this article, very appreciative. Anyway, my relations with him lasted for over twenty years.

The last time I met 'Allāmah Ṭabāṭabā'ī was at the height of the Revolution, with all the commotion and demonstrations in the streets in the fall of 1978. In our last meeting, he spoke of some political matters that I do not want to repeat here because it does not concern the subject at hand, but in any case we had the closest relationship. It is important for the historical record to mention that it was I who induced 'Allāmah Ṭabāṭabā'ī to write his books *Bidāyat al-ḥikmah* (*Beginning of Philosophy*) and *Nihāyat al-ḥikmah* (*End of Philosophy*),[61] which are now taught widely in Qom. For years, I used to say to him, "Ḥājī Āqā,[62] the *Sharḥ-i manẓūmah* of Sabziwārī is so difficult and was written in the last century. Why do you not write a text like this for present day students?" And he would say, "No, no, I do not have time." But he finally relented and wrote these two books. Zho'l-Majd Tabataba'i helped him a great deal financially to finish his Quranic commentary, *Tafsīr al-mīzān,* but meanwhile I was always nagging him about this matter. Finally he came one day with a serene smile and said, "*Āqā-yi Doctor,*[63] here is the book you kept asking me to write." He pulled out of his sleeve the manuscript of the *Bidāyah* and gave it to me.

This is also the case of *Qur'ān dar islām*[64] and *Shī'ah dar islām,*[65] which were commissioned by Kenneth Cragg[66] when he came to Iran to see me and said, "I want to have three books produced on Shi'ism. There is a new center at Colgate University for the study of religions, but there is nothing good on Shi'ism in English for the students to use." And so I accepted the responsibility and asked the 'Allāmah to write and direct them while I would undertake the task of translating and editing them for the Western audience. I edited and translated first of all *Shī'ah dar islām*[67] into English. For a long time, the translation of this book under the title *Shi'ite Islam* was the only book on Ithnā 'asharī (Twelve Imam)

Shi'ism in English, and even today, there is nothing like it. Most of what has come out after the Revolution about Shi'ism has been politically oriented in one way or another, or has not had the authority of this text, although a few good titles have since then seen the light of day. This work of 'Allāmah Ṭabāṭabā'ī is a purely traditional and classical exposition of Shi'ism which remains unique. As for *Qur'ān dar islām*, I was also translating it in Iran when the Revolution took place and my translation was lost. So, after the Revolution, somebody else translated it and I wrote an introduction for it.[68] The third volume was to be an anthology of the sayings of the Shi'ite Imams. 'Allāmah Ṭabāṭabā'ī chose the text, William Chittick translated it, and I wrote the introduction for it. It is still available[69] and is a very fine book. So that whole series, which introduced Twelve-Imam Shi'ism for the first time to the Western world in an authentic and authoritative manner, this being a major event, was carried out by 'Allāmah Ṭabāṭabā'ī at my instigation and with my cooperation and help.

R.J.: Was he considered as an innovator or as a conservative?
S.H.N.: You mean politically?

R.J.: No, no, I mean philosophically, theologically.
S.H.N.: I do not think that these categories really apply too much to him. He was in the line of the philosophers of the school of Mullā Ṣadrā; he was a Ṣadrian philosopher, but at the same time, he was not simply repeating Mullā Ṣadrā. There were many new issues with which he dealt, including what he wrote in his book *Uṣūl-i falsafa-yi ri'ālism*,[70] which marked the first serious encounter between traditional Islamic philosophy and Marxism. What he wrote on this matter is basically different from what has been written by so many Arabs and other Muslims who did not know Islamic philosophy, whereas Ṭabāṭabā'ī was a man who was well versed in Islamic philosophical teachings, on the basis of which he wrote on the relation between what he called "realism" and dialectical materialism. At the same time, what he wrote in this book, while based on Ṣadrian principles, is not simply a repetition of Mullā Ṣadrā and includes many hitherto undiscussed matters.

R.J.: So he read Marxism, Marxist literature?
S.H.N.: I will tell you how this book was written. When the Russians invaded northern Iran, 'Allāmah Ṭabāṭabā'ī, who belonged to a great family of religious scholars in Tabriz, faced a lot of problems there as many of the '*ulamā'* were attacked. So he left and came to Tehran first

and then to Qom. Nobody knew him in Tehran at that time. He went to Qom under difficult financial conditions. He came from a well-to-do family in Tabriz, but they lost their land and nearly everything else at that time. He began to teach Islamic philosophy and *tafsīr* (Quranic commentary) in Islamic seminaries in Qom, but many of the outward-looking *ṭullāb* (religious students) were against philosophy, and so they went to Ayatollah Burūjirdī[71] and complained that this man was teaching philosophy and this was *kufr* (infidelity). Ayatollah Burūjirdī met him and saw that 'Allāmah Ṭabāṭabā'ī was such a saintly man that there was no way of criticizing him for having any ambitions of a worldly kind. Seeing that he was such a remarkably saintly person, Ayatollah Burūjirdī said, "Whatever 'Allāmah Ṭabāṭabā'ī does is approved by me; he has my protection." Being such a powerful scholar that he was, he was able to protect him fully, and so 'Allāmah began to teach philosophy in Qom in peace.

At that time, the Tudeh (Communist) Party was very powerful in Iran. Its members were everywhere, and they were able to capture the minds of many intelligent, young Iranians, especially in the fields of science and literature. You know that until the Iranian Revolution, most of the Iranian writers were leftists, such as the well-known writer and social critic Al-e Ahmad, and many like him who were communists in the beginning. They were all pulled towards that pole. I was not in Iran at that time, but 'Allāmah Ṭabāṭabā'ī told me the whole story. He said that none of the *'ulamā'* dared to confront the Marxists intellectually during the period following immediately the Second World War because they were afraid of being assassinated. It was as simple as that. But 'Allāmah Ṭabāṭabā'ī was very brave, and he said, "I am an Azarbajani and I shall do this." So he came to Tehran from Qom and invited some of the philosophically minded ideologues of the Tudeh Party to debate. He wanted actually to debate with someone such as Taqī Irānī,[72] but the latter had been killed during the period of Reza Shah, having been considered as the godfather of the *panjāh-o se nafar* (an inner circle within the Tudeh) and had been their most intellectually inclined person. In any case, three or four people, who remained anonymous because the Tudeh Party did not want to give specific names to advertise that "these are our ideologues," were chosen, and they met with 'Allāmah Ṭabāṭabā'ī in Tehran in many sessions, discussing philosophically as philosophers the Marxist position, while he presented the position of Islamic philosophy of the Ṣadrian School, the school of Mullā Ṣadrā. Of course, there were many new issues that came up that were obviously not discussed in Mullā

Ṣadrā's works. Let us remember that 'Allāmah was a rejuvenator (*mujaddid*) of Islamic philosophy and not only a commentator of Mullā Ṣadrā; but 'Allāmah was not a modernist.

You know, in Islam, we have the categories of *mujaddid* and *muṣliḥ* now used in the sense of "innovator," meant as "modernizer" or "reformer," and employed for such figures as Jamāl al-Dīn Afghānī,[73] Muḥammad 'Abduh,[74] and men like them, but the 'Allāmah was not like them. He was really a renewer or *mujaddid* of Islamic thought like Mullā Ṣadrā himself, which is a very different matter. Just to turn to myself for a moment, I do not see myself at all to be in the line of reformers such as 'Abduh and so forth; but I do consider myself to be a humble reviver of Islamic thought and belonging, like 'Allāmah Ṭabāṭabā'ī, to the Islamic, philosophical tradition. Of course I have said many things with which Mullā Ṣadrā and Mīr Dāmād were not obviously concerned, but I belong philosophically to the same tradition; Islamic philosophy is a living, philosophical tradition, not a dead one.

Anyway, 'Allāmah Ṭabāṭabā'ī added many new elements to Islamic philosophy that had not been discussed before, but the principles he applied were those of traditional Islamic philosophy. The *Uṣūl-i falsafa-yi ri'ālism* reflects this reality more than his other works and represents the responses he gave to the Marxist theoreticians. The closest thing you can have to 'Allāmah Ṭabāṭabā'ī in the West is the works of a figure such as Gilson, who was a Neo-Thomist. Now, in his writings on art or the criticism of modern philosophy, Gilson was not just repeating Saint Thomas Aquinas but speaking from within the Thomistic tradition and as a Thomist while addressing new issues. This is the closest example in the contemporary West to what 'Allāmah Ṭabāṭabā'ī was doing in the contemporary Islamic world.

In any case, he was a very great man and had remarkable literary as well as philosophical gifts. He composed poetry, both in Arabic and Persian. He wrote well and also, besides his mystical and gnostic knowledge, he had these two dimensions of being a Quranic commentator and a philosopher. He was a first-rate philosopher and had a remarkable, philosophical mind as the discussions between him and Corbin reveal. As I said already, I acted as the chief translator of these discussions for a long time, succeeding Sepahbodi, who used to help, but of course he did not have much philosophical knowledge, although his French was excellent. So the main burden of translating remained on my shoulders for many years, while I was helped in later years by Shayegan. Consequently, I was a direct witness to 'Allāmah's philosophical acumen. What Corbin would do was to bring, when he would always arrive in September, issues that were being hotly debated philosophically or theologically at the time in France. He would present these issues as questions to 'Allāmah Ṭabāṭabā'ī and then 'Allāmah would provide answers, and discussions would follow. As already mentioned, later on, many other people came to these sessions, people some of whom are now famous *'ulamā'* in Iran, such as Khusrowshāhī and Makārim Shīrāzī, but the most important was Motahhari, who was always there.

Often the 'Allāmah would say jokingly, "Look at me, Āqā-yi Doctor Nasr, tell Āqā Morteza to continue his work on philosophy and to stop giving so many public lectures in all these places." 'Allāmah was alluding to the fact that even then Motahhari had become too much of an activist for 'Allāmah's taste, and he thought that that was really a shame, because Motahhari was so gifted philosophically.

Motahhari was to some extent a modernist. He was torn between the traditionalist and modernist positions, and he had not solved the problem completely in his mind, but he was very gifted. He started talking and giving lectures in Kanun-e Mohandesin (Association of Engineers), this *Kānūn* or that *Kānūn*, and so he did not have more time necessary to devote to philosophical works, and his serious philosophical activity was somewhat curtailed. For example, he never finished his commentary upon *Uṣūl-i falsafa-yi ri'ālism* as 'Allāmah had hoped. Nevertheless, Motahhari did write some important works, especially the book on the services rendered by Islam and Iran to each other.

R.J.: You were against all kinds of activism your whole life.
S.H.N.: I was opposed to political activism for myself but not necessarily for others. That kind of activism was not my vocation. It was not my function. I believe that the deepest reform comes from the top, that is, the intellectual and spiritual realm, and it is also in the intellectual realm that deviation first takes place. You know that we have a saying in Persian, "The fish begins to stink from its head," and as they say in Latin, *corruptio optima pessimi* (the corruption of the best is the worst). This is what happened during the process of the spread of modernism in the West. In the same way, for real reform in the serious sense to take place one has to start from the top. That is what Guénon wanted to do. Guénon was not at all an activist in the ordinary sense of the term. It is true that the *Figaro* published an article that made him sort of the ideologue of the French right, but that is total nonsense. A person who was so open to other religions of the world—how could he be opposed to

everything that was not French? Guénon was a universalist metaphysician and always emphasized universality.

Qazwīnī

Anyway, to go back to other teachers with whom I studied, it was one year after I returned to Iran that I met Sayyid Abū'l-Ḥasan Qazwīnī, who became my third great teacher of Islamic philosophy. He had been a teacher of Islamic philosophy for a long time, and a teacher of Seyyed Jalal al-Din Ashtiyani, among many others, and including Ayatollah Khomeini. As I said already, Ashtiyani and I had become friends immediately after meeting each other during the philosophical sessions with 'Allāmah Ṭabāṭabā'ī, and we remained close friends to the end of his life. If one were to put together all the introductions I have written to the various books of Ashtiyani over the years in both Persian and English, they would become a book. Ashtiyani had spoken very highly of Sayyid Abū'l-Ḥasan Qazwīnī, who would spend one term in Tehran teaching in a house in the bazaar and the rest of the year in Qazvin. Together Ashtiyani and I went to see him and I became his student. Often we would go to Qazvin to visit him, sometimes with Foruzanfar and Zho'l-Majd.

I also attended for several years his lectures on the *Asfār* (of Mullā Ṣadrā) in Tehran. He was the best teacher of the *Asfār* I have ever met. We used the lithograph edition of this work, whose pages were much longer than the ordinary printed page. He would first read a whole page as if he had memorized it, and then he would give a commentary on every single word and line in a manner that is called *taqrīr*. He was the most thorough teacher I had for the *Asfār*. Our lessons lasted for some five years, and then he became sick and died soon thereafter. There is an episode that is very facetious and is worth mentioning here. When Ayatollah Khomeini, who had been his student, started the Fifteenth of Khurdād uprising in 1963 (1342), Qazwīnī, who was himself young when he was Ayatollah Khomeini's teacher, said, "*omour be dast-e javānān oftādeh ast.*"[75]

Ayatollah Qazwīnī was a venerable old man, and it was really wonderful to experience his presence. He was the epitome of a really great traditional scholar such as Naṣīr al-Dīn Ṭūsī.[76] Qazwīnī was of course a great *'ālim*,[77] a *marja'-i taqlīd*,[78] and great authority in Islamic Law. When he went to the grand mosque in Qazvin, he was treated like a king. But in addition, he was an unbelievable philosopher. He was furthermore also a mathematician and an astronomer. He knew Islamic astronomy better than any Ph.D. student at Harvard studying the history of astronomy, and he also knew traditional medicine. That is why he reminded me of a figure such as Ṭūsī, with a remarkable expansion of vision and breadth of knowledge combined with depth. That is very rare indeed, especially in this day and age.

Other Teachers

To conclude this discussion about my traditional teachers, let me mention that for several years off and on, I also studied with Mahdī Ilāhī Qumsha'ī,[79] and we read and discussed mystical and philosophical texts such as *al-Insān al-kāmil* of 'Abd al-Karīm Jīlī[80] or his own *Ḥikmat-i ilāhī khāṣṣ wa 'āmm.* I studied these texts with him, sometimes alone and sometimes with two or three other people. He was a very gentle person, a poet and a mystic, and so whatever text we would discuss, he would not just teach what the text said, but would relate it to the discussion of Divine Love and love mysticism. He was like that, a very loving soul, a wonderful human being. I also studied for a while with Jawād Muṣliḥ[81] from Shiraz who was much more of a rationalist philosopher, who translated some of the works of Mullā Ṣadrā into Persian, including *al-Shawāhid al-rubūbiyyah*[82] and summaries of the *Asfār.* I studied the *Sharḥ al-ishārāt*[83] of Ṭūsī and Ibn Sīnā with him, and that is a much more discursive text of Islamic philosophy than let us say the *Asfār.*

These were my main teachers. But also occasionally I would have a lesson with Āqā-yi Maḥmūd Shahābī,[84] and sometimes I would sit down with Motahhari and we would have discussions together, mostly about Sabziwārī. Altogether, I had an extensive philosophical training in the traditional manner, because I wanted to receive, when I still could, the traditional education to complement the experience I had of Western education. I think that I am perhaps the first person to have ever had this kind of education, that is, learning not only modern but also medieval Western philosophy, along with Islamic philosophy from the greatest Western teachers such as Wolfson and Gilson, complemented by traditional Islamic philosophy learned from the greatest living masters in Iran. That training has served me profoundly throughout my life.

R.J.: It is rare to find somebody who is teaching and, at the same time, studying, because people, when they get a Ph.D., they finish studying, and you just went on studying.

S.H.N.: That is right. Oh my goodness, you cannot imagine how many people said, "Why are you doing all of this? Did you not learn anything at Harvard?" They did not understand my situation and needs. Even my own family did not understand why I spent so much time studying after finishing my formal education. But I wanted to be able to become competent in the *lecture* of traditional texts. *Lecture* means "reading" in Latin, and for me it meant the reading of a text in the original sense of the word. In order to be a good teacher in our philosophical tradition, you have to have a master. You have to have a continuity of the master-disciple relationship and be able to master the oral tradition that accompanies the written text. That experience of real masters helped me a great deal. I am still a student of Islamic philosophy, but at least I have had this experience and training.

R.J.: And you were transmitting this to your students at the same time.

S.H.N.: That is right. I have taught my students on several levels over these fifty years. One is the formal classes in the university and one is private lessons, or what is called *dars-e khārej* (outside lessons), which I gave in Iran, usually Sufi texts such as Lāhījī's *Sharḥ-i gulshan-i rāz*[85] and also in the United States, where I have had a number of choice students who have become quite advanced. Here I have taught among other works *al-Ḥikmat al-'arshiyyah* and *Kitāb al-mashā'ir*[86] of Mullā Ṣadrā to them using the original Arabic text with my own commentaries given in English.

Henry Corbin

R.J.: Now, among the other great philosophical figures whom you met in the late fifties and sixties in Iran was Henry Corbin, who was at that time the director of the French Institute for Iranian Studies in Tehran. What was the contribution of Corbin to your Islamic thought and your philosophical thought in general?

S.H.N.: I would not say that he made a contribution to my philosophical thought, but I learned a lot from him as far as the subjects of his scholarship were concerned. He wrote on certain philosophers, as I already mentioned, such as on Ibn Sīnā (especially on his Oriental Philosophy,[87] which I think is one of the most ingenious studies in Islamic philosophy), and of course there are both his edited texts and analyses of Suhrawardī and several other philosophers; I benefited from all these scholarly works. But as far as my philosophical position is concerned, I was not influenced by Corbin. In fact, we complemented each other rather than agreeing totally on everything. I had already come to know very well the writings of Corbin while I was in the United States before returning to Iran. As I told you, when I was writing my Ph.D. thesis in 1957 and 1958, I made extensive use of the writings of Corbin as far as Ibn Sīnā was concerned. When I came to Iran in 1958, very early that fall I met Corbin, and of course he realized my interests. We became good friends, and he asked to see my Ph.D. thesis, which was then in manuscript form, and I gave him a copy of it. He was elated by it and wanted to get it published immediately in the Bollingen Series at the Princeton University Press, but the Harvard University Press found out and said, "No, we would like to do it ourselves," and finally published it[88] although it took them a few years to bring it out.

Anyway, Corbin and I began immediately to discuss matters of mutual interest. At first, there was a certain friction between us, because he was opposed to the position of Guénon and the traditionalist perspective in general, which was mine. At the same time, however, he himself was really the reviver of many aspects of traditional philosophy. Once he made a few harsh criticisms including personal attacks and I became angry. His attack during a meeting we had at the Institut Franco-Iranien was not against Guénon but against Burckhardt,[89] who was a very close personal friend of mine. So I got up and left the Institute. Then Stella Corbin, his wife, called me up and apologized that Corbin had said these things. She said, "No, please, come. He wants to see you." In any case, after that episode, I always took great care not to discuss such matters with him and so did he. I understood his idiosyncrasies and avoided matters that he disliked.

From the doctrinal point of view, we continued to disagree on many matters as things went on. I must add that over the years he became more and more aware of the significance of traditional writings. I shall never forget that in the sixties Teilhard de Chardin[90] had become very popular, and Corbin was very angry with his whole approach towards theology and philosophy. At that time, Frithjof Schuon had written in the footnote of one of his books, *Comprendere l'Islam*,[91] that this kind of theology proposed by Teilhard de Chardin is the surrender of theology to the microscope, and he made a very severe criticism of him, which elated Corbin. He said, "I am going to quote this footnote in one of my writings, but that is going to cost me membership in the Académie de Belles Lettres in France," and that is exactly what happened. This shows you what kind of prejudice existed against traditionalists in academic circles in France at that time. Corbin also added, "*la vie est trop court*," meaning "life is too short" to care about the consequences of his action.

He definitely had sympathy for Schuon's writings. I also presented some of his books to Frithjof Schuon[92] and Titus Burckhardt, and they both thought that Corbin had discovered many important aspects of the traditional universe.

The main point of difference that I had with Corbin concerned the question of orthodoxy, which I interpret to mean not only formal and exterior orthodoxy, but also intellectual, metaphysical, and esoteric orthodoxy. Of course *ortho-docta* means to have the correct doctrine or knowledge of things. It means to possess the truth. In his youth, Corbin had had certain negative experiences *vis-à-vis* Catholic authorities, which had caused him to convert to Protestantism and to call himself heterodox, although what Corbin was talking about was at the heart of the orthodoxy of Shi'ism. We never came to an agreement over this issue. I was, however, in agreement with Corbin's criticism of the point of view of not only Western orientalism but also of modern Western philosophy in its disregard for the higher levels of reality and especially the imaginal world, about which he wrote so much, especially in his very important book written in 1956, *L'Imagination créatrice dans le soufisme d'Ibn 'Arabī*.[93] I was, of course, in accord with him on this subject.

Teaching with Corbin

Corbin and I formed a kind of team, practically speaking, and I "made use" of his presence in the following way: Corbin was a French man, and the modernized circles in Iran were not interested in what 'Allāmah Ṭabāṭabā'ī with a turban on his head was saying in Qom, but they would listen if somebody from France spoke of traditional teachings. I "made use" of him as much as possible in this context. Corbin himself also wanted to be used in that way to further the cause of the study of traditional philosophy in contemporary modern circles in Iran among people who had been educated in the West or influenced by Western thought. Needless to say, I also had the same goal in mind. Corbin was not only interested in making Islamic philosophy well known in the West, but was also very much interested in the restoration of Islamic philosophy in Iran. He always talked about bringing back to life Islamic philosophy in Iran itself and met often with traditional Persian scholars. Often we attended these meetings together, and so we formed, as I said, a kind of team. We also taught together for some fifteen years a seminar in Islamic philosophy at Tehran University to achieve the goal we both had in mind.

R.J.: Together?
S.H.N.: Together, and it went like this. Corbin would usually choose a philosophical text. For example, for several years it was the commentary of Mullā Ṣadrā upon the *Uṣūl al-kāfī* of Kulaynī,[94] which is a philosophical masterpiece to which no one in the West had paid attention before Corbin. The text of Mullā Ṣadrā is an incredible work, which was never completed. Corbin in fact compared it to *The Art of the Fugue* of Johann Sebastian Bach, which was also left incomplete in the middle of a fugue, but which is nevertheless a very remarkable work. Corbin would first read the text of Mullā Ṣadrā in French and then provide his own commentary.

R.J.: In French.
S.H.N.: Yes, in French, and then I would translate his words into Persian and add a commentary of my own; this would continue for some time. Then there would be questions and answers. As you know, Corbin was almost completely deaf and that is why the way he spoke French was very difficult to understand, and also the terminology that he used was not easy.

I will never forget that when we wanted to inaugurate the seminar, all the dignitaries of the Faculty of Letters came. Sadighi and Mahdavi did not like very much what was going on. They were too positivistic in their philosophical approach, but they did come, as did also Ali Akbar Siassi who was then dean. Of course Siassi was one of the masters of the French language of his generation in Iran, and he thought that he knew French perfectly well. When the two-hour session finished he said, "Dr. Nasr, how in the world did you translate Corbin into Persian? I did not understand anything he was saying." I said, "Corbin speaks in French, the angels understand him, then they transmit it to me in Persian, and then I express it in Persian to the audience," and we all laughed. These seminars were important because many people, including all of our own advanced students in the field of philosophy, graduate students, some of whom I have already named, such as Purhusayni, Davari, Davudi, and Mujtabavi, would be present along with many other people.

R.J.: Was it open to the public?
S.H.N.: It was open actually to the students and professors of the Faculty of Letters, and professors such as Isa Sepahbodi and Mehdi Mohaghegh would be often present, and later Shayegan joined us. But also a number of people from outside the Faculty were also given permission to attend. So it was really a remarkable event in the Iranian

cultural scene and had a major impact upon the teaching of Islamic philosophy in a comparative mode, as comparative philosophy East and West, you might say. Later on, when I became dean of the Faculty, I of course continued to emphasize very much the importance of this kind of study. In addition, as I have already mentioned, Corbin and I would meet with 'Allāmah Ṭabāṭabā'ī every other week during the fall when Corbin was in Tehran. Furthermore, I would meet him privately almost every week during the fall session, sometimes two or three times a week, and we would carry out joint intellectual and scholarly projects.

Projects with Corbin

First of all, I translated one or two essays of his into Persian in the late fifties and early sixties. Then one day he said, "The goal of my life was to edit in a critical manner the works of Suhrawardī, and I will not be able to complete the project by myself. Therefore, I want to ask you a great favor. I will put all the manuscripts that I have assembled over the years in your hands. Why do you not edit the Persian works of Suhrawardī, the shorter works?" And he added that he wanted to have included in this volume a text that was in Arabic, the *Risālat al-abrāj* (*Treatise of Constellations*). He said, "I had already edited it in my youth in Istanbul. You can go over them and add them to the others, which are all in Persian." I said, "All right," but I did not know what I was getting into. The task of editing these works and publishing them[95] took the next ten years of my life. It was a monumental task, a really monumental task. I received some new manuscripts from Istanbul and other places. In several cases it was only with the help of the Arabic text that I could establish the Persian text in question, because the manuscript of the latter was so faulty. The editing of these treatises was one of the major achievements of my life in the domain of the resuscitation of Islamic philosophy.

This task of editing critically philosophical texts is really a thankless one, since most people, especially in the West, think that it is an easy process, scholars just editing books and putting them in your hand. But of course it is in most cases very difficult. In any case, it is important to have first of all the best manuscripts and then establish a critical edition before one begins to analyze a work. In the West today, you do not have to worry about this matter, as far as modern philosophy is concerned. The works of Kant and Hegel and so forth have been critically edited sometimes several times, and now you can discuss these works on the basis of well-established texts. In our philosophical tradition, you first have to make the critically edited texts available.

R.J.: You knew already Suhrawardī, I mean, you had already read him.
S.H.N.: Yes. In the fifties and early sixties I had read mostly Suhrawardī's Arabic works such as *Ḥikmat al-ishrāq*[96] and other works contained in the two volumes that Corbin had brought out: the first in Istanbul, and the second in Tehran and Paris. But the Persian works were not easily available. Khānbābā Bayānī of the National Library of Iran had brought out a couple of these treatises, but the few texts available were scattered here and there, and furthermore they were for the most part faulty. I was, therefore, glad to edit the complete Persian works because it was a major contribution to Persian literature as well as philosophy in Iran. It was also an important step in creating greater awareness among Iranians of their own past.

Immediately upon publication of these treatises, interest in them spread like wildfire. The titles of these treatises, such as *Safīr-e sīmorgh* (*The Song of the Griffin*) and *'Aql-e Sorkh* (*The Purple Intellect*) came to be used even by cinematographers and painters. It is unbelievable how it caught on and what impact it had on the educated public in general. Corbin asked if I wanted him to write a French prolegomena for my volume,[97] as he had done for the other two volumes. I responded affirmatively, and then I wrote an extensive Persian introduction, and the work came out as an eight-hundred page book, which was then republished by the Imperial Academy after I founded it.

This was a project that caused Corbin and me to meet every week while the work was in progress and he was in Tehran. Corbin would also consult with me about other projects. For example, when he wanted to begin cooperating with Sayyid Jalal al-Din Ashtiyani on the *Muntakhabāt-e ḥukamā-ye elāhī dar Īrān*,[98] which was to be a seven-volume work, he consulted with me, and it was I who introduced Corbin to Ashtiyani for this task and vice versa.

R.J.: You went to Mashhad?
S.H.N.: Yes, I went to Mashhad and talked to Ashtiyani about the project, but I must say that I had brought Ashtiyani to see Corbin in Tehran years before, as Ashtiyani would come often to Tehran. I went to Mashhad especially for this project, and Ashtiyani agreed to cooperate. Unfortunately, because of the death of Corbin the seven volumes that were planned could not be realized, but four volumes did come

out. I was involved in nearly every major project that Corbin was carrying out at that time. Of course I also published a *Mélange* for him, which you must have seen.

R.J.: Absolutely.
S.H.N.: This is a very large volume and is a major work, one of the best things done on Corbin or for him. I asked the prime minister Amir Abbas Hoveida,[99] who liked Corbin's writings very much, to come to the celebration on the occasion of the publication of the book. We had a wonderful celebratory session for Corbin at Tehran University in which this book was presented to him. When I became the founding president of the Imperial Iranian Academy of Philosophy, Corbin was then retiring from the Sorbonne, and I asked him to become one of our professors. So, he continued to come to Tehran for the last four years of his life under the auspices of the Academy, being no longer formally associated with the Institut Franco-Iranien and no longer receiving a salary from it.

Corbin of course taught at the Academy, and this was an important part of the grand design I had for the Academy, which was to make it a major center for philosophy East and West, where different currents of philosophy were to be taught alongside our own philosophy, Persian Islamic philosophy, which was at the heart of our program. I brought both Izutsu[100] and Corbin to the Academy, and of course they played a very important role. Thanks to them and others, it was possible for many fine students to be trained there. The few years we had together was really the golden age of the Academy. Izutsu and Corbin as well as myself used to teach there along with many others, but we were the three main teachers.

Corbin and Mullā Ṣadrā

I also must mention that Corbin's attraction to Mullā Ṣadrā was caused to a large extent by what I said to him, and I pushed him in the direction of Ṣadrian Studies. The meetings with 'Allāmah Ṭabāṭabā'ī were also of course very important in turning the attention of Corbin to Mullā Ṣadrā, meetings that as already mentioned were also attended by me. Corbin in fact did not begin to write on Mullā Ṣadrā until after our meeting in 1958. All of the three major scholars who wrote on Mullā Ṣadrā in the West, that is Corbin, Izutsu, and Fazlur Rahman, everyone of whom were much older than myself, were introduced to the world of Mullā Ṣadrā by me.

Corbin and Religion

Corbin and I also had a lot of personal human contacts and common interest in various spiritual and intellectual matters, and I knew him very well on the human level. For example, we went together for *ziyārat*[101] of Jām-i karān, the site associated with the Twelfth Imam near the holy city of Qom. He considered himself a "Shi'ite," although I think that he never formally converted to Shi'ism. But he was inwardly converted to it. He always used to say, "*nous Shi'ites*" that is, "we Shi'ites." We also spoke about intimate, spiritual subjects together, about inner visions and matters like that, which I do not want to discuss here.

R.J.: What kind of man was Corbin, I mean, personally? I mean, did he practice his religion?
S.H.N.: That is a very good question. As I said, Corbin had been originally Catholic but converted to Protestantism because of the limitation put by his Catholic teachers upon his study of mysticism in which he was intensely interested. He was attracted to the study of mysticism since his youth, and so he began to study early in his life 16th- and 17th-century Lutheran mysticism and theosophy, and then he was led to the study of Islam and specially Suhrawardī. He discovered through Suhrawardī the Shi'ite Persian world, which he felt was his spiritual home. He had a very deep, personal attachment to the Twelfth Imam as well as to the other Shi'ite Imams. It was unbelievable to observe the love he had for the Shi'ite Imams as if he were a very pious Shi'ite; but at the same time, he was a French intellectual but not like figures such as Guénon and Schuon who embraced Islam formally and practiced what they preached in the sense that when they said you have to follow a tradition they themselves followed one. They got up in the morning and said their prayers but Corbin did not practice Islam on the formal level. I never saw Corbin formally perform *namāz* or something like that, but I definitely did see him pray. He was a religious man in the sense that he not only believed in God but also prayed to Him.

In addition, I think that Corbin was given a kind of divine gift of being able to be in contact with the angelic world. He was a kind of hermeneut of the angelic world in that he had a natural inclination towards that world and the ability to interpret its message for us. He was a kind of natural visionary. Whenever he looked at things, he looked behind them, not only at them. He always looked for the inner sense of things. That is what drew him to esoteric Shi'ism, and Sufism, to all of the

Persian sages and to spiritual hermeneutics, to the idea of *ta'wīl*,[102] which is at the heart of Corbin's whole worldview. The idea that the reality of things is not exhausted by their outer face was an evident truth for Corbin. He combined in himself a remarkable synthesis that is quite rare in the modern West, that is, the synthesis of philosophical rigor and a very strong mystical inclination. Corbin was a very serious philosopher. There is no doubt about it. He viewed all the texts he was studying in Persian and Arabic as a mystical philosopher and not as a philologist or a historian. He was a major thinker, and his significance is that in modern times, he was practically the first European orientalist in the field of Islamic studies who was also a keen philosopher, in the traditional sense of the term.

Corbin and Islamic Philosophy

R.J.: Is not that amazing being at the same time an orientalist and a philosopher?

S.H.N.: Not necessarily so. Look at, for example, the case of Indian Studies. People such as Heinrich Zimmer[103] and also Mircea Eliade, who wrote on Hinduism—these men were not only scholars of religion, they were really also philosophers, and you also have scholars like them in the field of Buddhism. In the case of Islam, it is in a sense a tragedy that most of the people who have come to the field of Islamic studies have done so either through philology of Arabic and Persian and/or history. Rarely have they been also philosophers. Often they have been missionaries at first who have hated Islam and have wanted to prove it false. There have been of course exceptions as we see in the case of H.A.R. Gibb. I am not saying that Corbin is the only philosophically minded Islamicist; but he was perhaps the only European scholar who was both an outstanding philosopher and a major Islamicist. Max Horten,[104] for example, who was a German philosopher and Islamicist in the early 20th century, studied from the philosophical point of view the books of Mullā Ṣadrā and those of Suhrawardī even at that time when nobody had heard about them in the West. He wrote that large book on the debate between Ṭūsī and Fakhr al-Dīn Rāzī. Yes, he was also a philosophically minded Islamicist, but he was not a major philosopher.

I think that Corbin in a sense is the beginning of a very important phenomenon coming at a time when modern philosophy in the West, which had developed after the Renaissance and had inbred within itself, being very sure of itself and rejecting every other philosophy, whether it be

Indian, Islamic, or Buddhist, began to crumble in the middle of the 20th century and is doing so more and more now. There are now many Western philosophers who are looking over the borders of the West in other places. In America you have dozens of them, professional philosophers who are interested in Hinduism, Buddhism, Neo-Confucianism, and so forth. Corbin opened this door for the Islamic world. So many people who had studied Islam, because of the long contact of Islam historically with the West, which did not exist in the case of Hinduism, Buddhism, Taoism, and Confucianism, were and are still to some extent dealing with Islam only as a social order and often as a military and political threat.

There still lingers in the minds of many people in the West memories of the Islamic period in Spain, the challenge of Islam to Christianity, the Crusades, the idea of Islam as "the religion of the sword," all of the pseudo-imagery, all kinds of half-truths which had been cast upon the minds of Western people since Peter the Venerable ordered the translation of the Quran into Latin a thousand years ago and even before. The fact that Islam played a very important role in the Western philosophical tradition and Western science is not emphasized enough in schools in Europe and America except in a dismissive manner. Few have wanted to study the Islamic intellectual and spiritual tradition in itself. Look, for example, at Bertrand Russell's *A History of Western Philosophy*. It contains a short chapter called "Arabic Philosophy," which he treats only in relation to Western thought. In the medieval West, you could not study Western philosophy without knowing Averroes, without knowing Avicenna. So people had to study them but they did not want to consider Islamic philosophy in its own right, and this attitude has survived to this day.

It was a very big struggle for both Corbin and also myself to try to turn the attention of the Western public to the philosophical significance of Islamic philosophy on its own terms. We tried to correct this historical error and to seek to study the integral Islamic philosophical tradition, reading its texts not philologically but philosophically. So Corbin marked the beginning of something very important. Today, we have many students even here in America interested in Islamic philosophy, although in America students are less trained in philosophy than in Continental Europe where they study some philosophy in secondary schools, for example the *lycée* and the *gymnasium* in France and Germany. Nevertheless, there are a number of students here who are doing their Ph.D.s in Islamic studies but who are seriously interested in philosophy and metaphysics and not just in philology, intellectual history, law, or poetry. There are also some students of this kind in Europe today. Corbin in a sense opened the door in the West to combining Islamic studies and philosophy.

Before him, Louis Massignon, another great French orientalist, had achieved the same to some extent for mysticism, and Louis Gardet[105] for theology. Gardet was a Catholic theologian and at the same time an Islamicist who wrote many important books. Of course, Massignon was a remarkable figure, not only an Arabist, but a Catholic mystic and thinker who was at the same time very well versed in Sufi mysticism and touched by it personally, and who introduced Sufism seriously to the West through his works on Ḥallāj and others. Corbin achieved that task for later Islamic philosophy, but he met immediately with great resistance from several quarters—first of all, from the Catholic scholars of Islamic philosophy. They looked with disdain upon Corbin for having left Catholicism. Furthermore, having been trained in a narrow understanding of "Arabic philosophy" ending with Averroes, they did not want to accept the integral tradition of the Islamic philosophy that has had its main home over the centuries mainly in Persia with some branches in India and the Ottoman world and that has continued to this day.

Corbin also met resistance from mainstream Western philosophers who did not want to consider seriously another branch of the tree that had produced the tradition of Western philosophy. This is the result of the absolutization, you might say, of Western thought in modern times culminating with Hegel, an idea that is still very strong in the West. If you accept that from the heritage of Abraham, Plato, and Aristotle there grew another branch of the tree of philosophy that produced people who were as important philosophically as Descartes but differed completely from him while being his contemporaries, that reality would destroy that absolutization of Western thought and the Eurocentrism that lies at the heart of the Western paradigm created in the Renaissance. That is why it is easy for most scholars in the West to study Ramanuja or some neo-Confucian philosopher such as Chu-Hsi as serious philosophy, but to study a figure in the 17th century from Persia talking about Plato and Aristotle within the context of a monotheistic revelation, as have our philosophers, is quite something else. It is very difficult for Western scholars to accept these figures as serious philosophers, because to do so means that the West has to rethink its own historiography of philosophy and its own philosophy of the history of philosophy. Therefore, it is a philosophical challenge to which the Western philosophical establishment has reacted for the most part through rejection.

Then there is the third factor that has come from modern Arab nationalism. The Arab nationalist interpreters of Islamic philosophy have clung to the Western category of "Arabic philosophy," which had a completely non-nationalistic meaning in the European Middle Ages. These nationalists do not want to hear of the Persian connections of later Islamic philosophy. They have continued to call Ibn Sīnā an Arab, but they know that we cannot call Mīr Dāmād an Arab by any stretch of the imagination. So Corbin met a lot of resistance from that corner and so have I. Corbin rendered a very great service to the integral tradition of Islamic philosophy by opening the door to the study of later Islamic philosophy, with its main home in Persia.

Corbin and Heidegger

R.J.: But how did he actually turn from his interest in phenomenology and Heidegger, whom he knew, to Mullā Ṣadrā and Suhrawardī? Did he ever talk about that with you?

S.H.N.: Oh yes, he talked about that issue often. He had actually met Heidegger both personally and through his books before he "met" Suhrawardī and Mullā Ṣadrā and figures like them. As I have already said, Mullā Ṣadrā comes later and Suhrawardī earlier in the life of Corbin. Corbin said that he was always interested from his youth, even before he went to meet Heidegger, in the inner meaning of things, and for him phenomenology had always meant the unveiling of the inner meaning of things, that is, *kashf al-maḥjūb,*[106] which is a special understanding of phenomenology that accepts the reality of the noumenon behind the phenomenon and the possibility of knowing this noumenal reality. For him phenomenology is the science of going from the phenomena to the noumena and rejecting the Kantian view of denying to human intelligence the possibility of knowing the noumena. So when he spoke of phenomenology, it was a very special understanding of it that he had in mind, very close to our perspective of *ta'wīl* and *kashf al-maḥjūb* as the unveiling of the *ẓāhir,* in order to reach the *bāṭin*[107] as our philosophers have taught.

Now, Corbin had gone to see Heidegger mainly because of his interest in phenomenology as Corbin understood it and also because of his great interest in being, in the whole question of ontology. As you know, he translated Heidegger into French, but he was not totally happy with Heidegger's philosophy, which did not fulfill his spiritual needs, you might say. He did not become a complete Heideggerian as some have claimed. So Corbin was still a man looking for philosophical answers. He set out to study Oriental languages to this end. He was very good in learning to read languages but not to speak them because of his deafness. He decided to learn how to read Arabic, Persian, and Pahlavi because from a young age he was looking actually for another world, for another way of seeing things.

Corbin Discovers Islamic Philosophy in Persia

Corbin told me that the turning point of his life philosophically came when one day he was sitting at the Sorbonne in a class of Massignon. Massignon knew Corbin's interest in both Islamic philosophy and Heidegger and the German school of *Existenz Philosophie* (existential philosophy, which must not, however, be simply identified with French existentialism) and was also fully aware of his student's interest in both spirituality and philosophy in general. At the end of the class, Massignon pulled out of his bag an old book and gave it to Corbin, saying, "This is what you are looking for." The book was the lithograph edition of the *Ḥikmat al-ishrāq* of Suhrawardī, the old bazaar edition published in the Qajar period in Tehran, which is very rare now but which in fact was widely used before Corbin brought out his critical edition of this book. Even afterwards this edition has continued to be used with its commentary by Quṭb al-Dīn Shīrāzī[108] in the margin. Corbin said that he took the book home. By that time he had already learned Arabic and his Arabic was pretty good. He said, "I began to read this book. My whole life changed and I realized that what I was really looking for was this philosophical tradition, and not only Heidegger." He alludes to this question in the French introduction, which he wrote to the *Kitāb al-mashā'ir* of Mullā Ṣadrā. This introduction is the most important work that Corbin has written on comparative ontology. It is short, but it is profound and an important text.

He discussed the question of existentialism with me personally and also in the seminars we used to teach together at Tehran University; it is too bad that there are no tapes from that time. He was much more critical of French existentialism than he was of *Existenz Philosophie*. Once Corbin said, "Existence for these [existentialist philosophers both French and German] leads to death, whereas in the philosophy of Mullā Ṣadrā and Persian Islamic philosophy, existence leads to transcendence; death always leads to higher levels of being." It is that discovery that changed Corbin's worldview completely. As I told you in the story of our going to Sainte Odile, Corbin was not that much interested in Heidegger in the latter part of his life, after he had discovered the later Islamic philosophy of Persia.

R.J.: Can one say that Corbin was the last true philosopher of Persia?
S.H.N.: No, no, first of all, he was not Persian.

R.J.: I know, but . . .
S.H.N.: Again, no, because first of all there are several notable Persian philosophers after Corbin. For example, there is Mehdi Ha'eri[109] who was a first-rate philosopher in the tradition of Islamic philosophy closer to the Ibn Sīnā school than to the school of Mullā Ṣadrā, a remarkable logician and thinker and an epistemologist. In his *Knowledge by Presence* he challenges Wittgenstein and Russell on the important question of knowledge by presence or *'ilm-i ḥuḍūrī*,[110] his position coming from the tradition of Suhrawardī and others. I can mention also Ashtiyani and the two Āmulīs.[111] There are also a number of younger Persian philosophers such as Gholam Hossein Ebrahimi Dinani and Gholamreza A'vani. Corbin died some thirty years ago, while all of us, people like myself, who consider ourselves to be rooted in the Islamic philosophical tradition and are thinking philosophically about various subjects, are still alive and belong to that tradition. So, I would not use the word *last* for Corbin. Rather, he is the *first*, I would say, European "Persian philosopher."

Corbin and Imamology

R.J.: That is interesting. How did Corbin get concerned with the themes of Islamic thought such as imamology and prophetology, and how did he relate them to the questions of the destiny of Western man?
S.H.N.: Corbin was a person who was very deeply drawn by his nature early in life to mysticism within the Christian tradition. Christ is himself the spiritual guide for the Christian mystics, although some also have had human guides, especially in the Orthodox tradition. In Islam, you have of course spiritual masters: the Sufi teachers, *pīrs*, *murshids*, *shaykhs*,[112] and most of those who follow the spiritual path have a human spiritual teacher. In Shi'ism, however, there is the possibility of guidance by the Twelfth Imam, and there are many Persian Shi'ite mystics, although not by any means all, who have claimed that they have had no human master but that their master has been the Twelfth Imam, because within the Shi'ite world it is possible, with the grace of Heaven,

for a person to have direct contact with the Twelfth Imam and to be guided spiritually in an initiatic way by him. I believe it is this aspect of Shi'ism more than anything else that drew Corbin to the study of Shi'ism and to the whole question of imamology.

Corbin wanted to have a spiritual guide but did not want to have a human guide. The whole ethos of this type of spirituality within Shi'ism therefore appealed deeply to him. I used to carry on debates with him on this issue all the time. I believe that Mullā Ṣadrā had a spiritual master, a human spiritual teacher, but Corbin always used to say "No, he is like Mīr Dāmād; he is one of those people who was guided only by the Twelfth Imam." He said that because he saw himself in that situation. I know that, for example, 'Allāmah Ṭabāṭabā'ī had had a spiritual teacher when he resided in Najaf; I mean a human being of flesh and blood who guided him spiritually.

In fact you have in Islam several possibilities. First of all, you have the possibility of regular Sufi orders, both Sunni and Shi'ite, such as the Qādiriyyah, Shādhiliyyah, Ni'malullāhiyyah et cetera, and then you have the possibility of Sufi orders which are not formally organized and have no distinct name. They are like what we see in the early centuries of Islam when there were individual masters guiding a circle of disciples. This latter type has definitely existed among Shi'ite and even Sunni *'ulamā'*. Because of the opposition to Sufism that came at the end of Safavid period in Persia, many of the Shi'ite *'ulamā'* were practicing Sufism without saying, "We are a member of this or that order." The word *ṣūfī* was not used, but initiation and spiritual guidance took place. This type included figures such as Baḥr al-'ulūm or 'Allāmah Ṭabāṭabā'ī who had an actual human teacher. And then there is in the Shi'ite context the third possibility, the possibility of direct contact with the Imam. The fourth possibility is that of the Uwaysī way, the possibility of being guided directly by Khiḍr, a prophet mentioned in the Quran and identified also by some with Elias.

All of these possibilities exist within the universe of Islamic spirituality taken as a whole, but Corbin was specially drawn to the possibility of being guided by the Imam. 'Allāmah Ṭabāṭabā'ī, who performed spiritual practice his whole life in addition to writing on philosophy and theology, was very well aware of that fact. He both praised Corbin's love for the Imams and also was critical that Corbin was not willing to submit himself personally to spiritual discipline. Anyway, I think that is the secret of how Corbin became personally involved in the study of what he called *imamologie*, *prophétologie*, and similar subjects.

Also, Corbin's vision of revelation in its inward aspect related to the guidance of the Imam even led him to a kind of Christology which was not orthodox and traditional from either the Catholic or mainstream Protestant point of view, but which was close in fact to Islamic Christology. It is in that vein that he studied the question of prophecy and prophetology, always tying revelation to inspiration, intuition, and illumination. That is why he studied Suhrawardī so avidly and used to refer to him as his master.

Ṭabāṭabā'ī and Corbin

R.J.: Was 'Allāmah Ṭabāṭabā'ī as close to this idea of illumination of Suhrawardī as was Corbin?
S.H.N.: Yes, but he was more attracted to Mullā Ṣadrā than to Suhrawardī. I would say that Corbin was on the contrary more attracted to Suhrawardī than to Mullā Ṣadrā, and even towards the end of his life, even after years of studying Mullā Ṣadrā, he continued to refer to Suhrawardī as "*notre maître.*"

R.J.: So how did the dialogue between the two, I mean 'Allāmah Ṭabāṭabā'ī and Corbin, go on? I think there had to be something more than a simple dialogue between two sides?
S.H.N.: First of all, there was a great deal of congeniality from both sides. The two were not identical in their thought, but there was certainly much common ground on many issues between them so that the dialogue could have gone on for another fifty years. I will tell you something from each side. 'Allāmah Ṭabāṭabā'ī saw in Corbin two characteristics that attracted him especially so that he was willing to spend so much time in dialogue with him. One was that he saw in Corbin a Western scholar sympathetic to the cause of Shi'ism, a person who could spread the teachings of Shi'ism to the West, being a kind of *porte-parole* for the expression of authentic Shi'ite teachings in Europe. Secondly, and the other way around, he saw Corbin as a person who could inform him of important ideas which were being discussed in the philosophical, religious, and theological circles of the West at that time. Do not forget that 'Allāmah Ṭabāṭabā'ī was always very much interested in what was going on intellectually in the world at large, because he wanted to provide Islamic answers for the questions of the day. In contrast, my other teacher, Ayatollah Qazwīnī, was not like that at all. Of course in political matters he was aware of what was going on in Iran, but he was rooted

firmly within his world of Ṣadrian metaphysics and was not interested in various philosophical ideas being discussed in modern Western circles.

As already mentioned, 'Allāmah Ṭabāṭabā'ī carried out dialogue in the earlier period of his youth with the Marxists, and this shows that he was interested in what philosophical and even ideological problems modernized people were facing and the questions that they were asking. He felt deeply that Islamic philosophy and thought had answers for all those questions. This was a major characteristic of 'Allāmah Ṭabāṭabā'ī that brought him close to Corbin.

As for Corbin, he also had several reasons for having intense interest in these dialogues. Firstly, 'Allāmah Ṭabāṭabā'ī was like an ocean of knowledge from which a scholar could draw so easily. Of course Corbin was a great scholar, but when he did have questions about some aspects of Islamic thought, he would turn with assurance of being answered in an authoritative manner to 'Allāmah Ṭabāṭabā'ī, who would provide very valuable clarifications, give references, provide the meaning of certain verses of the Quran and matters like that. So, he served as a major source of traditional Islamic thought for Corbin.

Secondly, because of his own personal and scholarly interest in Shi'ism, Corbin wanted very much to establish dialogue with serious Shi'ite thinkers. He was not interested in carrying out dialogue with Ahmad Fardid, Yahya Mahdavi, and people like that who were his friends. He knew them well, but they were for him European-trained Persian philosophers, and he could find plenty of people who thought like them in France and Germany. Why come to Tehran to have a dialogue with them? Rather, he wanted to have a dialogue with authentic representatives of Shi'ite thought, and he found the ideal solution in the person of 'Allāmah Ṭabāṭabā'ī. Mind you, he also had discussions with other people, including Sarkār-i Āqā, the head of the Shaykhī branch of Shi'ism. Corbin was also interested in that school and wrote much about it. The extreme form of love for the Imams, which characterizes Shaykhism, was especially attractive for Corbin. But no one else could provide what Corbin needed as did 'Allāmah Ṭabāṭabā'ī. Therefore, the latter was for Corbin a perfect partner for dialogue.

Thirdly, Corbin was also doing the same thing as 'Allāmah Ṭabāṭabā'ī, but the other way around. Through 'Allāmah Ṭabāṭabā'ī, Corbin could discover what was going on in Qom and other Iranian cities among religious scholars and subjects that they were discussing.

One last element that united the two was the following: Both men, from different perspectives and for different reasons, were very much interested in the revival of traditional philosophy in Persia and its continuation. Corbin was interested in this matter because he loved this philosophical tradition and did not want it to die out. He loved Iran and its culture and was deeply interested in its future. He always considered Iran to be his spiritual and intellectual home. Concerning Iran he would say, "*Mon pays intellectuel*" ("my intellectual home") and he felt as much at home in Iran as he did in France and intellectually even more at home in Iran than in his country of birth. He would always tell me that he felt more at home spiritually in Iran than anywhere else. He knew that it was very important for the traditional culture of Iran to continue to survive, and at the heart of this culture was this vision of the universe, the vision of reality with which Persian philosophers, metaphysicians, theologians, and Sufis had dealt over the ages. Therefore, Corbin was interested in the revival and a new presentation of Iran's intellectual tradition.

As for 'Allāmah Ṭabāṭabā'ī, he was also of course interested intensely in this matter. He himself was a great reviver of Islamic philosophy in his day, and this was the tradition to which he belonged. He considered Islamic philosophy to contain the truth, and he wanted it to endure not only for Iran but also for the whole world. I should also mention that both of them concentrated their attention upon myself as far as this question was concerned because I was also deeply dedicated to the task of the survival, revival, and presentation of the Islamic intellectual tradition. They therefore both saw me as a valuable link between them, and an aid in their efforts to revive that tradition.

Revival of the Islamic Intellectual Tradition

R.J.: And that was fruitful for you?

S.H.N.: Yes, it was very fruitful for me for several reasons. Since you have asked about this matter, I am obliged to talk about myself and why it was fruitful for me. First of all, I joined this dialogue as soon as I returned to Iran when I was only twenty-five years old. It was the beginning of my professional career, and I learned a great deal from these meetings. I was then learning certain new ideas (for me) in Islamic philosophy. Also, the question of comparative philosophical vocabulary was important to me. Of course my first European language is English and not French, which Corbin used, but it did not matter because I knew French well enough, and especially the philosophical vocabulary I know as well as English.

Let me cite you an example. In 1963, when Corbin was translating the *Kitāb al-mashā'ir* of Mullā Ṣadrā, for weeks he consulted with me concerning the translation of the title. Finally, we settled on *Le Livre des pénétrations métaphysiques*, which is a beautiful translation but not a literal one. Such an exercise taught me many things and certain French nuances, philosophically speaking, which Corbin was using, adding to my familiarity with philosophical French. Until then I had been familiar with the writings of the likes of Pascal, Descartes, and Voltaire, as well as with the traditionalists such as Guénon. Through Corbin I became familiar with a different style of French, which drew from the vocabulary of the Renaissance writers and certain other less used sources.

For me, the dialogue and my own meetings with Corbin were, first of all, occasions to learn. Secondly, I felt that I was taking a step in what I had set out to do, namely, to bring back to life our own philosophical tradition, which meant both to conceptualize and formulate it in a contemporary language and also to be able to face the issues that challenge it from the outside. Now this is a very important point that I need to mention again. When I went back from Harvard to Iran, I set out to try to bring back to life the whole of the Islamic intellectual tradition by remaining firmly faithful to it, but at the same time expressing it in a contemporary language, but I left aside the fields of law, politics, and matters like that. There were many other people working on these latter subjects, and these fields were not my specialty. So I concentrated primarily on three of the most important aspects of the Islamic intellectual tradition, that is, philosophy with all the different schools, doctrinal Sufism, and the sciences. I have written extensively on all of these three fields over several decades. The goal that I had set for myself stands still before me although much has already been achieved.

The role I played as translator and commentator during the meetings with Corbin and 'Allāmah Ṭabāṭabā'ī was in the very direction that I had to follow to achieve this goal. Therefore, I did the work of translator, interpreter, commentator, and intermediary for years with great pleasure and without ever asking anything personal in return. Through these efforts we produced many works which I felt were very much in harmony with my own goals and were much more important than any worldly return.

Let me ask you this question. In 1958, how many people among the educated classes in Tehran University, in other Iranian universities, or people in general who had studied in the West, were at all interested in Islamic philosophy? Practically no one. Such people had not even heard of Mīr Dāmād[113] and Mullā Ṣadrā, but twenty years later when the Islamic Revolution took place, look at the difference that had been created during this period. When I returned to Iran in 1958, there were two classes of people dealing with philosophy. People in Tehran University trained mostly in France, some in Germany, and one or two elsewhere. They were teaching and discussing European philosophy in the Persian language. The great contribution of Yahya Mahdavi among this group was precisely to emphasize the importance of the Persian language for philosophical discourse. Then there were the traditional philosophers in Qom, Mashhad, and Tehran, in such places as Madrasa-yi Marwī, Sepahsalar, et cetera. These two groups could have been on two different planets, but among the Western-educated Iranians, those who were interested in Islamic philosophy were very rare despite 'Allāmah Ṭabāṭabā'ī's earlier efforts. I do not want to say there was no modernized Persian interested in Islamic philosophy. There was one person here, one person there. Twenty years later, when the Revolution took place, Islamic philosophy was part of the general intellectual discourse; that is a very telling fact, and I take pride in having something to do with this transformation.

I will tell you this story, which is true and at the same time facetious, and its result is still extant in Iran. One day, when I was the dean of the Faculty of Letters, the Queen called me up and said, "Dr. Nasr, I want to change the name of Farah Avenue, which is in my name, to the name of some famous Persian figure. Please suggest someone." I said, "All of our great poets such as Firdawsī, Nāṣir-e Khosraw, Niẓāmī-yi Ganjawī, Ḥāfiẓ, Sa'dī, Khayyām, Jāmī, et cetera have avenues named after them, but for the philosophers the situation is very different. Why do you not call it 'Khiyābān-i Suhrawardī' (Suhrawardī Avenue)?" She called up the mayor of Tehran immediately, and within one week all the signs came down and the avenue came to be known by the name of Suhrawardī. Of course for a long, long time the taxi drivers would still call it Khiyābān-i Farah. In any case, today it is still called Khiyābān-i Suhrawardī.

Then, shortly before the Revolution when Tehran had expanded to the north, I was again asked by her to provide names for two major new boulevards. It is I who named Khiyābān-i Mīr Dāmād and Khiyābān-i Mullā Ṣadrā, choosing these names in answer to her request for these two important new roads. Even on a popular level you could not have imagined in 1960 that a major boulevard, not a little narrow street, in northern Tehran could be named Mīr Dāmād. Who knew Mīr Dāmād in northern Tehran at that time? But by the time the Revolution came, the most famous butcher's shop in Tehran was known by the name of Mullā Ṣadrā because it was located on that boulevard. Many people among modernized classes came to know of Mullā Ṣadrā's name by buying meat from a new butcher whose fancy shop was called Mulla Sadra butchery. There is now even a butchery by that name in Los Angeles.

I am telling you this story just as an anecdote, but it is a very telling story. Interest in Islamic philosophy among modern educated classes came about to a large extent through the efforts of 'Allāmah Ṭabāṭabā'ī, Corbin, and myself, on the one hand, and such younger traditional philosophers, not younger than I, as Ashtiyani, Motahhari, and Ha'eri on the other. Gradually, even younger scholars came to the fore. In addition to participating in the Ṭabāṭabā'ī-Corbin dialogues, I spoke often on the radio and television concerning Islamic philosophy, and we set out to publish many texts and studies which began to interest students at various universities as well as in traditional *madrasahs* in Qom and elsewhere. The Corbin-'Allāmah Ṭabāṭabā'ī dialogues were an important factor in this whole process. Not many people were allowed to participate in them. We did not allow more than about ten people, but two volumes came out in Qom concerning this dialogue. Other people began to read what had taken place, and interest grew rapidly from the reading of those texts. Moreover, Corbin, Motahhari, Shayegan, myself, and others who were present would often speak about the lively discussions between Western and Islamic philosophy held in these sessions to other audiences.

The Imperial Iranian Academy of Philosophy

R.J.: And this spirit of dialogue among the secularist Iranian intellectuals and the traditionalist school within Iran and also outside Iran was the idea that led to the creation of the Imperial Academy of Philosophy, because it was based on this idea?

S.H.N.: Yes, definitely, this was the central idea. We have not talked about how the Imperial Academy was founded, but if you were to ask me, I would talk about it.

R.J.: Yes, please do.

S.H.N.: You know yourself, since you have studied in France for a long time, that it is a very great honor to become a member of the *Institut International de philosophie* in Paris. It is the most important philosophical academy in the world, and it has no more than one hundred members at any time. Of course most of the famous European philosophers, including your friends Paul Ricoeur and Emmanuel Levinas, belonged to it. In the early seventies, I was elected to become a member of that Institute. At that time, Raymond Klibansky,[114] the famous philosopher, was its president. Of course it was a great honor for me to be chosen as the first Iranian member, and the news reached the newspapers. The Queen was very happy and congratulated me, as did Prime Minister Hoveida. It was an important cultural event for Iran. I was then the president of Aryamehr University and very busy up to my ears running a major university. Klibansky then approached me, as he always believed in the importance of non-Western philosophies. He said, "Now that you have been chosen a member of this Institute, why do we not hold one of the annual meetings of the Institute in Iran and why do we not establish an institute or an academy of philosophy in your country?" I said, "Fine." So I invited him to Iran, and first of all, we organized that major conference in Mashhad to which many of the members of the *Institut* who were important philosophers from France, Switzerland, Germany, and other places came and for which I was the host. This was the first important international philosophical conference ever held in Iran, and it turned out to be simply wonderful.

In addition to the conference, Klibansky himself came to Tehran and I took him to meet the Queen. He prevailed upon her, on the basis of what we had discussed together, that it would be important to establish a philosophical institute in Iran, which had always been a great center of philosophical thought. She agreed completely and accepted to become its patron. I had worked closely with the Queen on many other cultural projects, and she told me to start thinking about what to do about this matter. This was the end of 1973 and the beginning of 1974, when as a result of the oil boom there was a lot of money available, and therefore there was no problem with funding. So I assembled a number of people in the field or interested in general in philosophy and told them about the plan. Everyone agreed that such an institution should be an organization independent of the government and directly under the patronage of the Queen. The people consulted included Morteza Motahhari, Sayyid Jalal al-Din Ashtiyani, 'Abdollah Entizam,[115] Yahya Mahdavi, Mahmud Shahabi, Mahdi Mohaghegh,[116] Seyyed Ja'far Shahidi,[117] Jawad Mosleh, people like that, and of course Corbin.

I drew up the by-laws and the constitution for the institution, and Mahmud Shahabi suggested that the institution should be called the Royal Academy of Philosophy, like the royal academies in Britain,

Sweden, and other places. I had not thought of that title at that time and talked to Corbin about it. He said, "There was the old German Imperial Academy before the First World War when Germany was an empire, and this institution should be called the 'Imperial Iranian Academy of Philosophy.'" Anyway, we settled on the name *Anjuman-i Shāhanshāhī-yi Falsafa-yi Īrān*, which in English would be the Imperial Iranian Academy of Philosophy, and this met with the Shah's and the Queen's approval. And so the Academy was founded with its own board of directors. It was totally independent of the government financially and administratively. Although I was still the president of Aryamehr University, I also became the founder and president of this new academy.

The Queen said to me, "Any piece of land you want for the academy we will provide for you." I said, "I prefer to try to preserve as much as possible the old urban structures of Tehran, and if you allow me, I shall try to find one of these large old houses in the city and renovate it appropriately." She agreed with this proposal. After some search, I found the old house of Loqman al-Moulk[118] near Chaharrah-e Pahlavi; we bought the property from his children and had it renovated by traditional craftsmen. I also bought one or two other houses around it, and so in the middle of Tehran we created a large space devoted to philosophical studies. You should have seen how beautiful everything was when the renovation was finished. Isfahani craftsmen covered the inside with blue tile, and even specially designed furniture was ordered for it, and the garden was renovated. I wanted the ambience to be really Persian, an authentic Persian environment where philosophy would be studied and discussed.

We decided, first of all, that the Academy would not give degrees, because in too many places students come only to receive a degree. It would be like the Princeton School of Advanced Studies and several other places like that in the United States and Europe where people who have either finished their doctorate or are about to do so to come for advanced study while scholars would also come to carry out research. We would have students who were Persian or from other Islamic countries as well as students from the West and from the non-Islamic East, not only from Iran and the West, students who would hail from different philosophical traditions. We were anxious to have students even from Japan and China. Unfortunately, we could not get a student from China at that time because of political reasons, but we did have a couple from Japan, as well as from Europe, America, and other Islamic countries.

The teachers in the academy were to present different philosophical perspectives and included Corbin and Izutsu, who were great comparativists, one from the West, and the other from Japan, as well as Mirza Mehdi Ha'eri, Morteza Motahhari, who was also one of the members of the board, and myself. Ashtiyani was also one of the members of the board, which included what you would call secularist as well as religious figures. We also had a board of foreign advisors that included Naquib al-Attas, Raimundo Panikkar, A. K. Saran, Élemire Zolla, and T. M. P. Mahadevan. Hadi Sharifi, professor of education in Tehran University, was my deputy and played a major role in every way including helping with the publication of our journal and keeping contact with both the Iranian and the foreign board. We had people with traditional education as well as modern ones, people with a Western philosophical orientation, such as Yahya Mahdavi and Gholam-Hossein Sadighi, as well as those devoted to Islamic philosophy. Sadighi did not participate directly, but had his input, but Yahya Mahdavi played an important role.

We created an ambience in which these various perspectives came together and dialogue took place. There were all kinds of students, from William Chittick, who was then finishing his Ph.D. at Tehran University and who studied Ibn 'Arabī there with Izutsu and later on also taught there, to James Morris,[119] who is now a well-known American scholar of Islamic thought, to Igarashi, who, as you know, was later on killed in Japan over the question of the Salman Rushdie affair, to Peter Wilson who is a gifted American poet, and to the American poet Peter Russell, who also translated some Persian poetry into English, to *ṭullāb*[120] from Qom. Also, some of the advanced students from Tehran University would participate in the classes, which were open to everyone. It was really like the old traditional *madrasahs*.[121] You did not have to pay tuition. You did not have to register formally. All formal red tape was avoided. For example, I gave a class on the *Sharḥ-i gulshan-i rāz* of Lāhījī, which is in Persian with a few Arabic passages here and there. About half a dozen Persian women who had studied in the West and had become interested in *'erfān* (gnosis) were also present in this class along with both Persian and foreign students and scholars who were very advanced and who had studied Sufi and philosophical thought for years. It was a wonderful teaching ambience, and our publications also reflected the wide range of philosophical interest of the students as well as the faculty.

We published one of the most important books to come out in English in the 20th century on Zen, *Towards a Philosophy of Zen Buddhism* by Izutsu,[122] and at the same time many important texts and studies of Persian and Islamic philosophy, both in Arabic and Persian, as well as one or two works on Greek philosophy, all of which appeared within a short period of time. We had a five-year lifespan before the Revolution. During that time, we published some fifty important titles along with our multilanguage journal called *Jāwīdān-Khirad/Sophia Perennis*,[123] which soon became world famous.

R.J.: And it was read by people outside of Iran?
S.H.N.: Very much so. I did not know how much *Sophia Perennis* would be missed until after it ceased publication. Kathleen Raine,[124] who was a major English poet, writer, and philosopher, and a specialist on William Blake[125] began to publish *Temenos*, a very famous journal in English devoted to art and the imagination that came out for ten years in England starting in the eighties. She was also a friend of Corbin and a whole group of people in England interested in traditional art and the world of imagination. She said at the very beginning of the first issue of the journal that she hoped that *Temenos* would replace *Sophia Perennis* and fill the vacuum created by its demise. We sent the journal *Sophia Perennis* to many important academies and centers of learning all over the world. Its life was short, but its influence was profound. It is very interesting to note that the major effort made during the last twenty-five years in Iran to bring the *hawzah* and the *dāneshgāh*[126] closer together and also the avid interest of many of the *ṭullāb* in Qom, Mashhad, and Tehran who study Islamic philosophy to also study Western philosophy and matters like that, received a major impetus from the work of the academy and of course from the presence of 'Allāmah Ṭabāṭabā'ī himself, in our circle, and not directly in the Academy, as well as Motahhari.

Aryamehr University: Reconciling Modern Technology and Persian Culture

R.J.: So, you mention that at the same time you were the president of the Aryamehr University.[127] It is interesting, how you reconcile the fact of being the president of a modern scientific technological university and at the same time criticizing Western scientism.
S.H.N.: That is a very good point. You know that I have always criticized Western scientism, but I have never said that we have the choice of not mastering the modern sciences. I have said that we have to absorb Western science within our own worldview and try to criticize it and also

integrate and digest it within our own culture and intellectual tradition. I have also always been a strong critic of just blindly copying Western technology.

Now, as to the reason why I became the president of Aryamehr University; as you know, that university was then and still is the best scientific university not only in Iran but also at that time and still today probably in the whole of the Middle East. There was no university like it in Iran at that time with such high levels of learning and competence of its professors and students, although politically it was a very difficult place to run because of so many leftist students who were politically very active, and some even took recourse to violence. Those three years as the president of the university were some of the most challenging and difficult and at the same time fruitful years of my life. I was finally forced to resign when I developed heart trouble as a result of the continuous tension that was on me.

For years I had spoken to the Shah and the Queen about my views concerning science and Persian culture; I was never shy about that matter. The Shah was an ardent proponent of modern science and technology, of modernization, but at the same time he loved Iran. It was not as though he did not love his country, but he neglected the impact of modernization on our traditional culture, and thought that modernization was good for Iran. He did not realize all of its negative aspects. The Queen, however, was a great lover of different aspects of traditional Persian culture. Often times I would discuss the necessity of integration of modern ideas and techniques into our culture either with both of them or alone with her or with the Shah. When the Shah would introduce me to a foreign head of state, he would say, "Nasr is from M.I.T.," but would never say that I was also from Harvard, because M.I.T. was sort of his ideal, and he knew that I was well acquainted with Western science. I also knew what technology was, but at the same time was a great champion of Persian culture and a critic of any form of science or technology that would simply decimate our traditional culture. He knew that fact very well, and he also knew that I had written about the environmental crisis, against what we were doing to the natural environment as a result of modern technology.

I had been the vice chancellor of Tehran University and at the same time the dean of the Faculty of Letters of Tehran University under Alikhani and dean before him. When Nahavandi[128] replaced him, I did not want to be vice chancellor under him, but I wanted to go back to devote myself only to the Faculty of Letters. At that time with some five thousand students and more than half of Iran's great scholars, it was challenging enough to run that faculty.

One day, after I had returned to the deanship of the Faculty, I was called to the court and the Shah told me, "All of these years you have been speaking about the importance of the preservation of Persian culture, and I know that you have also had scientific training, and that at the same time you are an academic figure who has also been vice chancellor and dean of a major university. I want to give you an opportunity that is unique. There is no university that is dearer to my heart than Aryamehr University. See if you can run it well and also Persianize modern science and technology, making them more harmonious with our culture." Of course, it was an extremely big challenge, but a challenge that I accepted happily. As I have already said, those were among the most challenging but also creative years of my life. First of all, when I went there I knew that it was going to be difficult to change the view of four hundred Ph.D.s from M.I.T., Stanford, Berkeley, Imperial College of London, et cetera. I was not going to be able to change overnight the views of these people concerning science and technology. Yet, immediately upon becoming president, I was able to establish a department of humanities. I brought Haddad Adel and William Chittick, who were among the most brilliant of my students, along with several other gifted faculty to Aryamehr University to start this program.

R.J.: To teach there?
S.H.N.: Yes, to teach there. They all became instructors and assistant professors and we brought the whole dimension of the humanities to the university.

R.J.: Do you mean the Western humanities?
S.H.N.: No, not the humanities as now understood in the West, since they are mostly eclipsed by modern science and technology, but our own humanities. Today the humanities have themselves become downtrodden and marginalized in most Western universities as a result of the assault of scientism, at least here in America and to some extent in Europe. Anyway, I thought that this would be the first thing to do. All the students were required to take courses in the humanities and to think about matters of a nonscientific nature. I also began to introduce courses within the engineering and the science faculties on the assessment of modern technology and its impact on human society and on the environment, as one finds today in places such as M.I.T. I always believed that we should not be using only the crumbs from the table of the West, always getting what has been discarded, which is what the East usually receives, but creating our

own technologies based on our culture to the extent possible. And parallel with these programs, I began other major projects, both research projects and also teaching programs about alternative forms of technology including, for example, alternative energy such as solar power.

I had a great deal of trouble convincing the Shah to concentrate on solar energy and not to build the Bushehr nuclear plant, which was supervised to some extent by Aryamehr University. He would say, "One day, if we do not have any oil, we have to have this guarantee." He refused to accept my suggestion. It is very interesting that those students of the university, who were against the government, used to attack me for the university's supervision of that project. As soon as the Iranian Revolution took place, the project was closed, but years later it was started again with a loss of a couple of billion dollars. And look where this question now stands in Iran in its relation to the West! This is a very interesting fact. It seems that the attitude towards modern technology does not change so easily with changes, even revolutionary ones, in political regimes. I have written about this matter often.[129] From monarchies to communist governments, to revolutionary regimes, it remains the same. They all want to copy avidly Western science and technology without thought of their cultural, social, and environmental consequences.

Building the Isfahan Campus

Anyway, Aryamehr University began to do some wonderful things in ameliorating the impact of modern technology on our culture and environment and trying to revive as much as possible traditional forms of technology. Let me give you an example. It was at that time that we were building the Aryamehr University campus in Isfahan. I kept Mehdi Zarghami,[130] who was a very conscientious and patriotic person, in charge of the Isfahan campus. I kept him there in order to supervise closely the vast Isfahan project, which I would visit practically every week.

We bought more land for the Isfahan campus than the land of any university, including Stanford, and created, as far as I know, the biggest university campus in the world. Furthermore, when I saw the model made by the French architect for the university, I said, "This is not Persian architecture." It envisaged one tall thirty-story tower in the middle of the desert outside of Isfahan. So I went to the Queen and said, "Your Majesty, this tower does not belong there. If you have put me there at the head of the university, you should consider my views. We should build a campus that is based on traditional Persian architecture and uses traditional Persian materials, such as brick and so forth." She said, "Look, this is Aryamehr University. Go tell it to the king; I cannot interfere with this matter." So I went with trepidation to the king although the architect had said, "It has been approved by the king and nothing can be changed." I said to the Shah, "Your Majesty, the university has a wonderful view overlooking the most beautiful city of Iran, the city of Isfahan, and it would be a shame not to have an architecture that reflects that view." He said, "What do you mean?" I said, "There is a very high tower in the middle of the university which breaks completely with the Persian architectural tradition and they argue that this will hold a large number of people per square foot and will preserve land around it." He said, "Yes, yes, I have approved of that." I said, "Can we build a horizontal tower?" He laughed and he said, "What in the world are you taking about?"

R.J.: Instead of vertical.

S.H.N.: Yes, I said, "We have, 24 million meters of land, and why should we have all this energy wasted for elevators going up and down, for air conditioning, et cetera. We could have the same concentration horizontally and save much energy and be more in harmony with the surrounding environment." He laughed and said, "I never heard of a horizontal tower. All right, go change the plan and bring it to me." That was a very important matter that he conceded, and it gave us the opportunity to create a Persian design for the buildings. We started to build with brick; I got the best bricklayers in Yazd, Qom, and Isfahan, made our own kilns, and tried to revive old technologies. Of course I left after a few years, but the die was already cast, and my plans were continued to a large extent. Even from a practical point of view, I was not disappointed. Western technologies were coming into Iran anyway; so much the better that we should control them to some extent by our own know-how and with some knowledge of our own art and architecture, humanities, philosophy, and subjects like that. My goal was not to educate unidimensional engineers who fill the Middle East and the whole of Asia these days, but to train people who also would understand other dimensions of life and our own culture.

So as I said, I was not unhappy being president of Aryamehr University, although it was a difficult period of my life because, despite the heavy administrative burden upon my shoulders, I never gave up writing or teaching at Tehran University during all those years when I was the president of that university with all kinds of problems facing me, police coming in and going out of the campus, with all kinds of political difficulties at hand. Often times I would work until one o'clock in the morning.

Political Problems

R.J.: Was it difficult, I mean, I would like you to talk about this, was it difficult to be the president of the university? Were the students and professors very politically minded?

S.H.N.: Many of them were politically minded and furthermore anti-government. It was both challenging and difficult. It was much more difficult than the situation at Tehran University. In Tehran University, it was the students and not the faculty who were politically active and against the government, especially at the Faculty of Engineering. At the Faculty of Letters, the atmosphere was less politicized, but nevertheless we had student problems from time to time. In Aryamehr University, not only students, but also many of the professors, were not only politically minded, but some of them were very hot-headed, while some students even took recourse to violence. But also I had several advantages on my side.

First of all, I was a completely academic person. Nobody could complain and say, "Oh, they have put some minister at the head of the university," and things like that as happened often at Tehran University. Secondly, I had a deep grounding in the sciences as well as the humanities. Thirdly, the religious students there, who gradually became among the most hot-headed politically, knew that they could not outdo me as being more religious than I was. They could not accuse me of being, you know, just a modernized Persian drinking and flouting other Islamic teachings. Of course the students were not all religious; nor were the students, whether religious or not, naive. We had, in fact, organized leftist students such as those who belonged to the Mojahedin-e Khalq,[131] who had a secret organization within the student body, and so it was not only a question of using logic to speak to disgruntled students. They could say for example, "We want to have our exams delayed for several days," or something like that. What they wanted was not reasonable; what they wanted to do was to create commotion and disorder.

And then I did something that was dangerous and happened probably for the first time in Iran since the Second World War. When students in Iranian universities used to strike for various political reasons, they would come back to class after they finished their strike and nothing would happen. Consequently, the quality of education would come down. The very first day that I went to the university, I said, "I will not sacrifice the quality of education here for anything in the world," and I made that statement before the professors and also before the students.

Some time passed. In 1974 (1353), when the big riots in the university took place and the students led by the Mojahedin-e Khalq started a strike, I called a meeting of the university senate, which lasted two days of sixteen or seventeen, eighteen hours each day, lasting until two, three o'clock at night. We went home, slept for a few hours and came back the next morning. I had to convince the faculty to take the matter seriously, and some of them did not want to accept my proposal that we should give the students a notice, and if they did not come back to classes within a week, a second notice. If they did not come back by two weeks, then they would lose a term. We had a big computer that could make this possible. Other universities in Iran could not do it for technical administrative reasons besides lack of will. Moreover, some professors would resist because they did not want to have this serious action taken. They did not care if the strike went on.

I finally convinced the faculty to accept the plan and gave the orders the next day to execute the plan approved by the university senate. Hoveida, the prime minister, called me up and said, "You know, you are playing with fire. It is going to explode in your face. None of the other university presidents are doing it." I said, "Look, I did not accept this job in order to climb politically. I am an academic person, and if I am going to remain here I must take this matter, which concerns academic standards, seriously." He said, "I will not accept any responsibility. You have to go and talk to the Shah." So immediately I went and talked to the king. He approved and said, "I am glad there is somebody finally who is a university president and who is taking studies at the university seriously. You have my backing." The *Saziman-e amniyyat*[132] did things under the table. I did not know what they were doing. They themselves would be the cause of all kinds of instigations, and matters were not usually simple. The university was in the middle holding a rope and did not know who was pulling one end of the rope and who was pulling the other end. We were just holding the middle of the rope. I wanted to make sure at least that there would be no sabotage on their part. But even now I am not sure because they had their own *agents provocateurs*, who would do all kinds of things. Anyway, the two weeks passed after the beginning of the student strike, and university security began to prevent the striking students from coming in.

You cannot imagine what effect that had. First of all, they threatened the life of the head of the university guards, poor man, Major Nowrouzi, who was later assassinated. Then they put a bomb in my office, but it exploded half an hour before I came in because I had some business early that day and came into my office half an hour later than usual. That morning I came to the university at eight o'clock, instead of the usual seven thirty. That is what the situation was like. It was not song and dance, but I thank God that I succeeded in preserving the academic quality of the university in those difficult times. All of those students, even students who were causing disorder, were competent people in their own field, and they are now very happy that they received a serious education.

You know that in some Iranian universities, students would go to class for two months each term rather than four months and still they would receive their degrees. Students would not come to class for weeks, and the teacher would claim to make up what they had missed in two days. I had seen that at Tehran University many times, and so it was a great challenge to me to be very strict in the matter of classes at Aryamehr University. Perhaps this emphasis upon academic discipline was something that I had inherited from my father, who, as I mentioned, was an educator. I was also by nature an educator, and that is why I participated for many years in university administration both at Tehran University and Aryamehr University and later on at the Academy itself. But as I said, I never allowed this type of administrative activity to interfere with my teaching or my research and writing.

The Question of the Use of Force

R.J.: But did you have to use force to do that, I mean, as the president of Aryamehr?
S.H.N.: To do what?

R.J.: To calm the situation.
S.H.N.: Yes, but only by the university's own guards. We never allowed soldiers from the outside to come into the university. Sometimes students would start causing trouble, and even using violence in the dining room or the dormitories, and we had to send our guards to quiet things down.

R.J.: Yes. Because that is one of the reproaches they make of you as a spiritual man, to have used force to calm down the situation at the university.

S.H.N.: This is a misunderstanding of what spiritually is in reality. I will tell you this story, which is very amusing. The very first day when I came to the university, there was a big commotion in the dining room. So I went there myself and the students were very angry. They said, "They are supposed to have repaired the dining room, but look at the ceiling. It has not been repaired after months of supposed work. We have no place to eat." I said, "You are right; I shall get this fixed for you immediately." I came back to my office. A few minutes later, the head of the SAVAK himself called me up and said, "Dr. Nasr, you could have committed suicide. Why did you go there? You could have been killed." I said jokingly, "Because I am a *kashi.*[133] I wanted to prove to you that *kashis* are not afraid!" Then I called the contractors into my office and said, "You are not leaving the university until the ceiling is finished," and I called the guards at the gate and said to them, "These gentlemen cannot leave the university grounds until they have finished their work." At seven o'clock in the evening I left the university with my driver, and these people thought that I was joking.

The next morning when I came in, the head contractor, who had not as yet shaved and had not slept all night, had fixed the ceiling immediately after many weeks of delay. One of the contractors said, "Dr. Nasr, I thought you were an *'āref*—a mystic. But I did not know that you were an *'āref-e qaddārah-band* (a mystic with a sword)." I said to him, "My dear friend, you have not studied the history of Sufism. Did you know that many of the greatest wars in Islamic history were fought with Sufis riding on horseback in battle? You have not studied the other side of this story."

The decision to use force is sometimes unavoidable, especially when the other side uses force, as the Quran itself teaches. I mean, if you have students breaking windows and throwing television sets out of their rooms, which they were doing (these televisions were bought with taxes collected from the people of Iran and did not belong to a particular student), what were you going to do? Just sit there and watch? Somebody had to get up and say, "Do not do it." If they refused, you had to use force. Now, I was always on the side of the students, even at Tehran University. Many of the people who are now ruling Iran were among students whom I would go and get out of prison, and they are even now my friends. They knew that I was always on their side, but at the same time, if you had the responsibility for the lives of several thousand students in a university and a group of two, three hundred people was making life impossible for the rest, you had no choice. But first of all, you had to talk to them, admonish them, then you threatened them, but if nothing worked, you had to act with force to prevent them from causing havoc.

You know, a number of our students were killed, but never inside of the university. They belonged to underground organizations and fought the security forces outside of the campus. One of the events that I shall remember the rest of my life, and that still makes me very sad, is that one day, a father and mother from Mourcheh Khort, a town outside of Isfahan, came to my office. The man was obviously a peasant (*fallāḥ-keshāvarz*), and he began to cry, saying, "Our son is in the fourth year. He is about to become an engineer, and he has been imprisoned. He does nothing but study and he is a wonderful boy." I was so moved emotionally that I called the prime minister. I said, "So-and-so has been arrested. I want to have him released." He said, "I shall call you back in a few minutes." He called me back shortly thereafter and said, "Look, this person is a member of the Mojahedin-e Khalq, and he belongs to some kind of team that has been exploding bombs. I said, "Look, his parents are here and they are such nice people. I am sure that there is a mistake, and I guarantee his behavior." He said, "It is your responsibility." I said, "Fine."

So the next morning the boy was released and brought to my office. He was outwardly a very polite and humble-looking person, standing with his head down before me. I said to him, "Look, you are going to graduate in a few months. How much are you going to make?" He said, "Already people are giving me an offer of eight thousand *tomans* a month." At that time that was more than the salary of a full professor at Tehran University, which was around five thousand *tomans*. I said, "But why are you doing this?" He said, "I did not do anything. I am just very sad. My father only makes three hundred *tomans*. I have eight sisters and brothers. What about them?" I said, "When you jump from three hundred *tomans* to eight thousand *tomans* in one generation, that is a big jump. How fast do you think the country can move to be able to overcome certain economic problems it has inherited from the centuries past? With your job after graduation you will be able to support your whole family." And his father said, "Yes, please allow him to continue his studies."

I took his hand and put it in the father's hand. I said to him, "I am putting your hand in your father's hand; for their sake, go back to your studies. Do not do these things. You can reach your goals of making the country a better place if you are a person who is educated, who has a degree." Anyway, his father kissed his son and they left. A few days later a bomb was exploded in Cinema Capri in Tehran that killed fifteen, twenty people, and this boy had done it. This is the responsibility that I had to face. I believe in God and in the Day of Judgment and must accept the consequences for all my actions. Because I was soft-hearted, because I am by nature a professor, a teacher, and seek to emphasize above all else human qualities, I was so moved by the father that I pushed aside the warning of the government. I brought hundreds of people out of prison in Tehran by vouchsafing for them myself. Fortunately, none of them committed such an act as far as I know.

Some people may criticize me, but there was no possibility of running that university or any other university without keeping order. And if you did shut down the universities for several years in order to create a new, peaceful ambience, there would have been no higher education in Iran, and Iranian families, especially the families of the poorer students, would have been even more unhappy.

I will repeat this again for the record. Sufism was not always what many people think of as *darvishi*[134] today, as sitting in your house and doing nothing. Look at Amīr 'Abd al-Qādir, the great Sufi figure from Algeria, who also fought the French for decades. Of course, above all, you have the case of the Prophet (PBUH) and Haḍrat-i 'Alī, our great spiritual models, in whom rigor was combined with gentleness, justice with mercy, perfect activity in the world with perfect passivity towards God. They were spiritual knights at the highest level. The important thing is to be just and to administer justice. Surely I was much more of a shield for my students than a spear. It is I who protected them to the extent that I could. They would not even know how many times the SAVAK wanted to come to the campus and arrest somebody and I would say, "No." Sometimes, they, nevertheless, did it by going to homes of the students, but never on our campus. I would not find out about such cases until later, and I would not usually know what was going on beyond the confines of the university concerning such matters. When I did come to know about their intentions concerning a particular student, I would never allow the security agents to come into the university. Nor did I even allow outside police from Shahreza Avenue to come into the university. So my role was mostly that of a shield, but when you are a shield, of course, you are hit by a lot of arrows, and that is unavoidable.

Vocational Decisions

R.J.: So you never saw a contradiction between your spiritual life and your engagement as a university administrator . . .
S.H.N.: No.

R.J.: Being tired and saying, "I am going to leave and go back to my spirituality."
S.H.N.: There is always a tension between the ideals in one's mind and the realities of life, and the spiritual life itself is a journey through and transformation of this tension. There are different spiritual types. There are those who withdraw from the world, yes, that is one possibility. The other type is a person who lives in the world while being detached from it inwardly and who seeks to transform the world about him. My vocation is of the second type. That includes writing books and articles, giving lectures, and teaching, for which I have also been often criticized because of the nature of my ideas. This type of activity is itself a form of *jihād*. I could have avoided such attacks if I had refrained from writing. In the same way, I felt that I could be of service in the educational realm in Iran and many people thought the same. I still believe that what I did for education in Iran, in the Faculty of Letters, as vice chancellor of Tehran University, in Aryamehr University, and as the founder of the Imperial Academy of Philosophy is something that will last for a long time for the country, besides having produced many fine young scholars. It was a service that I had to render to my country. I could not have remained in Iran if I had refused even this kind of educational service.

I was offered a ministerial position several times going back to the time of Ali Amini,[135] when I was only twenty-eight years old. He contacted me when he became prime minister through my cousin Mohsen Nasr, who had become his minister. They were in fact very close friends. Amini said, "Hossein you have not had any administrative experience; become the deputy minister of education and in a few months I shall make you the minister of education." I said, "No thank you. I do not want to leave Tehran University." Later on, Hasan Ali Mansur,[136] whose father Mansur al-Molk was an old friend of the family and a relative, called me and said, "Look, I want you to head the educational and cultural part of our movement called *Kānūn-e moteraqqī* (meaning "Progressive Organization"). In six months we are going to take over the government and you will become the minister of education." I said, "Look, I have no desire to enter politics." And I introduced Hadi Hedayati to him, who was trying so hard to become a politician, and he in fact later became his minister. I was also offered an ambassadorship several times, but I turned them down. I say this because I want to point out that I had no ambition to enter politics or climb socially through it. But I could not have remained in Iran with the gifts that God had given me as both a scholar and a person who could administer things and not accept any position whatever. The pressure was simply too great.

For example, when the *Enqilab-e Farhangi*[137] took place in Iran, and reforms in the universities took place, they wanted to make me the president of Firdawsi University in Mashhad or Shiraz University. I went to Asadollah Alam and with great difficulty got out of it because I did not want to leave Tehran where I was engaged in so many activities, such as studying and working with 'Allāmah Ṭabāṭabā'ī. My request was accepted provided I would accept some other position. I said, "All right, I shall accept to become the dean of the Faculty of Letters of Tehran University" (where I was professor). If I had said, "I do not want to do that either," I could not have remained and functioned successfully in Iran. I would have had to pack up my bags and come back to the United States, go and teach at Harvard, which kept inviting me, or some place like that.

So, I avoided as much as possible entanglement in direct politics such as becoming minister, diplomatic ambassador, this or that, but I could not have, at least within the university system, refused to become the dean or president or something like that within that system. I also felt that being an educator was a part of my vocation, and so I am not at all sorry that I undertook such a task. University administration took a great deal of my time, but also I was able to create very positive structures in a creative manner even if administration did also have its downside. I could have been much more *jannat makān,*[138] one of those who sit on the side and say: "*lengesh kon.*" You know that when you go to the *zurkhaneh,*[139] you sit on the side and say: "*lengesh kon,*" meaning "pin him in wrestling"; that is part of our culture. People who have a hand in the world of action are expected to be perfect by those who never do anything themselves, but the world of action is not perfect. Those who just criticize do not get their hands soiled, but they do not accomplish anything in the active life either. In any case, I did not refrain from being active in the educational domain, and I am not sorry for it.

Mounting Political Tensions in Iran

R.J.: Is this why you got more involved by 1978—because there were all these tensions, and you went to the Empress Farah?

S.H.N.: I did not go to the Empress. Rather, it was she who asked me to become the head of her Special Bureau. What happened at that point is very important and needs to be explained. Let me deal with the background history of what happened. For years I was a well-known person in Iran. There was hardly anyone among the educated and political classes who did not know me. I had been president of a university for several years; I had been Iran's cultural ambassador; I was head of the Academy as well as a well-known teacher, writer, and lecturer. Even the *'ulamā'* knew me well, and among the *'ulamā'* who were politically inclined, my closest friend was Morteza Motahhari; I had also known Ayatollah Sharī'atmadārī, who was the great Shi'ite religious scholar and cleric at that time. Ayatollah Khomeini was in exile, and 'Allāmah Ṭabāṭabā'ī kept aloof totally from political matters. He was not interested to all practical purposes in any political issues whatsoever.

Let me tell you this story which is related to your question. Once, the Shah asked me to go to see him. He asked me if 'Allāmah Ṭabāṭabā'ī would accept to become the president of a new Islamic university in Mashhad. The Shah considered me to be a politically disinterested Muslim scholar and therefore ordered that I go to Qom to ask the 'Allāmah, who said, "No, I cannot accept to do it." The plan then changed and it was decided to establish the Islamic university in Mashhad, which would have been a major event in Iran, under my own direction. And this occurred while I was still president of Aryamehr university. The Islamic university was never established due to the opposition of the *'ulamā'*, although I had already bought some land for it in Mashhad. But the very fact that years before the 1979 Revolution the shah had asked me to supervise a project that could have changed the whole religious dynamics in Iran is indicative of the role that I played at that time as a link between the court and the *'ulamā'*, trusted by both sides although I had been critical over the years about many policies and actions of the government and delivered numerous talks on radio and television in defense of Islamic and Iranian culture, while criticizing severely modernism and its rapid spread in Iran.

I also knew Ayatollah Khwansārī and a few other very important religious figures, but of course, most of all, my dear friend Motahhari. On the other side, of course, the Shah knew me very well, and as for the

Queen, I had worked for years and years on many cultural projects with her even before I became the head of her Bureau. She consulted me on many matters, and I was intellectually close to her, because we had a common goal of trying to preserve traditional Persian culture. For example, the first conference on traditional architecture in Islam, held in Isfahan, which was so important, I organized with the support of the Empress. The same was true of the first conference on *ṭibb-i sunnatī*, or traditional medicine, held in Shiraz. Such conferences were all organized by me with her support. We worked together on such matters as preserving the old houses of Isfahan, the question of the pollution of Zayandeh Rud,[140] et cetera. You cannot imagine how many projects of this kind existed on which I worked with her.

With tensions building up in 1978, many figures among the *'ulamā'* were very worried about what would happen to Iran. They did not envisage a revolution taking place. They wanted the situation to be improved, corruption to be removed, and more Islamic norms followed; you know, less improper movies and books, et cetera. Motahhari himself was afraid that former communists had come into the government and might take over. Many former ministers had a communist background in their youth, and Motahhari and others were afraid that they might still have such leanings. Brezhnev was still in power and the Soviet Union had not as yet fallen apart. So when the rumblings in Tabriz took place, several of the *'ulamā'*, people for whom I had a great deal of respect and who were the props of the Islamic tradition in Iran at that time, said, "Look, you are the only person close to the court and to us who can act as a bridge between the two sides. You are the only person whom we trust, and who we assume is also a person whom the Shah trusts; you must come forward to play the role of a bridge."

When Sharif Emami came to power as prime minister, the Empress, who had wanted to remove Houchang Nahavandi for a long time as the head of her Special Bureau, found the opportunity she was waiting for. She immediately pushed him into Sharif Emami's cabinet and called me and said, "I would like you to replace Nahavandi." Of course this was a position that had to be approved by the Shah. By the protocol this was the highest position in Iran after the prime minister, the minister of court, heads of two houses of parliament, and the head of the king's Special Bureau. It was a particularly important position at that time, since the Shah was not physically well. In 1978, practically no one knew that he had cancer, but in any case, many state responsibilities were placed on the shoulders of the Empress.

With the condition of Iran being what it was, and with the views of the *'ulamā'* in mind, I accepted, but I had certain conditions. I said to her, "There needs to be a cleansing of the whole ambience of the court if I were to come." She said, "We are planning for that; some of the people in the court must be changed and these reforms be carried out." Anyway, I accepted because, as I was able to see it then, it concerned the future of the country. It was not that I was ambitious and wanted to get into politics or anything like that at that dangerous time, but because I felt that I was the only person who could act as a bridge to help to create a situation in which, for example, Ayatollah Khomeini would return to Iran, make peace with the Shah under mutually agreed conditions, and a kind of "Islamic Royal Regime" could be formed like the Safavid period, a regime in which the *'ulamā'* would have a say in the laws of the country, but the structure of the country would not be drastically changed. Many of the leading *'ulamā'* of that time also had the same goal in mind, being afraid like myself that the complete destruction of the existing regime could result in Iran being taken over by communists or the Mojahedin-e Khalq.

In any case, God had other plans, and what I did, instead of being seen in positive light, was evaluated otherwise later, at least publicly, although a lot of *'ulamā'* of that day who are still alive know that I sacrificed myself for an accord and peace which they themselves were seeking. Yet, none of them came to my defense after the Revolution. Of course I paid very dearly for acting as bridge as far as my material life was concerned, because my house, property, library, everything, was confiscated, and I had to start life all over again at the age of forty-five with nothing, materially speaking. Nevertheless, I am not either bitter or sad in any way, because at that time my conscience would not have allowed me to do otherwise.

I remember that in the fall of 1978 I called up Gholam-Hossein Sadighi, in contrast to what some have written, by the order of the Shah to accept to become the prime minister of Iran. Sadighi was a very patriotic person. He said to me, "Dr. Nasr, I am an old man and some people say I should not jump into this fire, but what do I want my life for if my country is in danger?" You know, at first, he accepted, but later on other conditions prevented him from following through. Well, I had very much the same feeling. I knew that it was a dangerous thing at that time to accept to become the head of the Empress's Bureau. I might even lose my life over it; but at the same time I could not have said "no" with people like Motahhari, who always encouraged me to accept positions of responsibility, in mind and with the future of Iran on the line. During that fall, Motahhari disappeared out of sight, went underground, an act that was unbelievable for me, since we were always in touch; but in any case he and many other people like him, including younger *'ulamā'*, were favorable to my acceptance of the position, and some even insisted on it. The only person among the *'ulamā'* who was not happy with my doing so was 'Allāmah Ṭabāṭabā'ī. In fact, he was altogether very unhappy with what was going on at that time in Iran.

The Death of 'Allāmah Ṭabāṭabā'ī

Let me mention a point which might be difficult to publish in Iran even now after all these years. The last time I saw 'Allāmah was in the fall of 1978. I said, "*Hāji Āqā*," (and I say it in Persian so you know exactly what was said) "*Hājī Āqā! Naẓar-e shomā dar barā-ye in sholūghīhā chist?*"[141] And he said, "*Kārhā'ī ke mīkonand dūn-e sha'n-e yek rūhanīst.*"[142] These were words of a person who was aggrandized as a great hero after the Revolution. In any case, he was very concerned for me and said that "The torch of Islamic learning is in your hands, and you must take very good care of yourself; be very careful."

Then when the Revolution took place, he fell sick and he died a couple of years later. Before he died, he called one of my very close friends, and that friend went to Qom. 'Allāmah Ṭabāṭabā'ī was lying on his deathbed. He always spoke with a low voice, and now with even a lower voice. He indicated with his hand for this man to come close to him. My friend came near him and 'Allāmah Ṭabāṭabā'ī raised his arm and took the lapel of his coat and pressed him down towards himself so that his mouth was next to his ear and said, "I have a message for you to give to Dr. Nasr. Tell him that I am so glad that he is not here. Tell him to keep the torch of *ma'refat* (gnosis) and *ḥekmat* (traditional philosophy) burning until one day when it can be rekindled in Iran." That was his last message for me.

R.J.: And you were clearly outside of Iran at that time, in Tokyo I think.
S.H.N.: No, no. I was in the United States. I never went to Tokyo. I was supposed to go to Tokyo. Perhaps next time we can speak about how I left Iran.

Part Four

Leaving Iran

R.J.: By January 1979, you left Iran for the opening of an exhibition of Persian art in Tokyo to which you did not go, and you have been out of Iran, living in exile ever since. My question is, why did you choose the United States as a place to live, and why did you not choose a Muslim country to go and live?

S.H.N.: That is a very good question. What happened was that there was a major exhibition of Persian art in Tokyo, which was supposed to be inaugurated by Iran's Empress. It was early in January 1979 when she told me that she could not go, and that they had decided that I should go to open the exhibition. My daughter was going to school in a place near the Parliament. There were constant commotions near the school, and it had been closed for two months. So I asked the Empress if I could first go to London to find a school for my daughter for a while, because she had been missing school for some time, and also to strengthen her English, and then to fly from London to Tokyo to inaugurate the exhibition. She accepted my request and added that since there was going to be a dinner with the Emperor of Japan, and the dinner was still going to be held, and since the Empress of Japan was also going to be there, I should make sure that my wife would be accompanying me. So on January 6, 1979, I took my wife and daughter to London, and we had just found a school for my daughter, Laili, when the government of Japan informed me that they had decided to delay the exhibition. I was about to come back to Iran with my wife when the Empress of Iran called me and said that the Shah and she were going away for holidays to Egypt and that I should stay in London and see how things developed. That was it! I did not return to Iran after that.

So I came out of Iran just prepared for a trip of several days, with a few suitcases containing clothing and things like that and especially some formal wear for Japan. Since I was always a patriotic person, I never kept any money abroad. I had just a few thousand pounds, which I had left in a London bank for my son Vali's tuition as he was going to school at that time in England, readying himself to go to Oxford the next year after finishing his A levels. All I had in the bank was his tuition for the next year and that was it. That was all the means that I had in the Western world. At that time I had not thought at all of going and living in another Islamic country, because I had no immediate contact who could help me find an academic position to support the whole family, and did not know where to go and what to do. I felt that since I had to provide for a living for my family—I had my wife and a son and daughter who were near college age, and they had to go to school—the most practical place would be Europe or America. Besides, there was war in Lebanon; in Pakistan, there was a lot of turmoil, and also it was dangerous and impractical for a person like myself at that time; the same was true of Turkey and even Egypt. So, I did not even think of those choices, and furthermore no invitations came up from any Islamic country. Perhaps, let us say, if at that time the Saudis or Kuwaitis had proposed that I go to become a professor in some Saudi or Kuwaiti university, I might have accepted, but that did not happen, and therefore I did not even think about such a possibility.

Since I had taught before in the Western world, I thought that I should try to find a teaching job there as soon as the old order collapsed in Iran. I knew that I would not be able to go back and would not be able to take anything out, because my house and library were plundered and bank accounts were all confiscated; materially speaking everything was lost. I just had to start life from zero from a material point of view. At that time my first choice was to remain in London. I would have preferred to live in Britain, but there was no position open for me there. The great paradox is that once I settled in the United States, the new chair of Islamic Studies at the University of Edinburgh was offered to me when I gave the Gifford lectures in 1981. Also, when Anne Lambton retired from the University of London, they asked me to apply for her position. They were seriously interested in my coming there. Also, there was the Spalding Chair at Oxford which was proposed to me, but all of these came later when I had settled in America and did not want to move to England. So I showed no interest when these offers did come. But in 1979, when it was my choice to stay in England, the possibility to do so did not exist, and I had to make a quick decision because of my dire financial situation.

Also, Queen Sophia of Spain, who had known me, realized what had happened to me. The Spanish monarchs were very kind, and they offered to give me a Spanish passport and also to find an academic position for me in Spain. My knowledge of Spanish was, however, not at all like my knowledge of French or English, and it would have taken me a long time to be able to master Spanish well enough not only to teach in Spanish but to also be intellectually active in the Spanish milieu. So, once I realized that Britain was not possible, I felt that the only possibility was the United States, where I had studied and taught for many years, where I had visited over the years, where I knew many people in the academic world.

It was a very bitter disappointment when the two universities with which I had worked most closely, Harvard and Princeton that is, in the fields of Islamic and Middle Eastern Studies and the like, showed no interest whatsoever in my coming there. Moreover, in the middle of the term it is very difficult to find an academic job in any university, but the president of the University of Utah, David Gardner,[1] and Khosrow Mostofi,[2] who was the head of Middle Eastern Studies, spoke together, and they took a special bill to the senate and made me Distinguished Visiting Professor. That was the only concrete position that came up at a time when my situation was really very difficult, because if another month or two had passed, I would not have had any money left to just buy bread. It was as simple as that for my family and for myself.

Moving to the United States

In any case, against my wish and the wish of my family, we moved to the United States. It was the only place where I could find a job and work. I left my family in Boston for a while. Vali, my son, was still studying in England and did not come with us, but remained in his boarding school where he was finishing his A levels and joined us only later. I went alone to Salt Lake City, Utah to begin to teach at the University of Utah, and that was the beginning of the new life that I was to establish. So the reason why I did not go to an Islamic country, to come back to your response, was the practical question of having to make a living immediately.

As for later on, when I was established in the United States, this possibility did present itself. I was offered a post as professor in

Malaysia. A couple of years later when I was at Temple University, there was a great deal of interest in my going to Malaysia to the institute founded by Naquib al-Attas. He had asked if I could just go there even for one year. I could have also gone, for example, to Pakistan, and places like that. But by then I felt that I could be of much greater service intellectually in America—even for the Islamic world itself. Any article I publish here these days spreads all over the Islamic world very rapidly and many of my works are translated into a number of Islamic languages; whereas if I had, let us say, settled in a place like Kuala Lumpur or an Arab country, where I would have preferred to go if I wanted to live in the Islamic world, my impact would have been less on the global scene.

There were also other problems. For example, Iraq was in turmoil and was fighting against Iran, and the level of universities in Pakistan had come down quite a bit; it was not like the old days, intellectually speaking. There was war in Lebanon, and Syria was isolated. Egypt is a country which I love very much. I could have perhaps gone to the American University of Cairo, but that did not really interest me because I did not want to teach in an American University in the Islamic world. As for places such as the University of Cairo, 'Ayn Shams or al-Azhar, there was no possibility for me to go to them and moreover they would not pay enough salary to enable me to rebuild my life, financially speaking. So I just decided to remain in the United States to teach, lecture, and write, while traveling often abroad.

Temple University

R.J.: And you have been very active during the past twenty-seven years. Actually, you have taught in different universities, and you have been involved in major projects, such as collaboration with the *Encyclopedia of World Spirituality*,[3] the edition of *The Essential Writings of Frithjof Schuon*,[4] the Gifford Lectures,[5] the Cadbury lectures,[6] the *Anthology of Philosophy in Persia*,[7] the production of a documentary on Islam in the West. How do you describe the impact of your works inside and outside Iran?

S.H.N.: Yes, these three decades, since I have been living in the United States, have been a very active period of my life. It took me a little while to settle down. I first had to provide for the basics of life, to be able to have a salary, find a house, and buy utensils and furniture again. But very quickly, even in 1979, as soon as I began to teach at Temple University I became again quite active intellectually. Actually, what happened was that since I had known Boston so well and had gone to school there, and had visited Boston often, and also since my wife knew the area well, I first decided that we should live in Boston. I was going to give one course at Harvard University, but there was no position open for me there or at M.I.T. The president of M.I.T., Jerome Wiesner, who was a friend of mine, because I had been his host when he came to Iran and had known him from the old days, asked me to go to see him, and he spoke to the provost about me. He said, "See if you can find a position for Dr. Nasr," but I could not have started as an assistant professor. I had to be a full professor, and that possibility did not exist there at that time.

Three possibilities did, however, come up. One was to stay at the University of Utah—they would offer me the world; the second was the University of Toronto (Professor Roger Savory[8] was there at that time, and he asked me if I were interested to come there, and they could make me a full professor); and finally Temple University. All of these positions offered to me were tenured, full professorships, not just one- or two-year-track positions. The University of Toronto was very attractive to me, but I thought I would be more effective and useful in America, and also I knew the United States better than Canada. So I decided against that and had to decide between Temple and the University of Utah. Temple was in Philadelphia, on the East Coast. Both of these institutions were major America universities, but Temple had a very large Department of Religion. I finally decided in favor of Temple, but I kept my family in Boston where we rented an apartment and lived for five years there, even buying later a house in a suburb called Newton. We made Boston our home so that my children could go to the best schools in the United States: Tufts, M.I.T., Harvard, and places like that.

For five years I commuted between Boston and Philadelphia, which was one of the most difficult things that I have done in my life—every week taking the plane going to Philadelphia and then coming back for the weekend to Boston. But a rhythm was created even in this difficult situation, and my intellectual life was not disrupted. In fact, a new phase of intense activity intellectually and academically began for me. First of all, I prepared the Gifford Lectures, which I had been invited to give while I was in Iran. These were the most prestigious and important lectures in the Western world on philosophy and natural theology, and so I did not want to just forget about them. I gave them in 1981 and wrote beforehand the text, which became one of my most important books, under the title of *Knowledge and the Sacred.* I was able to accomplish this task although I had a very difficult situation, having to commute between Boston and Philadelphia every week. Nevertheless, God had not taken away from me my concentration, so that I could work even on a plane and almost anywhere else. I also began to train new students, and then all the different activities that you have mentioned and many others ensued.

The George Washington University

In 1984, two new opportunities arose, one a university professorship of Islamic Studies at The George Washington University and the other a position of full professorship at Yale University. I decided to come to The George Washington because it was located in the capital of the United States, and also because this was a university professorship. So, it would give me complete freedom from any kind of academic administration. If I did not want to go to the faculty senate meetings and matters like that, I was free not to do so. I had had enough of that kind of activity as university administrator in Iran. Consequently, this position was very attractive to me. I accepted the position in 1984 and it has been now some twenty-five years since I have been teaching here at this university, which has afforded me further opportunity to concentrate my energies completely on intellectual and scholarly matters and the training of students, matters that have occupied me for the last thirty years more than anything else. But since my writings were well known even before I came to the United States, and as people discovered that I had come here, there was also a tremendous demand on my time to give lectures here and there, not only famous lectures such as the Gifford Lectures and the Cadbury Lectures, but individual lectures all over the United States and Canada.

Travels in the Islamic World

Needless to say, gradually I began again to make trips to the Islamic world, but until now not to Iran. We are neighbors of Pakistan and Turkey, and I used to travel there often in the old days. I was for some time the head of the governing board of the RCD Culture Institute and therefore traveled very often to Turkey and Pakistan in the sixties. I was especially close to intellectual circles in Pakistan from 1959 when I made my first foreign trip as professor of Tehran University to that country to attend the Pakistan Philosophical Congress. I was a very active member on the whole philosophical scene in Pakistan for many years, but strangely enough, when I came to the United States, certain events occurred that created a new situation, and I did not travel as much to Pakistan and India as before.

With Turkey, however, the situation was different. A circle of intellectuals gradually came into being in the eighties whose members knew my works and those of other traditionalists well. My writings began to be translated into Turkish one after another to the extent that there are today over twenty volumes, a whole library, of my works in Turkish, and so I began to go to Turkey more and more often and continue to do so to this day. I also began to go to Egypt regularly. In fact I have been going there for the last twenty years, every year. I have also visited Morocco from time to time. And then my writings began to be translated into Bosnian and had become well known among the Muslims of Sarajevo even before the tragedy of the 1990s. Then there is Malaysia, about which I have already told you, and Indonesia, which became a major opening for my works and where many of my books, including *Ideals and Realities of Islam*,[9] translated by the Indonesian president, Abdurrahman Wahid, have been published. I trained many students from those countries, especially Malaysia, where I have lectured many times.

So paradoxically my activity within the Islamic world increased after I left Iran. Of course, even then, when I was in Iran, several of my works had been translated into Arabic, and as I said, I had very close contact with Pakistan. In the case of Pakistan, in fact, the reverse is true, because once I came to the United States, I would go there much less often, although more than a dozen of my books have been translated or reprinted in Pakistan, and I still have a close relation with its intellectual circles. My life in America has become a period of my life when I have had a great deal of contact with the various parts of the Islamic world, as well as a great deal of lecturing in the United States and also in Europe.

Travels in the Western World

As far as Europe is concerned, I travel to England very often, and besides the Cadbury Lectures I have lectured many times at the University of London, Oxford, Cambridge, and other major British universities, and have been very much involved in many intellectual activities in

Great Britain including the activities of Temenos Academy and the creation of the Al-Furqan Foundation. Also I try to keep the close relation with France which I had had in Iran for many reasons: First of all, going back to my childhood, my vision of the Western world began with France, because my father knew French so well and the European books in his library were nearly all French. As I mentioned, that was the first European language I learned, and of course because of my long years of association with the writings of Guénon and Schuon, as well as Corbin, all of whom wrote in French, I have used French often, and my relation with France was fortified over the years. I continue to lecture in France from time to time, and have not let that relation die out. Over the years I have given many lectures at the Sorbonne, even on the French radio and at UNESCO, and of course my books continue to appear in French. I have tried to keep that dimension alive in every way possible. So, yes, it has been a very active period of my life intellectually, and as far as the global dissemination of my ideas are concerned, my coming out of Iran in a sense facilitated that process.

Self-Identity: Muslim, Persian or Global?

R.J.: So if you had to describe yourself, your identity, do you consider yourself first as a Muslim, or an Iranian, or a citizen of the world?

S.H.N.: Not a citizen of the world, although my concerns are global, and there are now people such as Robert Neville, who speaks about world philosophers and very kindly considers me one of them; that is, people who say something which has global significance and deal with subjects that are related to different traditions of the world. When I write something, it is often read even in places as far away as China and Japan; some of my works have in fact come out in Chinese and Japanese. But I do not like the idea of being considered a citizen of the world in the usual sense of the term. I consider myself to be an Islamic as well as a Persian thinker at the same time, and I do not see a dichotomy in this, as do many modernized Iranians, whose souls are polarized between the pole of some kind of Iranian nationalism and of Islam, often with a strong tension between the two. I do not feel that way at all. I definitely feel myself to be an Islamic thinker. Let us say I am giving a lecture in Pakistan or in Malaysia or in Turkey. Hundreds and even thousands of people come to hear me, because I speak about themes which are not only of concern to Iran, but concern the Islamic world as a whole. At the same time I feel strongly my Iranian identity.

It is very paradoxical that Iran and Turkey are neighbors of each other, but since the Middle Ages, no Persian has had as many of his works translated into Turkish as I have. One or two books of Foruzanfar have been translated after the Revolution, and also a few books of Ayatollah Khomeini and Sharīʿatī, all together perhaps a dozen books of this genre. But a whole library of my works has been translated, because obviously I am saying something that for the Turks is not just concerned with local Iranian problems. Let me say that I would consider myself a Persian Islamic thinker.

As for Iran, as you know, my works were censored there for a while, but they have a tremendous following in our homeland today. If I were saying something which was of interest only to people in Indonesia, Malaysia, or the Mauritius Islands, obviously people in Iran would not be interested. So I do not want to separate these two categories from each other. I consider myself both a Muslim and a Persian, and moreover a person also concerned with global issues. What you call a "world citizen" is right only in that sense, although I do not like the word *citizen* in this context and am opposed to a global view that belittles and even destroys local traditions.

I do indeed address myself to issues that are also significant for Hindu Indians as well as for the modern West. I write works which many Christians and Jews read. For example, *Knowledge and the Sacred* is taught in many Catholic universities in the United States such as Notre Dame. My works are also read by many Hindus. So I do not consider myself to be concerned only with questions pertaining to Iran or only to the Islamic world, but also I am not floating in the middle of the air without roots. I feel myself deeply rooted in the Islamic, and more specifically, Islamic tradition of Persia. I feel myself rooted in the teachings of Ibn Sīnā, Suhrawardī, Mullā Ṣadrā, Rūmī, Jāmī, but also Ibn ʿArabī and others, who have influenced me a great deal. But at the same time I am rooted in that universal truth or *sophia perennis*, which is not limited to either the Persian world or even to the whole Islamic world, but which is of truly global nature. I have written even on Native American religions, and have lectured to Native Americans on the Navajo reservation. I was once invited by the Navajos to talk about traditional cosmology, and it was a very exciting experience for me.

R.J.: So you do not have any problems reconciling between the universality of Islam and the particularity of Persian culture?

S.H.N.: Absolutely not, absolutely not.

Nostalgia for Iran

R.J.: Do you feel you have a sense of nostalgia for Iran?
S.H.N.: Very much so. Oh yes, I have tremendous nostalgia because even when I was in Iran, people who were like me, educated in the West, who knew Western languages and culture, of course loved Iran, but most of the things they loved were not Iranian. They loved European dress, European food, European cheese; they preferred camembert to *panīr-i līqwān*[10] and so forth. You understand what I am talking about. On the contrary, even when I lived in Iran, in addition to the general love we all had for Iran as our country, I loved everything Persian, the landscape, the culture, the music, our own cuisine, the traditional ways that people did things. I always preferred everything traditionally Iranian to what was coming from the West. So when people like me became exiled, they began to have nostalgia for Iran itself, but many of the things that they liked concretely, even in Iran, were not Persian things; whereas for me the object of my love remains both Iran and things Persian. It is also important to mention that, although I studied in the West, during the twenty-one years after I returned to Tehran, that is between 1958 and 1979, I was not only an Iranian in the ordinary sense; I was deeply concerned with nearly all aspects of Persian culture and most of the activities concerning Persian culture, from philosophy to architecture to practically everything else you can imagine. I read many works on the subject and wrote books about Persian culture as well as being active in the preservation of our culture.

All of these attachments are, of course, still within me, and I have a very deep nostalgia for Iran on several levels: first of all, the land itself, the beauty of the land. I used to travel a great deal in Iran in the mountains, mountain climbing away from cities to see the natural scenery of Iran and the great beauty that it has. Secondly, of course, there are the people and the language. I have been able to preserve the language very easily because we speak Persian at home all the time and have Persian friends, and I continue to write in Persian, but the ambience is not the same. Thirdly, there is the spiritual presence of Iran. I used to go several times every year to Qom and Mashhad. I miss that experience very much, the experience of holy places, the traditional music, the art, the mosques. I used to go particularly to Isfahan often, for several years nearly every week, and I know the main streets of that city like the palm of my hand. I miss those places even more than Tehran, or at least the anonymous, modern part of Tehran. When I think of Tehran, what I do miss, besides, of course, our own street and our own house, is not so much, let us say, Pahlavi or Takht-i Jamshid Avenues (I do not know their new names); it is most of all our old house by Shahabad Avenue, the Sepahsalar Mosque, the bazaar of Tehran, you know, this sort of thing, the old parts of Tehran, which had something of the *barakat*[11] of Persian culture in them. Yes, I have a deep nostalgia for Iran.

WHAT IS PERSIAN CULTURE?

R.J.: If you had to describe Persian civilization, Iranian civilization, to a non-Iranian, which aspects would you point out as the most important?
S.H.N.: This is of course a very deep and basic matter. When some years back, just a few years before the Revolution took place, the famous Canadian photographer Roloff Beny took the pictures for the book *Persia, Bridge of Turquoise*,[12] I wrote a long essay both in English and Persian as text for the book, dealing precisely with the question, "What Is Persian Culture?" I was surprised to see that the *Ettela'at*, the daily newspaper of Tehran, serialized that long essay that I wrote. They took the text of *Iran Pol-e Firouzeh*, the Persian version of the book. This issue is something that is difficult to summarize, but I would say that first of all, Persian culture has been marked by both continuity and discontinuity. Every Persian feels that there is definitely a sense of continuity in his or her society and culture covering a long historical era going back to the prehistoric period and the mythological ages that were described in the *Shahnameh*[13] and the dynasties before the Achamenians. At the same time, there is a discontinuity. Persian culture is profoundly Islamic, and all Iranians, even non-Muslims, have experienced the reality of that Islamic culture during the last fourteen hundred years and have lived in the general context and matrix of a Persian culture that had become deeply Islamicized.

Persian culture combines a sense of great refinement in almost everything with a sensuality that is at the same time spiritual. This wedding between the sensual and the spiritual is usually not well understood in the modern West, where the two have become dichotomized into opposing categories, and people cannot understand how someone can talk of the beautiful ruby lips of women, but be talking at the same time about Divine Qualities, as do Ḥāfiẓ and so many of our other poets. This is something that characterizes a great deal of Persian culture. The sense of beauty and refinement of both a sensual and spiritual nature, along with attention to that which is delicate and minute, is reflected in many types of Persian art, such as carpet weaving, miniature painting, calligraphy, illuminations, et cetera, and it is reflected, of course, in thought and language.

Also, I would characterize Persian culture as one which was placed from the very beginning at the crossroads of different civilizations and currents of thought, in contrast to the culture of a country such as Egypt, which also became Islamic, but which was like a fort with deserts on two sides, the origin of the Nile going into Black Africa in the south and the Mediterranean Sea in the north. Iran is just the other way around. It stands at a crossroad, roads crossing it from east and west and north, but especially east and west (but sometimes also the north, from which in fact the invasion of the Iranian plateau by the Aryan people most likely took place).

The geographical situation of Iran had consequences for Persian culture; it necessitated the quality of remarkable receptivity, plasticity, and power of absorption. The psyche of the Persians is not like the big branch of a tree, which is strong and does not bend, but if you pull it down with strong enough force it breaks. Rather, it is like a twig which bends without breaking. This remarkable elasticity that has been created in the Persian soul has allowed often apparently contradictory elements to be held within the being of a single person in ways that are astonishing to foreigners. Many people came to Iran and saw modernized Iranians and could not understand how they were acting in so many contradictory ways and with so many contradictory ideas. But this trait goes back to one of the characteristics of Persian culture which permitted people to be both malleable and receptive while preserving their identity in order to survive.

That does not, however, mean that Persian culture possessed only the quality of receptivity, as some people have said. It means that Persian culture has had a great deal of power of absorption which has been combined with the ability to synthesize. This trait was in fact strengthened by the coming of Islam itself, because Islam has a great deal of integrating power within itself. Persia was able to absorb not only people such as the Greeks, Arabs, Turks, and Mongols who came physically and settled there, but also ideas and practices, which is even more important, from India, China, the Mediterranean world, and elsewhere; and later on, of course, with the coming of Islam these sources increased. But Persians were always able to create a synthesis of these diverse ideas and practices with things Persian, which then themselves became new but still distinctly Persian modes of thought and culture. And in turn, Persia became also an important center for the dissemination of very important currents of thought and modes of culture including especially philosophy, art, and literature.

As a student of both Persian history and Islamic history in general, the more I study the more I realize how remarkable the synthesis created in Persia culturally during the Islamic period was for the whole history of Asia, of the Ottoman world, of all of India, of even Islamic China, of Central Asia, of Southeast Asia—that is, nearly the whole of Asia except for Japan, Indochina, and Korea. It is a really remarkable phenomenon of history. I do not at all agree with many of the evaluations given by modernized Iranians of their own culture when they say that Iranians are wishy-washy, they have no principles, they have no backbone and so forth. That is not true. This is not at all true, because the other element that is present is resilience, like that twig that you can bend, but when you let it go it straightens out again. We have had in Iran these phases of receptivity and absorption and then synthesis and reassertion. We have seen over and over again in our history up to the current period the phase of being docile, absorbing and passively accepting, and being run over, followed by reassertion, digestion, but also rejection of certain elements, through the Persianizing of things. That is what has enabled this remarkable culture to survive for so long with a distinct identity.

Also if I were to describe Persian culture to some foreigner, I would emphasize very much the incredible richness and diversity of Persian culture. There is an overall paradigm that dominates over all aspects of Persian culture. It includes among its components the keen awareness of transcendence, the love for light and illumination, which goes all the way from philosophy to the house we live in, and the keen appreciation of refinement and beauty in both art and thought. As I said, there is also this central relation between the sensual form and its spiritual essence. These traits are also to be seen elsewhere, but within Persian culture they have their notable concrete manifestations. There is remarkable diversity combined with authenticity in Persia in the field of philosophy, in Sufism, in different forms of theology, in various sciences, in different forms of art, in the diversity of musical expression. I do not want to give the impression that Persian culture is just a local culture like that of a small province or something such as you have within Persia itself in Baluchi or Semnani cultures. Rather, Persian culture is both universal and geographically extended. But Persian culture as a whole must be characterized by its remarkable diversity and also a combination of particularity and universality.

Traditional culture in Persia has, of course, always been strongly Persian. No culture could exist without particularity. But there are cultures that emphasize particularity more than anything else, whereas traditional Persian culture has always emphasized a kind of universalism within its own particularity. So, the two have always gone together. Even for certain Persians who do not consider themselves to be very Persianized and feel completely modernized, something of Persian culture survives in their soul, and both of these elements are still present to some extent.

Promethean Man and Pontifical Man

R.J.: It is interesting, because in your book *Persia, Bridge of Turquoise* you state that there is nothing of a Promethean nature in the Persian concept of the *anthrōpos*, especially in Islamic Persia, because of the characteristics of this culture that you were talking about.

S.H.N.: Yes. This is an important point, of course, and we could also make this comment about many other traditional cultures, but since I was talking about Persia in that book, I mentioned it in the context of our own culture. What do I mean by Promethean? First of all, this is a theme which I have developed extensively specially in my book *Knowledge and the Sacred* where I talk about and juxtapose the concepts Promethean Man and Pontifical Man—"Pontifical," of course, coming from the word *pontifix* in Latin, meaning "bridge," and therefore referring to a man who is a bridge between Heaven and earth. That is how traditional man saw himself or herself, whereas Promethean Man, going back to the myth of Prometheus, is the person who steals fire from the gods, and in the deepest sense rebels against Heaven. It is that aspect of Prometheanism that I had in mind, the kind of human rebellion against Heaven that comes to the fore in the West with the Renaissance and that characterizes so much of modern Western man's understanding of himself.

Now, in Persian culture, both in the Zoroastrian and the Islamic periods, a great deal was written about man, such as the doctrine of *insān-i kāmil*[14] about which Jīlī, Nasafī, Mullā Ṣadrā, and other great Sufis and philosophers wrote. But there was never this idea of rebellion of man against Heaven. As I have said before, it is interesting that in both Arabic and Persian, you do not have a word for "tragedy," and today in

Persian we use the word *trajedi.* Why is it that we do not have this word in Persian? We have so many terms for what was translated from Greek, and our language is so rich in the rendering of Greek words. Yet, we have no Persian or Arabic word for "tragedy" in the Greek sense of the term. The reason is that the Greek idea of tragedy was related to the idea of man fighting against the gods and against destiny, as we see in the great Greek plays. It is not accidental that we do not have this word in Persian, because the idea that man can rebel against the gods, against Heaven, is something that is totally against the Persian worldview.

Look at all the Iranian religions in the pre-Islamic period, that is, Zoroastrianism, Manicheanism, and later the Zurvanite interpretation of Zoroastrianism, and also Mazdakism, about which we know so little. To the extent that we know something of these religions, we know that the Promethean idea did not exist in them. The idea of Gayomarth (Kayūmarth or Primordial Man) as the prototype of humanity was always combined with obedience to God, to Ahura Mazda. There was not the idealization of rebellion of man against God, and we do not have a figure like Prometheus in our old Iranian mythology, a fact that is itself very interesting. We do have people like Zahhak.[15] There are figures who rebel, but they are forces of evil, and people identify themselves not with such figures but with a Kave-yi Ahangar[16] to be able to overcome such figures as Zahhak within themselves. So Zahhak represents the force of evil which we see in the mythology of every civilization, but such figures are not heroes who rebel against God in the Promethean sense, and therefore they are very different from Prometheus. In Iran, whether pre-Islamic or Islamic, you did not have a Promethean figure seen as hero; such a figure would never have been considered to be a positive one. He would be considered to be evil. Yes, in every mythology you have a way of presenting the reality of evil. You have it in Hinduism. You have it in the Chinese tradition, and we have it in the myth of Zahhak, and of course the figure of Ahriman (or the Devil) in ancient Persia. That is very different from what I am saying, that is, supporting the attempt to aggrandize man's rebelling against Heaven. Such a view was alien to our ancient, as well as our Islamic, culture.

R.J.: Maybe because the Greeks . . . I mean, tragedy in ancient Greece, ancient Athens, especially in the fifth century B.C. had a very political structure. It was related to democracy and the democratic situation in Greece at that time, and that was not the case in Iran during the same period.

S.H.N.: That is only partly true, because the Greek tragedies also have a very deep philosophical and religious significance. They were not only political, although of course the political element was there. Politics has of course always existed in other situations, but the fact that you have politics in itself, even one concerned with democracy, does not lead to this aggrandizement of the Promethean myth. You can go a step further and say that in ancient Greece the religion itself began to die out, and so the rebellion of man against the gods represents also the situation of the Greek religion itself that Plato himself criticized. In any case, whatever the reason, this Promethean myth did not exist in Iran.

R.J.: No, it did not exist, because actually the difference with Iran is that in Greece, men and the gods are equally bound by destiny, *moira*, and this is not the case in ancient Persian civilization.
S.H.N.: In a sense you are right, because you see, the Greek gods were not ultimately gods; *moira* was the god in the ultimate sense, and something happened in the Greek religion that brought about this dethroning of the gods. Hinduism was the sister of the Greek religion, both being Indo-European religions, and of course even Shiva is bound by the laws of time according to some interpretations of Hinduism; but the hierarchy of metaphysical reality and power were never destroyed in Hinduism as it happened in the Greek religion. First of all, you have Brahman, the supreme metaphysical Reality, the totally unconditioned Reality, and then you have Brahma, Vishnu and Shiva, various powers of the Divinity; and then you have all the gods, three hundred and sixty thousand of them, each with a divine power; whereas in the Greek religion during the classical period, the gods had become anthropomorphized already. That leads to the death of religion; it is the beginning of the end of the religion in question. That is why the Greek religion died out and the Hindu religion is still around. At the same time, the idea of *moira* is to be found *mutatis mutandis* in other religions including both Hinduism and Zoroastrianism.

Persian Joy and Sorrow

R.J.: Can we go back to your book *Persia, Bridge of Turquoise*, because I found it interesting when you say that there is a deep appreciation of life and beauty among the traditional Persians which is accompanied by a deep sense of joy. You remember when you wrote of joy, or *ṭarab*, and sorrow, or *ḥuzn*, and you say that this sense of sorrow is fortified among the Persians by the ethos of their religion and culture.

S.H.N.: That is right. You want me to comment on that?

R.J.: Yes, please.

S.H.N.: First of all, Iranians always have a *joie de vivre* as the French say, a sense of the "joy of life." They enjoy life and they put a great deal of their energy in making possible this sense of enjoyment. For example, when they set a table it is very elaborate and aesthetically pleasing. Persian women, even traditional ones before modern times, gave a great deal of attention to what they wore. Their love for beautiful clothing and so forth is not a modern phenomenon. What happened was that our love was transferred to Western fashions and Persian women became very *chic* in the French sense, an event that marked the decadence of our culture; but the love for beauty and refinement had been there before in centuries past especially among city dwellers, including in what is today Afghanistan, which was then part of Persia. In the sedentary centers of the Iranian plateau, I mean the towns and cities, women were known even in the old days for their refinement, beautiful clothing, jewelry, et cetera. Every civilization has had jewelry, but the emphasis upon such matters among Persians is notable. As I said, the elaboration of the cuisine, which is one of the remarkable aspects of Persian culture, points to the same sense of joy and beauty, as does the joy reflected in the arts. Altogether, in traditional Persian culture there has always been a great deal of joy in life.

However, this was not hedonism. There is a great difference between that joy, which was combined with asceticism and had a spiritual character, and, let us say, what we find in America today, where much energy of most people is spent on enjoying life in a form of hedonism. We are living in a hedonistic society where pleasure is practically divinized, where we have the reign of a kind of dephilosophized Epicureanism. You might ask, what is the difference? The difference is that in Iran that joy of life or *farah* was combined with the remembrance and nostalgia for our original spiritual home from which issues *hozn* or *ghamm*.[17] This truth is very beautifully reflected in Persian Sufi poetry and in Persian music. There is a remarkable sadness in Persian music, which, however, is not sadness in the ordinary emotional sense of, let us say, the *Pathétique Symphony* of Tchaikovsky. His Symphony Number Six is sad in the ordinary human sense, not in a spiritual sense. That is not at all the case of Persian music; let me cite you an example, which is very interesting. In modern Iranian television or radio, if you have a soap opera and the heroine dies, let us say, a twenty-year-old woman dies, the music that is played is not the *dastgah-e shour*,[18] but some piece from Tchaikovsky or something like that.

So this sadness must not be confused with ordinary emotional sadness. It is impossible to only enjoy life, because we suffer in life and we die. There is death; there is pain; there is illness; there is separation; there is deprivation; there is privation. These are all part and parcel of human life. Traditional Persian culture was fully aware of this truth, and this idea of *hozn* as spiritual attitude, and as I said a kind of nostalgia for our original home was present along with *farah*. This theme is prevalent in our mystical and philosophical writings, in such works as the *Risālah fī ḥaqīqat al-ʿishq*[19] and *Qiṣṣat al-ghurbat al-gharbiyyah*[20] of Suhrawardī. These works emphasize that as spiritual beings we are strangers to this world. This is why Persian art is so interiorizing. When we listen especially to classical Persian music, ordinary people of no spiritual qualification say, "Oh, do not put on that music; it makes me think of my debts. It is sad, and I do not want to be sorrowful." Obviously, no one wants to be sad in the ordinary sense of the term, as when one has lost a son or a daughter, or even a pet. So why is it that people listen to this music? Those who are qualified experience in that sadness also a great joy and sweetness because it is not sadness in the original sense, but being a spiritual sadness, it also contains within it joy. One of the remarkable complementarities in Persian culture is this combination of *hozn* or *ghamm* and *farah* or *shadi*.

Now, the aspect of *hozn* was, as I said, accentuated by the fact that after the Mongol invasion, gradually Iran became more and more Twelfth Imam Shiʿite until the Safavid period when Shiʿism became the official religion of Persia. And why is that so? There were many reasons, but one of the psychological reasons is that Shiʿism emphasized this element of *hozn* more than did Sunni Islam, since the former accentuated the martyrdom of the Imams and especially Imam Ḥusayn and the tragedy of Karbala'.[21] The encounter with the reality that this world is too imperfect to accept pure light, metaphysically speaking, is at the heart of the perspective of Shiʿism that always criticized Sunni Islam for accepting the imperfections of this world as far as political rule is concerned, and the response of Sunnism was that we first have to exist before we can do anything else, and this world is by its nature imperfect.

Shiʿism has always emphasized mourning, or *sougavari* (*sūgawārī*) on the everyday level of life, mourning for the death of Imam Ḥusayn but metaphysically for the rejection of the light in the Imam by this world and the tragedies that have resulted from this fact. That element that came with Shiʿism accentuated this strain of sadness in the Persian soul that is related to their historical experiences, and perhaps in some cases Persians went overboard. But if Persians did not have this element present in their culture, there would be the danger that the other elements of the joy of life would become over-dominant and they would become one might say too outgoing hedonists, people just after pleasure. Some human beings are given more to this tendency than others, like the Italians are in comparison to Swedes, who possess a different temperament. The Persians are more like the Italians and other Mediterranean people than like northern Europeans. The Persians are sort of "hot-blooded," and if that element of nostalgia, spiritual *hozn* and *ghamm*, were not to be present, then *farah* by itself would have become very soon transformed into an empty pleasure which no longer had any spiritual and philosophical significance, and they would have become simply sensualists and hedonistic, not capable of creating a major traditional culture.

R.J.: So you see elements of ancient Persia in the structure of Shiʿism?
S.H.N.: Not in the structure of Shiʿism, but in the soul of the Persians. This element of *hozn*, combined with the joy already mentioned, played a role in the molding of the souls of Persians and made them from the very beginning sympathetic to the tragedy of the Imams, who were not Persian, but Arabs. This element prepared the ground ultimately for the Persians to finally accept Shiʿism more than Sunnism. There were, of course, also other important factors. Let us not forget that during most of their history Persians were Sunnis, not Shiʿites. It is only during the last five hundred years that Shiʿism has become dominant in Persia.

R.J.: Yes, but I was referring to the fact that if you compare what Montgomery Watt called the "proto-Shiʿite" period with Shiʿism after the Safavid time, you see that there is a great difference between the two. I mean the attitude of Shiʿites towards how they see the facts of their worldview. No? You do not think so?
S.H.N.: What difference?

R.J.: For example, in the proto-Shiʿites you do not find this attitude of sorrow as you have said, and . . .
S.H.N.: That is a good point. First of all, there is some truth to this assertion. There is no doubt, however, that that element of sadness was potentially present from the beginning, but I think that in Persia it became more accentuated. It is interesting to note that Egyptians are

Shafiʿites, but they have very great love for the *Ahl al-Bayt*, the family of the Prophet. The head of Imam Ḥusayn is buried in Cairo, while his body is buried in Karbala'. So he has two major sanctuaries. The place, which is called *Ra's al-Ḥusayn*, that is, "the head of Ḥusayn" in Cairo is the spiritual heart of that city. It is around this sanctuary that al-Azhar University and Fatimid Cairo were built. In fact, the whole great city of Cairo with some 14 million people is built around that simple monument that is its heart.

Now, in the beginning of Muḥarram, the Egyptians observe some ceremonies of mourning for Imam Ḥusayn, as do the Persians, but most of the time their whole response to the advent of the history of Shiʿism is much more joyous than what we find in Persia. I was once speaking to an Egyptian and he said, "We are Shiʿites like you except yours is the *Shīʿah* of *ḥuzn*; ours is the *Shīʿah* of *faraḥ*," which is an interesting comment indeed. The aspect of sorrow and lament was there from the beginning in Shiʿism, but when it came to Persia, and especially during the Safavid period, it was accentuated. It became definitely more accentuated than before, complementing the *joie de vivre* that the Persians also possess deep within their soul.

Sacralization of Daily Life

R.J.: We are talking about a very important subject. I think that what has been lost amongst Iranians is the sacralization of life and the sense of duty that need to be accentuated among Persians. In which ways do you think that Shiʿism helps this sacralization of life and this sense of duty to be accentuated among the Persians?

S.H.N.: Oh, it helped a great deal, but even when Persia was mostly Sunni, Sunni Islam accomplished the same task in a different way. As far as Shiʿism is concerned, look for example at all of the various days of the calendar which are either *ʿids*[22] of celebration or days of mourning. These days were all accompanied by special religion functions, for example the *sofreh*,[23] a religious act, in which prayers were read and food given to the poor, or let us say *rowzekhani*,[24] which is something moving and beautiful, not to speak of the *taʿziyah*,[25] the passion play that includes the chanting of poems concerning the life of the Prophet, the Imams, and other elements of Islamic sacred history. All of these practices, along with of course the Islamic daily prayers and Islamic Law, were and still are definitely means to sanctify life and the rhythm of life of traditional Persians, which was and is even today governed in fact by the Shiʿite calendar.

You might say that in traditional society the days, months, and seasons were always combined with the sense of the sacred, both the happy days and the sad days. It is interesting that even Norouz, which is a pre-Islamic Iranian *'id* marking the beginning of our New Year, was of course totally Islamicized for ordinary Persians. Even today the ordinary people do not say that this is a Zoroastrian ritual, because for them it is really no longer Zoroastrian but Islamic. It is like many Christian celebrations which took over pre-Christian observances and Christianized them, so that they are now Christian. Norouz[26] was also thoroughly Islamicized and became more specifically, for Iran, as 'id became the Shi'ite New Year associated in a sense with the Imams, especially the eighth buried in Mashhad. To this day, many people in Iran go to Qom, Mashhad, and other holy places at the time of *taḥwīl* or the vernal equinox marking the beginning of spring. Definitely Islam both in its Sunni and Shi'ite form, and during the past few centuries especially in its Shi'ite form, has played a central and crucial role in the sacralization of the life of Persians.

Architecture and the Modernization of Iranian Cities

R.J.: Now, do not you think that when you look at Iranian cities today and you look at Iranians you have the impression (I mean you have not been back to this country recently, but you have contacts with it) that there has been a great change, and this sense of beauty that you talk about and this sacralization of life in *Persia, Bridge of Turquoise* has totally disappeared? When you look at Iranian cities today, Tehran for example with a population of 12 million, do you not see this reality?

S.H.N.: Yes, to some extent, but not totally. This process of creating ugly and secularized urban settings began not only in Iran, not only in Islamic countries, but in the whole of Asia and Africa in the 19th century with the onslaught of colonialism by the West and the emulation of modern Western architecture, city planning, et cetera, which were not based on spiritual principles. Even in Paris, the boulevards built by Hausman in modern times are very different from the narrow streets of Île St. Louis, and you have a very different feeling when visiting these urban areas. So this was a process that began in Iran in the late 19th and early 20th centuries, but it became more rapid in the Pahlavi period and even more so after the 1979 Revolution. What is very sad is that although when the Iranian Revolution came in the name of Islam, it paid little attention to Islamic art at the beginning, and the whole process of modernization of the ambience you see during the Pahlavi period was continued and became even further accentuated. The Tehran of 3.5 million people now has become a city of over 12 million people with all those tall buildings, skyscrapers, the destruction of the old gardens in Shemiran, and many other atrocious acts that make one very sad, because they have all contributed to the desacralization of the ambience.

Yes, but I think that this process is not the whole story. Although I have not been in Iran during the last three decades, I have had enough contacts to know first of all that there are a number of architects who are trying to understand again the principles of Islamic architecture and try to build accordingly, and secondly that there are a number of private houses and a few public ones that are now being built according to traditional principles. Also, there has been a renovation of some of the traditional architecture in Kashan, Isfahan Yazd, and some other places, which is very impressive. In the old days, we had a project in Isfahan to reconnect Meydan-i Shah to the river through that vast park which also contains the *Hasht Behesht* Palace. Some of the land had been bought and built up by private groups, and we had to re-buy the land and expand the park step by step. That project has apparently now been completed, and there has been a lot of renovation. So there are some people in Iran who are aware of the significance of preserving the sacred character of the ambience of urban life, but unfortunately the main forces in society remain totally blind to these matters as we also see elsewhere in the world.

I often receive letters from architects from Tehran, some of them Ph.D. students, others practicing architects, who, because I have written much on the philosophy of art and architecture, consult me on various matters. I had a letter some time back from someone which was very sad. He said, "You know that although everyone talks about Islam now, when it comes to actually implementing these principles of traditional Persian Islamic architecture and the like, the situation is worse now than it was thirty years ago." I hope that he is not right, but in any case I think your assessment is correct. I do not think that the resacralization of life and its ambience is completely forgotten, but it is certainly forgotten by many people. There are islands here and there, and groups within Iran of people who want to preserve and enhance the beauty of traditional art and architecture and the sacred quality of life itself.

What you have to do is to change the education of those who are going to create future urban settings and buildings, in the same way that by bringing the educational philosophy of the *Beaux-arts* of Paris to Tehran University and creating *Daneshkade-ye Honahra-ye Ziba*[27] the whole philosophy of building in Iran was changed. A new perspective began to dominate for the next sixty years.

What you have to do is to train our architects in such a way that even if they have to accept what the *karfarma* (*kārfarmā*) or employer asks them to do, and even if the employer wants something gaudy or lifeless, or even if only the element of greed parading as economic necessity dominates, the architect will not be able to do otherwise than what he has learned: to create good Persian architecture on the basis of the way in which he has been trained. Look at the late Qajar period when some Persians went to Europe and came back and wanted to build houses like European ones, but they could not bring with them French masons—it was too expensive; so they had to make use of Persian masons and Persian bricklayers and so forth, and although you got some European effects, by and large the technique of building remained Persian, because this was the only way that these people could build. It was the only way they could work. That is why for us today something like the Sepahsalar Mosque built during the Qajar period still looks beautiful, as do many of the stately homes of Tehran belonging to that period.

Now, we have to change our educational system to introduce seriously a way of looking at architecture and city planning Islamically, and this is something to which unfortunately little attention has been paid until now. It is one of the great tragedies not only in Iran but also throughout the Islamic world. There are now a number of people who have awakened to the importance of the preservation of Islamic architecture. But it is only now after all these years that in Jordan and one or two other places they are trying to create schools of architecture which would turn out architects who know the principles, the geometry, the materials involved in building according to the ethos of Islamic architecture. It is interesting to note that of all places it was in London that, because of the presence of Keith Critchlow, whom I invited to Iran many times (he is a great expert on sacred geometry and wrote on Islamic patterns), and with the help of Prince Charles, who is very much interested in traditional architecture, the Prince of Wales's Institute of Architecture was established with a branch devoted to Islamic art and architecture. This is the best and the most competent school for the training of traditional architects and artists, who are taught the principles of traditional architecture and how to build on the basis of these principles, not just copying let us say a Qajar building outwardly, but reapplying those principles to the circumstances in which they find themselves. If Iran wants to take its culture seriously and prevent its desacralization, urban design and architecture must be taken very seriously, because they determine the spaces in which people live. Of course many other factors are also involved in the process of sacralization or desacralization of the patterns of life, but art and architecture are, along with the prevalent worldview itself, among the most important. Therefore, I have confined my response here to them.

Needless to say, the Sacred Law itself has been primary to the sacralization of the life of Muslims throughout the world. The fact that I do not speak about it now is because the influence of Sacred Law seems obvious, and I do not feel that it needs to be emphasized or analyzed here.

Sacred Architecture in the Modern World

R.J.: I know that for you sacred architecture is important; you have written on it as sacred signs, but do you think that in modern times, I mean in modern countries such as Iran or Egypt or Syria or Lebanon, Islamic countries being modernized in the worst way, we can still have sacred art?

S.H.N.: Yes, we can. I am not being overoptimistic and saying that everything that will be built can be sacred architecture, no. Unfortunately, the forces of secularization, emulating the West, economic factors, greed, and increase in population, all of these factors are present as obstacles. And then there are governments, which need immediate housing and usually build the ugliest type of housing for the poor, houses which usually turn into slums later on. You see that in Cairo, you see that in Tehran, and also, you see it in Paris and New York. It is all over the world. I do not think that this is going to change all that rapidly, but Iran was always one of the great centers of architecture in both the pre-Islamic period and the Islamic period. Islamic architecture, of course, also has other great centers. We are not the only one. There is of course Egypt and then Spain, the Maghreb, Muslim India, and Turkey. But in any case, Iran has been always one of the greatest centers of Islamic art and architecture.

Now, the tradition has not been totally lost. What is important is first of all to continue to build sacred architecture, at least for sacred buildings such as mosques and not to build something like Masjed-e al-Jawad in Tehran and other monstrosities, buildings that have nothing to do with authentic Islamic architecture whatsoever. For mosques, for *khanqahs*,[28] for public institutions, such as the Iranian Academies or *Farhangestanha*, it is possible to try to use the principles of Islamic architecture. In Islamic-Persian architecture there is no absolute line of demarcation between the sacred and the profane. In Europe, church architecture was sacred architecture, palace architecture was profane architecture; but in Iran, Ali Qapu and the Shah Mosque of Isfahan, one sitting next to the other, both belong to the same style of architecture; so does in fact the bazaar, and one cannot call one sacred and the other profane. All traditional Islamic architecture was influenced by sacred architecture. Now, if we cannot build, let us say, a hotel in traditional architectural style, at least where it is possible to do so we should continue our architectural tradition and give the sense of the abiding reality of our architecture, which would be very significant for future generations.

I know that it is bad to build houses and offices that look as if they belong to Hamburg or Los Angeles rather than Tehran, but it is even worse to build these modernistic mosques that are monstrosities, having nothing to do with Islamic art. Few of the architects who make them know anything at all about the tradition of Islamic architecture. They might perform their prayers, but they do not know the principles of their own sacred architecture. In such cases it would be much better just to copy earlier mosques like the Egyptians do, which is a very wise thing. Egypt is a poor country and has some of the most depressing apartment houses in the world in Cairo built by Gamal Abd al-Nasser with the help of Russian engineers and architects, who built the ugliest buildings in the world you can imagine. But its mosque architecture is very beautiful because they usually do not give permits to build mosques to people who do not know anything at all about Islamic art, anything at all about sacred geometry, but just say, "But we are architects, we are living in the 20th century, and we must reflect it in our work," and so forth and so on. It is total nonsense to build whatever the modern age dictates from the outside and consider it as Islamic art.

I think that throughout the Islamic world there is now some revival of interest in genuine Islamic architecture and design. The situation is much better now than it was a generation ago, and this goes back to a large extent to the work and influence of Hasan Fathy,[29] the great Egyptian architect. I have already told you about what we did in Iran in that conference when we brought him to Isfahan. There are now in Pakistan a number of important traditional architects. There is a book by the contemporary traditional Pakistani architect Kamil Khan that has just come out on traditional Pakistani architecture. There is also Abdul Wahid al-Wakil, the famous Egyptian architect, now working from Britain, who has built several beautiful mosques in Saudi Arabia and elsewhere, and there are now a number of other architects such as the Egyptian Umar Faruq who are trying to revive Islamic architecture. The Aqa Khan Award in Islamic Architecture has also had some role to play in this matter, although not all those involved in the jury are fully aware of what constitutes authentic Islamic architecture.

R.J.: Yes, but how do you want an architect or a painter or a musician who does not believe in the sacred anymore, as did those old artisans who made Masjed-e Shah, and who believed in the sacred, to create works of sacred art? How do you want them then to create a sacred building, sacred architecture, without believing in sacred places?
S.H.N.: I do not want them to do that. They in fact cannot do it and should not do it. They should have the humility of not creating a building whose function they do not understand, whose meaning they do not share. Unfortunately, that humility does not exist very much among many modern architects. Most of the famous architects have very big egos, as do most modern artists in the world today, because the whole training of modern artists is not based on the training and disciplining of the ego but on expanding individualist tendencies and idiosyncrasies. I think that sacred architecture such as that of mosques, *husayniyyehs* or *takkiyehs*,[30] and things like that should be built in Iran by traditional architects who are still living within that world—until we gradually train architects, let us say in the Faculty of Fine Arts at Tehran University or someplace like that, who at least have faith in Islam and also understand the traditional science of geometry and what the ambience of the mosque implies. A person who does not believe in the sacred and does not possess a sense of the sacred cannot create sacred buildings.

I remember a discussion that I had in the 1950s with Walter Gropius, the founder of the Bauhaus in Germany, who was then in Cambridge. His office was requested to build a mosque for Baghdad University, where the whole campus was being designed by his firm. This man, who was one of the greatest Western architects of the 20th century, at least had common sense. He called me one day and said, "I can never build a building without knowing what its function is. What do you do in a mosque?" and we began our discussions from there. We had long discussions. We have always blamed the Bauhaus for all the monstrosities we all see all over Western cities, the glass boxes which go back to the simplification of architecture by the Bauhaus to what appears as pure geometry, but Gropius himself was truly aware of the shortcomings of such buildings for sacred use, and when it came to the creation of an Islamic sacred place, he said, "I cannot do it because I do not belong to that tradition." I think that this discussion points to the great crisis not only for architecture in Iran, not only in the Islamic world, but in the whole of Asia and Africa as you see in Hindu India, in Buddhist Japan, and many other places.

Persian and Western Poetry

R.J.: To finish this part of our discussion, I would like to know which part of Persian culture—I am not talking about Islamic culture, of course, and not Shiʿism—which part of Persian culture, Iranian culture, has most influenced your life, especially your intellectual life?

S.H.N.: First of all, I do not see any aspects of our present Persian culture that are separate from Islam. Let us take even *sizdah bedar*,[31] for example, which is part and parcel of one's life in Iran. When as a child I went out into the country and saw the trees blossoming and becoming green, I thought of the beginning of the *Golestan*[32] and the "emerald carpet" (*farsh-e zumorrodin*) that God spreads over the earth with the coming of the new year and the spring. And this phenomenon had an Islamic significance for me. In fact, I do not know of any element of our culture which for me was separate from Islam. Although I went to a Zoroastrian school both in the fourth grade and seventh grade, to Jamshid-e Jam and Firouz Bahram, even there, there was nothing specifically Zoroastrian that influenced my thought. As for what has influenced me most in Persian culture, it is first and foremost, I would say, Persian Sufi literature and especially poetry, and parallel with that, the philosophical works of the Islamic Persian philosophers, people such as Ibn Sīnā, Suhrawardī, Mīr Dāmād, Mullā Ṣadrā, and figures like them.

R.J.: And you yourself—we can talk about this shortly—you yourself have written poems in English and in Persian also which are very much Sufi poems, very mystical?

S.H.N.: Yes, I have, but I do not consider myself a poet. I am just a humble doodler of poetry, and I occasionally write a few verses here and there. Most of our philosophers throughout our history wrote a few poems on the side. Look at Ibn Sīnā, Naṣīr al-Dīn Ṭūsī, and Mullā Ṣadrā who have written some poems. Mīr Dāmād was a good poet, as were Lāhījī and Bābā Afḍal Kāshānī. Of course we have one person,

Nāṣir-i Khusraw, who was both one of the greatest poets of Persia and also one of its greatest philosophers. On another level, perhaps the same thing could be said about Khayyām. Yes, I have always been interested in poetry. As I said, I learned a great deal of poetry by heart as a child, and that definitely left an effect upon my mind and soul. Even when I write prose, people say that it has a certain poetic quality. This fact was noted even by some of my teachers at Harvard, including Harry Wolfson, who said that my Ph.D. thesis was in fact poetic prose. Poems occasionally come to me, but I do not force myself to write poetry. Sometimes poems will come to me as sort of a gift by the Muses, as the Greeks would say. Almost all of them are really Sufi poems, because they issue from my soul molded by the practice of the spiritual life. That is from where they emanate, and they are one expression of the link that I feel, of course, with the Persian Sufi poetical tradition.

R.J.: So, you read a lot of poetry yourself?
S.H.N.: Most of the poetry I have read over the last few years has been either from Ḥāfiẓ, Mawlānā, or Shabistarī,[33] unless it has been for my scholarly work. For example, if I am writing an article or essay on Jāmī, I read his poems, but as far as just taking a book of poetry and reading it, as I grow older I can live just with Ḥāfiẓ alone. But I do also read poems of Rūmī from time to time, but these two are practically the only ones to which I refer again and again. They are my constant companions, along with the *Golshan-e raẓ*. Occasionally, let us say, if there is a new edition of the *Golestan* or the *Bustan*[34] that has come out and somebody sends it to me, as happens from time to time, I may sit down for an hour or so and read some of the poems in the book. But what is an intimate companion of my soul, I would say, are the *Diwan* of Ḥāfiẓ, and both the *Diwan-e Shams* and *Mathnawi* of Rūmī and Shabistarī's *Golshan-e raẓ*.

R.J.: Yes. Do you think they are still relevant for our world today, both?
S.H.N.: Very relevant. Ḥāfiẓ is extremely difficult to translate, but Rūmī is so relevant that he is now the best selling poet in America, although some of the translations of his poems are often diluted and distorted. Nevertheless, there is no poet who is as relevant to the world today as Rūmī. I know of no one, no poet who is as timely as he, because he speaks of so many diverse spiritual questions, of the existential situation in which human beings find themselves today. He caters to the needs of a very diverse set of audiences. He is an unbelievable, universal poet. I think he is probably the most universal poet in all of Islamic civilization,

not only in Persian, but also in Arabic, Turkish and all the other Islamic languages.

R.J.: And you read non-Iranian poets? I mean, I am sure you have read . . .

S.H.N.: I read very extensively, first of all, English poetry when I was at the Peddie School. It was a very fine secondary school; so we had an in-depth education as far as English literature was concerned. I read many of thc plays of Shakespeare, which are the summit of English literature, and some of his incomparable sonnets. The plays are in prose, but nevertheless there are many poetic utterances in them. I read also the whole of Milton's *Paradise Lost* and *Paradise Regained.* John Donne, I read when I was in college. Going back to Peddie, we read many of the classical poetic works of the 19th century, that is, poets such as William Blake, Shelley, Byron, Keats, Wordsworth, and even lesser known poets, such as Addison, people like that. We also read some American poetry. When I went to M.I.T. and Harvard, I continued to read English poetry, and the poets who attracted me then besides these classical poets, and in fact to some extent more than them, were first of all Emerson and then the three great poets of the English language of the 20th century, that is, W. B. Yeats, Ezra Pound, and T. S. Eliot, whom I met personally, and with whom I had many conversations. His later poetry was very attractive to me, his critique of the condition of modern man . . .

R.J.: *The Wasteland*?

S.H.N.: Yes, *The Wasteland*, but also the *Quartets*, "The Love Song of J. Alfred Prufrock," et cetera. Then there was Ezra Pound's *Contos* to which I became attracted because of my interest in Dante. As for William Butler Yeats, I turned to him as a result of the influence on me of Coomaraswamy, who referred often to him. I also read Dylan Thomas, whom I knew personally. Then, in addition to these figures, I also began to read the poetry of other European countries. I read Rilke and Goethe, Hölderlin, and Novales; these German poets attracted me a great deal, especially, of course, Goethe, who is a great favorite of mine, particularly his *West-East Divan*, which is a late poem, and is very closely related to the themes of Ḥāfiẓ and Persian Sufi poetry in general. I also read French poetry, but strangely enough it did not attract me as much. I read some of the poetry of Victor Hugo, Baudelaire, Paul Claudel, and people like that, but French prose attracted me much more. Although I know French much better than German, German poetry attracted me more than French.

The Western poet who really attracted me most of all, and whom I read extensively in college, was Dante. I took a whole year's course with Georgio de Santillana on the inner meaning of the *Divine Comedy.* We spent a whole year just reading verse by verse the whole of this work, going through all the four levels of meaning, of which the highest is the anagogical. I also read many commentaries on the *Divine Comedy* and even learned some Italian just to be able to read the *Divine Comedy.* Of course my knowledge of Italian was not sufficient, because the *Divine Comedy* is such an incredibly difficult work. To this day, this poem remains for me the supreme poetical work of Western civilization. Then I began to read Arabic Sufi poetry while at Harvard. The poetry of Ḥallāj has always been very attractive to me. I have also read the poetry of Ibn 'Arabī, the *Khamriyyah* and *Ta'iyyah* of Ibn al-Fāriḍ, the poems of Shaykh al-'Alawī, et cetera.[35] These are the main poetic works which I have read often and whose poetic language I have enjoyed in the original. I have also read some haiku poems in translation and some classical Chinese poetry also in translation, but not that much. The haiku has always been interesting to me, but I would not say that it has been the center of my attention. I have also read some Spanish poetry, both in the original and in translation, and enjoy especially Saint John of the Cross. My first book of poetry[36] has just been translated by the distinguished scholar Luce López-Baralt into Spanish, and she tells me it sounds wonderful in that language.

R.J.: I have seen your books. You quote Dante very often . . .
S.H.N.: Yes, because I know Dante and I think that the *Divine Comedy* is the great synthesis of Western Christian civilization.

R.J.: Do you also quote from other poets?
S.H.N.: Yes, I have also quoted a few verses from Hartmann and from Goethe here and there, both of whom are German poets, and also, rarely, a few lines from French poets. I think that I once quoted a verse from Claudel, I do not remember. But yes, you are right, most of what I have quoted is English and Persian poetry. At first, when I was at Peddie, English poetry did not speak to me at all. I could not understand it as poetry. It took a long time before I began to appreciate English poetry, and to realize that English is poetically one of the richest languages. It is strange that we now identify English with this pidgin language that has spread all over the world. I think that for that very reason, now is the time to revive Shakespeare seriously. Shakespeare is

the poet of the age today because he is the greatest master of the English language, and English is spreading all over the world.

Yes, I do appreciate English poetry very much, but of course not every genre of poetry that has been written in that language. I have always looked in poetry for two things, inner philosophical wisdom and/or divine love. I also like good nature poetry because it reflects something of the wisdom and beauty of God's creation. Wordsworth, for example, was one of my favorite poets when I was young. I read a lot of Wordsworth, some of whose poetry I teach even now in courses that I give here on Man and the Natural Environment and also on Persian Sufi literature, East and West, a course which is probably unique in this country. This is a course in which the students are not required to know Persian or European languages other than English, but we do the work in translation. I teach something about Persian Sufi literature, especially poetry, and then its influence on the West, and I talk about many figures such as Emerson, Goethe, the English Khayyam, but also Wordsworth and Tennyson.

Another poet whom I like very much and used to read a great deal is William Blake. I have been concerned with Blake since my youth. Nowadays, I do not read too much Blake, but in my twenties and thirties I used to read a great deal of his works. As I have already said, I was a good friend of Kathleen Raine, the great English poet who died recently and who was also a major Blake scholar and wrote the book *Blake and Tradition.*[37] I am also a fellow of Temenos Academy, which was founded by her in London, and so through her I have kept my contact with Blake scholarship, but I do not read too much of Blake's poetry itself these days, although I have read much of Kathleen Raine's own poetry.

Sufi Poetry in the West

R.J.: I feel that there is something superficial in the way that many people in the West are becoming interested in Sufi poetry. I am not talking about those who study this poetry at the university level, the academic level, or on the spiritual level. I am talking of people for whom poets such as Rūmī are becoming "*à la mode*," very fashionable, often for the wrong reason, people who are not interested in the Sufi tradition that the work of Rūmī reflects.

S.H.N.: You are to a large extent right. Whatever becomes popular also becomes often shallow by virtue of that fact. It is interesting that in French we have the word *vulgarisation*, which has a positive connotation (meaning "popularization"), whereas in English, *vulgarization* has a very pejorative connotation. Unfortunately, often these days the two meanings go together: the French *vulgarisation* often leads to the English *vulgarization*; there is no doubt about that fact. There is nothing wrong with the popularization of Sufi poetry in the West as we find in the Islamic world itself, and in fact the impact that Persian Sufi literature has made and was bound to make globally is unavoidable. Look what happened when this poetry was first translated in the 19th century in Europe. At that time there were no pseudo-Sufis and gurus who could make a great deal of money from them, but it influenced people such as Goethe and Rilke, who were great poets. And also in England many poets such as Tennyson were influenced by it and that was unavoidable. What I mean is that once the poetic art and poetic depth of someone like Rumi or Jami is made available, people will want to read them. The tragedy in America today is that in many cases this has become commercialized and has become part of a kind of, you might say, spiritual consumerism in a society in which there is so much consumerism and everything in the society encourages consumerism.

For many Americans, not everybody, but many people in America, there is the feeling that everything must be available in such a way as to be easily consumable and digestible, like taking a pill. Then people grow weary of one product and throw it away to go to something else. For example, Zen was very popular in the United States after the Second World War, and then the Vedanta, and then Yoga, and so forth. They all marked the American landscape and have left their imprint, but then many people also have grown tired of them and have turned to watered-down Sufism. Many Americans have this unfortunate habit, again not all of them, of carrying within themselves this popular cultural trait of getting tired of things quickly; so now people have turned to Jalal al-Din Rumi. I think the fad aspect of this phenomenon is going to disappear. It is not going to last forever, but his popularity will leave, I think, a permanent imprint.

What is needed today is to make available, first of all, translations of Rūmī which are close to the original while being in a contemporary medium, and also to explain what this poetry really entails. Among the recent-day translators, a few are well known. There is Kabir Helmiski, who is the head of a branch of Mawlawī dervishes. He received his instructions and initiation in Turkey from Sulaiman Dede, the famous Mawlawī shaykh and spiritual teacher. Helminski has his own group, and they perform actually the Mawlawī rites, that is, the prayers, the invocation, and the sacred concert (*samā'*). They are Muslim, they perform their daily prayers, and then do their turning. He also translates Rumi, but unfortunately it is not from Persian but from the Turkish translation of the Persian of Rūmī. The other translators who are well known include Coleman Barks, Robert Bly, Andrew Harvey, and others like them who might be poetically gifted but do not know any Persian. They usually go to the Nicholson translation and they try to paraphrase his words from his style of English to modern American English to be able to reflect the flavor of contemporary American poetry. Sometimes they receive the help of a Persian or an Afghan whose mother tongue is Persian. But the great scholars of Rumi in the West, such as Annemarie Schimmel[38] and also my old friend William Chittick who wrote the book *The Sufi Path of Love*[39] on Jalāl al-Dīn Rūmī, have been very much opposed to this kind of translation. Yet, at the same time, as I said, the wide reception of these popular translations represents the reality of the thirst that exists in America at the present moment . . .

R.J.: For spirituality.
S.H.N.: Exactly, for spirituality, a thirst that is unavoidable, seeing the condition of human society in America today. This is something that is going to continue to exist. It is as if your blood pressure is high, you have a headache, and your face might turn red; so you seek medicine to bring down your blood pressure. These phenomena are similar. The task is, as I said, to try to present authentic spirituality to those who thirst for it. It is interesting that now there is a CD of the poetry of Rumi sung by famous Hollywood actors and actresses, you know . . .

R.J.: Madonna.
S.H.N.: Madonna, Demi Moore, and people like that, and it has made a fortune for certain people. Now, there is a Turkish company which also has a branch in this country. They asked me if I would record a CD of Rumi's poetry.[40] I agreed to do so if the original Persian poetry could be included, and if the translation were to be my own. I also insisted that only classical Turkish and Persian music would be included. The CD is now available, and I am very pleased with the result. Of course that act alone is not going to be able to erase the influence of this "popularism," because most people are attracted to what is easy and do not want to discipline themselves. They want the food in a capsule and are not willing to follow a difficult diet to get the necessary vitamins and other nutrients. They want to have just one little capsule to put in their mouth, and they are used to that way of living. Nevertheless, perhaps

this CD can help some people at least to understand what the poetry of Rumi is and also get a taste of the original Persian.

R.J.: I mean, they want spirituality without being spiritual.
S.H.N.: In a certain sense, yes. Well, they think that they are spiritual, but they want spirituality without the spiritual discipline that is needed to attain it. They cannot understand that if you want, let us say, to reach *nirvana* in Buddhism you have to spend thirty years in a Zen monastery doing *zazen* and praying every day, that you have to sit in *zazen* for four to eight hours every day remaining perfectly still; but they do not want to undergo that part of the discipline necessary to reach *satori.*[41] They just want to have the *satori*. In the case of Sufism, it is the same, but it is not possible to practice Sufism outside the cadre of Islam and the rigorous practices of the disciplines of Sufism. If this is not done, so-called spirituality becomes just a fad. A lot of clever "marketeers of spirituality" now find a big market for this kind of diluted Sufism, and so they are offering it to the public. They are attracting disciples who say that they are Sufis, but they are not even practicing Islam. They are not even performing their daily canonical prayers. "Spiritually" has become unfortunately to a large extent a market activity and has become commercialized.

Living the Spiritual Life

R.J.: Thomas Merton used to say, "Spiritual life is not to be known or studied. It is to be lived," and I have the impression that you spent more time in your life studying spirituality rather than living it directly.
S.H.N.: No. That is totally false. I have been concerned with living the spiritual life since my twenties. My association with Sufism is not only in writing about it but more than anything else by living it, besides, of course, practicing Islam which I do most assiduously. I have never missed a prayer a single day, a single time since I was twenty years old except for when I was in the hospital having a heart operation. But even then, I made up the missed prayers later. Nor have I missed fasting except when I have had stomach problems or been incapacitated otherwise. As for specifically Sufi practices, I have engaged in invocation (*dhikr*) every day of my life during the past fifty years. So both on the level of the practice of the religion and also on the level of spiritual practice itself, I have been associated with the practice of Sufism since my early twenties. Of course that is a private aspect of my life about which I do not usually speak. That is why for those who have only read my

books, it appears that I am more interested in the study of Sufism rather than in its practice. But since you asked this question openly, I must say that I agree completely with Thomas Merton as far as my own personal life is concerned.

As for Merton, he was coming to Iran to see me, but he died a few weeks before coming, while he was in Southeast Asia.[42] Yes, the spiritual life is not something you only study or write about; it is something that should be lived. The goal of all authentic spiritual writings is to lead people to the practice of the spiritual life. All these books that are written on this subject by authentic teachers have for their aim to lead a person to the point where he or she will begin to practice the spiritual life. So I am totally in agreement with Thomas Merton. Let me also again emphasize that it is only within Islam that Sufism can be practiced. The two have never been separated from each other in their reality and in fact are inwardly one, and certainly they have never been separated for me throughout my life.

Practicing Sufism

R.J.: This is an individual practice, but I think that Sufism could also be practiced fully collectively.

S.H.N.: No. The individual and collective practices of Sufism go together. When one enters a Sufi order, the most important part of it is the individual practice, which is based essentially upon the remembrance and invocation of God, which is called *ẕekr* in Persian, *dhikr Allāh* in Arabic; and to do that one has to perform certain forms of invocation of various Names of God or litanies drawn from the Quran as well as practicing Islamic rites fully. The *dhikr* must also be accompanied by various forms of meditation. One of course must also conform to certain ethical norms. Now, all of these elements concern the individual. But in addition to them, Sufis meet often collectively in what is called *majālis*,[43] which can range in their composition from a few to a very large number of disciples led by a spiritual teacher. The Sufi *majlis* is an important external support for the inner life and complements individual practice. It is not possible to be a serious practicing Sufi who wants to march on the path to God and just participate in the public gathering of Sufis. One also has to have interior spiritual practice. That is what is primary.

R.J.: So you are a part of the gathering also, I mean, a group?

S.H.N.: It depends on what you mean. If you mean a Sufi order, yes.

R.J.: So if you had to name in this context one or two spiritual figures, I mean, I suppose you would name Schuon, who impressed you most in your life, who would that be? Would it be Schuon?
S.H.N.: It would be first of all Shaykh al-'Alawī, the great Algerian shaykh of the Shādhiliyyah Order, whom I never met in this world, but I was deeply influenced by him indirectly through his writings and also through the grace that emanates from him; and yes, Schuon himself, who was his disciple.

What Is Spirituality?[44]

R.J.: When I think of spirituality it evokes the image of the bond, if you will, of universal forces of life binding together all human beings and other life forms, all genders, races, nations. Do you agree with this definition of spirituality?
S.H.N.: No. That is one of its consequences. Spirituality in itself is what the word itself reveals, that is, to be in contact with the world of the Spirit, and that transcends all particularities of the human state and of the material world. Some of the greatest spiritual figures in history—let us say Hildegard of Bingen, the 13th-century German mystic, and Rābi'ah, the eighth-century Sufi saint of Basrah—were women, while the great Milarepa was a Tibetan Buddhist monk. Such figures were not concerned with race, nationality, or gender. They were concerned with reaching the Truth. I mention figures from both a theistic and a non-theistic religion to emphasize that the ultimate goal of spirituality is really the same whether one speaks of God or *nirvana*. Everything else, including love and universality, flows from that ultimate Reality/Truth.

When it comes to the question of spirituality, I think that one of the great mistakes that is made in the modern world is to confuse the cause and the effect. To give a famous example, a spark from a fire proves that there is a fire, but there are also fires that do not give sparks. What is primary in spirituality is inwardness, the inward dimension which connects the human being inwardly to the Divine Truth and all of those external consequences, including love for others, or creation of poetry, or feeding the poor, flow from that inner realization. The external effects are not the same in every case. There are great saints, very highly spiritual figures, whose primary activity was not to feed the poor, for example, Shankaracharya, or Śri Ramana Maharshi, one of the greatest recent spiritual figures of Hinduism. Their function was to disseminate pure knowledge, to illuminate the world through knowledge. Others have been like Saint Vincent de Paul, whose whole life was spent on feeding the poor and so forth. So one must not make the mistake of creating external criteria for determining what spirituality is.

One of the unfortunate occurrences in our times is that *spirituality* has become a very vague word. It is a new word in European languages. It was not used in its modern sense until the 19th century, although the term *spirituel* was used. In French, *spiritualité* began to be used by certain Catholic theologians in the 19th century, and then the term entered into English and other European languages like what one might call "wild-fire." Nowadays here in America everybody talks about it, and many people say, "We are not religious, but we are spiritual." That term has indeed become very fuzzy and ambiguous. For me, the term *spirituality* remains clear, as that which is related to the Spirit, to *Rūḥ* or *Spiritus*. When I edited the two-volume work *Islamic Spirituality*, as part of that colossal twenty-five-volume *Encyclopedia of World Spirituality*,[45] I spoke at the beginning of the work of what I mean by "spirituality." Also, with the other editors, we wrote a few pages on the subject, the statement being put together by Ewert Cousins, the general editor, but with input from the rest of us as to what constitutes spirituality—not necessarily the point of view from one religion, but in the most general sense. We could not come to complete accord, but we did agree to a large extent. "Spirituality" has become one of these nebulous terms, and one must be very careful how one uses it in our present-day context; but within the framework of my thought, I have made it very clear that spirituality is related to the term *Spiritus* in Latin and is like the term *rūḥaniyyat* in Persian, related to the word *Rūḥ* in Arabic or Persian, as the term *spiritual* is related to the word *Spirit*. Today unfortunately there is a great deal of confusion between the world of the Spirit and the world of the psyche. Many people consider psychological phenomena to be spiritual, which is not at all the case, and I think that this is a very dangerous confusion. One has to be much more succinct and rigorous linguistically and philosophically as to what one means by the word *spirituality*.

Part Five

Spirituality: Esoteric and Exoteric

R.J.: In your introduction to the two volumes of *Islamic Spirituality*, you explain that there are two dimensions to the meaning of *spirituality* as used in Islam. One, it is mentioned, is expressed by the word *rūḥaniyyah* in Arabic and *ma'nawiyyat*[1] in Persian, both of which deal with the nature of the spirit and inwardness as opposed to the outward aspect of things; and the other, *barakat*,[2] which evokes the grace of God. So, how do you think that the esoteric dimension relates to the exoteric aspect of spirituality?

S.H.N.: The way I look at it is that there is an element of spirituality even to the exoteric dimension of religion and also of virgin nature, because there is nothing in the world which by the very fact that it exists does not reflect the Source of all existence. The perfume of spirituality can be found everywhere, especially in sacred rites and institutions even of the outward kind; but when it comes to man's life, especially religious life, I identify spirituality more than anything else with the inward dimension, with the esoteric dimension of being. As I said, there is an element of spirituality even in the exoteric dimension of religion. When a person prays, whether he be Christian, Jewish, Buddhist, Muslim, Hindu, or follower of another religion, or does good works or helps the poor, there is a spiritual element that is present. There is no doubt about that fact, but the heart of spirituality I identify exactly with how we understand it in Persian, the word *ma'nawiyyat*. As you know, this word comes from the word *ma'nā*, and many of the great Sufi masters have juxtaposed the outward form, or *ṣūrat*[3] to the inner *ma'nā*. When the term *ṣūrat* is used in this sense, it is therefore not to be taken in the Aristotelian meaning of the term, but means the outward aspect of something, and *ma'nā* its inward aspect. So in this sense, *ma'nawiyyat* has to do with the inner aspect of things, with the inward, with the esoteric. I think that spirituality identifies itself primarily with the inward and also with the reflection of the inward dimension of reality in the outward. That is how I see it.

Eso- and Exoterism in Christianity

R.J.: According to you, what are the main barriers, social, political, cultural barriers and boundaries that we have to remove to facilitate the bridge between the exoteric and the esoteric?

S.H.N.: First of all, the relation between the esoteric and exoteric is not the same in every religion, nor are the barriers primarily social or political. The structures of religions are different: for example, in Christianity, which began as an esoteric religion. Christ said, "My kingdom is not of this world," and "Give unto Caesar what is Caesar's," in a sense disowning the world of politics and the outward dimension and saying that the kingdom of God is within you and not in the external world. In a sense, he was the prophet of inwardness. Even in Sufism, we look upon him as such. Later on, however, when Christianity became the religion of an empire, an event that the early Christians did not expect, the situation changed. The early Christians thought that the world was coming to an end any day. But, when Christianity became the religion of the Roman Empire and had to establish a social order, it had to develop for itself an exoteric dimension. It took over Roman Law, since Christianity did not have a *Sharī'ah* in the sense that we have in Islam, drawn from the Quran. It took Roman Law, Germanic law, and common law and created legal and social institutions on their basis. Even the early ecclesiastical institutions of the Christian Church such as the episcopates were based on the structures and organizations of the Roman Empire. So Christianity became a kind of eso-exoterism in which the esoteric and the exoteric became wed together, and they were not completely distinct except for such currents as Christian Hermeticism and Christian Kabbalah.

Eso- and Exoterism in Islam and Judaism

In Judaism and Islam, however, the two dimensions, as far as practice is concerned, have been always distinct. In Judaism there is Jewish Law, the *Halakhah*, and then there are the Kabbalah and Hassidism, the mystical dimensions of Judaism. In Islam we also have the *Sharī'ah*,

Divine Law, which represents the exoteric dimension of the religion, and then of course the *tariqat*,[4] the inward and spiritual path, which represents the inner esoteric aspect of the tradition and is incorporated mostly within Sufism, but also within Shi'ism. It is interesting to note that the situation of Shi'ism is somewhat similar to that of Christianity, although not exactly, in that you have a certain mixture of the esoteric and the exoteric dimensions. Some of the great Shi'ite *'ulamā'* were also mystics. We have had in fact many of them in the history of Shi'ism, and some of the general practices of Shi'ism have a mystical aspect, but by and large in Islam and Judaism, as far as practice is concerned, the two dimensions are distinct; but in Christianity they are fused together.

Exoteric Barriers and Esoterism

Now, when it comes to the life of the individual, it is not only necessary, but also absolutely essential that on the social level, on the level of human action, the barriers and conditions established by the exoteric dimension of the religion should not be transgressed, because not everyone can follow the path of esoterism, the inward or mystical path. Not everyone is made for that path, whereas everyone has to follow a social pattern, a social norm to live in this world and in traditional societies, to be guided therein by the teachings of religion. On the individual level, what is important is that those who are gifted, those who have the propensity and inclination towards the inner life, should have such a possibility accessible to them. In classical Islamic civilization, including in our own country, Iran, as in other places, this possibility has been always there. A person who was born into a Muslim family and brought up as a Muslim performed his prayers, fasted, went to Qom, Mashhad, Karbala', Madinah, and Makkah, making pilgrimages and so forth. Only a few, however, were attracted so much to the love of God and quest for Divine knowledge that they would embark upon a spiritual path in the sense of the *tariqat.* Such a person would become member of a Sufi order or look for *'erfan* in its Shi'ite sense. But the path was always open; the door was not closed.

What happened in Christianity, which is a great tragedy, I believe, for both Christianity and Western civilization, and in fact for the rest of the world, is that after the Renaissance, gradually a wall was created, and Western Christianity's inner dimension became more or less inaccessible and to a large extent eclipsed. It is not accidental that during the last two hundred years, or even three hundred years, Christianity has not produced figures such as a Meister Eckhart, Tauler, or Saint Bernard of Clairvaux, and we could go down the list of hundreds of earlier great saints and mystics. Why is it that today so many people of Christian background look to Buddhism, Islam, and Hinduism for the inner dimension of religion? The reason for it is precisely what happened to Christianity in the West in modern times. Coming back to your question, a barrier preventing access to the inward was created, a barrier that has to be removed as much as possible. But that is something that each religion must do for itself.

As far as I can see, for a person like myself who is a traditional philosopher and practices the spiritual life, it is important in the present-day context to draw attention to the significance of the inner dimension of religion or esoterism in the real sense of the term, and not as the occult. The esoteric is not the occult. You must not confuse authentic esoterism with the "salon occultism" of France. Authentic esoterism has to do with the inner dimension of an orthodox religion. One must emphasize especially its significance, its importance at this time. There are certain questions that only esoterism can answer, and if religion remains bound to only its exoteric dimension and becomes what we call *qeshri* (*qishrī*) in Persian, clinging only to the shell and neglecting the kernel, or the *lubb,* then there are certain questions that it cannot answer for its followers, and it faces the danger of disbelief in religion, which happened to a large degree in the modern West.

Some of the most intelligent people, not all of them, but a large number of the most intelligent people in the Western world, left the Church and Christianity in the 17th and the 18th centuries. Why did they not leave it in the 13th century, or why did not the same type of people in India leave Hinduism in the 18th century? Were the latter less intelligent? No. It is just that the need for certain answers ceased to be fulfilled for many people by latter-day Christianity in the West, whereas this was not the case of either Islam or Hinduism down to modern times. It is very important to point to this truth today. Within the Islamic world itself, there is at this time a type of reaction to the West in the form of tendency to a kind of *qeshri*, or purely outward response, which is oftentimes called "fundamentalism" or something like that. I do not like this term very much, but anyway, you know what I mean. The emphasis on the outward alone can lead to the same crisis for Islam that has been faced by Western Christianity, except in a different form. It is very important, therefore, for religion to keep alive the reality and the significance of esoterism for people who have the capability and need to understand the inner or esoteric dimension of the tradition.

RELIGION'S RESPONSE TO MODERNISM

R.J.: Well, in your book *Knowledge and the Sacred* you talk about the challenges which actually face the religions today, and you talk about the challenges of reductionism and historicism. So how can religions today face these challenges?

S.H.N.: When you say religions, this statement needs to be analyzed, because you have two different situations. Two religions, Christianity and Judaism, I mean Western Christianity and also Judaism in the West (for a long time much of Western Judaism has followed Christianity as far as its reaction to Western sciences and philosophies are concerned) have had several centuries of experience with all the problems that have resulted from modernism and secularism. In fact these anti-religious currents grew in the bosom of a civilization which was until then a Christian civilization. For the other religions of the world, all of these challenges came from the outside and much later. You might say that although secularism along with reductionism and historicism were opposed to traditional Christianity, these challenges did not come from outside of the society in which Christianity had flourished and which it dominated for many centuries, in fact for a millennium and a half.

So, I would respond to your question by saying that we have two different religious situations: one, within religions in the West, and the other, within those in the East. In the West, the great problem that was created for Christianity from the 17th century onward and even earlier during the Renaissance was that religion began to retreat from one domain after another in order to accommodate the forces of modernism and secularism. One can point to the Galileo trial, after which the Church "lost the cosmos." In fact, the Church was right in many ways, because what Galileo was saying did not concern astronomy alone, but also theology, which was quite something else. As a consequence of this trial, the Church withdrew from its concern with the sciences of nature and no longer challenged what kind of science was developed, and suffered the results of accepting the reductionism and materialistic views of modern science. This process resulted in the complete secularization of nature and the cosmos. Many Christians, Protestants, especially, went even so far as to say, "We should dominate nature for economic ends; to create wealth is a Christian activity." That is what much of Evangelicalism in this country is doing right now. Many Evangelicals claim that to get wealthy is a kind of blessing from God. Consequently, many

Christians in the West joined secularists in the destruction of nature, at least until quite recently, and few were even aware of that problem.

It is strange that the religion of Christ, who had only one robe and lived in poverty completely all of his life, should suddenly become wed to the making of money and the domination over nature, which is one of the characteristics of wherever the West has gone since the Protestant Reformation. As for Catholicism, it followed suit to a large degree afterwards. The main reason, in fact, that Northern Europe is richer than Southern Europe is precisely that in the Protestant countries, this tendency was more accentuated and started much earlier. Anyway, the religious and sacred conception of nature was given up in Europe after the 17th century. Now after three centuries, when we are about to destroy our natural habitat, you have all of these Catholic and Protestant theologians scrambling to create a theology of nature and to fill the hiatus of three-hundred-some years of neglect of the issue of the sacred character of nature.

Both reductionism and historicism, which came with secularism, accentuated this process. They helped to reduce nature to purely quantitative and material elements and meta-historical realities, which are essential for religions, to mere historical and temporal events.

In many other fields, such as philosophy, where humanism and rationalism and later existentialism, in fact all kinds of -isms began to dominate the scene, many theologians kept taking different defensive positions, being on the retreat and trying to accommodate whatever came along. For example, we first have socialism, and then we have certain Catholic priests who would be leftist socialists, ending with liberation theology in Brazil, Peru, and elsewhere. Existentialism would become popular and existentialist religious thinkers such as Gabriel Marcel would follow. The same is true of historicism followed by attempts of Christian theologians to study "the historical Jesus." This process could not but end finally in making religion marginalized and placed in a ghetto. I do not like to be impolite towards Christianity, and I respect all the religions of the world, but it was in fact a Catholic thinker whose name I have forgotten who once said that in the West, religion has become "ghettoized" like the old Jewish ghettos. It has been pushed into a social ghetto; it no longer concerns public life except in some cases indirectly. Now religion is making a comeback in the West and especially in America, because its absence has resulted in such a chaos in the world that takes pride in being secularized.

Today in the West and especially in America, religion is stronger among many "intellectuals" than it was in more recent history, to a large extent because of all the events that happened in the 20th century. This is true despite the recent rise of an aggressive atheism among some Western scientists and philosophers. If one is honest one can no longer blame religion for the most devastating wars in history, for what Hitler and Stalin and others like them have done, for the atomic bomb and the unbelievable massacres of the two World Wars. These wars were not fought in the name of religion. So religion is now making a comeback; but nevertheless it is still in a weak position in Western-educated circles, particularly in Europe. There were few religious intellectuals, even theologians in the Christian Church, until recently, who would hold their own ground and not bend backwards all the time in face of the onslaught of secularist thought. The challenge of secularist thought can, however, be confronted only by reasserting the perennial wisdom that resides at the heart of all traditional religions and not through surrender.

In the other religions of the world, the situation is very different. I will talk about only three of them: Hinduism, Buddhism, and Islam. As for Confucianism, which is of course a major religion with over a billion followers (at least on some level) in China and other Far Eastern countries, its situation is complicated by the fact that already in the 16th and 17th centuries it encountered through Jesuits certain modern Western ideas, and by the 19th century in China, many considered themselves both Confucians and in a sense Western-style rationalists. This constituted the background for the rise of Marxism in the 20th century in China. In any case, the situation of Confucianism is a complicated one, which we will put aside for the moment. We shall also put aside Taoism and Shintoism as examples of non-Western religions and take the three above-mentioned major religions. It is, however, very interesting to note that Chinese religions are having a major revival in China today.

The religions I have chosen to discuss here, that is, Hinduism, Buddhism, and Islam, have kept intact to some extent their intellectual and spiritual resources in the sense that in India today we still have the representatives of Shankaracharya teaching the Advaita Vedanta metaphysics as a living school; and both on the popular level of faith and on the metaphysical, intellectual level, the religion is very much alive despite the encroachment of modernism and secularism. The myths are alive. You have had modernism among certain classes, but not the demystification, demythologization, in the manner that we see in Bultmann and all the other similar religious thinkers in the West who tried to take religion out of myth and myth out of religion. The symbols of Hinduism are still alive, for both the masses and for the intelligentsia. The intellectual dimensions of Hinduism are still alive; and also the crucial element, the spiritual practices involving Kundalini, Tantra, Japa, and other forms of yoga, are still alive and accessible.

Now, this is also true for Buddhism and Islam. All these three religions have witnessed encroachments of modernism within them as within Hinduism where you have had modernist movements in India with such figures as Śri Aurobindo[5] and all of the other 20th-century modernists. Likewise, we have had in the Islamic world such figures as Jamal al-Din Asadabadi[6] and Muhammad 'Abduh[7] and more recently 'Ali Shari'ati,[8] who sought to intermingle all kinds of modern ideas with Islam, and in the case of Shari'ati, interpret religion as ideology. You have also had this type of phenomenon in Buddhism, especially in Japan. There is no doubt about that fact. But the intellectual and spiritual tradition and the popular understanding of myth, appreciation of the significance of myth, as well as practice of orthodox religious rites remain very much alive in these three religions, except perhaps in Japan, where the intellectual tradition and spiritual practices are well preserved, but the general practice of religion on the popular level has waned to some extent since the Second World War.

For this reason these religions are in a better situation than Christianity to confront the intellectual challenges of modernism, but they are also in a more difficult situation from another point of view. They are in a better situation because they have the intellectual means of responding. If I were in Tehran or Lahore now, or even here, when I write on a specific Islamic theme, for example, a response to some modern philosophical attack against religion, basing myself on the teachings of, let us say, Mullā Ṣadrā, my response would carry a greater resonance among the general educated public in Iran or Pakistan (not the man on the street—these matters are never solved on the street, anyway) than if a French author were to try to respond to some religious challenge in France by having recourse to Saint Bonaventure or even Saint Thomas Aquinas. The last place of refuge for a continuous tradition of traditional thought in Europe was as a matter of fact Thomism, but even that school has gradually weakened since the Vatican Council of 1964. So, these non-Western traditions have better means of responding to modern challenges because their intellectual traditions have been better preserved, as have inward methods of spiritual realization.

They are, however, in another sense in a more difficult situation than Christianity, because there are very few people among the followers of these religions who are very deeply rooted in them intellectually and who at the same time understand in depth the challenges coming from the West, challenges which keep coming like waves from the sea, one after another, from somewhere out there beyond the borders of the non-Western world. These intellectual challenges, in fact, come almost always from the West; they do not come from within the non-Western societies themselves. If you are a Protestant minister in Texas or a Catholic priest in Belgium when, let us say, structuralism or deconstructionism or other philosophical ideas or scientific challenges suddenly come upon the scene, you see them as a part of your own society. Works on these subjects are published in English or French, which you can read firsthand. You probably know some of the people who have written on these subjects; you might have common students. These ideas sort of percolate within the world in which you live. But if you are sitting in Benares, or Qom, or Kyoto, these new challenges are coming from somewhere else beyond your society.

Japan, of course, is somewhat of an exception because it has become so deeply Westernized, but even in Japan, the priests of, let us say, the Renzai school of Zen Buddhism or something like that are not in the middle of all these modernist circles in Japan where such ideas are circulating. Yes, some say that there are more people studying Kant in Japan than in Germany. I understand that, but that is a small segment of Japan implanted within the larger Japanese society. In any case, if we put the case of Japan aside as an exception, in the rest of Asia, the dominant religions are at a disadvantage in that they do not usually know these modern challenges firsthand and in-depth, and therefore often provide very shallow responses to them. Let me repeat that they are also at an advantage because they can draw from the resource of a living intellectual tradition where traditional symbols and doctrines are still alive.

Let me give you an example. If you speak of the symbolism of the Holy Grail in the West, of course literary scholars will understand you; but in the mass media, for the ordinary people, this is taken only in a metaphorical sense, not in a symbolic sense as when they used to say that to run the mile in four minutes was the "holy grail" of running, or something like that; but the real meaning of the Holy Grail is known only to very few. But in Persian, if you write of the *Simorgh*,[9] a much larger audience will understand it in the symbolic sense. The traditional symbols are still alive in these societies at large in a manner that they are not in the modern West.

There are nuances that must be considered at this particular moment of history concerning how the various religions can respond to the challenges you mentioned. I think that what is going to happen in the next century, if we are still around and we do not blow ourselves up or destroy ourselves with all that we are doing to the environment, what is going to happen is that in the Christian tradition a number of people will begin to go back to their authentic spiritual and especially intellectual traditions, and not to feel so weak and have such an inferiority complex *vis à vis* all the "-isms" that come one after another from the secular part of their society. In the other religions, I think more and more there will be people trained who will know these "-isms" in depth, more and more people whom you could call "Occidentalists" who will be able to provide in-depth understanding of these matters for other members of their society, especially those who happen to be theologians or philosophers.

Tradition[10]

R.J.: So are you saying that the answer or answers for humanity are going to come from the East, because they are the only societies which can revitalize tradition?
S.H.N.: I would add a qualifier to what you say, although the answer is "yes." I say qualifier because the tradition of the West, which has been eclipsed for the last few centuries, will also play an important role. That tradition, however, has to be brought back to life, and it cannot be brought back to life except with help from the living traditions of the East. This was what Guénon was trying to do and what Coomaraswamy and Schuon tried to achieve. They had the greatest respect for the Western tradition, and they wrote some of the most profound pages about the Greek intellectual tradition, as well as traditional Christianity, along with later Western philosophy, science, cosmology, poetry, you name it. I believe very much in what they sought to achieve and did achieve. They did not say that (and I agree with them completely) all the answers are to be found in the East alone, but all the answers are to be found in the *Sophia Perennis*, perennial philosophy, and tradition as they understood it, tradition that belongs to both East and West. But it is in the East that traditions have been better kept. It is true that although now they are attacked so strongly in many circles, year by year there is greater understanding of their message even in the West. Yes, in order for the West to bring back to life its own intellectual and spiritual traditions, I think that those still-living traditions of the East are of indispensable help.

What Is Tradition?

R.J.: I think we have to define *tradition.* How do you define tradition in opposition, and contradiction to, modernity?
S.H.N.: This is of course a vast subject.

R.J.: Yes it is.
S.H.N.: As mentioned above, I have written in my book *Knowledge and the Sacred* a whole chapter entitled "What is Tradition?" The word *tradition* of course comes from the Latin word *traditio.* In the Catholic Church, it means the accumulated teachings of the Church over the centuries, going back to the Apostolic Age. As we traditionalists use it today, however, it goes back to the sense given to it by René Guénon at the beginning of the 20th century precisely in order to distinguish what we call tradition from modernism. I prefer to use "modernism" rather than "modernity" because modernism is a kind of philosophy and worldview, therefore an "ism," although of course the two are related.

Let us then talk about tradition and modernism. As for tradition, I accept one hundred percent the definition given by Guénon and Schuon, whose understanding I have expounded explicitly in that chapter "What is Tradition?" As used by us, "tradition" means truths of sacred origin revealed originally, with the different nuances given to them in different traditional religions, all of which agree that it means truths coming from the spiritual domain, coming from God or from Ultimate Reality, speaking metaphysically, with their elaboration and transmission within a historical religious civilization.

So you have two elements in tradition. One is truths that are of a transcendent order in their origin, that came from the Divine, from God, through the illumination of the Buddha, the descent of the Avatars of Hinduism, the prophetic reception in the monotheistic religions, and so forth. This is the first element. Then there is the continuity of tradition, which always implies transmission, continuity and application of the principles of Divine Origin over the centuries within the particular civilization that the original revelation creates. That is what we mean by "tradition." Therefore, it does not only mean religion in the ordinary sense of the word. Religion is at the heart of it, but you have traditional art, traditional dress, traditional music, traditional architecture, traditional science, et cetera, all of which are created on the basis of an original set of metaphysical truths and principles. There is also revealed traditional law, which covers all aspects of life in a traditional society.

Modernism

Now, "tradition" in this sense is juxtaposed to "modernism." To be modernist is not the same as to be contemporary, as I said before. The two are not at all the same thing. We, that is, the traditionalists like myself, use the term "modernism" not in a vague way as characterizing just things that happen to be around today, but as a particular way of looking at the world, a worldview that began in the Renaissance in the West with such components as Renaissance humanism, rationalism, et cetera. As I have mentioned already, modernism rejects the primacy of absolute and ultimate truth transcending the human order and descending upon the human realm from the Divine Order. It places man himself at the center of the stage as "the absolute." In a sense it absolutizes the human being in his or her earthly reality. Usually it does not come out and say so explicitly, but that is what it really means; that is, it takes the absolute away from God and puts it on the human plane, and therefore makes human reason, human perceptions, human interests the criteria of reality, of knowledge, of the truth, of the goal of human life. Therefore, as a consequence it substitutes the significance of the temporal and the transient for the abiding and the eternal. Modernism, philosophically speaking, is in a sense the "worship" of time and the transient, a kind of deification of time and becoming and all that flows in the temporal order. That is why it resulted quickly in historicism and evolutionism and the theories all of those 19th-century philosophers such as Hegel and Marx and scientists such as Darwin. Such people are very different from one point of view, but they all in a sense divinize history even if Marx rejected the category of "divine." The historical process is the reality that is dominant in modern thought. It is that which determines values and even reality today in the dominant Western paradigm.

Tradition's Answer to Historicism

Many today say, "Oh, this is the decade of the nineties or the 21st century," meaning that what is happening in this particular moment of time is what matters and what determines the truth. It means that history determines what is real, what is beautiful, what is true, and so on. Then one arrives at a new decade, and the previous decade and its thought and fashion became irrelevant. This is the very opposite of the traditional perspective. The gaze of tradition rests upon the sacred both in its immutable aspect and in its manifestations. Tradition does not only deal with the ossified or petrified, as has been claimed by its opponents, but with an ever-living reality. Look at yourself; you are the same person since you were born. During these forty years of your life, all the cells of your body have changed, but you are still you, even though you are living in time and space. So it is with tradition. Tradition looks at a traditional civilization as a tree. The root of the tree is permanent and firm in the ground of revelation, but the branches grow in different seasons and in different directions. Tradition does not deny the fact that if you have a harsh and dry winter, the next spring you have fewer flowers and that if you have a winter with more agreeable conditions, you will have more flowers. I use this metaphor to point out that different external conditions can affect the way that the tradition manifests itself; but what is important is to remember that every point of that tree is related through the sap to the roots, and a pear tree remains a pear tree through all the stages of its existence.

Moreover, tradition embraces the whole of life in its different circumstances, and therefore is not even to be reduced to the category of the sacred as an opposite to what is now called the secular. From the point of view of tradition, what is called secular in contrast to sacred is ultimately unreal. For example, you cannot say that tradition concerns only what we call sacred, such as religious rites, but that the secular is a legitimate domain outside the circle of the concerns of the sacred. In a traditional civilization both of them are encompassed in a unity, and what we call the secular today is also governed by the sacred so that the category of secular does not really even apply.

Let us talk for a moment about India, which you know well. Put aside all these modern developments and look at traditional and classical India of two or three hundred years ago. What was secular in India then? If you bathed, it was *puja* according to Hinduism. If you ate, you shared your food with the gods. If you heard music, all music had a very profound spiritual content. Whatever you were singing, even a love song to your beloved, had a religious significance. Everything was contained within the tradition. It is in that sense that we understand tradition, and in the heart of tradition, of course, stands the sacred in its most exalted sense as well as metaphysics and traditional philosophy, which we call the perennial philosophy, that is, the set of perennial teachings concerning the nature of reality. That is the heart of it. Those are the principles. But the principles have been applied over the ages to different circumstances. As long as that tree is alive, in all kinds of different circumstances there are produced from it and are born from it many different flowers and fruits. For example, Buddhism went out of India to China and from China to Korea and Japan, and in each place it produced remarkable results in the form of philosophy, poetry, art, architecture, social structure, and many other creations which were not identical on the formal plane but were united in being based on the principles of Buddhism.

Descartes' Break from Tradition

R.J.: But how do you see the birth of modern thought as we see it, for example, in philosophers such as Descartes or later in Kant? I mean, Descartes also uses the symbolism of the tree of which metaphysics is the roots, and it produces branches of science and every other thing, and for him metaphysics is the basis of thought.

S.H.N.: First of all, you could never have a complete and sudden break with tradition psychologically, philosophically, or artistically. There is always something that remains of that from which you have broken away. Suppose a young man breaks with his father, does not want to see his father again, and goes against all of the father's values. Nevertheless, something of those values remains within him. With Descartes it is the same way. The psychology of Descartes is almost completely the repetition of the psychology of Saint Thomas Aquinas. Gilson and many others have brought out this fact. However, when Descartes speaks of metaphysics, it is not traditional metaphysics that he has in mind.

I am glad you brought up the name of Descartes, for he marks the point of break with the medieval tradition much more than did Renaissance philosophers. What Descartes did, although he made use of this traditional symbol of the tree and that the sciences grew out of metaphysics, is that he substituted rationalism based on human judgment for intellection. The dictum *cogito ergo sum* means "I think (*cogito*, *je pense*), therefore I am." The "I" and the "therefore" that comes from the "I" as ordinary human consciousness in this statement is the ultimate criterion that determines the truth and even being and existence. All knowledge for Descartes flows from this assertion, which implies actually the cutting off of what Descartes calls metaphysics from whatever transcends the individual "I." You know that Franz von Baader, the 19th-century German philosopher, wrote a rebuttal to Descartes and said that he should have said *cogito ergo Est,* that is, *je pense donc Il est*, I think therefore God is. Descartes, by asserting what he did, cut himself off from traditional metaphysics, from the perennial philosophy which considers the origins of metaphysics to be not the "I" that can doubt a transcendent reality, and then say that I think, and that I cannot doubt my thinking—but what Hindu metaphysics called *Ātman,* the Supreme Self, that is, what we would call the Divine Reality as well as the *Buddhi* or the Divine Intellect. It is this substitution of human reason for the Divine Intellect, and the individual "I" for the Supreme Self in Descartes that marks the beginning of modern philosophy and the break between, intellectually speaking, modernism and traditional philosophy.

The Waning of the Western Tradition (Preparing the Ground for Descartes)

R.J.: I do not say that it is necessary, but could it have been otherwise? I mean, the fact that the whole Aristotelian system was broken down by Copernicus and Galileo in scientific and cosmological terms, and that then caused modern philosophy to be brought forth later. I think that the view of the man of the Renaissance and the man of the 16th and 17th centuries in Western Europe was changing completely. So could it have been otherwise?

S.H.N.: If an authentic metaphysical tradition had been preserved in Europe, the situation could have been otherwise. You know, what happened in Europe is very interesting. Long before Copernicus and Galileo, already in the 14th century, you had the rise of nominalism. Already in the Middle Ages, what people such as Gilson have called Christian philosophy began to wane, began to weaken. This event itself also had a lot to do with the eclipse, and also the persecution by the Church, of many of the esoteric dimensions within Christianity. Many of them went underground; many of them were persecuted; the Templars were decimated and destroyed, and other esoteric schools which arose were for the most part scattered or extinguished. And so a kind of vacuum was left, which then in the Renaissance, when you had a return of Greco-Roman philosophy, was filled by non-Christian philosophies.

In the 15th century in the Academy of Florence, manuscripts coming from Byzantium of Greek philosophical texts began to be translated for the first time directly from Greek into Latin or vernacular European languages rather than from Arabic into Latin, as had happened in the Middle Ages. Some people tried to substitute what is called Renaissance Platonism for medieval Christian philosophy, but that was no longer for the most part in the context of the main religion of the West, which was Christianity. It was not like the Platonism of Saint Augustine. It was a reassertion of Greek philosophy outside of religion in the West, and it could not sustain itself for very long, and in turn became criticized because it did not have a traditional basis, and because there were so many diverse currents going on. You have Montaigne with his idea of skepticism, and the works of Sextus Empiricus and others like him, people who were not known in the Middle Ages, were translated for the first time. Systematic doubt and skepticism from the school of Greek skeptics became part of the scene, and the traditional philosophical scene was already shattered before Descartes. I do not, therefore, think that it is so much the scientific discoveries but discontinuity in the Western philosophical tradition due to these series of earlier events that is the main cause of the appearance of modern European philosophy with Descartes. Had an authentic metaphysics survived in the mainstream of European thought, even the scientific discoveries of the day could have been interpreted very differently and not have given rise to philosophical rationalism. It is interesting to note that mainstream Westerners' scholarship has not paid too much attention to this process, but it is important to do so.

Western Philosophy's Dependence on Astronomy

When the new astronomy of Copernicus and Galileo reached the other civilizations of the world, let us say the Islamic or Hindu civilizations, it did not at all have the same theological and philosophical impact. This is an important fact to consider. The reason is that in the West, the purely metaphysical teachings, which made use of cosmology as a support, but were not based upon it, were replaced by an Aristotelian philosophy that in a sense rested upon Aristotelian and Ptolemaic astronomy; and once those views of the planetary system were destroyed, the metaphysics and philosophy bound to them also collapsed. But it did not have to be necessarily so. I want to indicate a point about which I have already written.[11] One of the tasks that Sadr al-Din Shirazi (Mullā Ṣadrā), who was a contemporary of Descartes, achieved was to point out that motion—which is such an important category for any philosopher who has to explain change and becoming, every philosopher from Heraclitus to Aristotle and to the medieval philosophers—in fact does not depend upon the movement of the first sphere, as you have in Aristotelian philosophy; because then once you have a different astronomy, the whole philosophical system based on it also falls apart.

Mullā Ṣadrā explained change through the theory of substantial motion within the very stuff of the universe itself, what you call in

Persian *harakat-e jawhari.*[12] Mullā Ṣadrā severed the dependence of philosophy on astronomy. This is a remarkable achievement with crucial consequences, because for those people who were philosophers of his school, if they learned that according to Copernicus and Galileo the sun does not go around the earth, and the seven heavens function differently, that would not affect their philosophical explanation of the nature of reality. And so you have philosophers such as Sabzivari[13] or Aqa 'Ali Mudarris[14] who lived after Mullā Ṣadrā and who had heard about Galilean and Copernican astronomy through works that had reached Persia from Bombay and Istanbul. Yet, they did not disregard Ṣadrian philosophy. It is not that such people were ignorant; far from it. They were extremely intelligent and brilliant men. They were first-rate philosophers, first-rate thinkers, with unbelievably logical minds. Why was it that they did not throw away the whole of what you call the medieval philosophical tradition, as Europe did after Copernicus and Galileo? The reason is the loss in mainstream European thought of the symbolic vision of the universe and of an authentic metaphysics independent of cosmology.

There were not people in Europe, in the central intellectual arena and not somewhere in the periphery of intellectual life, who could say that this whole concentric vision of the universe, or what we call *poust-e piyazi* (*pūst-i piyāzī*), that is, "onion skin," with one layer over another, only symbolizes the states of being and does not define and determine these states. In reality the "great chain of being" does not depend for its reality on any cosmological scheme. Nor were there metaphysicians in the true sense to explain the symbolic significance of the heliocentric system which Copernicus proposed. Such a response did not come about except in movements which were defined as a sort of occultism and pushed aside by mainstream religion, as well as prevalent philosophies and the science of the day. Such movements were ostracized and ghettoized, gradually becoming irrelevant and going underground and withering away. That, I think, is the main reason.

The Primacy of Philosophy over Economics and Politics

R.J.: Yes, but one of the points that I rarely see in your writings is the social, economic, and political aspects of modern Europe. I think of the changes that were happening in the social and political structure of Western Europe during the 16th and 17th centuries, for example the formation of the modern state. This pushed forward these kinds of philosophies which were not present at the same time in the Islamic world, because we were not dealing with a modern state.

S.H.N.: To some extent, you are right. I do not usually deal with economic and political theories and similar issues. First of all, that is not my field. Secondly, philosophically, I do not accept the Marxist assertion, accepted sometimes unconsciously by even many anti-Marxists, that economic and social factors determine philosophy and thought. I believe that it is the other way around, although these factors are also important. It is ideas that then percolate into society and create institutions. I am not, of course, one who would deny that once you had the gradual rise of the mercantile class in Italy, then you not also had a different outlook from, let us say, the feudal aristocratic class of the Middle Ages. I am not denying that at all, but I believe that it usually works the other way around. For example, one can ask why there is a rise of modern states in Europe and not in China or in the Islamic world. When you try to answer that question, it always comes back to philosophical and theological reasons.

If you are a Marxist and claim, "Because the economic situation was different in these cases, the political and even philosophical results were different because economics determines everything," I would answer that that view is itself based on a philosophical perspective that I do not accept. In my own mind, I am able to explain in a way that logically satisfies me why the rise of states in the way you have in mind, states that encouraged these more secularist and rationalistic philosophies, took place in Europe and not elsewhere. This event had everything to do with the destruction in Europe of the balance of power between the papacy and the empire, what Dante had already written about, as seen already in the imprisonment of the popes at Avignon. The appearance of the anti-pope, the attempt of the royal class or the aristocracy to dominate over the Church and the clergy, already upset the balance of Christian European civilization. And these are not matters of economics or politics alone in the secularist sense of these terms but involve ideas and philosophical and theological concepts.

The Disruption of the Political Hierarchy

You know, the Hindus have a doctrine concerning the four *yugas* (ages) that has been discussed in many texts. We are living now in the *Kali Yuga*, the Dark Age, according to Hinduism. The four castes that they have are the Brahmins, the Kshatriyas, the Vaishyas, and the Shudras, which stand in a normal hierarchy in the way I mention them. The norm is that spiritual authority, associated with the Brahmins concerned with spiritual and religious matters, should dominate over those who are men of action concerned with the affairs of state. This caste in turn should dominate over those who are merchants and deal with business, and they should in turn dominate over those who are workers, who cultivate produce and who work to manufacture things. As the *Kali Yuga* advances and as one comes to the end of the Dark Age, gradually you have the rebellion of the Kshatriyas against the Brahmins and then the Vaishyas against the Kshatriyas and finally the Shudras against the Vaishyas. This doctrine has, you might say, a symbolic sense that is very profound and not limited to the Hindu caste system, and I am not at all the first to have noted that fact. Its inner meaning can be applied elsewhere. Professor Ruysbroeck-Hussey, who was an English historian, has written something about this as it pertains to European history, but most of all Guénon has written extensively about this matter.[15]

This rebellion of one caste against another happened in Europe in a way that did not happen anywhere else. First of all, the aristocracy rebelled against the papacy (corresponding to the Brahmins) in the 14th century in France. The aristocracy (Kshatriyas) had already destroyed the normal balance in European civilization and therefore was itself no longer in a position to play its normal role and became gradually weakened, until with the French Revolution, the bourgeoisie (or Vayshias) toppled the aristocracy, and decapitated the king and the queen in France. But it itself was then challenged by the proletariat (the Shudras) in the middle of the 19th century, and finally with the Russian Revolution, that phase of the domination of the proletariat over the bourgeoisie was realized.

Of course, in none of these cases was the older order completely destroyed. Always something of it remained. There is no doubt about that fact. It is interesting that we are now in the "post-national-state" phase in Europe, which is moving toward a union of some kind of a supra-national homogeneous political structure. We shall see what happens in the future. In any case, there is no doubt that these national states in Europe arose from the background of the Middle Ages, which was dominated by the Holy Roman Emperor and the Pope and the local kings, who were under the aegis of a higher authority, and therefore did not constitute state authority in the modern sense.

The fact that change came about in only Europe, however, has a deep theological and philosophical reason, which I consider to be central. As I said, I do not at all negate the significance of these other elements, especially the social and the economic reasons for the rise of a mercantile class with its mercantile mentality, which then facilitated the rise of secular philosophies. But let us not forget, for example, that in the Islamic world, long before the West, there existed a mercantile class that was much stronger in the Islamic world than it was in medieval Europe. When you look at the year 1000 in France or Italy, there was no place which had a bazaar like that of Isfahan or Cairo. There is no doubt about that fact, but the *bazaari* class of Islamic civilization played a very different role from the mercantile class in medieval Europe and was certainly not the proponent of secular philosophies. I think, therefore, that economic and political factors taken by themselves are not sufficient, and that you have to take all of the different elements together, especially the theological and the philosophical.

Harmony and Dichotomy between Spiritual and Temporal Authority

R.J.: Yes. I agree with you—but two points. One, first of all, I do not know if you agree with me or not, but I think it has to do with the essence of Christianity, especially with the political theory of Christianity and the theory of the two separate authorities that we do not have in Islam. In Islam, you can correct me, we have the temporal and the spiritual, which go together, and we have the *khalifah.*[16] In Christianity in the Middle Ages, we have the theory of the two separate authorities. We already have somehow the separation between Church and state that was instrumental in the secularization of political institutions and the rise of individualism. We do not have the same situation in Islam.

S.H.N.: I think that the point that you have made is a good one. Of course, for a long time, Christendom was able to hold the two together; however, the fact that they parted ways was due to the existence of this possibility within Christianity. But let us also recall that as I said already concerning the law, Christianity had to integrate Roman law, and later on, when it came to Northern Europe, Germanic and common Anglo-Saxon law, into its legal structure. So for Christians, the law of society did not emanate directly from the same source as the spiritual and moral laws of Christian society. The New Testament does not say anything about how you should sell merchandise in the bazaar, or rule; it deals with purely spiritual matters; and in the political realm, of course, there was this idea from the very beginning of "Give unto God what is God's and give unto Caesar what is Caesar's." In Western Christianity, which we are discussing now, since Eastern Christianity has a very different structure, there developed the papacy, which in a sense replaced the old imperial power of the Roman Empire with its center in Rome. This city now became the center of Catholic Christianity. To this day one speaks of the "Roman Catholic Church." The word "Roman" has remained, and the pope took for himself the title of "pontifex," which was also the title of the old Roman emperors, and some refer to him as the Roman pontiff, he being also the bishop of Rome.

So one might think that in a certain sense the papacy replaced the imperial functions of the emperor; yet the papacy did not claim any temporal power for itself. There was no pope who claimed to rule over the Christian world as a caliph ruled over the Islamic world. Catholicism accepted that no pope could ever become king. So, although from one point of view the papacy seems to have replaced the older temporal power, in a basic way it did not do so. It transformed that temporal power into purely spiritual authority, which was that of the popes who nevertheless wielded great political power indirectly. And then you had the Christian emperor. Constantine established the Holy Roman Empire in Constantinople, and later on, when the Eastern and Western churches separated from each other, there was the Holy Roman Empire in the West, which survived in a sense all the way to World War I, after which the remnant of the Holy Roman Empire ceased to exist.

So you always had this dichotomy in European history between spiritual and temporal authority, but as long as that hierarchy remained, a harmony was preserved. But that harmony began to be destroyed in the later Middle Ages, as we see already in the works of Dante, especially *De Monarchia*, written in 13th-century Italy. One already observes at this time this rivalry and contention between spiritual and temporal authority, which became more accentuated in later centuries. More and more wealth and political power came to be concentrated in the hands of the nobility, and the new mercantile classes and this inclination towards the breaking up of the original harmony and creation of contention between various political classes and various kings increased, and divisions came about. So you are right. I would agree with you that the fact that Christianity was not based on one, but in a sense two sources of power, one related to this world and one to the other world, was an important factor. The fact that there was a separation of spiritual and temporal authority or church and state, not in the modern American sense, but at least in the theological sense, I think contributed to the possibility of the secularization of the public realm more easily in the West than in other civilizations, although in the Middle Ages the temporal order was also

Christianized and sacralized, as we see in the theory of the Divine Right of kings.

Muslim and Renaissance Interpretations of Greek Political Philosophy

R.J.: My second point had to do with the readings by Muslim philosophers and Christian philosophers of Greek and Roman writings. I suppose that you can correct me on that point too. I suppose that there have been two different readings; I mean the difference between the readings that were carried out in Islam and Islamic civilization of Aristotle, Plato, and Plotinus, and the ones that have been done by Christian authors. One of the points which I feel myself to be important is that most of the Muslim philosophers and metaphysicians do not place too much importance on the political philosophy of the Greeks and democracy in ancient Greece in the fifth century B.C. They give importance to Plato's and Aristotle's politics, but not to what happened in the fifth century. During the Renaissance and during the 16th, 17th, and 18th centuries in Europe, the reading they are carrying out of the Greeks had to do mostly with the revival of the ideas of Greek democracy or Roman Republicanism against the Middle Ages, as we see, for example, in the case of Machiavelli.

S.H.N.: This is a very complicated question. First of all, you can compare how the Muslims understood Greek political thought with how medieval Christianity understood it, and then you can also compare how the Muslims understood Greek philosophical thought with how the Renaissance and the 17th and 18th centuries understood it. These are two very different questions. Let me just turn to the second question. Of course Machiavelli was not interested in democracy. He was interested in pure power, he, Hobbes, and many others. But in any case, there is no doubt that in the Renaissance and the 17th century many people were reading Greek political ideas with the aim of strengthening their ideas of humanism and individualism, which are characteristic of the mode of thought that came into vogue in the Renaissance. Therefore, they, like later Western admirers of Greek political practices, talked, for example, about Greek democracy, but few mentioned the fact that Greek democracy was based upon slavery of a very intense kind, and that democracy was only just for a few people. Few spoke about that part of it, but they wanted to emphasize the idea of individual freedom while aggrandizing the Greeks.

It is also quite interesting to note that Greek philosophical ideas on politics were based on the experience of a state that was also a city. That is why both the word for politics and the force of authority to keep order in the city in French and English come from the Greek word *polis.* In contrast, of course, the experience of Muslims was of a vast world. The concrete experience of the city-state was irrelevant for them as basis for their political experience. Muslims thought in terms of the vast Islamic caliphate, whereas in Greek democracy one is talking about the small city-state such as Athens. Even other Greek cities such as Sparta were usually excluded from the discussion of Greek democracy. This identification of the reality of political life with the city was also something that appealed to the people in the Renaissance. They could identify themselves with such a type of political experience, especially in Italy, whereas Muslims saw the politics based on just a city as a kind of epiphenomenon compared to all that they were experiencing in the political world of Islam, stretching from Spain to China.

Nevertheless, Muslims *were* interested especially in the political ideas of Plato, if not so much of Aristotle. The book on politics by Aristotle was not known in Arabic, whereas his ethical works were very well known, especially his *Nichomachean Ethics*, which was very famous among Muslims. It was the *Republic* and *The Laws* of Plato that formed the foundation for political philosophy of people such as Fārābī as seen in his *On the Perfect State*[17] and all the way down to Ibn Rushd and other people farther down the road. There is also another very important point to consider, and that is that most Islamic political thinkers believed that they already had their own political philosophy drawn from the Quran and the teachings and practices of the Prophet. A type of political thought was developed by people such as Ghazzālī and al-Māwardī[18] that was not based on Greek ideas of the city-state, but on the idea of having a ruler who was the "prophet-king," like the philosopher king of Plato but ruling over a vast world, a person who was both ruler of this world and guardian of religion. This vision was based on what the prophets represented, not only the Prophet of Islam, but also Solomon and David and before them Moses: the monotheistic prophets, except for Christ, who did not have the function of ruling over this world.

Therefore, there are definitely differences in the reading of Greek texts, but these differences in the reading of Greek philosophical texts have to be understood in depth. As for Roman republicanism, Muslim thinkers hardly dealt with Roman sources on politics. I think that Islamic political thought is very rich. Many of the later sources have not as yet been examined, but even Islamic political philosophy cultivated by the Islamic philosophers rather than the jurists or theologians is certainly not simply a regurgitation of Greek political thought. What is interesting in Islamic political thought is the transformation that Muslim thinkers such as Fārābī sought to bring about in Greek political thought. In this context one must also mention Abu'l-Hasan al-'Amiri,[19] another great philosopher who hailed from Khorasan and who was the most important figure between Fārābī and Ibn Sīnā on the philosophical scene. The transformation they tried to bring about concerns the Platonic idea of the perfect city and the perfect ruler, but seen in the context of Islamic society. In the case of al-'Āmirī, attention is also paid to pre-Islamic Persian ideas. One can compare also that masterpiece of Fārābī *On a Perfect State* (*al-Madīnat al-fāḍilah*) with, let us say, *The City of God* of Saint Augustine, who also tried to make use of Greek political ideas in defining what the virtuous city was in Christian terms.

I think in fact that it is much more fecund from a scholarly point of view to compare the Islamic political philosophers' understanding of Greek political thought with that of figures such as Saint Augustine and Saint Thomas than with thinkers during and after the Renaissance. The method of these post-medieval thinkers in the West was for the most part selective. They chose certain elements of Greek political thought that suited their political agenda and interpreted them in a secular manner. That is why, for example, such people as Machiavelli and Hobbes were in fact opposed or indifferent to basic metaphysical elements of Greek political thought.

The Value of Tradition and the Critique of Modernism

R.J.: Going back to this idea, I mean, the contradiction, opposition, between modernism and tradition, what are the points that you think might be useful in traditional metaphysics for modernism?
S.H.N.: For modernism?

R.J.: I mean for modern civilization.
S.H.N.: Oh, that is something else, because modernism as a philosophy stands opposed to traditional metaphysics. Before everything it must be remembered that tradition is "useful" in the most profound sense of this term because it expounds the truth, and truth is truth, and to expound it is ultimately the most useful thing. Truth is like the sun. To state the truth is to state the real, for ultimately the truth and the real are the

same. I think that, because they are concerned with the real, all the elements of traditional metaphysics are very useful, but especially certain elements that are crucial for our present-day situation. First of all, there is need for an in-depth critique of modernism and the whole modern experiment that traditional teachings can provide. Many people even in the West have in fact been trying to carry out this criticism since Spengler wrote his famous book *The Decline of the West.*

During the last seventy years, many Western thinkers, from poets such as T. S. Eliot to philosophers and sociologists, have tried to write critiques of the modern West and of modernism, because they have observed and studied the experiences of the last few centuries and have realized that the modernist experiment has produced many things, but it has also landed humanity in unbelievable difficulties, and now has forced us to confront almost irremediable catastrophes. There is no doubt about this matter. You do not have to be a prophet to see that one of the first important and significant "uses," you might say, of traditional metaphysics is to provide the principles with which we can carry out this critique. Traditional metaphysics provides us with a view based upon thousands of years of human existence, upon how mankind has experienced the world, upon the wisdom of the ages which the greatest sages of the world have expounded, and it reveals the ways in which men have been able to live for a long time in happiness and harmony with themselves and with the natural environment. Tradition alone can provide us a sure guide for carrying out this critique.

Alternative Paradigm

Furthermore, this metaphysical worldview is able to provide an alternative paradigm to the paradigm that has been dominant for the past few centuries in the West, and with whose replacement many people are now struggling. Many know that the modern paradigm is falling apart, and they are therefore trying to create a new paradigm. In this endeavor some among them are turning to various traditional teachings. Many among them are not really traditionalists, but they choose a bit here from Hinduism, a little there from Buddhism, a little from Islam, a little from Taoism and God knows from where else, and then try to create some kind of a new paradigm. That kind of eclecticism, however, will never work. I think that the only paradigm that can replace this modernistic paradigm is an application to our contemporary situation of the perennial philosophy, the creation of a paradigm that goes back to eternal wisdom. This paradigm is not going to be identical in its expression with the various traditional formulations of the perennial philosophy. You have to deal with the modern social sciences, the modern natural sciences, the environmental crisis, this, that, a thousand new factors, but the principles and the total vision will be the same. I think that these are the two most fundamental elements, which are crucial, immediate, and urgently useful.

Psychology

There are also many other issues that need to be considered, for example, the whole question of the crisis in the way the human psyche is being studied in various schools of modern psychology. After the debacle of Freudianism and the realization of the limitations of the ultimately agnostic views of Jung, there is now a frantic effort on behalf of many psychologists to try to create a psychology which would not encounter all of the problems and the dead ends that psychoanalysis and other modern schools of psychotherapy and psychology have faced. Again, people here and there are now turning to the Sufi, Hindu, or Buddhist psychotherapy. Tradition alone can provide a whole and holistic science of the soul, which is urgently needed.

Philosophy of Nature

This also holds true for the field of the sciences of nature about which I have written a great deal. Only traditional metaphysics can provide an authentic philosophy of nature on the basis of which we can then try to solve the problems posed by modern science and its applications and the looming environmental crisis. Many seek to have recourse to better engineering, to what I call cosmetics, to solve the environmental crisis; but what we need is a change of view as to what the meaning of nature is, what our responsibilities towards nature are. And where are we going to obtain this "new" vision? Many people realize that they cannot obtain it from currently prevalent ideas in the West itself. So some turn to the American Indians or the native people of Australia and point out how wonderfully they lived in harmony with nature, for as we know, such people have lived for thousands of years in harmony with their environment and have developed wonderful philosophies of nature, to use our categories of thought, based on the profound harmony between man and nature. Yet others turn to other traditional cultures. That is exactly what we are talking about. For almost fifty years I have been trying to resuscitate the traditional philosophy of nature, which alone, I believe, can help people in the West to resuscitate their own philosophy of nature in such a way that we do not destroy ourselves and the natural environment around us. This is a very crucial and urgent matter, for we have very little time.

Controlling Technology

R.J.: Yes. I mean, which way can the traditional metaphysical view help us to control technology and the technologically based culture of today?

S.H.N.: Modern technology is the consequence of a particular view of nature and of man. Once we change our view as to what constitutes the human state and nature and bring back the traditional idea of man and nature as sacred, matters will begin to change. Let me give a shocking example. If you have a sister in your house, you do not rape her every morning if you are a normal human being, because you have respect for her and she is your sister. You have a human relationship with her. But it is the rape of nature that the modern world commits every day through its intrusive technology.

Once the awareness comes of what really nature is, that nature is not just an "it," that it is a living reality and has a sacred content, that it has an inner relation with us, with our own inner being, with what we are, then we will begin to respect her and not just rape her to satiate our never-ending thirst for power and wealth. We cannot destroy nature without destroying ourselves. Once that change of vision comes about, as a result of the change in our understanding of who we are, what nature is, and how we are related to nature, then the technology to dominate over her will also begin to change. We cannot any longer go on with the Renaissance and 17th-century definition of earthly man as the measure of all things, and as possessing the absolute right to dominate and destroy the world of nature, considered as simply resource, inert matter, and a vast mechanism. We have to go back to views expressed so profoundly in so many traditions, to what in the Chinese tradition is called the anthropocosmic view, based on an organic view of the relation between the human and the cosmos. We have its equivalent in Islam and in Hinduism. These are all subjects about which I have written extensively.[20]

Once we go back to the traditional view of man and nature, the question of the control of technology will be solved, but not before. Right now, we control technology only when our life is immediately threatened. For example, authorities do not allow people to drive more than sixty-five miles an hour on most roads, because it is seen to be dangerous. They do not allow the making of cars that can go two hundred miles an hour, because they know that ordinary people are not racecar drivers. But this kind of control is not at all sufficient. Our attitude is still to keep applying technology as much as we can to make money, to gain power, to become more dominant while thinking that we are going to become more comfortable and happy and extend human life. Much of this way of seeing things is daydreaming. Meanwhile, we are cutting into the whole structure and fiber of nature. The critique of technology on the external level is good and important, but the real critique must deal with the roots of the problem. We must reexamine our attitude towards nature, and ask again both who we are, what our real and not imagined needs are, and what nature is. Once that transformation comes about, I think the rest will follow suit.

The Environmental Crisis

R.J.: I understand that we can do that at the individual level, but how can you do that at the public level? It is so difficult in today's world.
S.H.N.: Yes, it is. I will make two comments about this matter. First of all, the journey of a thousand miles begins with a single step, as the Chinese saying goes. We have to take whatever step we can, and we cannot give ourselves the privilege of saying, "Well, since nothing can be done, I will not change anything in my life." The fact remains that we are in a very difficult and even critical situation in the world. Even if we can change one mind, it is important, because one can never guess what is going to happen. Somebody made a calculation once that if we just change the mind of one person towards this matter today, and he or she changes the mind of the next person the next day and so on, within just a period of a few decades, most people in the world will have a different attitude towards nature. Yes, it is a very difficult situation, and I agree with you on this point, but I think that those who can see the reality of the situation have to talk about it and write about it. That is my own view. Whether this will have a major effect or not, only God knows, but I think that it will have some effect. Even one person changing his or her way of thinking and acting can have an effect. I still have hope, but I see a major catastrophe lurking before us. Unfortunately, probably nothing is going to awaken people *en masse* without a major catastrophe.

R J: What kind of catastrophe? Nuclear catastrophe?

S.H.N.: Not necessarily. I mean the consequences of global warming or something like what happened in Bhopal, but on a larger scale. That event, which cost several thousand lives, was, however, in India, and few in the West cared. What would make people take notice would be if, God forbid, many thousand people suddenly died in the West as a result of an industrial accident or as a result of sudden climactic changes caused by human action. You know that in Chernobyl they said first that three people had died, then thirty-eight people; yesterday it was in the paper that 1 million people are going to die in the long run from that one accident. But since these deaths are stretched out, nobody changes his lifestyle as a result of it. Unfortunately, you need to have a bell that will wake people up at the present moment, when most people continue to talk about economic growth, globalization, et cetera, and sweep all the problems under the carpet.

Few governments want to act seriously on the problem of global warming, on the depletion of resources, and the destruction of the species and ecosystems. It is unbelievable, but just in the time that we have spent talking together, several of the species on earth have disappeared. Few in the mainstream want to talk about this mass ecocide that cannot but lead to suicide, there being some honorable exceptions. I think that a change will only happen if a major catastrophe, industrial catastrophe, or environmental catastrophe takes place. I do not mean a nuclear bomb; that is something else.

Apologists for modernism would say, "Nuclear disaster would result from a war; so let us not fight each other. Let us live in peace." In fact, peace as conceived today is in a sense more dangerous than war for the first time in history. What I am saying may appear strange, but consider the fact that if you had a war and millions of people died or something like that, the rest of the people of the world, and especially of the West, which is the main driving force for the spread of technology, would learn a lesson, and change their ways in order to survive; whereas, in present-day conditions, we use atomic energy with its radiation-causing problems which are unforeseeable, and we are constantly destroying nature and causing global warming while living "at peace." A little accident occurs in Japan and two people die. We become scared for a few days, but then everybody goes back to doing what they were doing before. The perceived threat is not great enough in a concrete way to make people change their manner of living. The tempo of our suicide is too slow for most people to take notice.

So, I am not optimistic that through lecturing or writing alone, gradually the necessary change will take place. I have been at this task for some fifty years. A lot of people are more interested in the environment now than when I began to speak as a lonely voice in the desert five decades ago. I gave a series of lectures at the University of Chicago in 1966 called "The Encounter of Man and Nature," which came out in a book called *Man and Nature*,[21] in which I predicted the environmental crisis, and I said then that its cause is primarily spiritual. At that time, my work was strongly criticized, especially by Christian philosophers and theologians in England. They said, "Who is this man from the Middle East telling us what to do?" and they were unhappy about it. Now, a generation has passed. Nearly every serious Christian theologian is interested in this issue. It has been and is being talked about in churches, in schools, and gradually younger generations are becoming much more sensitive.

And yet that alone is not going to replace this vast industrial complex that is based on wealth and power and that devours the resources of the world. I think, however, that if gradually the ambience changes and at the same time there is a jolt to wake people up, there might be some hope. Otherwise, we are just going to experience a slow death. Look at what is happening to the oceans. Already, as you know, the coral reefs of Australia, which are among the most beautiful in the world, are dying. The French oceanographer Jacques Cousteau wrote so much about this issue. He did a great deal to make people realize that even the oceans are not safe. We are killing the oceans along with life on land.

R.J.: Actually, I am very pessimistic, because I see exactly the opposite, because I see people having more and more greed in the West and in the East . . .
S.H.N.: That is right.

R.J.: People not paying attention as long as they have their Coca-Cola and their McDonald's and jeans, and even when I travel to India and back to Iran or countries in the Middle East, I see that people just want to continue to emulate what is going on in the West.
S.H.N.: You are right, and I could not disagree with you at all on this point. Those are all the trends that are going on, and they are parts of the generally negative currents prevalent today. As I have said, I am certainly not optimistic, but there is this other trend of becoming more aware of the dangers to the natural environment that is also going on, and this is happening more in countries that are also most responsible

for the destruction of the world of nature. It is interesting to note that the movement to create environmental awareness began first in America and then in Europe. You know that in Europe there are now Green parties. A lot of former communists became Greens. Forty years ago, except for Scandinavia, who in Europe was interested in environmental issues? Practically nobody. The United States, which is the most destructive nation of the world, environmentally speaking, in relation to its population, is also where the environmental movement began, although no Green parties developed politically in this country such as we see in Europe today, except perhaps the movement of Ralph Nader, which has not had much political impact. Let me add that now many mainstream politicians in America such as Al Gore are speaking about the environmental crisis, but few speak seriously of the sacrifices that have to be made, of the changes in lifestyle that have to take place.

R.J.: Why? Because they are more Puritan?

S.H.N.: It is not clear what you mean by Puritan, because Puritanism was based on a very disciplined life. As you say in Persian, you have to find the cure for a snakebite from the poison of the serpent itself. Because here in America the devastation of nature is so vast, and virgin nature had remained so well preserved until the last century, many people there are more aware of the destruction of nature than in most other countries and lament the loss of so much beauty. Europe destroyed most of its great forests several centuries ago. They in fact cut down many wooded areas a thousand years ago, whereas here in America, you are standing one day in a beautiful forest and the next day it is gone. The same could be said about pristine rivers polluted completely in just a few short years. So from the late sixties on, the environmental movement began here in America. The so-called hippie movement, which was very much interested in the natural environment, was too undisciplined to really get anywhere. It did not succeed as a political movement, but an element that involved the natural environment and was emphasized by them became without doubt stronger from day to day. Of course most Americans are not right now helping people in Sumatra not to drink Coca-Cola or not to pollute their rivers, but many are concerned at least with these issues as they concern thousands of people at home. I might also add that, although the environmental movement began in America, today it is stronger in Europe and meets less opposition than in the United States.

There is no doubt that the so-called Third World is, in a sense, in a worse situation than the industrialized world, because it is trying to just simply pick up the bread crumbs from the table of the industrial world, which is exporting to a large extent its leftovers to the Third World, and that in the present situation it is going to aggravate the environmental crisis much more in that world than in the West itself. Whatever happens to the Third World, however, is not going to change the situation in the West. What needs to take place as a warning is something that happens not in Bhopal, but in a place like Detroit. Then there would be a change of attitude; thousands of laws would be passed to protect the environment, and these laws would be seriously implemented rather than passing laws mostly with economic and social factors in mind. Only a major catastrophe would be able to bring about the needed change in the short time we have. The Western industrial complex would not change even if millions of people perished in Africa or India or some other faraway place. The population of the earth increases by millions every month, and such losses would be seen as a little drop in the ocean. But if something serious were to occur in the West, then that would turn upside down the currently held vision of Western people with regard to the impact of modern technology on nature. It would be something that would wake them up and perhaps help to stop this really suicidal course that modern civilization is currently pursuing and that the rest of the world is trying to follow.

The Sacred[22]

R.J.: Yes, and that brings us, to finish this part of our conversation, to the concept of the sacred, which is so important for you because it appears in many of your writings, as a title or as a chapter such as *Knowledge and the Sacred* and *The Need for a Sacred Science.* You mention the sacred every time in your writings, and I believe that it has to do with the fact—mainly the fact, not just because you are trying to talk about traditional metaphysics—that life is more desacralized in today's world. So, this is why you bring up so much the concept of the sacred. In which sense do you think that tradition is related to the sacred?

S.H.N.: Let me make a comment why I use this category so much. First of all, of course I have used other categories, but I believe that this very word, the word *sacred*, the Latin *sacra*, *le sacré* in French, *Die heilige* in German, all these are words that still resonate very deeply within the soul of the readers and speakers of these languages. They are living words. One of the greatest German philosophers of religion, Rudolf Otto, wrote a famous book called *Die Heilige* ("The Idea of the Holy"), which has been translated and is very well known in English and some other languages. In fact a lot of theologians in the West have tried to defend religion by taking refuge in this bastion of the sacred. I found through my experience of both teaching and lecturing in the West, and of course before that, studying in the West, how important this category is when you speak English. For example, in our mutual mother tongue, we are speaking Persian, we do not speak constantly about *qidasat*, *qoddous*, *qodsi*,[23] and so forth. We use such terms only once in a while, although recently their usage has increased to some extent. We use other terms and do not need to use the term *sacred* often, but in English and other European languages, I believe that the usage of this term is very important, and in fact it is used often. I am not the only person to employ it, but I have made it central to the language of my discourse.

What Is the Sacred?

Now, to the question you asked, what is the sacred? The sacred is the Divine Reality as it is in Itself and as It manifests Itself in beings in this world. So there are things that are sacred and then ultimately there is the "Sacred" as such with a capital "S." It is very interesting that in Islam, one of the names of God is *al-Quddūs*, which would be the equivalent of *Die Heilige.* God is *the* Sacred, and then there are things in this world that are sacred because of their relation to the Sacred. For example, we call Jerusalem *Bayt al-Moqaddas* or *Qods* (both using the word *sacred* in Arabic), and we refer to Christian saints as *qiddīs* in Persian and Arabic and many other words related to these forms. It is also used poetically in Persian as in the verse *ta'ir-e 'ālam-e qodsam* by Ḥāfiẓ, which means "I am in flight in the sacred world." In any case, the term *qods* and related words form a rich cluster in our mystical and religious vocabulary, although not used as often as in English, while such terms deeply impregnated with spiritual significance do remain in our own vocabulary. I use the term *sacred* in English in such a way that it pertains both to the very reality of God, as when you say *al-Quddūs* in the Quran, that is *the* Sacred as such, and to things that come from Him and are thereby sacralized such as *ta'ir-e 'ālam-e qods* or *amr-e qodsi*,[24] which we now use in Persian.

I feel that at the present moment in the history of the West, in order to resuscitate a sense of awareness of the spiritual world and of Ultimate Reality, the word *sacred* is seminal. The word *spiritual* has become too diffused. The word *spirit*, which is of course very important, has become confused, as I have already mentioned, with the psyche, and it is used in so many different ways that for numerous people it has lost its original meaning; but the word *sacred* has fortunately preserved its meaning more or less intact. Needless to say, sometimes it is used metaphorically, as when one says, "This matter is sacred to me." For example, "Visiting my close friend every Sunday morning is a sacred duty for me." That is a metaphorical usage of the term; but the way I use it is in its metaphysical sense, that is, that which pertains to the very Reality of God, the Eternal, the Immutable, and the manifestations and theophanies of this Divine Reality in certain beings and entities in this world.

Tradition and the Sacred

As for your question about the relationship between tradition and the sacred, the answer is that the relationship is extremely profound. Tradition is always sacred tradition. There is no man-made tradition, by our definition. Today, of course, in English the word *tradition* is used in the ordinary sense as "custom" or "habit." Supposing for five years you go to France for holidays every summer; then you say, "It has become a tradition for me to go to France every year." Of course, that is nothing more than habit or custom. But the way we use it, going back all the way to Guénon, Coomaraswamy, and Schuon, these seminal figures of the traditional school, is such that tradition by definition is sacred. The sacred is, however, different from tradition in its conceptualization in that tradition implies taking the sacred and transmitting it and applying it and making it visible and palpable through different channels and different means; while the sacred is the spiritual presence and reality that tradition transmits. So the two are really inseparable from each other.

In the same way that tradition is opposed to modernism and modernity as we use these terms, the sacred is opposed not only to the profane in the older sense of the term, but of course to the desacralization and secularization that characterize our world. It would not have been so necessary to use the category of sacred so often as you said yourself if the world had not become so secularized and desacralized. That is why, for example, in Persian we do not use the word *qoddous* so much, since this sacredness in the traditional culture has not been as yet taken away from everything so completely. But now that we live in a desacralized world, especially the secularized world in the West, it is very important to reassert the category of the sacred. We must try for spiritual reasons to cling to the sacred, which we find first and foremost in revelation, in the sacred rites of various religions, in initiatic and spiritual practices, especially in inward practices, in sacred art, in virgin nature, and, of course, in theophanies such as the Quran whose very form is sacred for us Muslims as the icon is sacred for Christians and the Buddha image for Buddhists. All these realities that emanate a kind of Divine Presence by their very existence are sacred.

Nature as Sacred

The sacred is a very fecund and living religious and spiritual category. For example, I have been trying to talk over the years about the revival of the spiritual understanding of nature, and one of the key terms that I have to use is precisely the sacred. If a Western person were to look at a tree as sacred with the same sense of reverence (because the sacred, as Otto said, always creates in us a sense of awe and reverence) as would a native American, he would not cut forests so easily. If a Christian were to look at a tree with the same sense of reverence as he does the cross in his church, his attitude to nature would change completely. Let us not forget that here in America, over 52 percent of the people go to church every Sunday, unlike most of Europe, where the practice of Christianity has become curtailed to a large extent in recent decades. The reason modern man does destroy nature with such impunity is that he looks upon it as a mere economic resource. Once he is finished with it, he throws it away like paper in the wastepaper basket. To change that attitude, we have to bring back the sense of the sacred in nature.

Science and the Sacred

Take a look at all this discussion that is taking place right now even by agnostic scientists about life, and especially human life, being sacred, and whether it is necessary to respect life. This whole way of thinking is of course logically meaningless from the point of view of modern science, and is, scientifically speaking, nothing but emotionalism and sentimentality. The category of the sacred of course does not have any meaning within the framework of modern science, and yet the meaning is there for the general culture. Even Einstein said that he had a feeling of the sacred when he looked at the universe, even if that was for him only sentimental.

From our point of view, however, the sacred is not at all the result of sentiments. It is part of the reality of things. In fact, to say reality in the metaphysical sense is to say sacred. It was to bring out this point that I wrote the book *The Need for a Sacred Science.* That was a very challenging title. I used it on purpose because as modern science developed in the West, the very term *science* became more and more narrowly defined, to the extent that even now as we sit here, the word *science* in English has a narrower meaning than the word *science* in French or *Wissenschaft* in German. For example, you have a department in the Sorbonne called *Sciences morales.* In English, *moral sciences* does not have the same significance. Science is reduced in English to the mathematical and natural sciences, to quantitative sciences, and only by extension to what we call the social sciences. The idea of sacred science thus appears as a kind of oxymoron in the minds of many people who ask, how can we have a science that is sacred? But this is exactly what I believe the West needs. The reassertion of the category of sacred science is today a necessity. Science does not have to be only a profane study of nature. One can study nature with exactitude and logically, but from the point of view of the sacred. As you can imagine, my book met with a lot of opposition from rationalistic and scientific quarters.

Knowledge and the Sacred

R.J.: That is why you disagree with Otto and assert that the sacred is not just irrational; hence the title *Knowledge and the Sacred.*

S.H.N.: That is right. I wanted also, in a sense, to respond to Otto and others like him and to confront the claim of rationalism. This brings us back to the point that I mentioned. In the West, many Christian theologians who are not able really to confront the assault of rationalism try to think about religion and even theology outside of the domain of reason, whereas I believe that this should not be the case. Of course, ordinary human reason has to bow before the majesty of the Sacred, for as Jalal al-Din Rumi has said: *Ziraki befrousho hayrani bekhar* (sell cunning reason and buy bewilderment). Here he is speaking of the partial intellect (*'aql-e jozʼī*), which is reason, and not the intellect, and does not mean that knowledge does not flow from the sacred, the intellect being the light of the sacred shining upon our minds. It is the intellect that illuminates the mind, illuminates reason. This brings up the whole question of traditional epistemology, which I have expounded elsewhere,[25] along with the relationship between reason and intellect. The differentiation of *'aql-e kollī* and *'aql-e joz'i* constitutes one of the main themes of the *Mathnawi.* This most notable work of Persian Sufi poetry deals in the profoundest and subtlest way with the important question of epistemology in the context of the sacred.

The Multiplicity of Religions

R.J.: Here is my last question because you are tired. In the same book, *Knowledge and the Sacred*, I saw one of your phrases, which is very important. I think you say that "The multiplicity of sacred forms has been used as an excuse to reject all sacred forms."

S.H.N.: Yes, of course. Since the 18th century, many of the secularists, rationalistic, and especially agnostic and atheistic philosophers of Europe have taken recourse to this argument that if religion were to be true, why are there then Christianity, Islam, Judaism, and other religions with different messages? According to them, the multiplicity of religions is therefore proof that all religions must be false. This line of reasoning is accepted by Karl Marx, and is one of his arguments for the rejection of religion. The fallacy of his argument lies in that these people identified the expression of the sacred within a particular religious universe with the Absolute itself, and since there have been other expressions of the Absolute in other religious universes, they were led to the denial of the Absolute itself, and to the claim that everything is relative and, therefore, there is no Sacred as such. Your question is a very important one, and I am sure we shall discuss it later. The basis of the whole philosophy of comparative religion, expanded by traditional authors such as myself and again going back to what was asserted by Guénon, Coomaraswamy, and Schuon is to assert that the very multiplicity of sacred forms in different religions, far from negating the sacredness of things, only confirms the richness of the Source of all that is sacred, the infinite creativity of the Divine Origin of all sacred forms. But that is a story for another day.

Part Six

What Is Modernism?[1]

R.J.: We are going to continue with the thoughts we had about Islam and modernity, and we will finish up with that. The 20th century brought change to the world at a rapid and unprecedented rate. The Islamic world had to face changes no less than anywhere else. Today, the problem for many of the Islamic countries is how to integrate change into society and into their lives. It is clear that for all of us, there is no longer one clear line of change and development from the traditional to the modern, but a series of ruptures and transformations. How do you think the gap between Islam and modernity can be bridged?

S.H.N.: I do not believe that the gap can ever be bridged if modernism is taken as the particular and distinct philosophy that it really is. But if you define modernity by the set of conditions that just happen to be prevalent at a particular moment of history, then there is of course no philosophical definition of what modernity is, and that is going to be a different question. As for the question of whether Islam can live with a particular new set of circumstances or not, the answer is yes, it can. But if you mean by "modernity" a particular way of looking at the world, a particular philosophical perspective (it is how I look at it, as I already mentioned) that claims for itself universality and rejects all that is opposed to it, then of course there is no possibility of harmony between Islam and modernism. I usually use the word *modernism* rather than *modernity* to bring out the philosophical character of this phenomenon.

Modernism does not mean simply change and newness; it is a particular way of looking at the world, a particular philosophy based on the rejection of the theocentric view of reality—that is, removing God from the center of reality and putting man in His place. In a sense, it is a substitution of the kingdom of man for the Kingdom of God, therefore paying special attention to the individual and individualism and to the different powers of the individual human being such as reason and the senses. Therefore, its method of cognition, its epistemology, is based essentially upon either rationalism or empiricism, and it makes human values, the values of terrestrial man, the supreme set of values and the criteria for all things. There are many other elements connected with modernism that I will not go into here, but it is this very cluster of humanism, rationalism, empiricism, worldliness, and anthropocentrism that characterizes modernism.

Authentic Religions' Opposition to Modernism

Now, not only Islam but also other authentic religions cannot close the gap between themselves and this worldview without negating themselves and betraying the truths for the sake of which they were brought into the world. This is so because modernism is the very negation of the traditional religious worldview. Every religion, especially Islam, about which we are speaking now, considers "ordinary reality" to be derived from the Ultimate Reality. It is, therefore, God-centered, theocentric. It considers man to be theomorphic and to possess the faculties of not only the senses and reason, but also intellect, spiritual intuition, faith, along with the possibility of the acceptance of a revelation, the possibility of reaching truth beyond the purely human. Moreover, it does not consider the individual as a merely earthly being to be of ultimate value even in this world. It considers the immortal soul of human beings to be of the highest value here on earth. It also creates a sacred collectivity, a sacred society of which the individual is a member. It creates a traditional civilization in which one finds various manifestations of the sacred in life and art. It is, needless to say, opposed to humanism in the ordinary sense of the word.

I think, therefore, that in this whole discussion between Islam and modernity, we must distinguish between two very different problems that are involved. One is the problem of how Islam, or for that matter Hinduism or Buddhism or any other religion, can function and be present in a world in which the parameters and the conditions are not those in which religions have lived until now, with those parameters and conditions themselves changing all the time. The other, the second problem, is how to understand the forces which are bringing about these changes and whether to accept changes that simply come along or reject them. Where I differ from so many modern thinkers, whether they be

Persians, Europeans, or others, is that for many of them, many but not all of them, modernism is taken as the norm, and the question then is posed as to how Islam or Hinduism or some other religion including Christianity or Judaism can accommodate itself to this norm, whereas I do not accept that at all. I believe that modernism itself is based on an error, an error in the understanding of who man is, an error in understanding the nature of reality both metacosmic and cosmic. Modernism is based on an enormous deception, which is leading us to perdition and destroying the world. Now that we have the environmental crisis, many people talk about our having only fifty years to save our very lives in this world, and that the way that we are proceeding leads to our committing collective suicide.

Critiques of Modernism

Some people are beginning to realize that all is not well in the Kingdom of Denmark, as Shakespeare would say, and this rejection of modernism in the 20th century by certain Westerners is itself a very important phenomenon to which people in the non-Western world should pay the greatest attention. Criticism was made of modernism before the Second World War by certain poets such as Ezra Pound and T. S. Eliot; and even certain French writers, who were not even very religious, including André Gide, began to criticize what was going on in the world around them. This criticism was carried out intellectually and spiritually on a much deeper level in the writings of René Guénon in such books as *La Crise du monde moderne*,[2] which has been printed numerous times in France, and especially his last book *La Regne de la quantité*,[3] which is also well known, and other works.

Then, in the second half of the 20th century, this criticism went so far that the Museum of Modern Art of New York changed its name to the Museum of Contemporary Art. I remember when I was a student at Harvard, several leading professors would say, "We should make a clear distinction between the contemporary and the modern." This distinction was made already several decades ago, and a number of thinkers pointed out that one should not associate everything that is contemporary with the modern. Why did these in-depth criticisms, based on the full understanding of the nature of modernism, begin primarily in the West? Because long before the advent of post-modernism many intelligent people in the West, where modernism was born and from where it was transplanted to other continents, were able to see more clearly than those living in still semi-traditional societies where the phenomenon of modernism was an alien one, what was wrong, although at that time the cracks in the wall of the modern world were not as evident as they are today.

I think that the role of any intellectual living in a spiritual and religious tradition such as that of Islam should not be to simply observe what modernism is and then try to accommodate the tradition itself to it, but first of all to provide a serious critique of modernism. Why is it that Islam or Christianity or any other religion has to accommodate itself to modernism? Why should not the modern world accommodate itself to the truths of tradition? This is a question few people ask. I once mentioned this question in Delhi in India in a famous conference in 1961, in the first Congress of Oriental Studies ever held in Asia, where they had an evening in which they were going to discuss the possibility of changes in Islamic personal laws for Indian Muslims. The government of India at that time wanted to change the Islamic personal laws with the claim that times had changed, and so should the laws. That night, I remember, Nehru was present along with Indira Gandhi and most of the leaders of India. In front of all of them, I said, "If we have to change with the times, what do the times have to change with?" This seminal question, which was then published in all the major newspapers in India the next day—English, Urdu, and Hindi papers—caused a big commotion and, in fact, stopped that planned process of changing Islamic personal laws for a whole generation. The question to ask, which I have always asked ever since I was a young man, is, "What are the principles by which change in society should take place?" If you lived in 12th-century France, why did you not ask this question? Yes, conditions even then had changed; the 12th century was not the same as the 11th century. But at that time each generation tried to apply the principles of the tradition to the world in which it found itself rather than changing the principles themselves to accommodate changed conditions.

Now, the cart is put before the horse. Social change is supposed to be independent of us, and then we are supposed to accommodate ourselves to this change. On the one hand, we say, "Man is free. He determines his own destiny." On the other hand, we say, "There are the conditions of the times, and we must follow the times." Modern historical determinism goes back to Hegel and Marx, but even anti-Marxists repeat it all the time under the rubric of the necessity to conform to historical conditions. But what are historical conditions? The whole idea of "the spirit of the times," the *Zeitgeist* of Hegel, can be philosophically criticized. What is the spirit of the times? Where does it come from if not from us human beings? Does it come from God? Does it come from the angels or from purely material facts and human factors? What does this *Geist* mean? When you use the term *Zeitgeist*, or the spirit of the times, you should always ask where it comes from and why we are forced to submit to it. I once said in Europe, "What modern Western man has done is to substitute for the *Heilige Geist*, the Holy Ghost, the *Zeitgeist*," and everybody laughed. What I meant was that in the old days, it was the Holy Ghost, *le saint esprit* in French, in whom the Christians believed, claiming that it provided guidance and protection for the Church and Christian life. Now, they have taken out *le saint esprit* and they have put in its place instead *l'esprit du temps*, the spirit of the times, which in a sense is now our master. We are in a deep sense slaves to this "spirit." We have absolutized time, although this is philosophically absurd, and now we search how we should accommodate ourselves and even our religion to this way of thinking. I am totally opposed to this point of view, and I have stood like a firm tree against a storm during over fifty years of writing on this subject. I have stood for the principle that it is we who must make the times in accordance with our sacred traditions.

I want to quote here something of Henry Corbin, whom we have already discussed. He was very much in accord with me on this issue. One day we were discussing this matter together when he made a wonderful statement. He said, "*L'Homme ordinaire est fait par les temps. L'Homme spirituel est celui qui fait les temps.*" (The ordinary person is fashioned by the times; the spiritual person is he who fashions the times.) I think that today, more than ever before, when the unprecedented crisis that modernism has created for the whole world has become so critical, is the moment to abandon these slogans on the intellectual level and to criticize in depth on the basis of intelligence, of tradition, of revealed truths, and of the wisdom of the ages, of the perennial philosophy, all the errors that together constitute modernism and its offspring post-modernism. That has to be done; otherwise, not only is modernism along with post-modernism going to destroy human civilizations, but it is also going to destroy the order of nature itself.

On the practical plane, an individual, let us say a Muslim, could take a plane and fly to Paris and learn to live as a Muslim in that situation so different from living in a village near Yazd. Yes, each religion has to provide instructions for its followers as to how to live in our present-day world. But to take this change itself as the "principle" which should drive us on, as if we were picked up like a horse and driven against our will, that is not only against religion, but also against everything for which the Western ideas of liberty and freedom have stood. You have this remarkable paradox in the modern world. On the one hand, people who are modern always talk about freedom, democracy, and so forth, and they say, "It is we who determine our future." On the other hand, modernists insist that we have to transform everything according to the times. We have to swim with the flow of the river. We cannot presume the validity of this or that sacred institution, idea or object, because this is the 21st century; this is not the 13th century. My response is to say, "So what?" The 21st century is what we as human beings make the 21st century to be, of course within certain confines, unless we are historical determinists, unless we are Marxists or something like that, or as materialists we believe that we are determined by our biological heritage; or on another level if we claim that we have no free will and that all is determined by the Divine Will (in which case we are not bound to a historical determinism). Well, let us declare our position in honesty. Let us declare clearly as philosophers our position vis-à-vis change, historical determinism, and free will. But to put this veil of ambiguity over such an important matter as is being done today, and always in the name of a particular century or a particular decade, is intellectually dishonest.

Nowadays, we no longer talk about centuries, but decades. Already in America the decade of the seventies is for many like the medieval period. You know that here things change very fast, and people now have nostalgia for the 1950s, the time when I was going to school, as if it were the age of Clovis in France or something like that. In the name of a new decade, everything has to be thrown away, discarded; everything becomes rapidly stale and no longer meaningful, and one has to become up-to-date to know what is going on and *belong* to the contemporary scene. I stand against this whole attitude and believe that this marks really nothing more or less than the ultimate suicide of civilization.

Modern Western Critical Thought

R.J.: Yes, but when you say that we have to be critical towards modernity, do we not find elements of criticism inside modernity itself? Because I believe that modernity has two sides. You mostly criticize the instrumental part of modernity, which is technology and capitalism; but I think modernity brought with itself also a critical rationality, which has been critical of modernity itself through the writings of many of the post-modern writers.

S.H.N.: Yes, but you must remember that critical thinking itself is not necessarily modern. It existed before, but not in the form of the Kantian critique. That kind of critical philosophy is logically absurd, because it uses reason to set limits to and to criticize reason. This position is logically very difficult to sustain, and therefore many post-Kantian philosophers in the West have also criticized it. Now, this type of criticism is part and parcel of modernity itself and is like the grease that makes it possible for the wheels of modernity to go around. This type of criticism itself comes only from the rational element of the human soul. It is not an in-depth intellectual criticism that clears the ground and opens the mind to the understanding of truths that are metarational. Those truths are not irrational, but metarational, and derive from intellection and revealed spiritual realities.

Occasionally, one finds in the West a profound metaphysical critique of this Kantian critical philosophy. For example, in his book *Logic and Transcendence*,[4] F. Schuon has a remarkable chapter in which he criticizes Kantian critical philosophy and the use of "critical reason." I am always on the side of that type of criticism, but I do not equate criticism with rationalism. Ibn Sīnā had also a very critical mind; the same with Bīrūnī. In Bīrūnī you see some of the most critical discourses in the sense of logical analysis of various issues, but what is called philosophical criticism in the Western philosophical schools today, and going back to Kant himself, is a very particular way of using this term. The use of "criticism" in this sense finally ends in an impasse. Consequently, one ends up with the assertion of Heidegger that "Philosophy ends with me." Or Richard Rorty, who says, "Philosophy is just conversation, and we are at the end of that conversation."

That is what has actually happened, and many Western philosophers feel that Western philosophy has reached an impasse. I do believe that the Japanese, Chinese, Indian, Persian, and Arab thinkers outside of the Western world should pay a great deal of attention to the critical appraisal that is made of modernism in the West, because it can help them to understand its shortcomings. Non-Western people have a lot of difficulty in understanding the problems that modern Western technology, Western science, Western psychology as a whole, and not only their instrumental part, pose. They have more trouble understanding the issues involved than do Westerners, who live within the confines of modernity.

Let us take the environmental crisis. Decades after the crisis became full blown (I wrote *The Encounter of Man and Nature* in the early sixties), there should be a lot of people in the East who would be at the forefront in the discussion of the deeper issues involved, but few do so because the majority do not realize in depth even now what the profound causes of the crisis are. The reason is that this is a problem created by modern Western civilization, and non-Westerners have greater difficulty seeing its inner causes. Most Eastern thinkers do not see what is "inside the box," and they think that the West will somehow solve the crisis because Westerners have the necessary technological know-how to be able to solve any problem; but that is not the case.

So I think that the criticisms made of modernism by certain Western writers, whether they are philosophers or *hommes de lettres* or sociologists, are definitely precious for non-Westerners. I think most of all of the great value of the criticisms made by Western followers of the traditional school, such as Tage Lindbom, the famous Swedish writer, in his book *The Tares and the Good Grain*,[5] which is one of the most profound criticisms of socialist and Marxist ideas written by a European. He himself was once the ideologue of the Swedish Socialist Party, and then discovered tradition and perennial philosophy and was able to apply the vast knowledge he had gained through his study of the principle of perennial philosophy to the philosophy of Marxism and socialism, which he also knew so well. He also criticized many other important elements of modernism, for his critique involved certain non-leftist modernist ideologies as well. In this sense, critical thinking developed in the West can be of much value, but what is important is that this critical form of thinking be informed by the light of the intellect, and not be critical philosophy only in the Kantian sense, which seeks to use reason to show the limitation of intelligence in the understanding of the truth. Nor can the relativism and nihilism characteristic of so much post-modern thought be of great help.

Modernism's Effect on Muslims

R.J.: Do you think that the challenge of modernity has shaken the confidence of Muslims in the metaphysical realities of Islam in Islamic societies?

S.H.N.: Yes and no. "Yes" in the sense that a number of people, Persians, Pakistanis and Muslim Indians, Egyptians, Turks, whoever they are who have become educated in the West or Western-style institutions in the Islamic world and who have become Westernized philosophically, have had their confidence in their own intellectual tradition shaken.

Moreover, many Muslims of a non-philosophical nature who became educated in the West or became Westernized at home did not study Western thought in depth. They simply adopted the hedonistic aspects of modern Western life without the philosophical aspects of it; and so their Western education did not concern itself with the study of Western thought and its principal criticisms. Among this group most do not anyway bother to concern themselves with metaphysical matters. But among the first group, yes, some have become skeptical about the metaphysical realities presented in their own philosophical tradition. It needs to be emphasized, however, that they constitute a much smaller number in the Islamic world in comparison with what we find in Japan and China. I said yes and no; this was the "yes" part.

The "no" part is that not only did Western thought not shake the attachment of the mainstream of Islamic thought away from its metaphysical worldview, but that during the last few decades, that kind of blind following of Western philosophical but anti-metaphysical thought by the few has dwindled somewhat in the Islamic world. We now have a whole new generation of Muslim thinkers about your age—Turk, Arab, Persian, Pakistani, Indian, Malay, et cetera—some of whom have been my own students, and I know them very well. They are brilliant young thinkers who know Western thought much better than their forefathers who were just talking about Bergson or Descartes and, you know, waving the flag of these figures of Western philosophy as we see in Iran itself. Most of this new generation of thinkers know one or two Western languages well, but at the same time, they are rooted in their own philosophical tradition. For example, if you were in what is today Pakistan or the Muslim part of India in the year 1900, a century ago, you could attend the universities, created by the British, such as the University of the Punjab or the University of Calcutta, these famous old universities in which only Western philosophy was taught. Both Hindus and Muslims who had studied in these universities were immersed up to their nose in Locke, Spencer, Mill, et cetera, and when many of them spoke about philosophy, they meant Western philosophy. This situation continued even after the partition.

In the 1950s and 1960s, I used to participate regularly in the Pakistan Philosophical Congress, and occasionally in philosophical conferences in India, but let us just limit ourselves to the case of Pakistan because it is an Islamic country. Now, in the Pakistan Philosophical Congresses, 90 percent of all the papers presented at that time were on Western philosophy, and even if there were a few papers on Islamic philosophy, they were written from the point of view of the Western study of Islamic philosophy. The reality of the Islamic metaphysical world was not taken seriously despite the fact that Iqbal, who was the ideological founder of Pakistan, had shown much interest in Islamic philosophy, although I do not think that he is really a traditional Islamic philosopher. He himself was influenced by Western philosophy, but at least was intelligent enough to realize the significance of Islamic philosophy. The problem with him was that he did not know Arabic well enough. His Persian was very good, but he could not read all the major texts of Islamic philosophy, which are written mostly in Arabic. Nevertheless, he wrote on the development of metaphysics in Persia, and he had some philosophical substance, much more than the other famous reformers who are mentioned all the time, such as Sir Syed Ahmad Khan or Muḥammad 'Abduh.

In any case, in Pakistan in the fifties and sixties, Islamic philosophy was not dealt with as a living, philosophical tradition. What was dealt with as a living school of thought was Western philosophy. Now, some fifty years later, the problem has not altered completely, but you have a number of Pakistani writers who are young philosophers for whom Islamic philosophy is philosophy and not only history or archaeology; and they feel that they belong to their own philosophical tradition. They are still studying Western philosophy, but they are studying it as Islamic philosophers.

So I think that the idea of confronting Western thought, the philosophical aspect of modernity, you might say, and then losing interest in one's own metaphysical worldview is still there in the Islamic world, but it was there much more so fifty years ago; and in fact, more recently the trend is towards taking the Islamic intellectual tradition more seriously. There is one exception to this trend, however, and that is that after the debacle of Arab nationalism, a number of secularized Arab thinkers, having no access to the earlier Islamic philosophical tradition except through Western eyes, in contrast to the living Islamic philosophical tradition, which has had a continuous life in such places as Iran, have adopted the view of Western rationalism. Then they have tried to look within the Islamic world for a figure with whom they could identify, and they have turned to Ibn Rushd, whom they are now interpreting as the last serious Islamic philosopher, who was also a rationalist. Many governments have been in favor of this trend, because they have thought that this would create a kind of secularism against the Islamic sentiments of the population and expedite modernism.

In recent years, there have been a number of conferences in Tunisia, Morocco, Jordan, and Egypt, as well as Turkey (which claims to be secularist), and other places on Ibn Rushd, trying to present him as the last Islamic philosopher and a rationalist to be used as a model by present-day Muslim thinkers. That phenomenon is there, I agree, but that is not the most important phenomenon, because most of the people who talk in these terms, although they are now popular in the Arab world, do not have that much of a philosophical substance to carry the day; nor is their thought connected to the worldview of their society.

I think that the challenge is still there for Islamic thought, but there is a great deal more awareness now of the Islamic reality, philosophically speaking, than there was among the Western-educated people in the Islamic world half a century ago. In the field of the history of Islamic philosophy proper, it is interesting to note that the whole idea of writing the history of philosophy in the modern sense was invented by the Germans in the 19th century, whether it be Western philosophy or anything else. In our own tradition we have works that speak about various Islamic thinkers and philosophers. We have a number of works in Persian and Arabic either by philosophers or historians dealing with philosophical or scientific figures, a page on Ibn Sīnā, a page on Bīrūnī, et cetera; but they are not really histories of philosophy in the Hegelian sense. The idea of writing the history of philosophy as philosophy began with Hegel's influence in Germany, and then it spread to France and England, and histories of philosophies began to appear everywhere in Europe and America.

As I told you already, the first histories of Islamic philosophy were written by Westerners, Munk, de Boer, Gauthier, and people like them in the late 19th century or early part of the 20th century, all written from the Western point of view. These books were studied and read by Muslims in universities in countries such as Pakistan where the language of instruction was English. We were protected to a large extent in Iran from this simple imitation because our language of instruction was Persian, and we could not understand European languages well. But where English or French was used, the Western view of the history of Islamic philosophy was fully adopted. Even the structure of the history edited by Sharif, *History of Muslim Philosophy*,[6] in which I participated and for which I wrote six long chapters, which were almost like a book in themselves, is based to a large extent on Western models. I participated in the project because when I first met Sharif in 1959, the first time I went to Pakistan, his outline of the project, which he showed me, had left aside the whole of the later development of Islamic philosophy. There was no chapter on Mullā Ṣadrā, nothing on Mīr Dāmād. Few had even heard of these figures except the *'ulamā'*, the classical *'ulamā'*, but not figures such as Sharif himself who had studied in modern institutions. Sharif was a prominent philosopher and a fine human being. So I talked to him and convinced him to add a few chapters on later Islamic philosophy. He accepted my proposal and asked me to write several chapters on the subject, but that did not change the general structure of the two-volume work. *History of Islamic Philosophy*[7] by Corbin, O. Yahya, and myself and the two-volume *History of Islamic Philosophy*[8] edited by myself and O. Leaman are the first works in Western languages in which the history of Islamic philosophy is seen from the point of view of the tradition of Islamic philosophy itself, and not from the Western way of looking at Islamic philosophy.

Yes, significant change has taken place in this field in recent decades. It is very interesting to note that in countries such as Indonesia and Malaysia, which had never been a center for Islamic philosophy, there are now many gifted, young philosophers, scholars, and teachers who teach Islamic philosophy from the point of view of the Islamic metaphysical and philosophical tradition, which was something unheard of in modern universities in the Islamic world a few decades ago.

Globilization and Diversity[9]

R.J.: How can Islam contribute to the global order in today's world? I mean, philosophically and also spiritually. And how can someone who lives in the modern world be a devout Muslim?

S.H.N.: These are two different questions. First of all, I do not believe in the reality of what is called the global order. I think that this is a slogan that began to be popularized by the first President Bush at the time of the Persian Gulf War. There is certainly no such thing as the global order in the realm of thought. You have a lot of global disorder, and people forget, right now as we sit here, how many wars are going on in the world, how many people are getting killed. Since the wars are not in the middle of Europe as it was with the war in Bosnia and Kosovo, and are far from America, people in the West think that order dominates more or less over the world, despite a few violent actions here and there. Look at what is happening in Africa, Kashmir, Palestine, Chechnya, and other places, terrible situations full of chaos and disorder. No, there is no global order. What we have is a tendency towards what is called "globalization," which I also believe will never be achieved totally, but there is a tendency towards that direction. I think that the role of Islam, as all the other religions and not only of Islam, should be to prevent the homogenization of humanity and destruction of local religions, cultures, and traditions in the name of global economic welfare. The present shibboleth of globalization is only a name—the poor getting poorer and the rich richer.

Globalization is not making the poor richer or spreading wealth globally. Look at the statistics, even within the United States, and look at the differences between what is called the "North" and the "South." Thirty or forty years ago, before this whole process was spoken about, what is called the gap between the rich and the poor was less than now. So even economically—and let us remember it is always in the name of wealth, money, and economics that everything is done today, not in the name of spirituality—when you look at the situation, greater economic justice has not been attained. Certainly spiritually, intellectually, and culturally it would be a disaster if globalization, which means really modernization in the Western sense and secularization, did succeed completely.

Even if globalization were to be achieved on the basis of equality, how would you like to have a garden in which you would have only one kind of flower all over the garden, no matter how beautiful that flower was? How impoverished humanity would become, if, in the villages of Java and Sumatra, people were doing the same thing, thinking the same thoughts as in New York. It would be a horrendous, horrible end for the diversity of human cultures. People say, "How wonderful, there would be no more wars. There would be peace," but this is not true. The whole culture of globalization is based on waste and fierce competition. It is based first of all on waging war against nature, against the natural world, leading to further environmental destruction of the worst kind. People in Tehran and Dacca may be polluting their own cities, but who is cutting all the trees of Borneo? Are not the Japanese and the Americans destroying the quality of water through copper mining and similar activities in South America, Indonesia, and Africa? Who has caused the destruction of so much of the Amazon? It is the peasants of Brazil who are mowing down and burning the trees, but it was the World Bank that encouraged such behavior. The demonstrations held fairly recently in Washington dealt with that very issue. Fortunately, the World Bank has now learned some of its lessons. Nevertheless, most people do not want to pay attention to the fact that the whole idea of development combined with globalization in the modern sense is based on aggression against the rest of creation. It is as simple as that, and globalization simply exacerbates the situation by spreading destructive economic and technological processes all over the globe.

And then there is the war within ourselves, because this globalization is based on intensifying the passions for possession, for acquisitiveness, for domination; so it is not going to lead to peace at all, but rather to homogenization, greater quantification, and the further destruction of the quality of life. The Quran states that God created us as different people with different characteristics, different religions and laws, and adds, "So vie one with another [in good works]."[10] The fact that we have different religions and cultures, different societies, different human types, different languages, different literatures, different kinds of music, different means of production, this is all a blessing from God. This diversity is a positive and not a negative reality, a diversity that must be preserved at all cost. What good would it be if you had only one kind of food that the world would have available to it? You would become bored after a while, obviously.

Fortunately there are now some people talking all the time about the importance of preserving diversity in the human family as well as biodiversity, because while we are spending just a few hours here talking together, more species of the world have been destroyed, and many cultures have taken another step toward extinction. The preservation of diversity is, I think, a very important duty on all levels and in all domains, including among and within the religions of the world, Islam included. Islam must emphasize its own inclusiveness and traditional diversity combined with inner unity and its uniqueness, not exclusivity and outward homogeneity, which means that it should accommodate other religions as well as its own diversity of schools of thought while maintaining its identity. It should create mutual understanding with other religions and also between various interpretations within itself. I have been at the forefront of dialogue with Christianity, Judaism, Hinduism, Buddhism, you name it, and to some extent Confucianism (trying to encourage Islamic-Confucian dialogue) for many decades, but I always emphasize that each religion must seek to preserve its uniqueness while respecting diversity, which, like its uniqueness, comes from God. Each authentic religion as well as traditional interpretations within it is like a beautiful flower in the human garden and should not, in the name of globalization, surrender what makes each religion, tradition, and culture, and all that goes with it distinct and unique. Let us take our own Persian culture. Our religion is Islam, and the vast majority of Persians are

Muslims. We are also a distinct cultural entity; we are culturally different from the Arabs or Turks, while being Muslims like them.

Islamic civilization should be preserved in all its rich diversity, and within that civilization various distinct cultures and schools of thought should be sustained and respected. Arabic is a marvelous language, a very beautiful and powerful language, but it should not take the place of Persian. Persian is also a marvelous and remarkable language, with supremely beautiful poetry, but it should not take the place of Turkish or Arabic and so on. Nor should one theological or legal school destroy all the others. Even within Iran, you can go one further step. I am not in favor of destroying Baluchi, Azari, or Kurdish in the name of some vague nationalism. Persian as the literary language can hold the country together as it has always done, but even in that situation the diversity of dialects and languages within Iran actually contributes to the diversity and the richness of the culture of the country, and this fact is not only true of Iran. There are many other countries such as India where even open conflicts are going on over language. Fortunately in Iran that has not taken place, but if all of India were only to speak only Hindi or Tamil, look at what India would lose from the point of literature, of language, of cultural habits et cetera. I think this is a very important issue and I am completely on the side of preserving not only biodiversity, which if we do not preserve will lead to our own destruction, but also cultural and religious diversity. I mean of course authentic and not pseudo religions and schools of thought. I am therefore opposed to globalization, which is another name for the homogenization of the world dominated by the modern Western worldview and civilization.

Muslims Throughout the World

As for how a Muslim can live in the modern world, Islam is the last major religion of this world, and God knew of course what He was doing in revealing it. He created Islam in such a way that it is perhaps the easiest of all religions to practice almost no matter where you are, if you really want to practice it. Its laws are such that you can always apply them to yourself. You might not be able to apply them to the whole society if you are a minority in a non-Islamic society, but you can certainly always practice Islam yourself practically no matter where you are. Its rites are such that you can perform them anywhere. You do not need to have, let us say, a priest officiating in a mass in order to participate in the rite of the Eucharist, which is the central rite of Christianity, or have a Brahmin to perform very complicated forms of sacrifice that you have in Hinduism and so forth. In Islam, every man and woman is a priest. All you need is some water to make your ablution and a piece of earth to perform your canonical prayers. You can perform them in Detroit or in Johannesburg, as well as in Cairo or Tehran. You can fast during the month of Ramadan wherever you are. No doubt performing these rites becomes more difficult in the modern world, because of the secularized ambience that is there, no doubt about it; but it is not impossible to live as a practicing Muslim anywhere, even in societies openly opposed to religion such as communist countries.

It is remarkable how rapidly just in the past few decades the Islamic presence has spread in North America and Europe and now more and more in South America. This is true of most parts of the world except for perhaps Japan, where there is not an appreciable Islamic presence. In India, of course, there are some 150 million Muslims. In China, God knows the number, which is estimated to be from 30 to 100 million. Even within Russia there are some 20 million Muslims. In the West during the last few decades, Islam has become such a reality that its presence is recognized by nearly everybody. For example, in the United States where there are more than 6 million Muslims most factories now give permission to their workers who are Muslims to take a few minutes off from their work to perform their prayers. It is like that also in much of Europe where there are now millions of Muslims.

So God has made it possible for a Muslim to live as a Muslim if he or she really wants to, no matter where that person happens to be. It is not that difficult. The difficulty comes from something else. The difficulty is a psychological and spiritual one, in the sense that since secular modernism appeals to the passions and it is against the sacred, it spreads rapidly and tempts many a soul. When you say that Western culture is spreading to Indonesia or India, it is not Plato who is spreading; it is McDonald's, pop music, and things like that, elements which appeal quite obviously to the passions and not to the higher reaches of the intellect or the mind, with the result that they weaken the faith of some Muslims. Even in movies, the vast majority of the movies that spread very rapidly in Africa and Asia are, as you know, based on violence and sex. If you make a very intellectual or spiritual movie, not many people in Zimbabwe or Bangladesh or for that matter the West itself are likely to see it or even have the opportunity to do so, although there are a few exceptions here and there.

You have this enticing characteristic of popular Western culture that attracts the souls of ordinary people when they come in contact with secular modernism. It is the soul within certain individuals that becomes no longer interested in practicing Islam, which is quite something else; but each person still has a choice even in the modern world to practice or not to practice his or her religion. God has put all of the responsibility on man's shoulders. There are both temptations and opportunities. Young people going to school today might be interested in sexual promiscuity and this and that action that incites the passions and not want to accept the constraints of religion, and that challenge is not unique to Islam. Every religion tries to discipline the soul. If you were to be a Buddhist, it would be the same way. Yes, some Muslims in the modern world do not want to practice their religion, but if they wanted, they would be able to do so. It is the challenge that modernism poses for all religions that must be considered. As to whether you can live as a Muslim in the modern world or not, the answer is yes, you can, if you have faith, and of course with God's help. It then becomes easy no matter where you are. As the Quran says, "With difficulty comes ease."

R.J.: For the Algerian thinker Moḥammad Arkoun, "the Muslim intellectual must today fight on two fronts: on the one hand against social science as practiced by orientalism in a disengaged, narrative, descriptive style," and on the other, against what he calls "the offensive, defensive apologia of Muslims who compensate for repeated attacks on the authenticity and the identity of the Islamic personality." Do you agree with him in what he says?

S.H.N.: I know Arkoun well personally; we are friends. But I certainly do not share his philosophical perspective. He does not speak from within the tradition of Islamic thought, not from within the tradition of Islamic philosophy and metaphysics. He is, of course, a Muslim from Algeria, but in a sense speaks more as a French intellectual who happens to be a Muslim, and he is a secularist in many ways. I do not accept his point of view of "higher criticism" that he is trying to apply to Islamic texts. As for the quotation which you posed, this is a bit abstruse. I certainly agree that Muslims should not accept the kind of social scientistic or orientalist interpretation of Islam, which is based on a premise very different from that of Islam; but as for the other side of the equation that he speaks about, that is why I said it is abstruse: What is he exactly talking about? If he is talking about the weak apologia that certain Muslims make for Islam, I would agree with him, and I am against such assertions as, "Well, Islam is wonderful because Goethe said so, because he was a great German poet," or, "Islam is wonderful because it gave science to the West," all this kind of nonsense. I think that this kind of nonsensical apology issues especially out of Pakistan and India (although not limited to these areas) mostly as a result of a long period of Western education. This type of phenomenon is also seen to some extent in other parts of the Islamic world. Yes, that kind of thinking is not serious; but this is not the only type of thought and scholarship that is now coming out of the Islamic world. There is a great deal of Islamic scholarship appearing these days that is based on very authentic studies of Islamic sources, and I think Arkoun seems to be against some of that as well. That is why I said that this quotation is somewhat abstruse, and he should clarify more what he means by this apologia. Maybe later on he made further clarifications, but anyway, from what you have quoted, the issue is not very clear.

Western Images of Islam[11]

R.J.: This brings us to my question, which is, how has the West imagined Islam through history, and how do you see the Western way of imagining Islam which started many centuries ago and continues until today?

The Arab Conquest

S.H.N.: Of course, this is a vast question. When Islam first began in the seventh Christian century, it was a remarkable shock to Christianity. Although Christ never said, "No prophet shall come after me," he did say that his followers should be aware of false prophets at the end of time. Nevertheless, Christians felt that theirs was the final revelation, Christ being the only Son of God, and that therefore there would not be another message from Heaven after him. Then suddenly like lightning, Islam comes out of Arabia, and within less than half a century, all of the Eastern Mediterranean lands and North Africa, which were Christian, become dominated by Islam, and most of the people gradually become Muslims. The Arab conquest was not only a matter of military domination. It was not like the Mongol invasion. The Mongols invaded Iran, but Iran did not become Shamanist or Buddhist. Some people say that the Arab invasion was just a military conquest, but this is not so. Rather, it was accompanied by a profound spiritual transformation that took place wherever Muslims went and settled down.

As you know, by the beginning of the eighth century, Muslim armies had come all the way up to northern France. I shall never forget when for the first time I went to Poitiers, where Charles Martel is said to have defeated the Islamic armies in 738, a century after the rise of Islam. I realized only then that Poitiers is only a two-hour drive from Paris. So Islam reached right to the heart of Western Europe. Consequently, the first experience that Christianity had of Islam was one of fear. At that time and obviously even before Islam reached France, Islam, on the basis of the teaching of the Quran, spoke about the Christians and the Jews as the People of the Book and respected the Hebrew prophets and Christ. In fact, according to Islamic Law, Muslims were and still are commanded to protect the lives and property of Christians and Jews.

John the Damascene

When the Umayyads established the Umayyad dynasty with its center in Damascus, creating an empire stretching from China to the Pyrenees, an incredible feat was achieved politically, although religiously, of course, they fell away from the original perfection of the first few years. At the beginning of the Umayyad period, there was a man called John the Damascene[12] who was an Eastern Christian theologian living in Damascus and who wrote a book against Islam. Can you imagine that? Under the nose of the caliph, he was allowed to write and disseminate this book, and nothing was done to him, although his work was a scathing attack against Islam. That book came to the West, and so the West began to look upon Islam as a kind of parody of Christianity, as something that was a deviation from the Christian norm. Christians could not understand how Islam could spread so rapidly. Because Islam spoke about Christ and the Virgin, Christians were even more uncomfortable about it. So many people in the West thought that the Prophet of Islam had been an excommunicated Roman bishop, and all kinds of unbelievable stories were concocted about him in an atmosphere in which the physical fear that soon Islam would take over the whole of Europe was ever present.

The Middle Ages

The Christian attitude towards Islam began in that setting, and over the centuries during the early Middle Ages, whenever Western Christianity felt insecure, there also appeared an eschatological idea that the coming of Islam was the sign of the end of the world and the appearance of the Antichrist, who was identified by some with the Prophet himself.

When Christianity felt more secure, matters became a bit calmer, but even the translation of the Quran made under the direction of Peter the Venerable,[13] a thousand years ago, was done in order that the Christians could answer the Muslims more readily; it was based on a very combative anti-Islamic attitude. There were, of course, exceptions, especially among a few monks here and there. There were a number of Christians who would even come to Spain and study with the Muslims, and numerous Christians lived under Muslim rule peacefully for centuries not only in the heartland of the Islamic world, but also in Spain and Sicily. The Muslims did not massacre the Christians in Spain as later on the Christians were to massacre or expel the Muslims and Jews in 1492, after the reconquest of the Iberian Peninsula. In any case, putting Spain and Sicily aside, there was in the northern and western parts of Europe, that is, France, Germany, England, et cetera, this trepidation and feeling of threat, while at the same time Islam was regarded as a heresy of Christianity; yet, this attribute was combined strangely enough with respect for Islamic civilization, thought, and culture, which led to the translation of so many works into Latin from Arabic.

The Renaissance

During the Renaissance, another negative element was added. In the Middle Ages, although Christians feared and disliked Islam, they at least respected Islamic science, philosophy, and the arts. Saint Thomas Aquinas quotes Ibn Sīnā, Ghazzālī, and Ibn Rushd some five hundred times. Many Christian scholars learned Arabic. For example, Roger Bacon was an Arabist at Oxford, and Albertus Magnus, the teacher of Saint Thomas Aquinas, knew Arabic. There existed a world where one could see an unbelievable symbiosis and relationship between Islam and the West in the fields of science, philosophy, theology, the arts, literature, and of course technology and music, you name it. There were influences emanating from the Islamic world in all these fields, and the West accepted them mostly with open arms. In fact these influences played a major role in the creation of the civilization of the European High Middle Ages.

Can you imagine that there were medieval European miniatures of the Virgin Mary in the style of Islamic miniatures? First of all, the illuminations in these miniatures are very similar to Quranic illuminations, and secondly, often the mantle of the Virgin, which is blue with gold margins, contains in the margins pseudo-Arabic writing, that is, patterns that look like Arabic, but they are not Arabic, because the scribe did not know any Arabic and simply copied patterns similar to Arabic calligraphy. To that extent was Islamic art emulated. All the way from art to mathematics, from philosophy to astronomy, there were notable influences, because there was an opening in the mind of Westerners for things Islamic based on respect for Islamic civilization. In the Renaissance, the earlier hatred that had existed religiously continued, along with a new hatred of Islam as a civilization.

One of the great mistakes that modernized Muslims make today is that they think that Islam brought about the European Renaissance, and that the Renaissance is proof of how wonderful Islamic civilization was. In fact, during the Renaissance, Arabs and Muslims were hated more than in any other period of European history, as you see in the writings of a major writer of that period, Petrarch.[14] This reality can be seen in black and white if one only pays close attention to the writings of that period. Not everybody, of course, joined in this opposition to and hatred of things Islamic. The universities of Bologna and Padua in Italy continued to be centers of Averroism. In the 16th century, Averroes was translated again in Italy into Latin, but that is a more local phenomenon. And then you have the modern period.

The Colonial Period

Modern scholarship about Islam began in the late 18th and early 19th centuries mostly when the two major colonial powers, France and England (along with others such as the Dutch), because they had Muslim colonies, sought to know better what was going on in their colonies and therefore supported scholarship on the Islamic world in the form of orientalism. Of course there are many exceptions of scholars who were not simply servants of colonialism. But many of the early orientalists were at the service of a colonial power, and some of the most influential books written on matters Islamic came from their pens, for example, about Sufism in North Africa, a subject on which several works were written by agents of the French secret police trying to keep an eye on what was going on in the Sufi orders, to discover where they were, who their members were, what their doctrines were, et cetera.

The same was true in India. It is interesting to note that Persian writings, in contrast to Arabic works, first came to Europe not through Spain, not through Sicily, not even through Persia itself, but through India. It was in the late 18th century and especially in the 19th century that once the British were established in India, they realized that for the Muslims, the main language was Persian, while for the Hindus, it was Hindi in the north and Tamil, along with several other languages, in the south, with Sanskrit their common religious language. The British school of orientalism then began to translate works from these languages including Persian. Such scholars as Sir William Jones began to make important Persian and Arabic works available in English. Consequently, in the 19th century, for the first time since the Middle Ages there began to appear a new serious interest in Islam in the West thanks most of all to the new Arabic and Persian texts that were coming out in European languages.

A number of very prominent Europeans, chief among them Goethe, whom many people think secretly converted to Islam, were drawn to matters Islamic. There is a new book out in German showing that in some of his letters, Goethe began with *Bismi'Llāh al-Raḥmān al-Raḥīm* in Arabic letters, which is itself absolutely amazing. In any case, he had great sympathy for Islam, especially in his last work, *The West-East Divan,* which was deeply influenced by Ḥāfiẓ and has sections with such Persian titles as *Sāqī-nāmah*, et cetera. This great love for Ḥāfiẓ and Sufism is also to be seen in Rückert, the German poet. In America, Emerson, perhaps the most important of all American philosophers, wrote a long poem called "Saadi," and loved Sufism, as did the whole of New England Transcendentalism, whose members were called "the Persians of Cambridge." It is really amazing what was going on at that time in both America and in England, where the famous translation of Khayyam was made by Fitzgerald. Of course Khayyam was misinterpreted to a large extent in this translation and was presented as a hedonist and fatalist, but this was part and parcel of the peculiar interpretation of the whole cultural wave coming from the East into 19th-century Europe and especially Victorian England.

The Romantic Era

Also during the Romantic Era another view of Islam again came to the fore, that is, not the mystical and Sufi aspects of Islam, but the aspect of Islam as the enemy, as a harsh religion of the desert to be confronted and combated. The Christian missionaries had an important role to play during this period in denigrating Islam and writing pejorative accounts of it. For example, biographies written against the Prophet by them often followed the themes of earlier works written to denigrate the

Prophet in the Middle Ages. That genre of writing has continued into modern times against all objective scholarship. Neither missionaries nor secular scholars accepted the Islamic revelation as authentic revelation, but at least the scholars sought to be scholarly. The missionaries tried to explain the Prophet's message away and all of the old medieval accusations against the Prophet, that he was an epileptic or that he was sexually uncontrolled or undisciplined, all kinds of idiotic accusations that had been mentioned in earlier days were revived and continued into the 20th century.

Modern Times

Since 2001, these ignorant accusations have in fact been again revived in certain extremist Christian circles in America. In the 20th century and continuing today, however, another voice began to be added in the West, and that was the voice of individuals in the Occident who, for the first time since the Middle Ages, had gained direct access to the Islamic revelation. Most of these people embraced Islam and became secretly initiated into Sufism. The most important voice in this group, a voice which in fact is unique, was that of René Guénon in the early 20th century, followed by other traditionalist authors who have written about Islam, such as Frithjof Schuon, Titus Burckhardt, and Martin Lings,[15] all of whom I knew well. These figures are among the great spiritual and intellectual luminaries of the 20th century. They and many others were Muslims, but at the same time they had a universalist perspective based on the perennial philosophy and of course knew Western thought and the Western language of intellectual discourse perfectly well. Consequently, they opened a new chapter in the understanding of Islam, which is the most important since the Middle Ages, but they were not alone in achieving this goal, although their intellectual significance is central and unique.

There are also a number of orientalists going back to Louis Massignon, who have also opened a new chapter in the authentic academic study of Islam, because they have been scholars who have had empathy for Islam and deep understanding of it. Massignon returned to Catholicism in a sense through the grace of Islam, through his mysterious "meeting" with Hallaj,[16] and he was not alone. One can also mention the French scholars Louis Gardet and Henry Corbin, and Annemarie Schimmel, the famous German scholar. They have been in turn followed by a whole group of younger scholars with deep empathy for Islam whose number continues to grow in the West.

Today you have several approaches to Islam in the West. You have the traditionalists such as Guénon, Schuon, Burckhardt, Lings, et cetera, whom I have already mentioned. You have both Catholic and Protestant and also Jewish scholars who are sympathetic to Islam and have some understanding of it. And then you still have missionaries who write about Islam, but they are not now as important as the secularists who, you might say, have taken on the mantle of Western missionary activity in a new form as missionary activity for anti-religious secularism in the name of scientific scholarship. You also have sociologists who write about Islam from the point of the Western social sciences including political science. They are not interested in revelation, in religion as such, but in secular social science or anthropological, social, political, and economic analysis. You now have an army of political scientists writing on Islam. And then there are the scholars of comparative religion, but they have made relatively little contribution to Islamic studies. Mircea Eliade himself once said that for philosophical and methodological reasons, most scholars of comparative religion have paid most of their attention to Hinduism, Buddhism, Taoism, or the primal and ancient religions, and have not made that much of a contribution to Islamic studies. Finally, one must mention the works of Muslim scholars' writings in Western languages. The latter have produced in recent years an important body of authentic works on all aspects of Islam.

The image of Islam in the West has been forged from what is contained in all of these different sources along with the picture presented by the mass media, to which has been added, since 1948, very important elements created as a result of the partition of Palestine and since 2001 extremism and terrorism. There is today a strong political dimension to Islamic studies in the West coming from both the rise of what is called "Islamic fundamentalism" and the confrontation between Zionism and Islamic and Arab interests in Palestine, and these types of studies have created proponents and opponents in different countries. For example, in France, you have a man such as Maxim Rodinson who was a Marxist and leftist, and who was not interested in religion as such; but at the same time he defended many Islamic causes, and he was for Palestinian rights to some extent. And then you have scholars who have tried to attack Islam to further Zionist causes, and since the tragedy of September 2001, to express anger against the Islamic world. You have all kinds of situations created as a result of the intractable political conflicts of today. Of course, the mass media have a very important role to play in this matter and in feeding the fire of what is called "Islamophobia" to protect certain interests of the West.

So the image of Islam in the West is on the one hand better than it was before. On the other hand, the obstacles to improving the image are also much stronger and much more difficult to overcome than before. Today there is more authentic knowledge of Islam available in the West, along with a torrent of ignorance, misinformation, and disinformation.

Part Seven

Art[1]

R.J.: Let us turn to the question of art and spirituality. The question of art and its relation to spirituality has always been at the center of your philosophical thinking. How do you understand the philosophy of art in its traditional sense, and in what way do you think it differs from the modern interpretations of art?

S.H.N.: First of all, let me say that one of the reasons why the spiritual dimension of art, or the philosophy of art, has always been at the center of my philosophical worldview is that art itself has been one of the important elements of my personal life since my childhood. I was always attracted very much since my early years to beauty, to the beauty of nature, to the beauty of music and calligraphy, to art forms of various kinds, and this attraction has remained with me all my life. Even while I was at M.I.T., before going to Harvard, I would go to Harvard University and study with Professor Benjamin Rowland, who was then the leading scholar of Oriental art in the United States and had been a student of Ananda Coomaraswamy. I took almost all of his courses on Hindu, Buddhist, and Chinese art; unfortunately he did not teach a course on Islamic art. I also studied earlier European art with him. At the Fogg Museum at Harvard where Rowland taught, there was a very large collection of slides of various traditional art objects. This collection complemented for me the Coomaraswamy Library in which, as already mentioned, I studied for years, and I had open access to a remarkable collection of images and works on Oriental art. During that period of my life, that is, in my twenties, the intellectual understanding of what constituted traditional art was complemented by my existential attachment to that art and its direct experience. I could say the same especially about music, both Western and Oriental.

Traditional Art

Now, I was always attracted, in earlier days even before I knew that there was "traditional art" as defined by Coomaraswamy and others, to this art and not to modern art—and by modern art I do not mean only 20th-century art, but most of Western art from the Renaissance onward. I had never been attracted to naturalism, art simply trying to emulate the external forms of nature, nor to modern abstract art. Then as I undertook the study of these subjects with Rowland, combined with my own reading and experiencing of many forms of traditional art, my taste became more and more refined, and I came to know the symbolic meaning of, let us say, Hindu art, the meaning of various gestures of the divinities of the Hindu pantheon, of its various designs, symbolic forms, and patterns. The same held true for Buddhist art, and of course, our own Persian Islamic art, and in fact Islamic art in general. So I began to study art not simply for the sake of aesthetics in the usual sense of the word (because *aesthesis* in Greek has to do with sensation), but in order to discern the deepest spiritual meaning of art.

Later, when I went back to Persia, influenced a great deal by two figures—Coomaraswamy and Burckhardt, who had been the first person in the West to expound seriously the inner meaning of Islamic art—I continued my studies, and I turned to a large extent to the literary and philosophical study of the meaning of art, as well as to discourse with living masters of traditional Persian art. As you know, in Persian and Arabic philosophical works there are very few texts devoted separately to the philosophy of Islamic and Persian art as you have, let us say, in Benedetto Croce[2] in the West. You have to find the philosophy of Islamic art in pages here and there, and especially in Sufi texts, as well as through oral tradition.

I believe that the *Mathnawi* of Rumi is probably our most important source for the philosophy of art in the Persian language. I turned to these sources, such as Rumi, Awḥad al-Dīn Kirmānī, and others, who had written about the importance of symbolism and the beauty of forms, and parallel with that type of study, I immersed myself much more in our own artistic tradition. That is why also during the twenty-one years when I lived in Iran, between my leaving Harvard and returning to America in 1979, I was at the forefront of many important projects for the preservation of traditional Persian art. I organized the first conference on traditional architecture in Isfahan. I was also a member of a secret committee chosen by the Empress for the preservation of Isfahan and its traditional arts. I was also a member of the Supreme Council of Arts and Culture of Iran for some fifteen years. Furthermore, I always tried to be in contact with great masters of traditional art who lived and worked in Isfahan and other cities in different fields such as, for example, book binding, which was a great art in the Safavid period, but which was being gradually lost. We just had two or three masters left in such arts. Therefore, we tried to get some students to study with them, to learn from them the secrets of the art, and to spread their activities. So my practical concern was also very extensive. As I said before, even bringing Hasan Fathy, the greatest 20th-century Islamic architect, from Egypt to Iran—that was my doing.

I do not want to discuss too much in detail what I did in these domains, but I want to tell you that my interest in art followed, in a sense, two parallel paths. One was the study of the intellectual, philosophical, and spiritual meaning of traditional art, and the second, actual engagement in the process of preserving these arts, at least in my own home country, Iran. Needless to say, I could not do the same directly in other countries, although I did play a role in the foundation of the Prince of Wales Institute of Traditional Architecture in London. During all this time, of course, I was fully aware of the very profound distinction that exists between various traditional art and nontraditional or modern art, which constitutes most of the post-medieval art of the West, and I tried to point out these differences in my writings and lectures. These differences are much greater than those between various forms of traditional art. When we look at traditional art, let us say, we look at a piece of Persian or Arabic calligraphy or a Persian miniature, it does not look like a Chinese landscape painting or Japanese calligraphy, but the principles that are involved are much closer than, let us say, the relationship between a traditional Persian miniature by Behzad[3] or Reza 'Abbasi[4] on the one hand and some of the modern painters by Iranians on the other hand; although the latter belong to the same country and speak the same language, their language of expression and content of their paintings are no longer that of the traditional Persian world.

I began to realize this truth more and more, and delved into further study of traditional art seriously with the help of the works of Coomaraswamy and Burckhardt primarily, but also of Schuon and other perennialist thinkers, as well as a number of Western art critics such as Hans Sedlmayr, the famous Austrian art critic, people who were fully aware of what had happened to Western art. Sedlmayr is the author of several remarkable books such as *Art and Truth*.[5] I read such works in French, German, and English, along with works of those traditional authorities whom I mentioned, and it became more and more evident to me why the *David* of Michelangelo, one of the masterpieces of Renaissance art, is so different from the sculpture of the Chartres Cathedral in France. What had happened to bring about this radical change? This question became of great interest to me, and I have developed this subject in many of my writings throughout my life.

R.J.: In other words, you see a great difference between medieval art and Renaissance and post-Renaissance art in the West?

What Is Traditional Art?

S.H.N.: Yes, I do. Traditional art, at the heart of which stands sacred art, is an art in which the creator of the art, the artist, is an instrument for the expression of certain symbols, of certain ideas in the Platonic sense, which are beyond the individual and are executed artistically through traditional techniques. The ultimate origin of forms, contours, shapes, colors in all traditional art is not the individual psyche of the artist. It is the metaphysical world, the spiritual world that transcends the individual artist, and that is where the great difference between traditional and modern art comes from. Even in the West in the old days, when a Christian painter wanted to paint an icon of Christ or the Virgin—and this practice continues in the Greek Orthodox Church to this day—he would fast for forty days, prepare himself, be in a state of spiritual presence, and then he would paint the icon. And the icon was always based on certain laws, certain regulations, which the Christians considered to have come originally from Saint Luke and the archangel; that is, they had come from Heaven and then been transmitted for two thousand years. You cannot put your own ego into the art of the traditional icon. If you did so, it would no longer be an icon.

It is interesting to note the case of El Greco,[6] the famous Spanish painter who hailed originally from Greece. He brought certain techniques of iconic painting to his art, but he painted in an individualistic style. Therefore, you can always tell that his paintings are individualistic, and you can detect the profound difference between the traditional painting of an icon and the painting of the Christ images which he created. Some of these paintings are powerful, but they are no longer icons. Now, this is a very important point of difference that must be noted.

The icon painter in traditional Christian art is like any traditional artist. He does not try to express his own feelings and ideas; he does not say, "I am trying to express myself," as does a modern artist. A traditional artist would say, "What good does it do, and of what interest is it, for you to express yourself? There are another 6 billion people living on the surface of the earth. Why is my self more interesting than the self of the other 6 billion people, and what do I achieve by expressing myself?" In contrast, the traditional worldview is based on the idea that art must convey the truth, it must convey beauty, and it must convey meaning, a meaning that is ultimately universal precisely because it stands above the realm of the individual. It is universal and not bound to the ego of the individual artist.

In viewing many a modern canvas, often times you and I will not be able to understand its message. We might try to be a snob and say, "Oh yes, how interesting," but it does not have any meaning for us. We might enjoy the colors or shapes or something like that, but it does not convey any ultimate meaning in the metaphysical and spiritual sense. The artist has to go along with the painting to explain it to us or to say it has no meaning at all. He or she might even say that he or she did not want it to convey any meaning, and not even reflect beauty. These days in the West beauty has become separated even from much of art. Many modern artists believe that art does not have to be beautiful, whereas traditional art is always, as I said, a conduit for the presence of the sacred and the beautiful. That art is the reflection of a Platonic paradigm, idea, or archetype, in the Platonic sense, in the world of physical forms.

Naturalism

Another very important difference is that traditional art never emulates the external forms of nature; it is always against naturalism. Saint Thomas Aquinas expresses this truth in his exposition of the philosophy of Christian art. The same principle is of course to be found in Oriental art of all kinds, as well as in medieval European artistic forms. I mentioned the Chartres Cathedral. The figures in the sculpture of the Cathedral do not look like people walking on the streets of the town. The faces are elongated; they are not naturalistic. In Japanese or Chinese painting, a beautiful butterfly is painted, but the painting captures the essence of butterflyness, you might say; it is not simply an external emulation and copying of the natural shape of the butterfly. The same can be said of Persian art, which created one of the greatest schools of painting, although in Islam painting is not as important as it is in the Far Eastern and the Western traditions.

Calligraphy is much more important in Islamic art as embodying the "Divine Word." But let us just concern ourselves with traditional Persian painting. You look at these beautiful Timurid and Safavid miniatures that mark the peak of the Persian art of painting. You look at a mountain; it might be pink. I am sure you recall such a scene in your mind right now. You look at trees; they are "idealized," or what some people today call "abstract." They are not simple emulations of trees in the garden. They are prototypic trees, trees of paradise reflected here on earth, as are mountains, streams, and animals.

The decadence of Persian miniatures and Islamic paintings in general in Turkey during the Ottoman era, and in India in the Mogul period and somewhat later in Persia begins as soon as the figures and the space of the paintings become naturalistic. That change marks the beginning of the decadence of Persian, Ottoman, and Indian miniatures. The same is true of China in the Ming Dynasty as the forms painted on Chinese vases become more and more naturalistic. Japanese art became decadent much later and preserved its remarkable vitality within a traditional framework better than Chinese art. When you go to India and you see a statue of Vishnu like the beautiful medieval Vishnus of Nepal or Northern India, you realize that there is a whole science of how the body of the god is sculpted. Its result depicts life coming from within the sculpture without any naturalism. Likewise, the Buddha image of earlier periods is never meant to look like a man on the street. But with the decadence of these arts they become gradually naturalistic, as you can see in so much modern sculpture of India and the Buddhist world.

You might say that modern Western art of the past century and a half is not naturalistic either, but there is a very important difference. Western art rebelled against its own traditional past by turning towards humanism and naturalism. There appeared in the Renaissance a few great geniuses in art, such as Leonardo da Vinci, Raphael, and Michelangelo, who gradually transformed the high art of the Middle Ages into a more humanistic art, and many people in the modern world consider that to be great progress. But if you put these few individual geniuses aside, you realize better what was happening. The art was gradually becoming "humanistic *cum* naturalistic" rather than being symbolic. The famous paintings of the Virgin by Raphael are very sweet, very gentle, but in these canvases the Virgin looks like a sweet gentle girl taken from the streets of Florence or Milan and painted; whereas the figures of the Virgin done in the Middle Ages, the ones that are considered to perform miracles even today and that Christians go to visit as pilgrims in such places as Poland, do not look like an ordinary woman at all. They are symbolic iconic figures and not at all naturalistic.

So what happened in the Renaissance is that art tended more and more towards humanism *cum* naturalism, and this process continued until the 17th and 18th centuries, when naturalism reached its peak and became so heavy that people grew tired of it, and in a sense it crumbled under its own weight. How long can you go on painting naturalistic forms of human beings, trees, and animals and things like that as if they were in the natural state, while being in reality deprived of life and the reality of that state? Islam opposes so much naturalistic depiction and painting of life forms because of this reason, for these naturalistic forms become spiritually opaque and finally crumble.

After Naturalism

For a while you have this very ingenious new wave of impressionistic art which tries to capture some of the qualities of nature without being naturalistic: Renoir, Dégas, Monet, Van Gogh, these painters used light and colors to bring out certain spiritual qualities of nature without simply emulating the external forms of nature. But even that was a transient phase, and soon the whole world of form broke down from below, and you had 20th-century art starting with Picasso and continuing to our own day. In modern art you have the dissolution of form, and you have such schools as cubism and surrealism, which is really subrealism, for it falls below rather than transcends natural forms. Instead of breaking the natural forms from above like all traditional art, these forms are broken from below. So art becomes more and more psychological, subjective, and individualistic. At least a face painted in the 17th century looked like a face; but now gradually you begin to get a disintegration of natural forms. So there is a very profound difference that is involved between the opposition of traditional art to naturalism and that of modern art to it.

The different understandings of art are not simply a question of ethnicity or nationality, but of worldviews. We both come from a country which is very artistically gifted. There are now Persian painters painting in a modernistic style like their Western counterparts, but that does not make them traditional Persian painters. They are in fact painting in the style based on another philosophy of art that they have imported from the West. There are many other points to mention, but I think that I have said enough on this question to at least set the background for you to understand why it is that I have been so much interested in the traditional philosophy of art.

Form

There is, however, one more point that I want to add to this answer, one which I think is quite important, and that is the meaning of form itself. Today, form, as understood traditionally and going back to *morphos* in Greek and *forma* in Latin, is often confused with shape, and this is a widespread error. The traditional philosophy of art is a philosophy that deals with the meaning of forms in the traditional philosophical sense, because normal art deals with form as understood traditionally. Even the musical art has its own musical forms. There is a lack of attention to form as traditionally understood, in its ontological sense, in much of modern Western thought, starting with science from the Scientific Revolution onward.

In modern science, especially in physics, the forms of nature are disregarded in the name of mathematical forms which are invisible. Consequently, visible forms are no longer considered as the appropriate subject for scientific study except in the descriptive sciences. But in physics, the mother of the modern sciences, one is not interested in the form of the rock but in its mass, in its geometry, in its velocity if it is moving. These parameters are not form as we understood it either in the Platonic or the Aristotelian sense of the term. This banishment of form in the sense of *morphos* by modern science had a great deal to do with the destruction of the traditional philosophy of art.

Recently, a number of Western philosophers of art have tried to resuscitate the meaning of form in art, but they have not been able to recapture the meaning of it as understood in the mainstream of traditional thought. Therefore, the traditional philosophy of art, whether it be Persian and Arabic in the Islamic world, Japanese and Chinese in the Far East, Hindu and Buddhist in the Indian world, medieval Christian in the West, among the primal people of the Americas, Australia, and Africa, who in a sense belong to one family, has remained marginalized in the modern world. If you ask today what art is, what its function is, what the meaning of art is and why one should create art, the answer given oftentimes by Western philosophers of art and those who specialize in modern aesthetics is "art for art's sake." The modern response is that you just create art for the sake of art; but this was never the answer of traditional civilizations where one created art for both the sake of attainment of inner perfection and for human need in the deepest sense—because the needs of man are not only physical, they are also spiritual. We are as much in need of beauty as of the air that we breathe.

Utility

So in traditional civilizations, art was never separated from life, from utility in the deepest sense of the term, and not in the sense of the philosophical utilitarianism of the 19th century. I mean utility in the sense of something which is needed by human beings in the deepest sense and is therefore very important for them to survive as human beings. Art was always associated with life itself; in traditional civilizations, art was life and life was art. I remember a wonderful sentence by Coomaraswamy. He said that in the modern world the artist is a special kind of man, whereas in traditional India or in the traditional world in general, every man was a special kind of artist. It is this truth that has become forgotten. It is this vision that we have lost: the vision of the identity of art with life itself. That is why we have museums, and that is why traditional civilizations did not need to have museums. That is why objects of everyday life, the utensils that your grandmother and my grandmother took to the public bath with them, the cloth they wrapped around themselves while there, you could put in a museum today. Any 19th-century carpet from Iran is now seen as a work of art, because it was made by hand according to certain principles with natural dyes and *is* art in the highest sense. Traditional art extended itself to the whole of life and left an imprint of beauty upon the everyday existence of human beings rather than being concerned only with paintings that we put in museums and at best visit a few Sundays each year.

Beauty

R.J.: So we have become alien to art because we have become alien to life?

S.H.N.: In a certain sense, yes, to normal life. We no longer live normal lives. The great tragedy is that many people in the West, including thinkers who should have known better, have made beauty into a luxury. Marxism especially did a great deal of harm in identifying beauty with wealth and luxury, and its followers often said: "Oh, once your stomach is full, then you can think of beauty," but that is not at all the case. We need beauty as much as the food we eat and the air we breathe. It is part of our basic needs in order to live normally as human beings. Yes, there was disease, and there were poor people in traditional societies; there is no doubt about that. But even poverty then was not ugly in the way that poverty is ugly today in modern industrialized societies. If you go to a poor village in India—I do not mean the big cities which have already become Westernized, I do not mean Calcutta with thousands of cars in the street—but if you go to a traditional village in India which by Western standards appears to be poor and compare it with some of the slums around Paris, of Harlem in New York, or Anacostia in Washington, you will see the qualitative difference. That poverty of the Indian, Bangladeshi, or Moroccan village is still close to nature. There are still things there that are beautiful even if there is not much wealth, and there are aspects of beauty associated with life itself.

In contrast, in the modern world, unfortunately most people cannot afford what they would call beautiful things, so that the ordinary things of life are much uglier than in the traditional world. Look at, for example here, at the United States, the richest country in the world. Put aside a few gadgets such as cars, trains, refrigerators, computers, and the like that are of so much concern to people today. Take, for example, the clothing that people wear and compare that with the traditional clothing still worn in parts of the world mentioned above that have not become modernized. Obviously the traditional clothing is much more beautiful than what most of us wear and its material usually finer. Here, you have to be pretty rich to buy good quality wool or cotton or have somebody bring it for you from India, and not everybody can afford it. Poor ordinary people here wear mostly nylon and all kinds of artificial materials like that. What only the rich can afford was possessed by ordinary people in traditional societies if we look at the quality of things and not only their quantity.

As for the food that is eaten, there is a lot more food here, but look at the quality. Again you have to be rich here to buy natural food, which was the ordinary food that everybody ate in earlier times. The presentation of food and the carpet that you sat on to eat it in nearly every home in Iran, even in the villages, were more beautiful than we see in the industrialized world today. Now they sell those carpets for a few thousand dollars on Wisconsin Avenue here in Washington, and you have to be pretty wealthy to afford a piece to put in a place of honor in your home. I could go on and on. The hat one wore, the shoes, the utensils, everything in days of old were made with art and were beautiful. They were made with human hands and not machines, but now objects of the same quality have become a luxury. When an object is handmade it becomes much more expensive to purchase. In this sense, beauty has in fact become reduced to luxury. Yes, I think we have really lost the meaning of life itself. We live below ourselves in ugliness, unaware that the need for beauty is as profound in the human being as the need for food, water, clothing, and shelter.

R.J.: Does it have to do also with the concept of the sacred, which is so important in your thought, and does it have to do with the fact, as you said, that beauty is no longer sacred and we do not relate any more the sacred to beauty? If you agree with this, how do you differentiate between religious art and sacred art? Is there a differentiation?

S.H.N.: First of all, let me answer the first question, and then we will come to the second. In the deepest mystical sense, Beauty with a capital "B" belongs to God. We have the *ḥadīth* of the Prophet: "God is beautiful and He loves beauty." The name *al-Jamīl* in Arabic, which means "The Beautiful," is one of the Names of God in Islam. Therefore, by its very nature, beauty in itself is sacred, but when it is reflected in this world, precisely because it is sacred, it is liked a double-edged sword. On the one hand, it can lead us to Beauty as such, to the Sacred. On the other hand, it can itself become for us a snare, a substitute for the sacred that separates us from the Divine Source. A certain strand of Western Christianity in modern times emphasizes this aspect of the truth exclusively, often with unfortunate consequences. It emphasizes the good above the beautiful, and one of the reasons why so many 20th-century Catholic thinkers have allowed and in fact praised building ugly churches which are like factories goes back indirectly to this view. They say that Christ was born in a manger, forgetting that he was not born in a Detroit factory. These modernist Catholic thinkers have given the argument that in the Middle Ages also the churches looked like the municipality building, forgetting that then it was the municipality building that looked like a church. In any case, this idea exists in certain Christian circles that beauty in a sense is a veil for the soul and can distance one away from God, and that it is not necessary for human life here on earth. In the Islamic perspective, much more emphasis is placed upon beauty, and this is also true of the Eastern Orthodox Church. I think that in fact the farther east you go from Europe to the Islamic world, the more does beauty becomes central in the theological sense. The *Philokalia*, which is an essential text of Orthodox spirituality, means "love of beauty."

Anyway, there is this double aspect to beauty. For example, a person can fall in love with a beautiful woman, and the attraction of female beauty for the male, because it is really a reflection of the Beauty of God, can itself become ensnaring and often a distraction from God. It can capture the mind and soul completely unto itself. Therefore, the importance of detachment and asceticism have always been emphasized in various religions and not only Christianity in order to enable human beings to understand that all beauty comes from the Sacred—but that to reach this truth, one must, first of all, practice detachment from what one might mistake for the Source of beauty while that entity is but Its shadow. This legitimate attitude must not, however, be confused with the modern "cult of ugliness" accepted in certain Christian circles that I criticized above for from the metaphysical point of view, from the Sufi point of view, of which I speak, all beauty is a reflection of Divine Beauty and can lead to the Source of that reflection. When the Sufis speak of metaphorical love and real love and also beauty, they are referring to this distinction between the Source and its earthly reflection. This is a very profound distinction made by the Sufis, and great masters have written about this subject. For example, Awhad al-Din Kermani[7] was one of the key figures in the exposition of the meaning of metaphorical beauty and metaphorical love as reflections of real beauty and real love concerning God.

In truth there is no love in the universe which is not ultimately the love of God, of the Sacred, and no beauty which is not the reflection of Divine Beauty. Even a person who thinks that he is an atheist, when he says, "I am an atheist, and I do not believe in anything," he has actually transferred his religious love and devotion to something else other than formal religion, but the search for love and beauty still exists in him even if he is unaware of their transcendent Source. When such a person, if he is sensitive to music, listens to Johann Sebastian Bach or Mozart, he wants everything to be very quiet, concentrating completely with his whole soul in a state of devotion. In fact what he is doing is searching for the Sacred in this beautiful music, but he is not aware of the real source of this attraction for his soul. What is it that is attracting him to Bach or Mozart "religiously"? Why is he so much interested in this musical experience? Where does this state in his mind and soul come from? Often he is not aware enough to really sit down and seek to discover what the source of this "feeling" is.

From our point of view every beauty is associated with the Sacred, but not everyone is aware of the levels of the reflection of Beauty, which is one of the attributes of the Sacred as such. When Plato said, "Beauty is the splendor of the Truth," he made a statement that is very close to Sufism and the Islamic perspective. As I said, Islam asserts that one of God's Qualities is Beauty, a basic truth that Plato was affirming in his statement "Beauty is the splendor of the Truth." Beauty is light emanating from the crown of the Sacred and is in its essence celestial. Beauty is in fact the splendor of Reality as such.

Religious Art and Sacred Art

As for your second question, "What is the difference between religious art and sacred art?" I am glad you brought up this question. If you had lived 500 years ago even in Europe, I would say that there was no basic difference, and that sacred art was the religious art at the heart of the art of Christian civilization, an art that was traditional in nature; but now, 500 years later, there is a very important difference, because traditional art has been replaced by humanistic and even subhuman "art." What we now have is a religious art that is no longer traditional and certainly not sacred art. In the present-day context, religious art is an art whose subject is religious, but its manner of execution, its methods and its language, are not that of sacred art, and it does not possess the same symbolic significance. Until the 19th century, it was only religious art in the West that was not sacred art; now you have the same situation to some degree in other civilizations with the global spread of modernism which started in the West.

Supposing you have, let us say, a Marc Chagall, a Jewish painter painting angels floating up from the earth. I am sure that you remember such paintings. Now, that is religious art, but it is not sacred art, because its subject is a religious one, namely angels; but his execution and formal language are not those of traditional Jewish art. On the Christian side, there are all of these paintings of Christ, such as the famous Christ of Velasquez, the 19th-century Spanish painter, which is in the Prado Museum in Madrid and is one of the most famous paintings of Christ. These are religious art and not sacred art. Or take the painting of the Virgin by Raphael, or the scene of the Last Supper by Leonardo da Vinci. These are great masterpieces from the human point of view, but they are not sacred art; they are religious art. So, modern religious art is the large category of art which pertains through its subject matter to religious themes, but not by its means of execution and the use of symbolism, which transcend the individual order and belong to the suprahuman realm, which is the source of sacred art.

The origin of sacred art is considered by all traditions to be the Sacred itself. If you look, for example, at Islam, the highest sacred plastic art is Quranic calligraphy, since it is the depiction of the Word of

God. Muslims believe that calligraphy originated with 'Alī ibn Abī Ṭālib and that he was the first calligrapher who used beautiful Arabic script. Whether this assertion is right or wrong historically is irrelevant, because we can never prove or disapprove it; but the fact that this claim is made, which means that Muslims saw calligraphy as originating from the person who, after the Prophet, was the most important spiritual figure of Islam, is what is significant. Let us turn to Buddhism and the Buddha image. The Buddhists believe that the beauty of the Buddha image saves. They believe that the origin of the Buddha image is not simply human. Rather, its origin is the Buddha within. It is based on a vision resulting from enlightenment which allows the artist to "see" or to emulate previous visions and subsequently to depict that vision externally in forms of celestial origin. Buddhist art is highly stylized and traditional, with the protrusion on the top of the head and elongated ears, et cetera of the Buddha figure. The Buddha image is not just a fancy of a particular artist issuing from his psyche but issues from the Buddha nature itself. As I mentioned, in Christianity, the origin of the icon is considered to be the archangel who revealed it to Saint Luke. It is not a man sitting in Athens who decides to paint Christ according to his own imagination and not as he has been painted as an icon for two millennia.

Sacred art, according to those who produced it and those who lived with it, comes from the Sacred itself; it does not have a human origin. Its origin is either anonymous or is associated with an angel or an exceptional spiritual figure such as 'Alī and so on, whereas religious art has a ordinary human origin. From a philosophical point of view it is important to make this precise distinction. If you say that religious art is art dealing with a subject of a religious nature, then, of course, sacred art would be a branch of religious art. But in order to make our definitions clear, I think it is better to distinguish the two, because "religious art" as the term is understood today is very different from sacred art. Today in the West and to some extent elsewhere, sacred art must be clearly distinguished from the religious art that is being produced precisely because much of what is called religious art is no longer traditional but individualistic and psychological. I think that once we consider these examples carefully, its becomes clear how sacred art is distinct from religious art in the post-medieval West and also outside of the Western world since the 19th century, in fact wherever you already have had the decadence of the traditional arts.

In India, for example, both Hindu and Islamic art in the form of painting began to decay as a result of European influence in Delhi and other big cities, but Islamic and Hindu architecture, as well as the traditional symbolic representation of the pantheon of the Hindu gods, was still preserved to a large extent. I mean that Ganesh still looked like the traditional depiction of Ganesh. It is only since the last century that if one goes inside a modern Hindu temple, one sees that both the paintings and statues of Krishna have become naturalized. This naturalistic art is Hindu religious art; it is not Hindu sacred art. It is not like the Dance of Shiva from the 11th century or the medieval sculptures and paintings of Krishna. This basic distinction was made by Coomaraswamy and Burckhardt among others. Also I have written an essay on religious, traditional, and sacred art[8] in which I make a clear distinction between these categories of art.

R.J.: Is it impossible to understand sacred art without penetrating into the religion that has produced this art?
S.H.N.: Again I have to answer yes and no. It is not possible to understand fully in the sense of becoming totally transformed by the sacred art that belongs to a particular universe other than one's own unless one knows and is able to penetrate in depth into the religion in question, but one can become deeply affected. For example, a devout Muslim contemplating an icon of Christ can have an appreciation of that icon, but he will not be able to assimilate it fully without being open to the spiritual universe that produced that art, and in any case he cannot use it ritually. Likewise, a Buddhist from Japan who visits a medieval cathedral can have a profound experience of its beauty but cannot fully understand it without full comprehension of Christian theology and cosmology. So on that level, I would say no.

On the level of spiritual empathy, however, a certain degree of understanding and participation in depth is definitely possible in principle, because it is possible for human intelligence to understand things by anticipation. Once you understand what traditional art is, it is also possible to understand the language of another sacred universe and to participate in its presence to a great degree and be moved and even transformed spiritually by its beauty without being fully immersed in that universe.

The same holds true for human language but in a different way. You and I, our mother tongue is Persian, but we have studied for years, let us say, English, French, and a few other languages, but I am sure that you and I cannot appreciate and enjoy fully the poetry of our third or fourth language like the person who is a native speaker of that language, although we can enjoy it to some extent. You and I understand fully Persian poetry, but for someone in the West who has even studied Persian poetry for years, it is hard to fully understand Ḥāfiẓ as you and I do; but it is not impossible. I know a few Americans who, without being Persian, have mastered Persian so well, and penetrated so deeply into the spiritual world that this poetry represents, that when they read a verse of Ḥāfiẓ, they can say with their heart, "How beautiful," and this poetry really penetrates into their soul.

Now, this example can be transposed to sacred art itself. A man such as Burckhardt wrote *Sacred Art in East and West*,[9] each chapter of which deals with one of the major schools of sacred art: Hindu, Buddhist, Taoist, Christian, and Islamic—these five major traditions. Each chapter is really a masterpiece penetrating into the meaning of the sacred message of the sacred art in question. His description of the spiritual message of a Taoist landscape painting is considered by many Chinese to be incredible. Yes, it is possible intellectually, spiritually, and also artistically to understand other forms of sacred art than one's own; but it is not possible to be fully transformed and saved in the religious sense by these sacred arts unless one is able to penetrate and "live" within their sacred and spiritual universe. Let us not forget that because the function of sacred art is to help in our salvation and deliverance, it is there to convey a message that transforms and saves us. Sacred art possesses a presence that can penetrate us and help lift us to the Divine Empyrean beyond the realm of earthly existence.

You are a Persian, and when you visit one of the great masterpieces of mosque architecture in the Islamic world, you observe numerous worshipers and see thousands of pilgrims standing or sitting there, or in a state of prayers. The beauty of the ambience penetrates into them. They know that they are in a sacred ambience and have a feeling for the sacred itself, but they do not say, "Oh, this arch is from 14th century," or "Look at that cobalt color, how beautiful it is." Many years ago I took some twenty of the leading European philosophers, who were extremely cultivated men but were educated in the West, to the mausoleum of Imam Reza in Mashhad. They were fascinated by the remarkable architecture and calligraphy, and they were analyzing the art, but they were not being transformed by the sacred presence of that art, because they were not living within the same spiritual universe, and most did not even have a sense of the sacred. I remember that there was a Jewish philosopher among them, the famous Emmanuel Levinas. He stood by the wall silently for some time; I said to him, "Why do you not come with us?"

He said, "I am just trying to be quiet and let this space penetrate into me." He had a sense of the sacred presence of the ambience, but obviously the rest of group was not like the ordinary pilgrims, who did not have one hundredth of the education of these men; but they were traditional Persians, and so the sacred presence which emanates from this ambience created by this art was able to transform them. That is the real function of sacred art. It was not made to be put in a museum. It was not made to be appreciated only aesthetically. The beauty in such an art is the vehicle for the Sacred itself; the beauty of such art is the ladder to Divine Beauty. Sacred art cannot transform us until we participate in the spiritual universe that has created it.

R.J.: Sacred art is also very much related to the mythological point of view.
S.H.N.: Yes, that is true in many but not all traditions.

R.J.: The mythological point of view in which, as you know, the Divine has become personified. What kind of relationship do you see—because you did not talk about myths—what kind of relationship do you see between the sacred and myths?
S.H.N.: That is again a vast question, one that does not deal with only art, but with philosophy and religion as well.

R.J.: Yes, but especially with art?
S.H.N.: Sacred art does not have to be mythological in order to be sacred art. It depends how the truths of the revelation of the religion in question are expressed. The reason is that the sacred art of a religion is related not only to the principal truths but also to the forms in which those truths are revealed. Let us take two sister civilizations, the Hindu and the Islamic, which are geographically neighbors. Hinduism was expressed through myths, Islam through metaphysical ideas. Both such forms of expression of the sacred are possible, and both religions developed sacred art of vast proportions. In India the two came together in a single land and side by side. So the idea that sacred art is only of a mythological kind dealing with the iconography of divine beings is not true. To express the sacred, one can also make use of abstract forms of sacred geometry, which symbolize the intelligible world, as in Islamic art and in certain other forms of art, such as that of the Native Americans in this country. Certain Native American tribes developed a very geometric art, which is sacred. Even the beautiful sand paintings they make on the ground, and put people in the middle of it sometimes for healing

or to aid in spiritual realization, are pure geometry. Much of this art is like Islamic art and is of an "abstract" and geometric character, and that is a possibility that has been realized in more than one tradition.

That possibility can, however, be understood only if we do not commit the error that has been made, I believe, in the last few centuries in the West, the error of seeing an irreducible dichotomy between *mythos* and *logos*, an error that we see in so much recent Western philosophy. Philosophers who speak of this dichotomy are right to some extent when they say that modern civilization has killed *mythos*, but they are not completely right, because they then reduce *logos* to simply reason, and pit *logos* as reason against *mythos*. If we do that, we can no longer understand the relationship between sacred art based on myth and nonmythological forms of sacred art, because we are excluding the importance of the intellect as traditionally understood, which is related to both *logos* and *mythos*.

Myth and symbol are interrelated. I would agree that without symbol, there is no sacred art at all; but without myth, as I said, there is a possibility of a sacred art that is based on a nonmythic expression of the truth. But if myth and symbol are taken together as one reality, then of course they become a necessity for sacred art. Myth is symbol that is lived and acted out. The meaning of myth and symbol and their relation was brought out in 20th-century thought in the West by a number of scholars, especially Mircea Eliade, in such books as *Mythes et symboles*, which has now also come out in English[10]; and also by a number of other writers, all of whom were directly or indirectly influenced by the traditional writers such as Coomaraswamy and Guénon, whose *Symboles fondamentaux de la science sacré*, which also has a fine English translation,[11] is particularly significant for this subject. These authors make clear that symbols are not man-made signs or images.

If you understand symbol as the reflection in the lower level of reality of a reality of a higher order, then the symbol in its dynamic form corresponds to myth and in its static form to what we usually mean when we use the word *symbol*. Let us take the symbol of the cross or a circle or spiral, or something like that. In its dynamic form, it becomes myth, which is enacted in sacred history. A myth is really a meta-historical enactment by mythological figures of a basic truth. It is a truth that is enacted, but not in ordinary time. So myth is more real than historical reality, and the fact that we have debased the word today when we say, "Well, historical reality is what is real, whereas this or that is only myth," which means that it is false—this is due to the fact that we have lost sight of truths that are meta-historical, and nontemporal. Now, if we take the meanings of symbol and myth together, in the sense that I have defined them, then you can say that myth is itself a symbol emphasized in the art of civilizations whose founding religion has a mythic character; whereas nonmythic symbols are also a major possibility. Any civilization which loses its understanding of myth and symbol can no longer produce sacred art. This is what happened in the modern West except among certain marginal figures outside the mainstream.

The famous painter Rouault,[12] a very important religious painter in France in the 20th century, painted some moving images of Christ which are modernistic, but they are very deeply impregnated with a sense of piety which he had. He once said, "Although I am a painter, I would be willing to have my arm cut off if I could live within a world in which symbols were alive and which could be used in painting." In medieval European civilization or in our own Islamic civilization or that of India or any other traditional civilization, symbols were alive as well myths, as particular kinds of symbols, and there was a common language of discourse based on them. For example, in our Persian poetry symbols are still alive. When we read of saki (*sāqī*) and wine, they still form a part of a common symbolic language which most people still understand. Persian Sufi poetry is almost like sacred art and marks the peak of the Persian poetic tradition.

I think that the question that you ask is important, and I want to make it clear why I have not in my own writings referred much to mythology, occasionally making references to it here and there. The reason I have not done so is that I have not really felt the need for it, because it has been discussed so thoroughly and profoundly in general already by such people as Coomaraswamy and Eliade, and as far as India in particular is concerned, by Heinrich Zimmer and Alain Daniélou, among others; but I have always been aware, of course, of the importance of mythology. Personally, I have always been more attracted to the nonmythological expressions of metaphysics. For example, when I was studying Greek thought, what really attracted me was the early Greek philosophers especially the pre-Socratics, then Socrates, Plato, Aristotle, and the later Neoplatonic School, particularly Plotinus and Proclus.

Greek mythology held little attraction for me. I would keep reading about it, but it seemed to be less satisfying to read about all those anthropomorphic gods fighting against each other on top of Mount Olympus than to read the metaphysics of Plotinus. But of course that was the decayed form of the religion of the Greeks, emptied of its original meaning. It took many decades, after I had studied so many philosophical explanations of the Olympian religion and of Greek mythology, to gain some interest in it and to take it seriously. Still, the formal expression of Greek religious mythology did not and does not attract me as much as "abstract" intellectual expressions. As far as India is concerned, I was again much more attracted to, let us say, the *Gita* and the Upanishads, than the great epics, but nevertheless I read the epics and understand the beauty of the mythological perspective; but it is not my own. I am more interested in symbolism in the other sense of it, although I have the greatest respect for mythology.

So the fact that I have not written so much about mythological subjects has not been due to my opposition to them, not at all. No society can live without myths, even Islamic society. Many of these modernized Islamic thinkers who are trying to become rationalists and who try to demythologize Islamic myths in the sense that I use the term are totally wrong. They are secularizing the world around them. To kill myth is to secularize the world, to kill the sacred. But that does not mean that every tradition has to express its truths only in purely mythological terms; and yet no tradition can be complete without myths. For example, the *mir'āj* of the Prophet of Islam[13]—this is both a historical fact and a metaphysical reality, but it is also a myth in the true meaning of the term in that it concerns a transhistorical reality that has been re-enacted over the ages by those making the spiritual journey. That is why Sufis of every century have tried to emulate it, and so many have written about its symbolic and esoteric meaning.

The Sacred in the Modern World

R.J.: Can we go back to the meaning of the sacred in the Western world, because I know that you do not agree with it, but I would like to know your point of view. For some contemporary anthropologists, there are such places as Disney World, which has become a ritual space for people where they can experience the "sacred." So when you ask them, they will say that Western culture is not devoid of sacred objects. I know that you are against this and you think that the modern world is largely devoid of the sacred. What do you think of the way people try to find the sacred in the modern world? Since they cannot find it anywhere else, they try to find it in places such as Disney World, for example.

S.H.N.: Yes, this is a good question. Let me first mention that Eliade once wrote, "Modern man will not stay put until he has killed all the gods"—that was his expression, in the sense of destroying all that is sacred, as he mentions in his book *Le sacré et le profane*, translated into English as *The Sacred and the Profane*,[14] and he is quite right. One of the characteristics of modernism has been to try to remove all traces of the sacred from human life. For example, like a vacuum cleaner, the positivists in the Vienna Circle[15] wanted to remove all the "cobwebs" of metaphysics, philosophically speaking, from Western thought, while also destroying the sense of the sacred. In contrast, traditional man possessed a "symbolist spirit," to use the words of Frithjof Schuon, by which he meant that traditional man was able to "see" sacred symbols everywhere. Modern man can no longer see symbols; he only sees facts. Is it not interesting that in the Persian language there is no word for "fact"? You have to say *amr* or something like that; that is also true for Arabic. We have been able to get by for thousands of years without having a word for "fact." This is very significant because it shows that traditionally one lived in a world dominated not by fact but by symbols, whereas the modern world has lost the sense of symbols and the sacred, and symbols are reduced to facts.

I do not, of course, mean that this is so for everybody, because there might be a small village in Ireland, Italy, France, or someplace else in the West where religion is still strong, and the sense of the presence of myths and symbols in life has survived; and this is true not only in the Catholic world but in the Protestant world as well. In a sense, however, Protestantism helped to secularize the world around it, much more than did Catholicism, and tried to concentrate the sacred in the act of faith, in the relation between man and God, while the world outside was allowed to become to a large extent secularized. I do not want to get into all the historical forces that led to this secularization of the world and the loss of the symbolist spirit and the vision of the Source of the sacred, for it is a very complicated matter, but I mention it briefly by way of coming back to the question you asked, because it is so significant.

The imprint of the sacred upon the human soul cannot be erased so easily. One can "kill the gods," if I can quote Eliade again, but one cannot destroy the space which they or, in other expressions of the sacred, occupied within the soul. Modern man, having succeeded in killing the gods, you might say, and in destroying the sacred, cannot destroy the space it had always occupied in its soul. Soon he tries to substitute something for it in order to fill that space, and that is what we observe today. For example, take mountain climbing, before we get to Walt Disney. This kind of heroic mountain climbing that we see today, trying to climb the side of a mountain which is almost a straight wall and seeking to subjugate the mountain, takes place now when people no longer climb the spiritual mountain. Besides the idea of humiliating nature and subjugating it, modern mountain climbing also signifies a kind of substitution for spiritual mountain climbing. Flight into space became possible with the invention of the airplane, and many have a yearning to fly. Of course, the Shamans do not only have the yearning to fly for they do so every day although it is in spiritual space. The experience of flight exists in fact in all traditional civilizations—except that before, you had to train yourself spiritually in order to be able to fly instead of just buying a ticket from Air France. You can go down the list of many activities carried out today which are attempts to replace the loss of the spiritual and the sacred.

What has happened in places such as Disney World and even the malls in the United States is, in a sense, to attempt to create substitutes for the cathedrals and sacred spaces of traditional Western civilization. People used to go on Sunday, not to the mall, but to cathedrals and churches. Some people, of course, still go to church, but a large number of people prefer to go to malls or theme parks like Disney World, which have become centers of secularized life and determine for many what life is all about today. To that extent, I agree with you. But such places are not sacred; they are false substitutes for the sacred, and that is why they are, spiritually speaking, ugly. That is why so many intelligent persons with spiritual sensibility are put off by them. The intelligent person in the 13th century was not only not put off by the cathedral, but felt at home in it. Saint Thomas Aquinas had no trouble going to the cathedrals of his days. Even the University of Paris itself, the Sorbonne, where you studied, was a very beautiful place in the Middle Ages. It was like a cathedral and had traditional architecture.

The Chapel of Saint Louis, the saintly French king, was also visited by many of his entourage, who were very learned men and highly cultured, but they did not, obviously, feel disturbed or offended in visiting it, just the opposite. That chapel is so beautiful that today people pay money just to see it. The most intelligent and well-educated tourists in Paris go inside the Ministry of Justice to experience the beautiful space of the chapel, which is also a sacred space. Medieval France did not need a Disney World to keep its people occupied and amused. Now, why is it that a person like you, who is an educated person, if you go to Disney World you want to run away after a few minutes, unless you go for the sake of your child or go to Epcot Center where there are replicas of the traditional architecture of Morocco or India? It is interesting to notice that once you go there, you feel that outside these recreations of traditional ambiences, anything else is all superficial, all these objects made of plastic, with all these balloons, all this artificiality, all this noise, all this crowding. I went there once just to see what it was like, but I went especially to see the Epcot Center, dedicated to various traditional cultures. I refused to visit any of the other "attractions," and I know many highly educated persons with some spiritual sensitivity who have done the same. Traditional societies created an ambience that attracted and held within its grasp all members of society, from the most educated to the least educated, from the saint to the ordinary person in the street, in contrast to what we see in the modern world.

These modern substitutions for the sacred do not really satisfy the spirit; that is the evident problem. Practically every American parent wants to take his or her children once to Disney Land or Disney World, but if an ordinary American were to go there every day, he or she would be put off after a while. In contrast, in the traditional city, people would visit sacred places every day during their whole life and would not become bored or tired of it. So, obviously, even from an anthropological and sociological point of view, you are not dealing with the same reality. I think that it is important to emphasize that all of such modern places signify the creation of false substitutes to compensate for the loss of the sacred.

R.J.: Yes, but apparently this experience does not prevent the emergence of the fact that art is dying at some point. I really want to know how real, after all, should be our philosophical worry about the fact that art is dying in the world today. I think that even if we can no longer produce sacred art, we can still preserve it in our own memories, because we are still preserving it in museums. We are preserving art in our memories like the literary tradition, which is preserved in the memory of characters. For example, we see the film of a civilization where they can burn books and people become books themselves, because they have to preserve this heritage in their memory. For example, one becomes part of *War and Peace* of Tolstoy by reading it or seeing its film, and I think that today sacred art has become like this. I mean, we have become living memories of sacred art. As you said, we do not truly live it anymore.

S.H.N.: First of all, let us come back to the first part of your comment. We live in a world in which not all art is dying. It is not really all of art, but only traditional and sacred art that are dying. Today, people just create anything and say, "Well, this is art." What is the difference between, let us say, the people who go to the junkyard and pick up a few pieces of a junk car, put them together, weld them together, and create modern sculpture, and traditional Hindu sculpture and the statues of the Buddha or something like that? Of course, I do not agree that both are art in the same sense. It is true that in the modern world traditional art is on the retreat. Wherever modernism goes, it tries to destroy the traditional arts. This process has also a lot to do with the question of making money, of greed, because modern industrial society wants to substitute the products of the machine for things that are man-made. Why is it that people go all the way to the island of Bali? It is because on this island you still see the vibrant living tradition of making things by hand along with traditional music and theatre, and they wish to escape even for a short while from a world in which the products of the machine have replaced art made by human hands. Nearly everything in Bali is authentically artistic, and that is why it is so famous. There are other places in Java which are similar but not as well known. One finds there and also elsewhere artistic traditions that have survived, but modernization means for the most part the destruction of these traditional arts and their banishment to the margin of society, to museums, to memories similar to the banishment of live sacred and traditional music from the everyday texture of life and its relegation to the concert hall.

That, however, is not the complete picture. There is another current that is going on which is quite interesting. If thirty or forty years ago, someone spoke about the demise or death of the traditional and sacred arts in many parts of the world, it would be closer to the truth than now. I am not trying to belittle the tremendous challenge that modern industrial society poses for the traditional arts and the destruction of so much traditional art by the products of the machine; but I think there has been a certain amount of comeback of traditional art here and there, although in general the eclipse and marginalization of the traditional arts has gone hand in hand with the spread of modern industrialization.

Let us take the Islamic world itself. From the 19th century until about fifty years ago, in the middle of the 20th century, those who should have been the patrons of the arts were as before either the rulers and wealthy aristocracy or the well-to-do merchant class. There was also patronage from the Sufis and the '*ulamā*' for certain arts, but for the moment let us put that aside. Most of the rulers and the aristocracy along with wealthy merchants, who were the major patrons of the arts, had, however, become almost completely modernized by that time. In our own country, Persia, forty, fifty years ago in the house of the rich there would be nothing Persian except the carpets. The rest consisted of objects, things that were second-rate French, or other European objects of the modern period, from furniture to porcelains and paintings. Those who had been patrons of the traditional arts were trying to run away from their own traditional culture. Few cared about the fact that if you do not buy a piece from a Persian craftsman, gradually his art would die, and his son would not follow his father in mastering the art. The same can be said for the rest of the Islamic world.

Now fifty years later, the situation of the arts in the Islamic world is somewhat better, not worse, and this fact itself is quite remarkable, considering the rapid process of industrialization that has gone on. Two countries, Iran and in Morocco, took the lead in reviving traditional arts because a situation was created in which the patronage for such arts existed. In Iran, the former Empress was a great patron of the traditional arts; she loved these arts, and people like myself took advantage of that fact and pushed for the preservation of the traditional arts and for their revival, and in these efforts we were supported by her. In Morocco, the late King Hasan was a great lover of traditional art and architecture and built beautiful palaces, mosques, libraries, et cetera all over the country, each of which used numerous craftsmen and artists, and this activity revived many of the traditional arts that were dying out.

In general in the bazaars of most of the Islamic world even today, about seventy or eighty percent of the material for sale is practically junk, made of plastic in China or in older days in Japan. Now Japan is too wealthy to make such products; so it is now China that has taken its place. But gradually one is beginning to observe a trend in the other direction. The objects that we find today in the bazaars of many Islamic countries such as Syria and Indonesia, and not only Iran and Morocco, include many beautiful traditional objects—certainly more than what we could find a few decades ago. The picture is not completely satisfactory, but there is today a certain amount of energy that is being used in the Islamic world for the preservation and revival of the traditional arts, more so than fifty years ago. I know that you have been to Iran often in the last twenty years, and I have not, but I know that such a revival is still going on there, on the basis of what we tried to establish in the 1960s and 1970s, to revive the traditional arts and crafts, stucco work, brick-laying, architecture, painting, textile, you name it. And of course at the heart of this effort stands the revival of sacred architecture and sacred calligraphy, the sacred arts *par excellence* of Persia, Morocco, and other Islamic countries.

In India the situation has been in a sense a bit more difficult because of financial factors, but even there, one sees to some extent a movement for the revival of traditional Indian arts despite the rapid modernization of

India. The foundation of the Indira Gandhi Centre for the Arts in Delhi had for its very purpose the study and preservation of the traditional arts of India. And of course you have the case of Japan, which is very interesting. The most industrialized of all non-Western countries is at the same time a country which, until a few yeas ago, tried everything possible to preserve its traditional arts, especially its sacred arts, such as the Zen garden, the Buddhist and Shinto temples, and traditional music, dance, and theatre. Of special interest here is the central Shinto temple of Ise,[16] which is rebuilt every few years from scratch on a completely traditional basis. The Japanese have been able to preserve their traditional art quite well until now. As for China, its case is very problematic because of its Marxist regime, which for a long time denigrated traditional art, but Chinese art had a large market. So they began to produce *en masse* a lot of cheap imitations of traditional art; but even in China there exists the realization that a Chinese vase done on a purely traditional basis has a better international market than cheap and second-rate imitations. So gradually even in China matters are improving, and some fine objects of an artistic nature are now being produced.

To conclude this answer, I would not say that modernization has been destroying all of the traditional arts. It has certainly destroyed much and done a lot of harm; there is no doubt about it. But there has been a kind of countermovement, during the last fifty years, which is very heartening. Needless to say, what I have said about these non-Western civilizations does not hold in the same way for the West itself, where the traditional arts remain much more marginalized. And this is, of course, a cause for great concern.

R.J.: So you are saying that we are starting to see clearly, in the sense that reminds me of what John Ruskin[17] said. I have a quotation I found in one of his works, which is very interesting. He says, "The greatest thing a human soul ever does in this world is to see something and tell what it saw in a plain way." So, for Ruskin, to see clearly is poetry, prophecy, and religion. So art for him is a matter of seeing clearly, and you are saying, I think, that we are trying to see clearly now after we have been blind for so many years.

S.H.N.: It depends who the "we" is. Yes, there are a number of people in the non-Western world who are now able to see more clearly. In the West also some people "see" more clearly, but so much of traditional art has been destroyed there that it is more difficult for it to make a major comeback, although we are observing a comeback here and there. A number of objects are now being made by hand here in Washington and in Alexandria where people make pottery, traditional weaving, et cetera, but they are still in the margin of society and their products are minor compared to all the products of the machine sold in Wal-Mart and in similar places. Nevertheless, there is some momentum in the right direction here, which we also observe in certain European countries.

In the non-Western world, however, there is a lot of traditional art that still survives, and there is a lot that needs to be preserved. It is unfortunate of course that most political and social leaders of recent times in this world have been for the most part blind to the significance of traditional art and its preservation. Now, there are more people in the position of authority and power who can see the value of preserving traditional art than before, as you see in lands as far from each other as Indonesia and Oman, China and Morocco. I am not saying that everyone now sees the light, and the subject "we" must be defined, but there are within almost every country, even Egypt—which was so impervious for a long time to its own traditional arts, although it is one of the great centers of Islamic art—those who are now more aware of the importance of preserving the traditional arts than before.

When Hasan Fathy was young, no one paid attention to him. He built a whole beautiful village very cheaply along the Nile based on purely traditional architecture, an unbelievable place, but the Ministry of Housing of Egypt refused to have people live in it, because of course you could make a lot more money by having modern contractors making ugly things. There was the possibility of greater financial corruption in not following Hasan Fathy, because when you build traditionally, you use traditional materials and local labor, which is cheap and, therefore, there is not as much possibility of corruption. The Ministry that refused to have people living in that village was profiteering from its decision. Now, however, Hasan Fathy is a great national hero in Egypt. I was very pleased when, just a few years ago, I went to the area of Lake Fayyum, which is about two hours from Cairo. It is a very beautiful lake in Northern Egypt, the only one of its kind in that area. I saw a number of houses of doctors, professors, and lawyers, professionals who had come in and built places for themselves along the lake for the weekend, and these houses did not at all look like an ugly invasion, like the usual unfortunate invasions by urban dwellers of the countryside, because almost all of the houses around Fayyum were built in the style of Hasan Fathy, totally integrated into the landscape. I had the feeling of being in both traditional Egypt and at the end of the 20th century. It was really remarkable. I was very moved by the observation of this development.

There are a number of people in Egypt today as in other Islamic countries who "see" in the sense that John Ruskin said, but I do not agree that everybody "sees." No, in every Islamic country and also in India, China, and other parts of the world, even in Japan, there are many who do not "see" clearly; but there are now at least some people who do so. That is why I said that the situation has changed. Even in secularized Turkey, where secularism tried to curtail Islam, tried to destroy the sacred itself to the extent possible, many now realize that beautiful Turkish architecture, calligraphy, even calligraphy of the now banned Arabic, Persian, and Ottoman script, the tile work of the Ottoman period, et cetera are very important even to attract tourists, and so there is a lot of effort made to preserve their traditional arts. There are Turkish calligraphers, amazingly even women, people in their twenties and thirties studying calligraphy—that is the sacred art *par excellence* of Islam. Many of the new mosques in Turkey emulate purely Ottoman style, such as the new mosque in Konya and new mosques even in the capital of secularized Turkey, Ankara, and are thereby built on the basis of traditional sacred architecture.

So there is a battle going on, and it is not a one-way street. During my whole adult life, one of the great battles that I have fought has been precisely to try to revive the traditional arts, and some of my own writings, specifically the book *Islamic Art and Spirituality*, and many essays, have had some influence in places such as Turkey, Jordan, and Egypt, not to speak of Iran where some of my works on art were translated by someone whom I did not know, but apparently he was a famous figure in Iran after the Revolution who was apparently killed by stepping on a land mine.[18] He must have been quite a remarkable person in his understanding of traditional art. My works on traditional art have been read by many Iranian architects and artists, and I am surprised by how many letters I receive from Iran practically every month from Ph.D. students in architecture and the arts—not in philosophy—who are doing work on the metaphysical and cosmological principles of sacred architecture and art. And they write to me to ask questions concerning the principles involved. I am, of course, very happy that these ideas are spreading more and more.

The Meaning of Islamic Art

R.J.: Let us now go to the substance and the spiritual message of Islamic art. In your book on Islamic art and spirituality, you wrote that if one were asked what Islam is, one could not answer better than pointing to the Mezquita or the Cordova Mosque, the Ibn Ṭūlūn Mosque in Cairo, or the Jāmiʿ Mosque of Isfahan. Does this mean that from your point of view, traditional Islamic art represents itself the quintessence of the message of Islam?

S.H.N.: On the visual plane, yes, definitely. It might seem paradoxical that art, at least the plastic arts, dealing with substances of the material world, with physical substances, with brick, stucco, wood, paint and color, and so forth, should reflect the deepest aspect of religion. But let us recall the famous Hermetic adage, "that which is lowest symbolizes that which is highest." That is a very profound and important principle and applies very much to this situation. The art of any religion is not created on the basis of the social and legal aspects of that religion but issues from its purely inner dimension. In the case of Islam, for example, Islamic art is not created by the *Sharīʿah*, by the Divine Law. The *Sharīʿah* sets the conditions within which Islamic art is created. For example, if you are an architect who wants to create an Islamic building, there are certain laws of the *Sharīʿah* concerning the right of neighbor, privacy of intimate family spaces, relation to the street, and so forth which you must consider. The fact that you have to have your house protected from outside public spaces so that women can move freely in their home must be accepted, but the *Sharīʿah* does not lead to the creation of Islamic art directly. Islamic art comes from the inner dimension, the *Ḥaqīqat*[19] of the Islamic message, which lies at the heart of the Quran. It issues from the heart of the Islamic message. In all climes in the world of forms, sacred art reflects that which is deepest in a religion.

I gave examples of mosques built of stone and brick, tile and stucco. If you have a bulldozer, you can of course destroy them all easily, and then ask if this act also destroys the inner meaning of the religion. No it does not; it only destroys the visible manifestation of that inner reality. These works, although perishable, reflect the deepest abiding message of Islam which one experiences in the presence of these sites much more than reading a text of law or even theology or philosophy. Philosophy deals with concepts. Theology deals with the defense of religion on the mental plane. Law deals with the world of action. But sacred art deals with the world of the Spirit, pure and most inward. This is why those people in Islamic civilization who have sought after the innermost dimension of their religion have included among their ranks its greatest artists, architects, as well as calligraphers, poets, as well as musicians.

It is not accidental that nearly all the great poets of the Persian language are Sufi poets; they are with a few exceptions mystical poets. The most universal poet of the Persian language is not a panegyrist and writer of profane poetry. For someone sitting in China or Japan, France or America, what interest is there in matters pertaining to the everyday life of those living in Khorasan a millennium ago or the adventures of their rulers? But everyone is interested in the poetry of Rumi, as you can see for yourself in the world today. This remarkable Sufi poetry was written by men who were seeking God and the inner dimension of their religion, and who therefore presented an essential, and at the same time universal, message in their poetic art. Most of the great calligraphers of the Islamic word were also Sufis, people who were devoted to the inner life and had spiritual discipline.

Most of the great architects and calligraphers participated in the spiritual life of Islam, and many were associated formally with Sufi orders. In architecture, in fact, there was a whole esoteric, inner message that was handed down orally from breast to breast, as we say in Persian—that is, orally from person to person, from master to disciple. Much of this teaching has not been written down even today. The purely inward, esoteric teaching and science allowed these people to build those remarkable monuments, to create those stunning objects of art. The building of such works seems to be outwardly easy, but where does the knowledge upon which it is based come from? I mean for example, knowledge of the dyes that created the cobalt color of, let us say, the tiles of the Sultaniyyah or Gawharshad Mosques in Iran or the spaces of these mosques, the acoustics, et cetera. What science made possible the building of those domes in Isfahan that have resisted earthquakes for seven hundred years? How did the architects attain such knowledge?

Few are willing to ask such questions, because such questions challenge our prevalent way of looking at things, and people therefore do not usually want to ask them; but they are plain logical questions. If today you want to build a dome like those of old, you have to have knowledge of modern physics and engineering, of the science of materials; otherwise the dome will fall down on your head. But these people did not know 19th-century physics and engineering; so how did they then build those domes? These are unavoidable questions. It was in fact an esoteric knowledge that was involved, as was also the case of the cathedral builders in the West. There is a sacred geometry, a sacred science that is hidden, and this science is precisely related to the inner, esoteric dimension of the tradition, which was then reflected in the world of external forms by traditional artists and architects. But today we remain for the most part impervious to the presence of this sacred science. Theology is important; philosophy is important; law is important. Of course they are all important. But none of them reflects directly the inner dimension of religion as much as does sacred art.

Understanding the Sacred Art of Other Religions

R.J.: Can one appreciate the beauty of Islamic art without knowing anything about Islamic spirituality?
S.H.N.: Yes, in the sense that I already explained to you. There are certain Westerners who have such a sense. You must have a deep intuitive grasp of the world of the sacred, including sacred forms other than your own. You must also have empathy for that "other" world. Otherwise you pass it by, even if it is present before you. It is interesting to note that Egypt, which is a major center for both Islamic art and, of course, the art of the great Egyptian civilization of antiquity, is visited by several million tourists from the West every year. Over 90 percent, I would say, never even notice the presence of Islamic art there and are not interested in it at all. They go to the pyramids, Luxor, Aswan, and places like that. That small percentage, however, which constitutes many thousands of people, who are European and American, and who are not usually Muslims, but who have studied traditional art—perhaps their own cathedrals, perhaps Indian or Japanese art—they are able to "see," as John Ruskin said, with the eye of the mind and appreciate Islamic art. Often they have at least studied its history, and they come to these mosques, where they stand in awe of their remarkable beauty, even without having much knowledge of Islamic spirituality.

If I can speak of the reverse situation, in my younger days I used to go to traditional cathedrals in Europe as often as I could; it was like a pilgrimage for me. Even now when I go to Paris, never does a single time pass without my going to the Notre Dame Cathedral. There, all the Japanese tourists are clicking away their cameras. Nevertheless, the presence of that sacred place is still there. And there are the stained glass windows, which I especially love. The color of the glass is very beautiful. I sit down and contemplate the sight, and appreciate it very deeply, because I know sacred art. I am not a Christian but appreciate traditional Christian art, and this I did even before I knew Christian spirituality. God has given us intuition and the power of empathy, of penetration into another sacred universe with our intelligence and even with our feelings without formally belonging to it, and has enabled us to appreciate the sacred art of another tradition without having penetrated into the depth of its spiritual teachings—although of course penetration into those teaching facilitates and intensifies our understanding of the arts that reflect those teachings on the level of form. In any case, sacred art has the power to transform us provided we are aware of our own roots in the Sacred as such.

R.J.: Do you see this empathy as a gift of God, or can we be educated to cultivate this gift?

S.H.N.: Both elements are necessary. We need God's help, and we certainly have to develop our understanding and to educate ourselves. Of course there are people for whom this gift does not exist, so that no matter how much they study the subject, it does not do them any good as far as inner understanding is concerned. It is like the case of music; there are some people who are musically deaf. Aristotle just did not understand music; that is why he did not appreciate fully what the Pythagoreans were saying, although he was a very great philosopher. But once you have a musical ear, which is a gift, then you will appreciate music; but still you have to cultivate your taste and educate yourself. It does not mean that just having the ear is enough. You must educate your musical taste and train yourself to appreciate fully Bach, Beethoven, and Brahms and furthermore learn the language of Indian music in order to appreciate it. You have to develop your understanding, to cultivate your taste in order to comprehend the language of the musical traditions in question. You cannot say just because I have a musical ear, I will turn on the radio and listen to a symphony or a *rag* and expect to appreciate both fully. So, both of these elements have to be there. Appreciation of art is both a gift from God and something to be cultivated.

Art and Education

R.J.: Maybe that is why someone like Plato said that the basis of education was art. I mean education through art, through music, through painting . . .

S.H.N.: I do not believe that art is the only element, but I certainly would put art at the center as one of the bases of education. Art would not be the only element unless you define art in the vastest sense of the term. The original Latin word *ars* means to make, like the Greek word *techne.* It is interesting how the two terms have parted ways in modern times. Today art is on one side and technology on the other side. In

Persian when we say *san'at* (*ṣinā'ah* in Arabic), it contains the meaning of both current terms. We use the term *san'at* when referring to the Ministry of Industries and Technology. At the same time when you say *san'at-gar*, it does not mean the person working in a steel mill, but someone making a plate or an inlaid frame by hand. If you mean art in that general sense, including doing or making anything correctly, and according to principles, and also thinking correctly and mastering the art of correct thinking along with correct acting, then yes. But if you mean art in the sense of the cultivation of music, painting, poetry, and so forth, I would place that at the very heart of education; but it is not the only basic element, because besides training the eye, there is also the very important element of spiritual, intellectual, and moral education. The modern world tends to separate the aesthetic as currently understood from both the intellectual and the ethical, a point that many philosophers have discussed, but there are today many people who have no ethical concerns but have a strong aesthetic sense. Traditional civilizations never separated the aesthetic, the intellectual, the moral, and the spiritual.

R.J.: Is that not the case for Plato, because he said, "Truth is beauty, beauty is truth"?

S.H.N.: I know that remarkable assertion with which I concur completely, but what I am saying is that in addition to training in the arts, you must have moral, spiritual, and intellectual training, which means also the training of the mind, of the faculties for abstract thought as provided in such disciplines as philosophy, logic, and mathematics. If you call these art, because everything has its art, then yes; but if you mean by art, let us say, painting, sculpture, music, and poetry, and things like that, then although these are extremely important, they have to be complemented by the training of mental faculties related to abstract thought, the training of intelligence along with moral and spiritual education. I have always emphasized this unitary vision in my works.

In our tradition, in the Islamic tradition, it is interesting to note that a true philosopher was often also an artist. It is remarkable how many Persian and, more generally, Islamic philosophers from Ibn Sīnā to Sabziwārī were also poets. They were not all great poets, but a couple of them were both great poets and great philosophers. Let us recall here the names of Nāṣir-i Khusraw and Afḍal al-Dīn Kāshānī. Even if you compose a few verses of poetry, that means that your soul has a poetical aspect to it, a poetical quality. In fact the very exposition of traditional philosophy in a serious sense is an art, and such an expositor is both an artist and a philosopher. Especially in the Islamic tradition, but also in

India, China, and Japan there are many examples of the wedding between what we call philosophy and art. In the traditional world, the training of the "mind" was never divorced in the expression of concepts and ideas in beautiful forms, as you find, for example, in Zen. This is to be found on the highest level in such sacred scriptures as the Quran, the Psalms, Tao Te-Ching, and the Upanishads.

So, I would complement what you said by stating that yes, art is central; but if you do not mean "art" in the most universal meaning of the term, but if "art" is understood in the more particular meaning of it, then you need these other forms of training to be added. Of course physical training should also be included, and Plato talks about it in the *Republic*. I think that the training of the body is related to all those other elements, especially to art. Take for example the Hindu temple dance and yoga: the two are not separable from art and also the training of the mind. Mental concentration is also related to the training of the body and to moral training. So, I would say that physical training, especially when sacralized, is also an important part of a complete education.

Traditional Islamic Art

R.J.: Talking about Hindu art, you touched on this problem. What distinguishes Islamic art from Christian and Hindu art, which are presented by icons and as you said by images, but Islamic art is devoid of iconography, and this brings some scholars to say that there is no place for art in Islam? I mean, I am not myself one of them, but I have seen some people like that who have declared recently that there is no distinctly Muslim traditional painting.

S.H.N.: First of all, this is from pure ignorance. Art is not only painting. If we define art as only painting, then of course a civilization that does not emphasize painting does not have any serious art. But this is absurd. It is like saying that only meat is food, and therefore anyone who does not eat meat does not eat any food. Certainly that is an absurd assertion. How can one say that there is no such thing as art in Islam when there is such great architecture and calligraphy and even the remarkable schools of miniature painting, when there is the very artistic psalmody of the Quran? In fact, Islam, like Judaism, never considered painting as a sacred art, but it did have and continues to have its own sacred art. In the main tradition of Judaism, like Islam, sacred art is aniconic. Now one must understand this truth, that the sacred art of Islam is an art which is aniconic, but nevertheless sacred and also art.

In contrast, Christian and Hindu art are iconic, and they are iconic in the sense that at the heart of both of these arts stand the depictions of the divine image. In Hinduism there are the images of the gods and in Christianity of Christ and the Virgin. In the case of Buddhism also, there is the image of the Buddha, which is central to Buddhist art. At the heart of Islamic art stands an art that seeks to point to the Divine without an image, without making use of an icon. We call that aniconic art. This aniconic art was a possibility that was realized in Islamic art as well as in Jewish sacred art. What takes the place of images in such an art is a stylized form of geometry, of arabesques, and of calligraphy. These elements make possible the presence of the spiritual world without the use of images. Islam being based on the One, the Absolute, on the absoluteness of the Divine Principle, could not have produced an iconic art for the same reason that one finds in Judaism, where the Torah says "The Lord is one." God is one, and if you really take the oneness of God as the central doctrine, then no image in the world can depict it, because we live in the world of multiplicity, and no image can be adequate for the representation of the transcendent One. In the case of Buddhism and Christianity, these two religions are based on the manifestation of the Divine more than the Divine in Its absoluteness transcending all images and forms. One can see this truth in the case of Buddhism, in the Buddha, and in Christianity, in Christ, who are the central realities of their religions rather than the Absolute or the "One" Itself, although of course these religions are ultimately also manifestations of the Absolute. That is why Christianity is called Christianity and Buddhism is called Buddhism, but Islam cannot be correctly called Mohammadism and Judaism cannot be called Mosaism. This fact is very significant. To say that Islam has no art, because painting is not central to its art, is a meaningless statement. If we define art as I have defined it, the assertion is totally absurd. I can never accept such a view.

Master and Apprentice

R.J.: Islamic metaphysics states that the universe is made up of various levels of existence. I read it in your own writings. In what way do you think that the Muslim artist can distinguish between these levels when he or she is doing his or her work? Is there a relationship between the artistic activity of the Muslim artist and Divine Creativity?

S.H.N.: There are two levels, that of masters and that of their apprentices, who constitute most of the artists. The ordinary artist or craftsman (the two being the same in a traditional civilization) learns through a master the techniques and methods of creating a particular form of art such as calligraphy or ceramics. What he or she is doing is to master the form and technique that he or she learns from somebody else. The ordinary artist and craftsman does not have to know all the symbolic science, all the cosmology, all the metaphysics, that is involved in what he or she is creating. But because the art that he or she is creating is based on traditional channels of transmission, even a person sitting simply in a bazaar and making a comb is aware through apprenticeship of the spiritual significance of his or her work and derives spiritual benefit from it without the complete awareness of the levels of reality that you mention.

And then there is a second level, that of the master, the master craftsman, the teacher. He or she is the person who produces forms which are then emulated by the apprentices, and the master bases what he or she creates upon a wisdom that is related to knowledge of metaphysics, cosmology, and symbolism. Such men and women have always had this knowledge of the levels of reality and a vision of the archetypal world and have been able to translate that knowledge and vision into physical or audible forms. More specifically, they have had a vision of the imaginal world, what Islamic metaphysicians call the intermediate world of forms, which stands above the physical world. Such knowledge and vision come through spiritual experience, which enables them to be in contact with that world. What is the origin of these forms, which are universal yet produced within a particular civilization, forms that are beyond idiosyncrasies and individualistic limitations? It is forms that belong to the meta-individual realm to which the master is able to gain access.

There are, therefore, two types of creativity: one is this second type, which is that of the master who is able to have a vision of the higher realities and in a sense to swim in the higher reaches of the imaginal world, which themselves reflect the purely intelligible world, and then to bring these forms down to the level of the physical world. The second is the creativity of the first type, comprising the creative activity of those who are able to emulate these forms and repeat them faithfully in new works of art. Now, people in the modern West think that this is not creativity at all. But again going back to John Ruskin's quotation that you made, any true vision of things is itself creative. Newness or what we call originality today and real creativity are not the same thing. We live in a world in which the two are considered to be identical. To be creative is thought today to mean the creation of something different, and therefore to be original in the ordinary sense of the term—but that is not necessarily the case. I have always said that originality is authentic only if it refers to the Origin, to the Origin of things. In a traditional civilization, the original artist was a person who was able to go back to the Origin, to go back to God, to the spiritual world, and not to just produce something different out of his own ego for the sake of being different. That was the highest form of creativity. But there was also a secondary type of creativity, that of a person who mastered the traditional forms and was able to create works of art on the basis of those forms, an activity that nevertheless always includes an element belonging to the soul of the particular artist in question.

Let us take the style of *nasta'liq*,[20] the most common Persian style of calligraphy. A person wanting to master this style has first of all to study with a master the very precise geometry that is involved and cannot just make up his own rules. You and I know Persian calligraphy. As soon as you see good writing, you can recognize it. But to be able to master that style and to repeat it, which does not mean simply a mechanical repetition, is also a creative art. In fact in every calligrapher there is also a certain individual element that is involved, because God never repeats anything twice, and there is no repetition in creation. It is said in Arabic *la-takrar fī tajallī* (there is no repetition in manifestation) and that also applies to the creations of man. Nothing ever repeats itself exactly in this world. Traditional art is in this sense like nature. Trees give forth leaves, blossoms, and fruits each spring. For a particular tree, the same fruit is produced this year as last year. A pear tree will not give you prunes next year but, at the same time, the pear this year is not exactly the same fruit as what you picked last year. In the new season the fruit will be bigger or smaller and the color could be different, but the pear remains a pear. We thus have two kinds of creativity which are not equally essential, but they are both transforming. They transform the artist as well as the person using or appreciating the art in question, because they put the artist in touch with the reality that transcends the realm of the ego and individual consciousness, opening up the soul to the universal order, thereby also transforming those for whom the art is meant.

Representations of God

R.J.: Is this why God is beyond all figurative representations in Islam?

S.H.N.: This is not the only reason; there are other more central reasons. But this is one of the reasons. If you conceive God as His

Self-determinations or incarnations, then you can create an image that depicts the Divine. Islam, however, is not based on the Self-disclosure or manifestation of God, but on God Himself, or God as the Absolute, the Infinite and the perfectly Good, the Reality that transcends all limitations and thus all forms and images. Therefore, no form can depict that absolute Reality. Forms can reflect spiritual realities which will lead us gradually to the Formless, as we see in Hindu art; but even in Hindu art there is an aniconic art such as certain Tantric types of art that are not iconic, have no images. It is important to mention that this is true even of Hinduism, where the mythological form of religion can be seen everywhere. As for Islam, it is based on a view of art that refuses to "imprison" the Divine in any finite form, and certainly not in any anthropomorphic form, because there then is the danger of mistaking the form for the Formless, for the Absolute, and falling into anthropomorphism. As Burckhardt has pointed out so correctly, there is the danger of man seeing himself in this anthropomorphic form and then anthropomorphizing the divine image more and more. There is this psychological interplay between man and the divine image and the danger that the divine form will become totally anthropomorphic, as it happened in the post-medieval West. And that can be true for any religion, as we can also see in the Graeco-Roman antiquity.

Persian Art

R.J.: Now to get to Persian art, you consider Persian art as the peak of Islamic art. I read from yourself . . .
S.H.N.: I said one of the peaks . . .

R.J.: But even if we accept this, that it is one of the peaks, is not Persian art more in conformity with the sensibility of the Persian people rather than with Islam? I mean, somebody can ask you this question.
S.H.N.: Yes, this is a plausible question. I would, however, criticize the word *rather*. The sensibility of Persian people during the past fourteen centuries has been related to Islam, since they were and remain Muslims, but it is not identical with the sensibility of, let us say, the Malay or Egyptian people, or Indian Muslims. That is why you have different forms of Islamic art. They are not identical, but at the same time, they all reflect the same principles and are all Islamic art. I have had this discussion a great deal with many Persians, and I have said that the categories of Persian art and Islamic art are not mutually exclusive. We also see this in Buddhist art. Now, the Buddhist art of Japan is certainly

Buddhist, but this art is not identical with the Buddhist art of Sri Lanka or Indian Buddhist art; yet they are all Buddhist art. The same holds true for Islamic art. The two categories are not mutually exclusive.

Definitely, Persian Islamic art corresponds to the sensibility of the Persian people and is at the same time Islamic art, and that is the whole point. Persian Islamic art is both Islamic and Persian in the same way that pre-Islamic Persian art was both Zoroastrian and Persian. Moreover, there are certain elements of Persian Islamic art that are typically Persian. Persian art is also the most diversified of all forms of Islamic art; that I will accept. It is not only one of the great peaks of that art, but also the most diversified, its creativity manifesting itself in many diverse forms of Islamic art. Persia has produced the greatest paintings of Islamic civilization. The Persian miniature is in a class unto itself. The Mogul and Turkish miniatures which were originally of Persian inspiration never really matched it in finesse, although Turks and Indian Muslims also produced great works of the art of the miniature. In calligraphy, however, Persian art is not supreme; Turkish calligraphy in the *thuluth* and *naskh* styles is also one of the peaks of that art, as are some forms of Iraqi and Egyptian calligraphy, not to speak of the *maghribī* style of Spain and Morocco, which is also very beautiful. Also in architecture some of the greatest works of Islamic architecture are to be found in Persia, but one cannot say that the mosque architecture of the Maghrib, Egypt, Turkey, or Muslim India represent also anything less than great peaks of architecture. So one should not be a chauvinist—but at the same time, one should assert that Persian art is the richest and most diversified form of Islamic art and its influence is the most extensive, because most of the art of Islamic Asia and the Ottoman world was influenced directly by Persian Islamic art.

Unity in Diverse Schools of Islamic Art

R.J.: For a non-Muslim, or even for a Muslim who does not know much about Islamic spirituality or Islamic art, he or she has difficulty to find the unifying principles which bring together the Taj Mahal and the mosques of the Maghrib.

S.H.N.: First of all, if one does not have proper sensibility and comes from a foreign culture, that person will nevertheless sense a unity in the diverse forms of Islamic architecture. If you bring a Swede into two traditional buildings from the areas you mention, he senses that they belong to the same universe. Secondly, for a Persian who has just been used to Persian Islamic art, if he transcends his ordinary habits, he will experience in the forms of architecture from India and Morocco a distinct sense of unity, use of sacred geometry, crystalline space resting upon itself, opposition to naturalism and anthropomorphism, the particular use of light, the relationship between the inner space of the building and the world of nature, and the symbolism of colors. All of these elements are extremely important in non-Persian as well as types of Persian Islamic architecture. If that person looks at these different types of architecture closely enough, he will detect that these are basic elements that are common among various forms of Islamic art. He will see diversity reflecting unity, diversity that is related to various ethnic types, as well as considerations of climatic conditions and other external factors which together have created diversity, but a diversity that nevertheless reflects unity in Islamic art and architecture.

Part Eight

Sufism[1]

R.J.: I think it is time for us at this moment in our conversation to discuss your interest in Sufism, and let us start by defining Sufism. Martin Lings, whom you knew very well, has said in his book *What is Sufism?*[2] that "Sufism is a kind of mysticism, and mysticism by definition is concerned above all with the mysteries of the kingdom of Heaven." Is this a complete definition of Sufism for you?

S.H.N.: It is a very fine definition, but of course not an exhaustive one, because it does not embrace all the different aspects of Sufism, which in fact cannot be expected in any brief definition. If you understand the word *mysticism* in its original sense of dealing with the Divine Mysteries—the word *mystery* itself and *mystic* are words derived ultimately from the Greek word *muen*, which means "to keep silent, to keep quiet"—then it corresponds very much to the famous Persian poem, "Whoever is taught the mysteries of God,/ His mouth has become sealed and his lips sewn"—the silence of which the Sufis speak. This silence is of course in reference to the esoteric, to the inward, and the truth that leads to the inward, to the truth about which one remains outwardly silent. That is why the term *mysticism* should really be understood in its etymological sense, and not in the modern sense of something ambiguous, vague, and illogical. If we understand mysticism in that sense, then of course Sufism is mysticism in the deepest sense of the word, but I do not always use the term *mysticism* precisely because of all of the difficulties which have come about through the misuse of the term, and also because the term *mysticism* in the English language is impregnated with the sense of the Christian mysticism of love. Now, the Christian mysticism of love is an important form of mysticism, but Sufism is not to be completely equated with it. There is an aspect of Sufism that corresponds to it, but Sufism itself embraces more than anything else the path of knowledge which is always combined with love.

To clarify further the very beautiful definition given by Martin Lings, I would say that Sufism is the inner, esoteric, and mystical dimension of Islam, and for that very reason it partakes of the nature of the Islamic revelation of which it is the heart. Rather than basing itself on sacrifice and love alone, as does most of Christian mysticism—although not all because there is also a sapiential form of mysticism in Christianity—Sufism is based more than anything else on *gnosis* in its original sense, on illuminative wisdom and the realization of the oneness of God, a realization that is not possible without love. After all, the very statement that defines the oneness of God in Islam, namely the first *shahādah*,[3] is a statement of knowledge. It refers to the knowledge of God, to the oneness of Ultimate Reality.

Sufism in the Safavid Period

R.J.: In a chapter called "Shi'ism and Sufism" in your *Sufi Essays* you write that Sufism changed its name in the religious circles in Persia from *taṣawwuf* to *'irfān* because of the great difficultly encountered during the Safavid period by Sufis. Now there is, among Iranians especially, the use of a language in which sometimes a differentiation is made between the two and sometimes not.

S.H.N.: Yes, this is a question that is more or less peculiar to the Persian world and to Shi'ism. First of all, the word *gnosis*, which I usually translate as *'irfān* in English, must not be confused with Gnosticism, which was a sect of the early Christian period. The word *'irfān* does not have exactly the same meaning in Arabic and in Persian. The word in Arabic that corresponds to it is in Persian *ma'rifah*, but the word *'irfān* is not used with exactly the same meaning in Arabic. The reason why the word *'irfān* has come to be used in this way in Persian, sometimes as equivalent, sometimes in opposition, and sometimes as complementary to Sufism, is due to special historical reasons. It has to do with the opposition of the later Shi'ite *'ulamā'* in the Safavid period to Sufism. In principle and going back to the roots of Sufism, it could be said that Sufism, like every authentic and integral spiritual path, possesses at once a doctrine and a method—that is, a truth concerning the nature of Reality and a method for reaching that Reality. The doctrine of Sufism could be called *'irfān*. It is the theoretical aspect of Sufism which must, however, be combined with practice, which is the method. If you look at the early works of Persian Sufis using the Persian language, such as those of Hujwuri,[4] or figures such as Kharaqani[5] and Imam Qushayri,[6] who used mostly Arabic and who had a strong *'irfānī* aspect to their writings, no such ambiguity or dichotomy exists between *taṣawwuf* and *'irfān* or *ma'rifah*. Nor does one find such a distinction in early Sufi works in Arabic written by non-Persians.

As I said, the problem that you posed in your question goes back to the Safavid period. With the coming of the Safavids, two important events took place. First of all, the head of a Sufi order, the Safavid order, that is, Shah Ismā'īl, became the ruler, the king, of Persia. Secondly, Twelfth-Imam Shi'ism was declared as the official school of law of the state. Of course the official religion was Islam, but Shi'ism became the official interpretation of Islam by the state, and these two events led to the following.

First of all, in order to strengthen the hold of Shi'ism upon the nation at that time, since the majority of Persians were still Sunnis, a large number of Shi'ite *'ulamā'* who were Arab were brought from outside of Persia from such regions as the Jabal 'Amil in Southern Lebanon and Syria, from Hillah and certain other areas of central Iraq, and from what was then called Bahrain, which is now the name of a small island, but at that time referred to the whole area of the southwestern region of the Persian Gulf. These *'ulamā'* did not know any Persian, although they gradually learned the language. Their being Arab was one of the reasons why one sees a return of greater use of Arabic, for some time after the establishment of the national state in Persia by the Safavid, in the fields of philosophy and theology, in comparison to the earlier Il-Khanid and Timurid periods. These *'ulamā'*, most of whom were not inclined towards Sufism, gradually began to gain strength and power in Iran, and so a struggle was created between them and the Sufi orders, for political and social power.

Secondly, since the king at that time was also the head of the Safavid Sufi order, and human nature being what it is, many people tried to do what Americans call "jump on the bandwagon," that is, to join Sufism for worldly reasons in order to reach a position of prominence, to gain political advantages, et cetera. Consequently, a lot of people claimed to be Sufis who did not at all have the spiritual discipline and virtues that a Sufi should have. Many of them became indifferent to the external rules of life as promulgated in the *Sharī'ah* and committed all kinds of acts not worthy of spiritually disciplined people. Meanwhile, other Sufi orders came to be opposed to a large extent.

These factors together led to opposition to Sufism by many of the Shi'ite *'ulamā'* and the Shi'ite hierarchy, which did not wield direct political power and rule directly as has occurred since the Islamic Revolution of Iran, but shared political power with the Safavid kings in addition to their having complete religious power. This situation caused the *'ulamā'* to begin an active campaign of opposition to Sufism in the later period of Safavid rule. First, the Safavid Order itself tried to eliminate its rivals, especially the Ni'matollahi Order,[7] which was highly persecuted, and many of its members fled to India, not coming back to Persia until the time of the early Qajar kings. That is why you have a hiatus in Persia in the history of Sufism from the late Safavid to the early Qajar period. Opponents of Sufism, which gradually came to include much of the political establishment, tried to eliminate various Sufi groups. Although they did not succeed completely, they were nevertheless certainly successful in making many of the Sufis to go underground or be marginalized or persecuted.

Then the Shi'ite *'ulamā'* themselves began to attack Sufism from a religious point of view. In the ambience thus created during the second part of the Safavid period, the word *Sufism* began to lose its positive connotation in the circle of religious scholars as well as sometimes among ordinary pious people, and a situation was created which had not existed before in Persia and did not exist in the Sunni world at all until the rise of the anti-Sufi *salafī* or modernist movements. If you are in, let us say, the city of Cairo, you can see that an ordinary pious Muslim looks upon the Sufis as being very pious members of the community. He does not understand their esoteric doctrines, but he understands them to be morally upright persons devoted to the love of the Prophet and of God. But in Iran in the late Safavid period, due to the instigation of many Shi'ite *'ulamā'* against Sufism and also in order to prevent corruption of the religion in the name of Sufism, the ordinary people were told that Sufism was against Islam, and Sufism was attacked in books and from the pulpit. A kind of polarization took place that was not, however, able to eliminate the importance of Sufism by any means, since it was too deeply rooted in the soul of many Persians. That is why in the Qajar period Sufism makes a notably important comeback to the extent that one of the Qajar prime ministers became a member of a Sufi order, and one observes the remarkable flowering of Sufism in the early 19th century. Nevertheless, as a result of those events in religious circles, many people shunned using the word *taṣawwuf* or *Sufism*, especially in religious centers such as Mashhad and Qom. In fact, those among the *'ulamā'* who were attracted inwardly to the reality of Sufism began to use the word *'irfān* as a substitute. They denigrated *taṣawwuf* while praising *'irfān*.

It is interesting to note that despite those events, the reality of Sufism did not disappear among the *'ulamā'* because Shi'ism itself has a strong esoteric dimension. In fact, there were a number of *'ulamā'*, such as Baḥr al-'ulum,[8] who was one of the greatest Shi'ite scholars of the 19th century, who were Sufis. But this verbal distinction that had come about between *'irfān* and *taṣawwuf* became prevalent. And if you were a religious scholar or if you came from a very pious religious family, rather than saying, "I am a Sufi," you would say, "I am an *'āref*," or more likely, "I am studying *'erfān*." It is interesting to note that down to our own century and the last few decades, some of the most important figures of Iranian religious history have been associated in one way or another with what in English we would call Sufism and in Persian *'erfān*. A prime example is 'Allāmah Ṭabāṭabā'ī and also Ayatollah Khomeini, as well as a number of other well-known religious scholars of recent times who were drawn to Sufism and wrote on *'irfān*. Some of them also practiced Sufism secretly, but they never spoke about this matter publicly and would only say that they were immersed in *'erfān*.

Shi'ism and Sufism

I have made a study of this subject as far as Shi'ite Persia (and by extension Iraq) is concerned, leaving aside Afghanistan, which represents the Sunni half of the older Persia. In Iran and Iraq, as far as Shi'ites are concerned, there is a complex pattern concerning the relation of Shi'ism and Sufism, but let us just stick to Persia, since I am a Persian and know more about it than I know about Iraq. In Persia we have first of all several Sufi orders such as Ni'matollahi, Dhahabi,[9] Khaksar,[10] et cetera that are still functioning with many followers, similar to what we find in the Sunni world, including the Sunni parts of Persia, such as Kordistan and Baluchestan, where the Qaderi and Naqshbandi orders are active.

Secondly, you have what is called Shi'ite *gnosis*, or *'erfān-ī shī'ī*, involving Shi'ite thinkers who have gained access to authentic metaphysical knowledge corresponding to Sufi doctrine. This category includes some of the greatest philosophers of Persia such as Mullā Ṣadrā and Sabziwārī. These are figures who in addition to being philosophers were also gnostics. Let us remember especially in this category Aqa Mohammad Reza Qumsha'i,[11] who was called the Ibn 'Arabī of his day, and who was the greatest gnostic of the last century. Closer to our own period we have Mirza Aḥmad Ashtiyani,[12] Seyyed Mohammad Kazim 'Assar[13] and others who belonged to this category.

There is, moreover, another category in Persia that is more hidden, and that is a regular Sufi chain of transmission of the power of *walayat*[14] from master to disciple and going back to the Prophet of Islam and finally to God through the Archangel Gabriel. You cannot have Sufism without that chain or *silsilah*. There also does exist a chain based on regular initiate transmission among certain Shi'ite *'ulamā'*, although it is very much hidden. We have not discovered all the documents concerning this chain because it has remained such a hidden matter. Among this group one can name Baḥr al-ulūm during the Qajar period and 'Allāmah Ṭabāṭabā'ī in our own time. These people not only prayed to God for guidance and were aided by the Twelfth Imam, but they undertook the regular spiritual practice of invocation and meditation as one finds in various Sufi orders but without the name of Sufism being used. This hidden chain continues to this day, especially among the *'ulamā'* engaged in the intellectual life in centers of religious learning such as Qom and Mashhad, but also among others. In answering your question, all these categories must be considered in seeking to understand in depth the religious history of Persia during the past few centuries.

Sufism and Pacifism

R.J.: I see a contradiction here when you say that some of the *'ulamā'* who have been engaged in politics can be Sufis at the same time, because I thought that Sufism is always pacifist and very much against violence by its essence. So how can one be a religious thinker who is engaged in politics and who has political aims, and at the same time a Sufi? Does Sufism have a political aim?

S.H.N.: The question you pose is a very important one. The aim of Sufism is to reach God, but Sufism is not necessarily pacifist. Usually Sufis shun external political turmoil, but also during the history of Islam there have been cases in which Sufism has had an active role in the establishing of a just order in society, or even fighting against foreign rule, as we see in the case of the Sanusiyyah[15] fighting against Italian colonialism in Libya or Amir 'Abd al-Qadir al-Jaza'iri,[16] one of the greatest Sufis of the 19th century, battling against French colonialism.

The figure of the warrior-saint, which is for the most part alien to Christianity, exists not only in Islam but also in Hinduism. There is a notable prejudice in the West that has to be overcome, and that is to identify spiritually with pacifism. That is why people in the West do not usually mention the Prophet of Islam as one of the greatest spiritual figures of humanity but in this context always talk about Christ, the Buddha, Saint Francis of Assisi, Gandhi, or someone like them who represents the first possibility, which is that of withdrawal from the external strifes that characterize a part of human life here on earth, or participation in passive resistance as we see especially in the case of Gandhi.

There is, however, this other, possibility, which is precisely that of the warrior-saint, you might say. Now, as I said, if you want to really understand the second possibility, you do not have to look only at Islam. Consider the *Bhagavad-Gita*, one of the greatest spiritual documents of Hinduism and certainly the most accessible. All of this sublime teaching about renunciation mentioned in the *Gita*, where did it take place? It took place on the battlefield. Krishna tells the hero Arjuna to fight the good fight, while instructing him about Divine love and knowledge. Yes, there is also this aspect to Sufism, and there is not a contradiction here. Sufism in general has shunned political power, but there have been exceptional cases when it has entered the realm of external political conflict. What it did shun absolutely was personal ambition and fighting for selfish ends. But if there were a just cause for the preservation of society, of religion, of justice, then depending on the vocation of a particular Sufi order, or a particular saint, that battle for justice, or what you would call violence, was joined in exceptional circumstances. Violence is inseparable from certain aspects of human existence, although Sufism and, in fact, Islam itself, have always sought to limit it. When we get up every morning and start the day, our body has to wage war against all the bacteria trying to attack it, and when we go out and make a living, if we cut a tree, we are waging war against the tree; and when we take medicine we are waging war against germs in our own body. This is a vast issue that has to be analyzed much more extensively and not reduced to simplistic alternatives.

Let me give you an example of participation in battle from the history of Sufism. When the grandson of Genghis Khan, Hülagü, reached the gates of Samarqand, he had already heard of Najm al-Dīn Kubra,[17] the founder of the Kubrawiyyah Order, which is one of the greatest of Central Asian Sufi orders. He was a Persian Sufi, the author of very important treatises, and was called "the maker of saints." Many of his disciples, such as Najm al-Din Razi,[18] were famous Sufi authors. At that time, Najm al-Din Kubra was very old, in his nineties, or maybe even a hundred. So the Mongols camped in front of the city and sent an emissary to the city to bring out this saintly figure, and so he came out of the gate of the city to face Hülagü. According to historic accounts, Hülagü came to him and said, "I have great respect for you." (It is very interesting to note that the Mongols, despite their great cruelty, had usually respect for Sufis and religious scholars wherever they went.) In any case, Hülagü stated that he was going to lay siege to the city, and before doing that he wanted Najm al-Din to come out with all his followers, so that he and they would not be harmed. Najm al-Din smiled and said, "All the people of Samarqand are my followers." He then went back to the city, put on his armor, came out at the head of the army, and was killed immediately.

This incredible event must be understood in its context. Najm al-Dīn Kubrā was not preaching violence or participating in politics in order to become rich or powerful; but he performed a very important political act, which is remembered in history 700 years later, since we are now talking about it.

Let us consider a second example. The French were crushing Islamic culture in North Africa, destroying the whole fabric of Islamic society in the 19th century. The Algerian prince Amīr 'Abd al-Qādir, who was a great Sufi, arose and fought for twenty years against the French with great magnanimity and chivalry. His chief opponent, a French general, wrote to the French government and said, "How is it possible to fight against a man who is like the prophets of the Old Testament, who is a saint?" Anyway, finally he was surrounded in the mountains by a large French army, but they were afraid to kill him; so they captured him and sent him to France, where the French army officers received him as a hero. He was finally exiled to Syria, and when he came to Syria, practically the whole city of Damascus came to meet him. This man, who was both a prince and a Sufi saint, probably the most famous active Sufi of North Africa of his day, was wealthy. But when he went to the house of the nobility and dignitaries of Syria, he would always remove the cover of the seat where he was to sit if it was made of silk. He would sit either on simple cloth or on the floor. He remained an ascetic despite being a prince, and this manner of living continued until the end of his days. He published many important books on Sufism in Arabic, some of which have been translated into French and English. So you have the incredible image of this man who was not fighting a war in order to become ruler or king of the country, for the sake of his own ambition, or to become rich or powerful; not at all. He fought for justice and was inwardly detached like the warrior about whom Krishna speaks in the *Gita*.

To cut the story short, participation in politics and external battles which of necessity sometimes involve struggle and violence is by no mean central to Sufism, and most of the great Sufi masters have shunned external activism. But at certain times in the history of Islam, certain Sufis were placed in situations in which the very protection of their society, of their people, of justice, of religion, of morality depended upon their entering into the realm of action on the social and even political level—but they did so with inner detachment. For the most part, however, you are right. Usually the great Sufi teachers shunned political power and violence and never went to sultans to ask for favors. It was in fact the other way around. In our own country when Nāsir al-Dīn Shah went on pilgrimage to Mashhad, he went to meet on the way Sabzivar, who was both a great Sufi and a notable philosopher. This is an example that is seen over and over again. Sufis were not people who debased themselves for worldly gain. They did not bow before a worldly power in order to gain access to power or wealth. Cases when Sufis did enter the political and social arena must not therefore be confused with the participation by ordinary people in that realm for the sake of worldliness and in order to gain worldly ends.

Sufism and Sunnism

R.J.: Why do you think that Shi'ism is more favorable to the rise of Sufism than Sunnism? Does this have to do with the theory of the Imamate and the fact that in Shi'ism we have this doctrine that we do not have in Sunnism?

S.H.N.: I do not agree with the assertion that you have made. There are many people who say that, but they confuse two levels of reality. If you look at the Islamic world today, putting the *salafi*[19] movement aside, which grew out of the Sunni world and which is against both Sufism and Shi'ism, the vast majority of Sunni Muslims are traditional Sunnis. The acceptance and love of the spirit of Sufism among them is, if not greater than in the Shi'ism world, certainly as great as it is in that world. Look at, for example, Senegal. Senegal is completely Sunni, and most ordinary people there have never even heard of Shi'ism. Yet, probably over half the population has some kind of affiliation with the Sufi orders. In Egypt and Syria, likewise one sees the deepest respect for Sufism, which is very widespread. The only Sunni countries where Sufi orders are having problems are countries where the political and to some extent religious conditions are opposed to Sufism, such as Libya and Saudi Arabia, where there are either extreme forms of government or strong Wahhabi and *salafī* opposition to Sufism. In such places Sufism is more or less banned and usually has gone underground, but in more traditional Islamic settings in the Sunni world, Sufis are numerous. So it is not true to say that Shi'ism as such has always been more open to Sufism than has Sunnism.

The Imams

This is, however, only one level. On the level of doctrine, Shi'ism is closer to Sufism in the sense that Shi'ism has within its ordinary religious structure certain esoteric teachings. In the Sunni world, a person attracted to esoterism goes to Sufi orders. The exoteric dimension, that is, what concerns the belief system, doctrines concerning the law and theological matters, are more distinct from the teachings of Sufism than in the case of Shi'ism. Occasionally there have been important figures in the Sunni world, such as Ghazzālī, who have been both outstanding doctors of the law as well as theology, and in addition great Sufis. In the Shi'ite world, however, the very structure of what we would call exoteric religion and theology have certain esoteric elements in them related definitely, as you said, to the Imam, who represents a continuation of the Muḥammadan Light and has definitely an esoteric as well as an exoteric function in Shi'ism. The fact that the Imams are biological descendants of the Prophet is secondary. What is primary is the transmission of Muḥammadan Light to them down to the Twelfth Imam. And through the Twelfth Imam this light that obliviously possesses an esoteric dimension continues to be available and accessible to qualified Twelve Imam Shi'ites to this day.

In the Sunni world, the term *imām* is used in many ways including for the ruler of the community and in that case is another word for caliph. There are of course other meanings of *imām* in the Sunni world, only one being the ruler of the community. Another of course is an honorific title given to a number of great scholars, such as when we say Imam Ghazzālī. *Imām* is also used for the founders of the schools of Sunni law. But in none of these cases is the term associated with the esoteric doctrine of Muḥammadan Light, which we also have in Sufism. In contrast, in Shi'ism the Imam is not only the ruler—at least in principle, because after the death of 'Alī none of the Imams actually ruled over this world, and yet the Shi'ites accept them as the rulers of this world—but they are also experts in the Divine Law. They were in fact the most perfect interpreters of the Law, which the caliph does not have to be in Sunni Islam, where this function resides in the hands of the *'ulamā'*. The Imam is also the esoteric guide, the spiritual guide. He is really like a Sufi master in a Sufi order on the highest level, and it is not accidental that the Imams of Shi'ism up to the eighth Imam are all poles of Sufi orders in Sunnism in addition to being Shi'ite Imams.

Look at the role of Imam Ja'far al-Ṣādiq. Not only is he the founder of Shi'ite Law, which we therefore call Ja'farī Law and which we have in Iran; not only was he the teacher of Imam Abū Ḥanīfah and had a very important role to play in the formulation of Sunni Law; but also Imam Ja'far has played a very important role in Sufism. He is the author of the first esoteric commentary on the Quran that has survived at least in part, that of 'Alī having been lost. Imam Ja'far also plays an important role in many Sufi orders, including the Naqshbandiyyah, which is the only Sufi order not to originate with 'Alī directly. All of the other Sufi orders trace their *silsilah* back to 'Alī. But even that one order that is not attached to 'Alī directly is nevertheless attached to him indirectly through his descendant Imam Ja'far. Therefore, the reality of the Imam does not only have a legal and theological aspect, also, but above all, a metaphysical and spiritual one, and it is this aspect of the reality of the Imam that is the source of the link between Shi'ism and Sufism. I need to add here that in the ambience of Twelve-Imam Shi'ism the title Imam has been used exclusively for the twelve inerrant (*ma'ṣūm*), although it can also be used on rare occasions for an outstanding leader who is not among the twelve *ma'ṣūm* Imams as we see in the case of Ayatollah Khomeini. The issue of the relation between Sufism and Shi'ism is indeed complicated, but at the beginning they belonged in a sense to the same world, that of Islamic esoterism. It is not accidental that 'Alī is the first Shi'ite Imam and is also considered by the early Sufis as their patriarch, as their link to the Prophet.

The Source of Sufism

R.J.: Some seem to believe that a few of the early transmitters of *ḥadīth* actually became in the late eighth century the pioneers of Sufism. You know that because they did not just recite the traditional text but also believed that they could achieve spiritual transformation through emulating the teachings contained in the *ḥadīth*. Do you agree with that assertion, that is, that we have Sufism coming out of these transmitters of *ḥadīth*?

S.H.N.: No, Sufism came into being from the inner dimension of the Quran and the inner being of the Prophet of Islam and his instructions—but not only instructions; rather there was also the spiritual power of *walāyat* that emanated from him and that is so important in both Shiʿism and Sufism. Sufi initiation, which transmits this spiritual power, originates with him. He initiated ʿAlī and certain other companions such as Abū Bakr. But for Sufism the most important figure is ʿAlī. Then these teachings and the power of *walāyat* were transmitted to the next generation, to Salman-e Farsi[20] and later Hasan al-Basri[21] and also the Prophet's two grandchildren, especially Ḥasan, who was also the second Imam. These figures are very important for all of Sufism. It is this transmission and the spiritual knowledge and experience made possible by it that became crystallized later as classical Sufism. Needless to say, Ḥasan and certain other early transmitters of *ḥadīth* were also Sufis, but that is something else.

Of course the *aḥādīth* are of great significance, but Sufism could not be created by simply reading any part of the *ḥadīth* or even the Quran. You cannot become a Sufi just by reading the Quran unless God helps you in a special manner, since there are, of course, always exceptions made possible by Divine Mercy. What is needed in Sufism is initiation and guidance by a spiritual teacher, and that does not come from only reading a text. The text is always complementary to spiritual practice. The text is, of course, very important, especially the text of the Quran, which is sacred and extremely significant, as are on another level the esoteric *aḥādīth* of the Prophet, especially the sacred sayings or *al-aḥādīth al-qudsiyyah* that along with certain verses of the Quran are foundational for the doctrine of early Sufism. They are of central significance for meditation and doctrinal and practical guidance, but by themselves alone they do not constitute Sufism on the operative level. There has to be in addition to sacred texts the actual living spiritual power of *walāyat* transmitted from the Prophet generation by generation through various Sufi masters to the disciple seeking guidance. And of course there must be spiritual practice and the attainment of virtues made possible by the power and *barakah* associated with *walāyat*.

R.J.: Do you agree with those who believe that Sufism grew out of Eastern Christianity, as some historians believe, as a result of contact with Christians and the borrowing of their mysticism?

S.H.N.: This is a well-known theory of Western orientalists which I have repudiated in very strong terms in my writings. Putting the historical texts aside and just looking at this matter from the point of view of logic, and not even talking about Islam, let us consider a Christian saint who would go, let us say, to Africa, like Saint Augustine or like Saint Odile, who went to France and Germany and converted the Northern Germans and French to Christianity. If that person were to have no relation to Christ, how could he convert people to Christianity? If that person had become a Christian saint only as a result of having studied Plato and Plotinus or Manichaean texts, then how could people become Christian as a result of his influence? There is no logic in that. Likewise, millions of people over the centuries have embraced Islam and become devout Muslims because of Sufism, and this would not have been possible if Sufism had not issued from the heart of Islam.

There are people who have claimed that Sufism is the result of the influence of Christian monasticism, others who have said that Sufism is the result of the influence of Hinduism, or of the Iranian religions, or of Neoplatonism, or of the Aryan reaction against a Semitic religion. These theories that began with figures such as von Kremer and others in the 19th century are recycled all the time. Massignon was the first European orientalist to accept the fact that the roots of Sufism are to be found in the Quran, in the Quranic revelation. I do not want to disparage what he had said, but I think that although there is much truth in it, it is not complete, for there is also that spiritual presence or power which was given to the Prophet by God through the Archangel Gabriel, and which complements the spiritual presence and the message contained in the Sacred Text itself. But what Massignon asserted is of great importance for the West, for he was the first notable orientalist to have written that it is enough to read the Quran and meditate upon it to discover where the origins of Sufism are to be found.

The origin of Sufism is the Quranic revelation and the spiritual power that was transmitted through the Prophet, the power that makes its practice possible. I will say, moreover, that the mysticism of every religion is not only rooted in that religion, but that it is the heart of that religion. Later on it can always submit itself to certain external influences. It is especially important to remember that Sufism is the esoteric dimension of the last plenary revelation of our world, that is, Islam, which is the seal of previous revelations and therefore has great power to synthesize what came before it. That is why like Islam Sufism has such a strong synthesizing power and has integrated diverse elements from different mysticisms into some of its doctrinal structure and language, while the roots and the sap of the tree of Sufism have always been and remain Islamic. The teachings of Sufism contain all the possible dimensions of esoterism from the perspective of the Vedanta to that of Saint John of the Cross and everything in between, and therefore Sufism has also been always open to exchange of influences on the level of the formulation and crystallization of doctrine, et cetera with other traditions, including of course Christianity.

There is no doubt that Neoplatonism provided a very suitable language for the expression of Sufi metaphysical vision as it did for Christian and also Jewish mystical thought; but Sufi metaphysics does not come only from Neoplatonism. People who say such things confuse realized knowledge and mental formulations of knowledge. They do not understand that realized knowledge is not only concepts but is like a light shining within one's being. It is what we call "tasted knowledge" or "presential knowledge." There is no doubt that Ibn 'Arabī and others discovered in earlier mystical and metaphorical works a suitable language along with Quranic teachings to express their experience of the Divine Reality, but that experience itself did not result from reading the Neoplatonic texts. I always give the following example: Supposing you have a Native American who has climbed one of their sacred mountains in New Mexico ten times. Now he wants to write about his experiences, and he discovers a book on mountain climbing in English which explains very well how to describe mountaineering and so he uses the language of the book to describe his own experience of mountain climbing. Now, that book did not cause or enable the Native American to climb that mountain, but provided a convenient language for him to express his own experiences of having climbed the mountain.

Also, it is not only Neoplatonism, but also Christian monasticism that was very moving and attracted many early Sufis. The monks were usually spiritual beings. The Prophet loved the Christian monks and said that Muslims should be respectful toward them and kind to them—but that did not mean that Islamic spirituality came from Christian monasticism. On a more profound level, Christ himself plays an important esoteric role in the Islamic universe. In this question Islam is not like Christianity. In Christianity you do not ask prophets other than Christ to help you before God. In Islam, you have the prayer of Abraham which you recite when you go to the town of al-Khalīl in Palestine where he is buried or even when you are praying in your own mosque in, let us say, Cairo. In Shi'ism the names of all prophets including Christ are recited in famous prayers. In Sufism, Christ is the symbol of spirituality and inwardness. He is in fact the prophet of inwardness. Sufis saw this love for Christ and the presence of Christian spirituality among the monks as an expression of an aspect of Islam itself and had a great deal of affinity with it; but Sufism did not come into being as a result of this contact. Otherwise, everywhere Sufism spread people should have become converted to Christianity. That would be the logic of it, but they did not. More than half of the Islamic world has become Islamic as a result of Sufism.

When the Sufis went to Senegal in the 19th century right under the nose of the French colonialists, only a few percent of Senegalese people were Muslims. The Christians sent all of those Catholic missionaries to Senegal and the French government supported them and their schools and other institutions for over a century. When the French left Senegal as colonial masters, however, 83 or 84 percent of the population was Muslim and a small percentage Christian. Now, if all of these Sufi orders which spread Islam in Senegal were originally the result of Christian monasticism, how is it that when they went to Senegal, they were the cause of the population becoming Muslim and not Christian? There is no logic to the assertion that Sufism is the result of the influence of Christian monasticism or anything else outside the Islamic revelation any more than the assertion that Christian mysticism came from Neoplatonism. There is of course the possibility of influence on Sufism of certain ideas and symbols drawn from early Christianity, Neoplatonism, Buddhism, Hinduism, Zoroastrianism, et cetera, and you can also see that process the other way around. Everybody talks about the influence of Sufism on the *bhakti* movement in India. I would also defend the religious authenticity of this movement and say that the *bhakti* movement was not created by Sufism in India—otherwise it would not be Hindu, but that *bhaktism* was influenced in many of its expressions, in its poetry, in its attitudes, by the presence of Sufism in India.

Interreligious Dialogue[22]

Sufism and Interreligious Dialogue

R.J.: Do you think that Sufism can play a great role in the dialogue of religions today?

S.H.N.: Very much so. The whole subject of dialogue between religions is a major problem with which we have to deal. Often this dialogue is carried out for political expediency, which is fine on its own level, but not sufficient. Many people of good intention ask that we not fight with each other and that religions meet together like in the United Nations, where one sees all kinds of governments, from monarchies to republics, from the left to the right, dictatorships, democracies, everything. But they all sit down together in order to try at least to avoid conflict to the extent possible. I am not against such an endeavor, but that is not enough when it comes to religions. What is needed is mutual understanding, unity, and empathy between religions, and that is not possible on the formal level. The form of each religion is distinct and exclusive, but also sacred; it comes from Heaven, and I am the last person in the world to say that we should destroy these forms in the name of world peace or something like that, even if it were possible to do so. It is these forms themselves that we need in order to reach real peace in the Formless, in order to reach the Sacred. And yet harmony is not possible on the formal plane. Where harmony is possible is on the level of the supra-formal, that is, of the Reality that transcends forms. That level is the inner, esoteric dimension of each religion, and for Islam that is Sufism.

It is not accidental that before the contemporary period, when so much interest is being shown in comparative religion, comparative philosophy, comparative mysticism, et cetera, during earlier historical periods, in the Islamic world it was primarily the Sufis who spoke about universality of the truth and of revelation. It was figures such as Ibn ʻArabī and Rūmī who had a vision of the Formless which allowed them to see the truth in forms other than those of their own religion. There were other Muslims who had knowledge of other religions and some studied the subject very carefully and scientifically, such as Bīrunī[23] in his book *India*, which many people have called "the first book on comparative religion." But when it came to the question of trying to create empathy and understanding across religious frontiers, among Muslims it was the Sufis who were the pioneers.

One of the reasons why it is so difficult to have in-depth religious dialogue today is that on the Christian side, where this dialogue began, the esoteric, inner dimension has been to a large extent absent. Christian mysticism has been to a large degree eclipsed in the West in the last few centuries even in the Catholic world, and so it is more difficult, I believe, to have the Christian mystical tradition present in religious dialogue—but there are exceptions, as in the case of Thomas Merton. On the Islamic side, however, the most profound doctrines that have been formulated concerning the plurality of religions and the relationship between them have come from sources inspired by Sufism directly or indirectly.

It is interesting to note that in Europe itself, many of the traditionalists, who have been at the forefront of speaking about the authenticity of all the great religions of the world, their relation with each other and the transcendent unity of the Truth, people such as Guénon and Schuon, belonged to the Sufi tradition. Guénon used to quote the Arabic phrase *al-tawḥīdu wāḥid*, that is, the doctrine of Unity is itself unique; therefore you cannot have two truths with a capital "T." There must be only one single Truth, and that single Truth must have manifested itself in all the different authentic religious universes. Otherwise God would not be merciful and just.

Christianity Confronts Other Religions

R.J.: You said that this dialogue started in modern times because of an inner need within the Christian religion. Does this inner need exist also for Islam, or does Islam not sense this necessity for dialogue?

S.H.N.: Islam also needs religious dialogue, which is at the heart of civilizational and cultural dialogue; but Islam is not theologically threatened by the presence of other religions in the same way that Christianity is. But over time engagement in religious dialogue becomes more and more a necessity for Islam as well. Let me explain this point. Christianity experienced the withering influence of secularism before Islam. In the Middle Ages, Christianity filled the whole living space of Western man, as did Eastern Christianity for people of Eastern Europe; but I am concentrating now only on Western Christianity, and we shall put the case of Eastern Christianity aside. With the rise of modernism from the Renaissance onward, as you know, philosophy, the sciences, the arts, social ideas, and even the field of ethics became gradually secularized. In a sense Western Christianity was not in the same situation in its world as Islam, Hinduism, or Buddhism were in theirs when the encounter between different civilizations and religions occurred in modern times and became especially accentuated in the 20th century.

Now, Christianity has almost always claimed that there is only one truth and that it is the Christian truth, and that there is no salvation outside the Church. The Catholic Church has made this claim over the centuries, and its formulation in Latin as *extra ecclesiam nulla salus* (no salvation outside the Church) is well known. How different is this from the Islamic view, for the Quran asserts clearly that people who do good works and have faith will be rewarded for their actions and will be saved, but does not say that this is true for only Muslims. There are some exclusivist and short-sighted Muslims today who believe that anyone who is not a Muslim is an infidel and will go therefore to hell, but that is not the traditional Islamic doctrine and goes against the text of the Quran. This exclusivism according to which only Christians are saved is a view still held by many more Christians than Muslims, especially Evangelical Christians among Protestants, and not only among Catholics. It is also held by most in the Eastern churches, which have been much less interested in dialogue than Western churches until quite recently. It is only now that they are beginning to show interest after the tragedies of Bosnia, Kosovo, and Chechnya, all of which involve Islam and Eastern Christianity. In any case, although the claim to exclusive truth was shared by the different churches, it was in the West that as a result of secularization a religious vacuum was created into which non-Christian religions entered, posing a direct challenge to Western Christianity and its exclusivist view of religious truth.

As you know, after Vatican II, the papacy itself issued the famous encyclical *Nostrae Aetate* and created a whole secretariat for non-Christian religions, which was headed for many years by Cardinal Pignedoli and later by other cardinals including Cardinal Arinze who is an African. This was more the result of the recognition of the challenge of other religions and the necessity for religious dialogue than anything else. Many Westerners no longer accept Christianity and seek knowledge of other religions, which have become a living presence in the West. As a result of both this interest and also migration, other religions play an unprecedented role in the Christian living space in the West. Now you might say, "Did this not happen also in the 12th century in Spain, France, or Italy?" Yes, but there is a big difference. If you were a Frenchman living in Paris in the 12th century when Islamic ideas were spreading, or even a Christian living in Muslim Spain, your whole world was filled with Christianity, and you viewed Islamic ideas from a completely Christian point of view and as foreign. You felt no need to seek after the truth outside the confines of Christianity. It was not this half-empty world, religiously speaking, depleted to a large extent of religious presence that we see today in the West. It was a very different world over which a homogeneous worldview that was Christian dominated.

It was into this half-secularized world that came translations in the 19th century of the Quran and *Ḥadīth*, of works on Sufism, of Upanishads, Buddhist *sutras*, et cetera. And gradually it became increasingly difficult for intelligent Westerners, who were still in a sense Christians but who also felt that their inner spiritual and intellectual space was not completely filled by Christianity, to remain totally indifferent to the truth of other religions which they now encountered. Many people in the West began to write about other religions, and from the early 20th century more and more Westerners realized that it was necessary to take other religions seriously. Intelligent and sincere people who were studying these other religions also came to meet more and more members of those religions who were highly spiritual and even sometimes of great sanctity and became afraid that if they denied them, they would have to deny their own religion. India had a very important role to play in this process, especially with the spread of the Ramakrishna movement[24] in the 19th century to the West and the journey of many Westerners to India. Even popular writers such as Romain Rolland[25] wrote books on India, and such famous figures of Hinduism as Vivekananda,[26] Gandhi, and Maharshi became well known in the West. Moreover, there began to appear in the West in museums and elsewhere objects of sacred art of various religions that attracted many spiritually sensitive people.

Christianity began to feel threatened by the presence of other religions as a result of these diverse factors in a way that these other religions did not. The other religions were threatened in a very different way by Christian missionary activity and the financial and political power that was behind the Christian missionaries as well as, of course, modern secularism coming from the West. I will not call their activity forced conversion but very strong persuasion, resulting in what is sometimes called in Asia "rice bag conversion." In India, Indonesia, and Africa especially, people often talk about this matter; they say that because these missionaries did not come with only the Bible but also brought syringes so that they cured cows through vaccination, provided of course the farmers would show an interest in Christianity. Behind all the medical and educational activity has been the desire to convert the people of the East.

The question in such cases is one of confrontation and not dialogue, because the invading religion, that is, Christianity, has been supported by economic and political power, and this was especially true in the Colonial period. During that period, no matter how much the European governments became secularized, they supported Christian missionaries as if they were Charlemagne ruling over a Christian society. It is interesting to note the paradox that after the French Revolution when priests in France were being killed, the French government was supporting the Christian missionaries in North Africa. The question of Christianity for Islam and other Oriental religions has been marked by confrontation for a long time. Other religions have felt threatened by Christianity on the basis of a power structure that has supported Christian missionary activity, and still does in many direct and indirect ways.

This is very different from the way that Christianity has felt threatened by other religions in modern times. Hinduism, Islam, or Buddhism have not had any armies or worldly assets, schools, medical cures, and hospitals with which to lure people towards them. They have not had any of those means, and therefore individuals in the West who have been attracted to them have been so because of the presence of spiritual practices and metaphysical doctrines which the non-Western religions have still preserved, while the more intellectual, spiritual, and esoteric dimensions of Christianity have become ever more inaccessible.

In the 20th century you did not have a Meister Eckhart,[27] a Saint Thomas Aquinas, or a Saint Bonaventure[28] living in any Western countries. There were a few spiritually speaking great people such as the Italian Padre Pio.[29] There were a few exceptions here and there, but by and large, the mystical dimension of the religion, especially its intellectual dimension, had become, to a large extent, enfeebled and eclipsed as a result of the thrust of the Enlightenment and subsequent 19th-century philosophies. Suddenly these other religions appeared on the scene with an intact metaphysics and a very powerful mystical, spiritual, and intellectual presence, along with techniques for spiritual realization. This was a very great challenge for Christianity. A number of leading European intellectuals who were not totally Christian in the sense that they were wooed away from Christianity by secularism and modernism became attracted to these other religions, including Islam, despite the hatred that existed in the Middle Ages in Europe against Islam, which has received the worst treatment in the West in comparison with other non-Western religions. But even in the case of Islam, someone like Charles de Foucauld[30] had empathy for the spiritual aspects of Islam, and Emile Dermenghem[31] would go to North Africa and write as a young Catholic but with spiritual sympathy towards Islam, while others such as Vincent Monteil[32] embraced Islam openly. I have already spoken of Massignon and Corbin. Here I am mentioning only France, because you lived in France for so many years, but one sees a similar situation in England and Germany as well as America, which came somehow later upon the scene.

Although the West won the Second World War, after the war, Far Eastern influences and also Indian influences began to come into the United States much more openly. It is true that in 1927 D. T. Suzuki[33] had already published his essays on Zen Buddhism, which introduced Zen into the West, but at the beginning only a relatively small circle of people were interested. After the end of the War one observes in the West a wave of interest in Oriental spirituality, especially Zen Buddhism and the Vedanta; and many leading intellectuals such as Alan Watts,[34] Gerald Heard,[35] and Aldous Huxley[36] begin to write about Eastern religions. It is this movement during the period after the war, a movement often combined with the dilution of authentic Oriental teachings, that led to the New Age religions which began in American in the sixties, and which has now spread into Europe, and about which the Church is very worried now in France and elsewhere. But before what is now called New Age religions, these earlier movements brought about the actual presence of non-Western religions, some in a less adulterated form, right into the bosom of the West. There was first the Vedanta Society, and the propagation of the Vedanta. Then came Zen, and then upon its wake came Sufism.

Most of the people in the West who have become attracted to Eastern religions have been attracted to the esoteric, inward dimension of these religions. Many people in the West talk about Hinduism and most among this group have read the *Gita*, but I always say, practically no one has read the *Laws* of Manu. These Western seekers are not interested in purification rites, what you do with cows, and sacrificing before the gods and so forth. They are interested in the pure metaphysical and spiritual ideas of the remarkable celestial works that are *Gita* or the Upanishads. Sufism was in a sense very fortunate in that for some time at least it was spared this pseudo-spirituality, much of which came in the form of pseudo-Zen, pseudo-Vedanta, et cetera mixed often with commercialism and usually taught by questionable gurus, with finding a market for people selling pseudo-spirituality to those weary of modern civilization and looking for so-called Oriental spirituality without wanting to dedicate themselves fully to it. Anyway, Sufism came upon the scene later and was saved much of the earlier profanation of Oriental spiritual teachings. But later, people such as Idris Shah,[37] who tried to divorce Sufism from Islam, did appear on the scene and did try to present Sufism as a spiritual practice independent of Islam for those who did not want to practice religion seriously.

So, all of these developments have marked a challenge that Christianity has been forced to face, and therefore some Christian writers began to study these matters in order to provide a response. Soon you had books such as *Zen Catholicism* by Aelred Graham,[38] who was a Benedictine monk from England. You had Bede Griffith,[39] who migrated to India and lived like a Hindu in an ashram, but was a Christian and began to write on Hindu meditation from a Christian perspective. There were also Christians who wrote on Buddhism and continue to do so today.

The most influential of all American Catholic writers of the 20th century, and perhaps the most influential of all Catholic writers of the 20th century anywhere, because his books are so widely read even in Europe in other languages than English, was Thomas Merton,[40] who studied Zen Buddhism fervently and also studied Sufism. He was coming to Iran to see me when he died in Thailand. He was very much interested in Oriental religions, trying in a sense to incorporate certain elements from these religions into Christian contemplative practices, elements such as methods of meditation and so forth, which had been lost for a long time in the West but preserved in such traditions as Buddhism and Islam in their mystical teachings, such as Zen and Sufism. All of these efforts represent the attempt on the part of Christianity to respond to the presence of other religions, and through dialogue provide means for Christian thought to respond to the challenge posed for it, which is very different from the challenges Christianity poses for other religions. All of these factors must be considered when one tries to discover why Christianity became so much interested in religious dialogue.

Islam in the West

I must say something about Islam itself becoming a notable presence in the West. Of course for centuries Islam has existed in such places as Bosnia, Kosovo, Macedonia, and Albania, but the culture of these lands was completely separated from Western Europe's mental space. It was only after the Second World War that the presence of Islam in the West became a major factor through both immigration and conversion. Having lost their colonies abroad, European nations had to create in a sense colonies inside their countries in order to have cheap labor, and so they had to open their doors to a large number of emigrants. The French opted of course for the North African colonies, or former colonies, and many Algerians, Moroccans, and Tunisians came to France to work. Today you find hardly any railroad station in Paris being swept by anyone except North Africans along with some from Black Africa. The

French themselves, like other native Western Europeans, do not perform such tasks. Germany chose Turkey, and a large number of "guest workers" were brought from that country. Great Britain also chose mostly its former colonies, primarily people from Pakistan, India, and Bangladesh, although a number of Black Africans were also allowed to come to Britain to work, many from the Caribbean.

The situation in the United States and Canada has been somewhat different in that Muslim emigrants to these countries have been usually better educated and wealthier than those who migrated to Europe. But in North America, also millions of people migrated from the Arab world, Iran, Turkey, the Indian subcontinent, and elsewhere in the Islamic world to create, along with converts to Islam, especially those from the African American community, a strong Islamic presence which had not been there before the Second World War. In any case, as a result of these events there occurred suddenly the growth of a large, relatively speaking, Islamic population in Europe and America. In France today, there are a lot more Muslims than Jews, five hundred thousand Jews, and between 5 and 8 million Muslims. In Britain there are some 2 million Muslims, and in almost all European countries, Islam is the second largest religion after Christianity. In America there are between 6 and 8 million Muslims. All of these events along with other factors, coming one after another, forced Christian theologians to consider seriously the challenge of the presence of other religions and especially of Islam; and since Christianity had almost always rejected the possibility of salvation outside of Christianity, this new situation has been a difficult one to confront and has posed one of the most intractable problems for Christianity, theologically speaking.

Islam and Other Religions

Now, to come back to your original question, this was not the case for Islam. Why? Because Islam, besides coming at the end of the major cycle of revelations, had had an experience of the different religions of the world before modern times. I have always said that Islam is the only religion that had direct contact with nearly all the major families of religions of the world outside of the matrix of modernism. That is a very significant fact. If you lived in Persia a thousand years ago, you would probably have had Christian and Jewish neighbors or friends and probably would have known and had as friends some Zoroastrians. Furthermore, you would certainly have heard of Buddhism and Hinduism, and stories, ideas, and even sciences of Indian origin would exist in your society. If you were a scholar, you would have read Bīrūnī's *India.* If you lived in the Safavid period, you might have even read the Persian commentary of Mir Findiriski[41] upon the *Yoga Vasishtha*, a notable work which is one of the most important books on comparative philosophy and religion before modern times, a work whose complete and critically edited text is still not available. The Upanishads were translated into Persian first before being translated into Latin from the Persian by Anquétil-Duperron.[42]

The premodern Islamic world was very different from the France or Germany of the Middle Ages or Renaissance as far as awareness of other religions is concerned. If you lived several centuries ago in Strasbourg, you would have heard of Islam and might have known the small Jewish community there, but you would have had no awareness of the presence of other religions. In contrast, Islam had contact with all the major families of religions before modern times, except for Shintoism, and of course the Native American religions, and those of Australia and other faraway places. Islam had contact with African religions in Black Africa in such places as the Niger Valley and Sudan, and contact with Christianity and Judaism, throughout the Islamic world. It had contact with the Chinese religions in China and with Hinduism and Buddhism in the eastern regions of the Islamic world. The eastern provinces of Persia were Buddhist and not Zoroastrian when Islam first came there. The Barmakid[43] family was originally Buddhist, and its members before the coming of Islam keepers of a Buddhist temple. Islam had contact with Hinduism from the very first century of its existence in Sindh and Gujarat. Later within India for a thousand years Muslims and Hindus interacted with each other in countless ways. Thousands of works in Persian were written in India, mostly by Muslims but also some by Hindus. Many classics of Islamic thought were rendered into Sanskrit and other Indian languages, while many masterpieces of Hinduism and to a lesser degree Buddhism were rendered into Persian and also to some extent Arabic and other Islamic languages. Also one should not forget that it was through Persia that Buddhism reached China before the rise of Islam.

Islam also had contact with the Shamanic religions. The Turks were originally Shamans who converted to Islam even before they came to Iran. Muslims, therefore, knew something about Shamanism, and certain ideas of both Turkic and Mongolian Shamanism survived for some time within the Islamic world. Furthermore, Islam has been present in China since the first century, and certainly during the past six or seven hundred years it has had a major presence in China. Chinese Islam is a distinct zone of Islamic culture. The Chinese Muslims wrote in Arabic and especially Persian for a long time. The first books written in Chinese on Islamic thought but in the language of classical Neo-Confucianism were written by Liu Hsi and Wang Dei-Yu, contemporaries of Descartes, in the 17th century. Such Chinese Muslim scholars had in fact a deep knowledge of Neo-Confucianism, and although not every Muslim had great knowledge of these matters, Islamic civilization as a whole had vast knowledge of other religions, which included the Chinese.

There was a great deal of exchange of ideas among Muslim scholars all the way from Morocco to China during the *hajj* in Makkah, and there was a remarkable facility for the exchange of ideas within Islamic civilization, so that knowledge of other religions spread easily from one end of the Islamic world to the other. The presence of other religions is therefore nothing new to Islam as it has been for Christianity, and the multiplicity of other religions does not pose the same kind of theological challenge for Muslims as it does for Christians.

However, having said all of this concerning the historical background of this question, I must add that religious dialogue is absolutely necessary today for Muslims, as well as for Christians. Awareness of this necessity began first in Christianity because Christianity was threatened by the presence of other religions, but today religious dialogue is also necessary for Islam, because to the extent that modernism spreads into the Islamic world, it necessitates paradoxically knowledge of other religions. I believe that in the deepest religious sense, the presence of other religions and their truths, which confirm the teachings of one's own religion, is a kind of divine compensation for the loss of the homogeneity of the religious ambience which modernism and secularism have brought about.

R.J.: Yes, but I mean, Christianity is a religion of the West, and the West today dominates the world economically through globalization. So I think that other civilizations feel this necessity to go and have a dialogue with the West, at least not to be dominated, but to live in a balanced way, and they find the spiritual and ethical guarantors of the West among Christians, because otherwise businessmen cannot be spiritual guarantors. This is why somebody like, for example, Khatami[44] talks about the dialogue of civilizations. I suppose he means that he wants to start the dialogue not just on an economic basis, but especially on a spiritual basis, to find this balance between the West and Islam.

S.H.N.: I think that your comments are quite just except that they need to be modified in a certain sense. You said that Christianity is the dominant religion of the West, and therefore as the West dominates the world through globalization, Christianity will do the same. But although Christianity is still the majority religion in the West, it does not have total dominance over the West. Unfortunately, the dialogue with the West is not identical with the dialogue with Christianity, and that is what makes dialogue even more difficult. Of course every civilization was created through a religion, and there is no exception to this truth. But in the present state of Western civilization, this civilization is no longer a Christian civilization; and Khatami, as a Muslim, or for that matter someone from India, as a Hindu, must recognize the fact that the other side of the civilizational dialogue, which is the West, does not belong to a predominantly religious civilization, as it was in the past, although religious elements continue to survive in it today. Despite this fact, however, I still think that at the heart of dialogue with the West stands the dialogue with Christianity, even if there are many other forces, mostly secular, present in the modern West.

Also I want to say that through the very process of globalization, the West is becoming less and less "Western" in a certain sense; that is, Eastern elements, elements from other religions and cultures, are becoming present in the West itself, as in the United States, where the Islamic presence is now an important factor in many areas. Islam has now become a mainstream religion in America and is no longer marginal, while the process of globalization has been continuing. The same phenomenon is also occurring more or less in Europe, where, as in America, Islam is gradually becoming, despite much opposition, a mainstream religion, like Judaism.

Part Nine

Modernism and Its Effect on Christianity

R.J.: Why do you think that modernity affected Christianity more easily than Islam, since we are talking about this?

S.H.N.: This is a very complicated matter. Let us remember first of all that modernism did not affect Eastern Christianity in the same way that it affected Western Christianity. As far as Western Christianity is concerned, there are several reasons: As Christianity became the dominant religion of the West, after the fall of the Roman Empire—to which it itself contributed—and as it created a new civilization, which is what we call Western civilization, it was not able to nullify completely the influences of the Greco-Roman antiquity and its pagan and antireligious aspects. As you remember, before the rise of Christianity, the late phase of Greek and Roman civilization and cultures present us with the only known case in history before modern times in which you have a fairly extensive, if not complete and total, rebellion against religion. Both the Greek and Roman religions had decayed, and it is in the late Greek period and among the Romans that you find agnostic, or even atheistic and materialistic philosophies that deny any transcendent principle, such philosophies as those of the New Academy, the Epicureans, the Skeptics, and groups like them. Even before the later period of Antiquity there were the Sophists who were a class of principle-less dialecticians against whom Socrates had spoken already, men who were willing to argue in favor of anything because they did not believe in anything. One just could pay them to argue for the truth of anything that one desired. You do not meet that kind of phenomenon in either ancient Persia, India, or China, all of which possessed great civilizations.

Although Rome did not have the same strong philosophical tradition as Greece, nevertheless aspects of hedonism, skepticism, and this-worldliness which characterized much of the late Greek culture were also to be seen in Rome. And as the Roman religion became gradually enfeebled, various Eastern religions began to fill this vacuum, including the cult of Isis and Osiris, Mithraism and Manicheanism from Persia, and of course Christianity, which won the day. It won over all of these other religions and eclipsed all the secular philosophies of the day, but it was not able to fully neutralize the negative influence of various existing philosophical and religious movements. There was a great deal of skepticism, naturalism, and rationalism that remained in a latent state and that with the weakening of medieval Christian philosophy and theology manifested itself with fury during the Renaissance.

The case of Islam, or for that matter Buddhism, was very different. When Buddhism went to China, it also encountered a vast civilization with a remarkably long philosophical tradition—Confucianism, Taoism, schools of logic, et cetera—but that was not the same situation at all, because these schools were traditional in nature and did not deny the spiritual dimensions of reality. As for Islam, it inherited the metaphysical aspects of Greek philosophy and not its skepticism, agnosticism, naturalism, and rationalism, which survived in the West in a latent state even after the triumph of Christianity. These tendencies were not totally neutralized and began to raise their head again in the Occident as soon as they could.

Naturalism, Rationalism, and Nominalism

Now, how did that revolt come about? I believe that it came about after the 13th century in the West, when Christian theology and Christian thought in general became more and more externalized. Christian theology in Western, in contrast to Eastern, Christianity introduced an element of rationalism into theology itself, although it was kept at bay in the 13th century. By the 14th century, when you have the nominalist denial of Platonic realism, and Ockham's razor which in a sense substituted logic for metaphysics, in many circles the intellectual hold of Christianity became weakened. And as usual, as the famous Arabic and Persian proverb states, "the fish begins to stink from its head," or the corruption of the best is the worst (*corruptio optima pessimi*), as a Latin proverb asserts.

Always when intellectual decline takes place, it begins from the top. In the West, even after the Middle Ages the ordinary people still remained very pious and faithful to Christian rituals and doctrines. Even if certain pre-Christian religious practices and symbols had been integrated into Christianity, such as various Druidic and Germanic holidays, and even the Christmas tree, they were still seen as Christian by the ordinary people. Needless to say, there had been no Christmas trees in Palestine. The integration of pre-Christian European religious practices on the popular level did not, however, bring about the advent of modernism and secularization. The problem began on the intellectual level with the intellectual elite, with the weakening of Christian theology and Christian philosophy. In fact, nominalism in a sense destroyed the metaphysical aspect of Christian philosophy and weakened mystical theology in the West. Therefore, the ground was prepared for those older elements of skepticism and rationalism of Graeco-Roman origin that had remained latent to raise their head again. During the Renaissance, there was the rise of paganism in the real Christian sense outside of Christianity, not as one sees in the early Christian period when Saint Augustine and others integrated certain elements of Greek thought into Christian theology. Their interpretation of Greek thought was not independent of Christianity and was not pagan.

The rebellion that took place against Christianity in the Renaissance among a large sector of the intelligentsia did not occur in the same way in any other world religion, in any other global civilization, until quite recently. The Renaissance was in a sense the rebellion and triumph of the paganism of the decadent world of late Antiquity with its naturalism and rationalism over the Christian culture of the West. Christianity, no longer having full authority within the whole of society to make use of its own intellectual tradition, and having turned against much of its own more profound metaphysical teachings, was to a large extent helpless before this onslaught.

Other Factors in the Secularization of the West

It is important to ask this question, which most European scholars do not usually ask: Why it is that in the 11th, 12th, or 13th centuries, when you had this very powerful traditional current, both mystical and intellectual, in Christianity, this rebellion against religion did not take place in Europe? I should mention two figures, Saint Bonaventure and Saint Thomas, very different from each other but almost contemporaries. They represented at the highest level the mystical, intellectual, and philosophical dimensions of the Christian tradition and Christian responses to Greek philosophy. Why was it that this later challenge of Greco-Roman paganism could not be answered by Christianity? It was because the Christian sapiential tradition was still strong during their time and not after the Middle Ages. It was not that there were not Roman statues around in Rome; they had been around since Christianity came to that city, but they did not serve as sources of inspiration for medieval sculptors. The spiritual and intellectual traditional climate of Christianity was strong enough so that the weeds, you might say, of decadent Greco-Roman culture, which were under the ground, did not find the right atmosphere, the right conditions to shoot out of the earth and start killing many of the plants of Christianity; but this happened gradually when that tradition weakened.

There are also many social and political elements that are involved in this process, as I have already mentioned. First of all, the weakening of the papacy by the imprisonment of the popes at Avignon by the French kings, and secondly the oppression caused by the papacy itself against many of the mystical dimensions of Christianity, along with a worldliness that crept into the Catholic Church and its hierarchy and which caused the Protestant Reformation were also very important. All of these factors were significant in the secularization of the West. The Protestant Reformation itself is a unique event in religious history. Religions have had diverse interpretations, such as Mahayana, Theravada, and Tibetan or Vajrayana Buddhism, or Shivite and Vishnuvite Hinduism, or various schools of Islam, such as Sunnism and Shi'ism, but they do not represent the same thing as Protestantism, which came 1,500 years after the founding of the religion, and which was a direct revolt in the name of the Bible against the central authority and structure of the Western Christian religion. And why did that come about? It was because of some of those excesses and a kind of worldliness that contaminated the papacy during the Renaissance.

One of the great tragedies that occurred is that Catholicism, which had been responsible for having created Western civilization, continued to defend it even when this civilization became secularized and worldly. It is only now in the 20th and 21st centuries that finally the Catholic Church is beginning to disassociate itself at least to some extent from modern Western civilization, which is no longer a Christian civilization, but one that has produced nearly all the antireligious forces that have wreaked havoc upon the world, from Karl Marx to Freud, to atheistic existentialists such as Jean-Paul Sartre, to relativizing deconstructionism. People who created such antireligious philosophies were not Persian or Japanese. They were all Westerners whose ancestors were either Catholics or, in the case of Karl Marx, Jewish, but living within a Western context, not being Arab or Persian Christians or Jews.

The tragedy was that Catholic Christianity as a religion, instead of disassociating itself from what was going on, just went along with it and so became deeply affected by secularism. Look at what happened to Catholic art. I use the words "Catholic art" here on purpose, for it was this art that began to incorporate in such a clear fashion the worldliness of the Renaissance; and as we see today, the Vatican is not like the Chartres Cathedral, but more like a 16th-century Roman palace. It does not have the otherworldliness of Gothic or Romanesque art. And as Catholic art became more humanistic and worldly, many of the most intelligent and sensitive people left the Church. One can think of someone of high intelligence in the metaphysical sense and spiritual sensibility feeling at home in the Cathedral of Rheims or Strasbourg, but it is very difficult to imagine them feeling at home in one of those decadent Baroque churches. This can also be seen in the realm of thought. So, as Christianity in the West went along with much that was going on around it, it lost a lot of its most intelligent followers, although there were of course exceptions, and something of traditional Christianity survived even within this ambience.

In a sense, the wedding between intelligence and piety became more and more rare in the West—not that it became totally inaccessible, but it became exceptional and remains so even in our own day. It is hard to find today many persons in the West who are both very intelligent and very devout, although fortunately there are still some. Such was not the case in other civilizations or during the European Middle Ages.

Protestantism's Secularizing Influence

As for Protestantism, its reaction was the other way around. Protestantism claimed that it had nothing to do with medieval and Renaissance culture and disassociated itself from classical Western civilization and "civilizationism," claiming to go back to the Bible, and also going against 1,500 years of the Christian tradition in the West. One positive aspect of this attitude was that it did not have to associate itself with all of the worldliness that was going on within the Catholic Church during the Renaissance. But its position also helped to destroy the sacred ambience of medieval Christianity. It became further more and more opposed to mysticism and traditional Christian philosophy, and of course to sacred art, sacred literature, sacred music, et cetera. There was Protestant religious music, but not sacred music like the Gregorian chant. All of this had a notable role to play in the further secularization and weakening of traditional Christianity. Of course the early Protestant movement accepted certain of the deepest elements of medieval culture and civilization; it had no choice. For example, Johann Sebastian Bach was a Protestant, a Lutheran, and even though he wrote the *B-Minor Mass* in Latin, he was a German Lutheran who composed some of the most profound and beautiful Western music of a traditional character. And there are also other examples, including the early Protestant theosophers up to Jakob Böhme.

The net result was, however, that Protestantism, especially in allying itself with capitalism and helping its rise, helped to secularize the world in which Christianity functioned. Many Protestants, even to this day, do not even want to view the matter from this perspective, but there are others who resent that they now live in a secularized world. Many Protestants in the United States are serious Christians, but the world in which they live is not a totally Christian world, even though they remain strongly Christian in their personal lives. Furthermore, Christianity itself does not seem to have at the present moment the intellectual strength to re-Christianize society, even in America where religion is much stronger than in Europe, although there are now movements afoot to revive Christian thought and to re-sacralize the Christian mental space in both Europe and America.

Another element that is very important is that as a result of the creation of Protestantism and the Counter-Reformation within the Catholic Church, Protestants and Catholics began to fight against each other, and these incredible wars of religion in Europe lasted well over a century. That is a long time, and God knows how many hundreds of thousands of people were killed. You know these stories in France, what they did to the Huguenots and the other way around. On both sides there were mass killings, and these actions naturally bothered the conscience of many Europeans, many of whom as a result, drew away from religion altogether. These wars definitely helped to weaken Christianity a great deal and to help the rise of secularism. One does not see the same situation in other religions of the world to the same extent. There was a unique situation in the West in which the factors mentioned above, as well as others, joined hands to weaken religion as a total way of life and to make possible the domination of secularism.

Secular and Sacred Law[1]

R.J.: One of the main factors in the encounter between Christianity and modernity was the rise of secularism. I mean that today when we see the Christian churches, we see that most of them have accepted the difference between God's laws and secular laws in their societies. I know that you do not agree with secular ideas, but there is a debate going on in Islamic societies today because of our encounter with the modern world. In which way do you think one can apply this separation of church and state, which is fundamental to the secular ideology in the Western world, to the Islamic world?

S.H.N.: The question that you are asking is of course important to consider. Let me first turn to the question of God's laws and secular laws. One of the reasons that Western Christianity became weakened as no other religion has in history except for the late Greco-Roman religions, whose decay led to the death of these civilizations of which they were the dominant religions, is that the laws used by Christian people in Europe were not drawn directly from the source of Christian revelation and the fountainhead of their religion, except for spiritual laws and personal moral codes such as the Ten Commandments. What do I mean by that? I mean that Judaism, like Islam, has a religious law that embraces all of life, and traditional Judaism holds exactly the same position as Islam in this matter. There is no such thing as secular law as we understand today in these religions. Let us look at Jewish society. I do not mean modern Israel where there are many agnostic Jews from Europe and there is a major battle going on between Orthodox and secularized Jews, which itself is very telling; for it is the battle again of certain aspects of secularized Western civilization with now another religion. But let us say Jewish society in the time of Solomon and David. At that time there was no distinction between the laws of God and the laws of a secular political authority or what the New Testament refers to as the laws of Caesar.

It is Christ who said, "Give unto God what is God's and give unto Caesar what is Caesar's." In the New Testament there are very profound spiritual teachings, but there are no instructions for how to rule society and how to carry out economic transactions except by being good and just on the level of individual human beings. It has been written that, in a sense, Christianity is the religion of a society of saints; but for ordinary human beings, they had to devise laws drawn from somewhere else. So, as we already discussed, when Christianity came to the West, it incorporated Roman law and later Germanic and Anglo-Saxon common law. These laws became integrated into the body of law of Western civilization and are still foundations of modern law. Even though law today is called "secular," originally it was related to ancient religions. Roman law originated from the Roman religion, but for Christianity it appeared as secular law, because it did not issue from the revealed sources of Christianity. There remained a hiatus between the two. There was always a kind of chasm between spiritual laws mentioned in the New Testament such as "Love thy neighbor," and the Ten Commandments, which Christianity accepted, although revealed to Moses, on the one hand, and how one should rule a country—political laws, economic laws, social laws, et cetera—on the other.

Now, Christianity and to some extent Buddhism are the only major world religions with such a situation. Not only Islam, but also Judaism, Hinduism, Shintoism, Confucianism, and many other religions are religions in which the law of society and what we call the rule of God do not belong to two different domains. Look at Confucianism: the laws of classical Chinese society and Confucian-inspired laws were the same. Look at India: we find the same situation there, and in this matter there is little difference between Hinduism and Islam. For many Persians, whom you probably have in mind, because many of them have not thought enough about these issues in general, the only question is the situation of Iran today in relation to the West. But let us look farther afield and take even the case of Buddhism, which in many ways is similar to Christianity. When we look at a country such as Tibet, where the Dalai Lama was both the head of Buddhism and the king of the country until 1951, and is still considered the ruler of Tibet by most Tibetans, who do not want to be colonized by the Chinese, we see a unity between spiritual and temporal power and also religious and social laws, even if the latter often drew on Hindu sources. One finds a similar situation in the other Himalayan kingdoms such as Bhutan and Nepal. Buddhism was able to create a unity that avoided the dichotomy between the religious and the secular that one finds in the West because of the nature of the laws that Buddhism incorporated into itself, although it has certain structural resemblances to Christianity.

In the case of Christianity, there always existed a dichotomy between religious and secular law, even in medieval times, and between the authority of the pope and the emperor, about which Dante spoke. The temporal and spiritual authorities were always different and distinct, and this became later transformed into the question of the relation between the state and the Church after the medieval synthesis, which had held this division together in a higher unity, was destroyed. The state in its modern sense is a child of the French Revolution, but it also corresponds to the older political structure, which had been subservient to the papacy, to the spiritual authority in the Middle Ages. The emperor received his legitimacy from the pope and the kings of France were anointed by the "Rite of David." People who discuss the question of the relation between church and state are not often aware of its roots in the particular experiences of earlier European history, in which there were two different authorities and not one single authority as there were two sources of law. Such was not the case in most other major civilizations. The Emperor of China, before the Ching Dynasty came to an end, was the bridge between Heaven and Earth. He was both the premier authority of Confucianism and the supreme authority of the state. The Emperor of Japan, until McArthur helped create the modern Japanese constitution, was (and is still for many Japanese) the descendant of the Sun God of Shintoism and the center of Shinto religion.

The idea of looking at the relation of spiritual and temporal authority in other societies as being the same as the relation between church and state in the West is really a very parochial way of looking at this matter. In all these other civilizations there existed a single authority, and only in the West were there two authorities who gradually parted ways, leading to the gradual breakup in the West of the close relation which had existed between church and state and religious law and what is now called secular law. Of course had laws of Western society not had different sources from those of religion in Christianity, and if there had existed a situation like that of Judaism and Islam, a dichotomy would not have existed between religious and secular law to start with.

The very word *secular* does not exist in Persian and Arabic, and we have to make up words for it. Today Arabs use the word *'ilmāniyyah*, which has no basis in classical Arabic. In Persian we say the new term *dunyāgarā'ī* or something like that. In either case, we are using recently coined words. There are no classical terms for secularism for us because there was no separation between the religious and the secular in classical Islamic civilization, or as far as Iran is concerned even in the Zoroastrian period.

Church and State in America and in the Islamic World

Now, with this background in mind we can turn to the question of church and state, which are in fact very clearly Christian categories. Although we talk about them all the time, especially in the United States, where people speak constantly about the separation of church and state, these two institutions did not even exist in other civilizations in the way that the modern West conceives of them. *Al-dīn* and *al-dawlah*, which are the closest terms in Arabic to "church" and "state" and which many people have written about, are not, however, at all the same as church and state. What corresponds to "church" in the Islamic world where there is no pope, no priesthood, and no religious hierarchy is in a sense the whole of Islamic society or the Islamic people (*ummah*). You and I sitting in this room are as much priests in Islam as any Catholic priest. We can marry people, we can perform the rights of burial, and when a child is born read the *shahādah* into his or her ears, et cetera. There is no organization called the church in Islam, and the mullas or *'ulamā'*, whatever you like to call them, are not members of the priestly class. They are not like the Brahmins of India. Those people, who instead of studying, let us say, dentistry, study Islamic Law, have no authority over you and me as far as liturgical functions are concerned. They simply have knowledge of Islamic Law and therefore we have to learn from them as far as this Law is concerned. If you want to perform your prayers, you stand before God, and there is no one between you and Him. Church and state as complementary institutions simply do not exist in Islam.

The *'ulamā'* have ruled over Iran since the Islamic Revolution, and therefore Iranians talk about this matter all the time as if this were the first time that religion and politics have become intertwined in Iran. But look at before the Iranian Revolution. The Iranian kings were not simply secular figures. They were supposed to be protectors of religion and were even called the shadow of God on earth even through the Pahlavi period. In the Iranian Constitution of 1906, it is said that royalty is a gift bestowed by God. In fact, kingship in any civilization can never be completely secular. Even before the Revolution it was not as if you had the body of *'ulamā'* as the church and the monarchy as the state, which were separate as church and state are separate in the United States. The situation was not like that at all. You have to consider what the realities are within a particular civilization.

Even in the West, the so-called separation of church and state does not hold true in the same way for all nations. In England, the queen is the head of the Church of England and in principle there is no separation of the church and state at all in that land. In Sweden, the most secularized of all societies in Europe, the Lutheran Church was the official church of the country until a short time ago. Now, they are planning to change the laws because there are not only Christians, but also Muslims, in Sweden today, and consequently you have different religions which have to be considered in their relation to the state. In Germany the churches receive financial aid officially from the state. It is only in France and the United States where one keeps speaking about the separation of church and state in a categorical manner. In France the complete removal of religion from the political realm was the result of the French Revolution with it strong anti-Catholic bias.

As for the United States, it came into being, first of all, as a result of the influence of Freemasonry, which was highly anti-Catholic, and secondly, because of the persecution of many religious groups in Europe, which then migrated to America, with the Quakers settling in Pennsylvania, the Puritans in New England, et cetera. These people did not want to have a single church dominate over them, and so established the separation of church and state, although religion still played and continues to play an important role in politics in America. There is these days a crisis in the United States because many people now interpret that separation to mean that religion should have no role in the public arena, while others argue against this view. Until now, the ethics of American society have been Protestant ethics, and the major crisis of this country in so many problems, ranging from abortion to euthanasia to homosexuality and other major social issues, is a result of the confrontation of the existing Protestant ethics with secular ideas held by many sectors of society.

I think that the whole question of the relation between church and state must be considered more profoundly if we want to solve the problems involved. There was no such thing in the Islamic world as the institution of the state, in the French sense of *état*, which did not come into being even in Europe until the 19th century, only after the French Revolution. The term *dawlah* does not mean the same thing. We spoke already about the Safavids. Shah Ismāʿīl was the head of both "church" and "state" in Persia in the 16th century. He created the national identity of modern Iran, and modern Iranian nationalism is based on the "state" created by him. Obviously, even for secularist nationalists, he should be their national hero; but this man was also the head of the "church," if you were to speak in the Western sense of this term.

So I think that this whole debate should be formulated in another way as far as Iran is concerned. The question is not the separation of church and state; the question is who should wield political power in society? The direct rule of the *ʿulamāʾ* as we have in Iran today is a recent phenomenon, and we never had such as thing in the history of Islam before. We have had the rule of Sufi orders before, for example, the Safavids in Iran and the Sanūsiyyah in Libya who ruled until 1971 when Ghaddafi overthrew King Idrīs. And there were other instances, for example, in Portugal, where a state was created by Sufis in the early European Middle Ages. But we have never had the *'ulamā'* ruling directly as a class, either in the Sunni world or the Shi'ite world before.

Because people often do not think clearly enough, they confuse different categories with each other. For example, the American press calls Egypt a "secular state" because the so-called Islamist "fundamentalists" are opposed to the present regime. But is the regime of President Mubarak really secular? Absolutely not. The government could not change the *Sharī'ah* in Egypt nor disregard religious values. The government has to be protective of religion, and certainly there is no separation of church and state in Egypt. I think that one of the big traps into which contemporary Western political thought concerning the Islamic world has fallen is precisely the idea of applying the category of "secular" to domains where it does not really apply. Even such a maverick as Gamal Abd al-Nasser, the father of modern Arabic nationalism, was certainly not an imam or caliph, but you could also not say that he was a purely secular figure. He always made use of Islamic terms and spoke about Islamic unity. Even his brand of Arab nationalism had a religious color.

The Islamic world is in a major political crisis because its traditional institutions of rule have been destroyed, first by colonialism and later for many lands by Ataturk, when he destroyed the Ottoman sultanate. After these events, many traditional monarchies which had ruled for centuries were removed in favor of foreign institutions. Now one cannot pull a new institution out of the hat. Some people talk about an Islamic Republic, others of secular Republicanism, and yet others of Islamic monarchy. Right now all of these different ideas and institutions are in a state of flux, and there is turmoil as far as the political realm is concerned. One can ask what kind of political institution is properly speaking Islamic. The Quran, being God's Book, contains, of course, the deepest wisdom in not defining Islamic political institutions in the same way that it defines certain economic institutions. In the Quran it is stated exactly that when a person dies how much inheritance should go to his son, daughter, and wife, but it does not say exactly what form of government one should have. But the principles are there to be applied to different conditions, and Muslims have to carry out that task now. In any case, whatever prevails in the Islamic world, there will never be the separation of church and state in the American sense because these categories do not really apply to Islamic societies.

I think the sooner thinkers, whether they consider themselves to be religious or secular, begin to face the reality of the situation and study things in depth and see what issues are really involved, the better it is for Islamic countries. Today the whole debate that is going on in the American and European press and media, in books written left and right, is to a large extent misplaced and is based on confusing categories. The same holds for much of the writing coming from the Islamic world itself. For example, in Iran, there are certain people who want to separate the government from religion in the sense of removing the *'ulamā'* from ruling directly; but that does not mean necessarily secularism. Pakistan is an Islamic Republic often ruled by the military and not the *'ulamā'*, but you could not say there is a separation of church and state there. This statement is meaningless. There is no Islamic country from the left to the right, except to some extent Turkey, where you really have a separation of religion or of "church" and the state; and Turkey itself is half paralyzed because while the majority of its population is devoutly Muslim, it claims for its ideology secularism, or what in French is called *laïcisme*, which in a sense is even more totalitarian than the term *secularism* in English. But has Turkey succeeded? No, because most people are still deeply religious, and as Muslims their religion concerns not only their private lives but the public realm as well, because society as a whole never accepted the *laïcisme* forced on it from above. If you go right now to Turkey, you can see how many people go to the mosque to say their prayers at noontime. What are the ethical codes? They remain Islamic. For example, the Turkish government tried in decades past to ban Islamic Law, but one cannot destroy Islamic Law in a society where people still believe in Islam. The question what the future of Turkey will be remains an open one as far as the role of religion in public life is concerned. But, in any case, Islamic forces are much too strong in Turkey to be simply ignored or marginalized, as recent events have shown clearly.

You have a similar situation in India, where fifty years after Gandhi there was until quite recently a government that claimed itself to be a Hindu government, and secularist parties such as the Congress Party of Nehru had lost much of their power, although they have now made a comeback. In any case, the dominating political forces in India cannot be understood simply on the basis of the separation of the church and state. I mention India to show that the phenomenon of relating religion to the public realm is not limited to the Islamic world. I think that in all non-Western societies and civilizations, we have to cast the whole question of the relation between church and state in a way that is different from what is prevalent in the West and especially in America today. I am not saying that there are not problems to be faced. On the contrary, there are many problems; secularism is now present in these societies, and its relation to religion must be studied. But the way it is often discussed in terms of separation of church and state is, I think, the wrong way to go about it. These are categories which do not really mean anything in other contexts, not even in Japan, whose constitution was dictated by the United States after Japan's defeat, when its emperor was reduced to a figurehead, at least on paper. Even there you do not have the same idea of separation of church and state as you have in the United States. One can also mention China, whose government is Marxist but is now encouraging Confucian ethics.

Certainly for the Islamic world, no matter what happens and which institutions come to power, I think that for the foreseeable future the political institutions will have a religious dimension along with the political one, and they cannot claim to have nothing to do with religion, as many in America claim for their government. (Of course, not even in America is this true, especially during the last few years.) No government will come along in the Islamic world and claim that you cannot have prayers in schools any more because it is against the freedoms guaranteed by the Constitution. This is not going to happen in the Islamic world in any foreseeable future.

The Resistance of Islamic Governments to Secularization

R.J.: Do you not think that in Islamic countries there is going to be a change, many people asking for more democracy and the democratization of Islam? Do you not think the idea to take Islam into the private sphere and to keep the public sphere more secular can work in Islamic countries?

S.H.N.: No, it will never work, because if you limit religion to the private sphere, then according to what principles do you rule the public sphere? The reason this "privatization of religion" has worked in the West until now is that without saying it, Western societies have continued to be based to a large extent on Christian ethics. Remember, Dostoievski asked in *Crime and Punishment*, where does the respect for life come from? He conjectured that if you have a "useless" person in society like a beggar in the street, why not kill him? It would be much better for society. But we do not accept such an idea no matter how secularist we are. But where did we get this idea of respecting human life? In the West it came from Christianity, and it is only now that this

Christian ethics is being challenged and to some extent destroyed, with the result that we see such a crisis within Western society. I think that the destruction of Islamic ethics is not going to happen within Islamic society in the near future. It is true that you can remove the *'ulamā'* from power and claim that the government is based on the voice of the people; but because of the strength of Islam among the people themselves, the government will still reflect the Islamic reality if and especially if you have more democracy.

What you have in the Islamic world today is just the reverse of what you might think. You have many governments supported by the West that speak about democracy all the time but that are against the will of their people, but they are supported by Western governments anyway because they support the interests of the West more than those of their own people. If you had real democracy in the Islamic world, almost all of the present-day Islamic governments, especially pro-Western ones, would fall, because most of these governments are a heritage of the colonial period, with Western support ruling over the vast majority of Muslim people with another worldview. Few talk about this matter, because it is not in the interest of Western powers to do so. The West for the most part is not interested in real democracy in the Islamic world because such a democratic government will not necessarily be pro-Western if the interests of the West are opposed to those of the Muslim peoples. And if an Islamic country, perhaps Iran or Indonesia, develops a real Islamic society with democratic institutions in the sense of being based on both God's laws and the will of the people, then such a government would not have to be necessarily secular, but could be both religious and democratic. Democracy has different meanings for different societies; even between France and England the meaning is different. If Iran can create a government based on the voice of the people who are, in the majority, deeply Islamic, and therefore create an "Islamic democracy" in the authentic sense of the term, it would be a model for the whole of the Islamic world. A major experimentation is going on in Iran, as in certain other Islamic countries, at the present moment in this realm, and I can only hope and pray that it succeeds in creating and maintaining an order both acceptable to its people and pleasing to God.

Notes

Part One

1. Shaykh Faḍl Allāh Nūrī hailed from the village of Nur in Mazandaran, which lies south of the Caspian Sea. He studied in both Iran and Iraq and became the most influential Shi'ite scholar (*'ālim*) in his homeland. He opposed the Constitutional Revolution in 1906 on the issue of the role of religion in public life. As a result of political machinations including foreign collusion, he was arrested and hanged in Tehran in 1908. The government allowed his body to be taken to Qom, where he was buried. He was very much vilified by modernists in the late Qajar and Pahlavi periods but has been considered a great hero since the advent of the Islamic Revolution in Iran in 1979.

2. One of the most notable scholars and political figures of the late Qajar and early Pahlavi periods, he became prime minister several times. He also had the greatest role in introducing Iranians to European philosophy through his very popular book *Sayr-i ḥikmat dar Urūpā* ("The Development of Philosophy in Europe"). Moreover, he did much to revive classical Persian literature and also produced works on Islamic philosophy in eloquent Persian. He died in 1942.

3. Muḥtashim al-Ṣalṭanah Isfandiyārī (d. 1945) was another major political figure during the rule of Reza Shah and became the head of the parliament for many years. He was also deeply rooted in classical learning and much interested in Persian literature.

4. These four poets are among the greatest of Persian poets. Sa'dī (d. 1292) is Persia's greatest moral poet and the author of the *Gulistān* and *Būstān,* which have defined the norm of eloquent Persian for the past seven centuries. Ḥāfiẓ (d. 1389), known for his incomparable *Dīwān*, hailed like Sa'dī from Shiraz. He is considered by many as the greatest poet of the Persian language. Rūmī

(d. 1273), the author of the *Mathnawī* and *Dīwān-i Shams,* is the greatest mystical poet of the Persian language and originator of the Mawlawiyyah Sufi order. Firdawsī (d.1020) is Iran's greatest epic poet and the author of the *Shāh-nāmah.*

5. Niẓāmī (d. 1209) is Iran's most celebrated lyric poet and the composer of celebrated romances. His best-known work is the *Khamsah.* His poetry is somewhat more difficult and is therefore usually learned after the works of the above-mentioned authors who of course have also composed some very difficult verses.

6. Hādī Ḥā'irī (d. 1993) was the son of a famous Sufi master and himself a member of the Ni'matullāhī Order. He was an incomparable authority on the poetry of Rūmī and himself a gifted poet.

7. Badī' al-Zamān Furūzānfar (d. 1970) was professor of literature and dean of the Faculty of Theology of Tehran University. One of Iran's most outstanding men of letters, he was known internationally as a great authority on Rūmī and wrote many works on him as well as editing critically for the first time his *Dīwān-i kabīr* or *Dīwān-i Shams.*

8. Sayyid Muḥammad Kāẓim 'Aṣṣār (d. 1974) was one of the great philosophers and gnostics of his day, who after studying the religious sciences in Najaf in Iraq settled in Tehran where he taught Islamic philosophy at Tehran University as well as in the Sipahsālār *Madrasah.* His few but exceptional works have been collectively printed in *Majmu'a-yi āthār-i 'Aṣṣār.*

9. Reza Shah was the founder of the Pahlavi Dynasty. As an army officer he carried out a revolution, becoming first prime minister and then in 1925 the king of Iran. He was exiled from Iran by the Allied Forces that had invaded the country at the beginning of World War II, and died in exile in South Africa in 1942.

10. Belgian philosopher (d. 1949), many of whose writings had been translated into Persian and were popular among the modern educated classes. Although a playwright, he was also a philosopher and mystic as can be seen in his *Wisdom and Destiny.* He also wrote on natural philosophy, his best-known works being *The Life of the Bee* and *The Intelligence of Flowers.*

11. Famous French philosopher and scientist-mathematician (d. 1662), Blaise Pascal was popular among those Persians who were religious believers because he was a believer as well as an important scientist, seriously interested in modern Western science. His most influential work is *Meditations,* which is also a significant literary work.

12. Descartes' *Discourse on Method* was the first work of a modern European philosopher to be translated into Persian (from the original French). Altogether, Descartes (d. 1650) is a pivotal figure in the introduction of European philosophy into modern Iran.

13. This book was published posthumously in 1960 (Tehran: Ibn Sīnā Press) and consists of a number of essays in Persian by my father with an introduction by my uncle Seyyed Ali Nasr, who was himself a famous writer as well as

statesman and diplomat. Because of its profound message and literary quality, the book won the Royal Book Award.

14. Ṣadīqa'lam (d. 1978) studied in America and England and rose in the ranks to become minister of education. He was also professor of education at Tehran University and one of the major figures in the field of education in Iran during the modern period.

15. 'Alī Akbar Siyāsī (d. 1990) was one of the founders of Tehran University and for many years its rector as well as being dean of the Faculty of Letters of the University. He also served as minister of education. He was trained in psychology in France where he developed a positivistic outlook, philosophically speaking. He was one of the most influential figures in the introduction of Western and more particularly French ideas into the Persian educational system.

16. Mīrzā Muḥammad Ṣādiq Ṭabāṭabā'ī (d. 1985) was my mother's maternal uncle and for many years the head of parliament.

17. 'Alī Akbar Dāwar (d. 1937) was one of the major political figures of the early part of the reign of Reza Shah and as minister of justice responsible directly for the codification of civil laws in Iran. He fell out of grace and committed suicide.

18. 'Ali Aṣghar Khān Ḥikmat (d. 1980) was a well-known scholar of Persian literature, professor at Tehran University, and minister of education and later of foreign affairs during the reign of Reza Shah and his son Mohammad Reza Shah.

19. Ismā'īl Mir'āt (d. 1950), like Hekmat, worked under my father and later became minister of education.

20. Aḥmad Qawām (d. 1955) was one of Iran's most powerful prime ministers, who played an important role in saving the province of Azarbaijan from the communists.

21. Manṣūr al-Mulk became prime minister under both Reza Shah and his son and died soon after the beginning of the reign of Mohammad Reza Shah.

22. Sayyid Muḥammad 'Abduh (d. 1905) was a preeminent authority on both Islamic and civil law and exercised great influence on the codification of law in modern Iran.

23. An Islamic scholar is called *'ālim* (pl. *'ulamā'*). More specifically, this term is applied to the religious scholars in the Islamic world who are sometimes called *clerics* in English.

24. Shaykh 'Abd al-Karīm Ḥā'irī Yazdī (d. 1937) was the foremost Shi'ite scholar of his day in Iran and source of emulation (*marja'-i taqlīd*) for most Shi'ites. He founded the religious school of Qom, which today is the center of Shi'ism in Iran with students from all over the world.

25. Sayyid Ḥasan Mudarris (d. 1936) was a well-known religious as well as political figure who went into opposition to Reza Shah and was put to death.

26. Fāḍil-i Tūnī (d. 1961) was one of the foremost authorities on Islamic philosophy and gnosis of his day.

27. Malik al-Shu'arā' Bahār (d. 1951), the poet laureate and one of the greatest poets of the Persian language in recent centuries, was also for some time minister of education.

28. Jalāl Humā'ī was one of the leading literary authorities of his day and an accomplished poet as well as one of the foremost teachers of Persian literature at Tehran University.

29. Sa'īd Nafīsī (d. 1966) was the author of numerous books on Persian literature and history. He was also a professor of literature at Tehran University and one of Iran's major men of letters.

30. Aḥmad Bahmayār (d. 1955) was another major authority in Persian literature and professor at Tehran University.

31. Nūr al-Dīn Kiānūrī (d. 1999) studied architecture in Germany, then returned to Iran just before World War II. Soon he joined the Tudeh (Communist) Party, rising in rank and finally becoming its general secretary. He fled Iran during the reign of Mohammad Reza Shah and returned after the Iranian Revolution in 1979. After a while he was imprisoned, but finally freed. He died shortly thereafter.

32. Īraj Iskandarī (d. 1993) was from the Qajar nobility but became a communist and one of the party's most eminent members, for a while becoming a minister. He also fled Iran and finally died in the West.

33. Firaydūn Kishāwarz (d. 1985) was a competent physician who also became a communist and for a while even minister. Like many other members of the Tudeh Party, he fled from Iran and spent the second half of his life in the West.

34. See for example my *Islam and the Plight of Modern Man* (Chicago: ABC International, 2001) and *A Young Muslim's Guide to the Modern World* (Chicago: Kazi Publications, 1993).

35. Muslims are obliged after entering into adulthood to turn five times a day, from before sunrise to the night, in the direction of Makkah and perform prayers in Arabic, which also include movements of the body. These prayers, based on the model of the Prophet and his instructions, are called *ṣalāh* in Arabic and *namāz* in Persian and other languages of the eastern Islamic world.

36. Haḍrat-i 'Abad al-'Aẓīm is a major shrine near Tehran often visited by the pious from the capital, while Qom, located about 100 miles south of Tehran, contains the tomb of Haḍrat-i Ma'ṣūmah, the sister of the eighth Shi'ite Imam Mūsā al-Riḍā, and is today the religious center of Iran.

37. Traditional Islamic cities have water fountains for the public that are usually adorned with highly artistic tile decorations and sometimes mirrors and paid for by religious endowments. These sites have also gained a religious character. Examples of *saqqā-khānah*s can still be found in many Persian cities and in other Islamic countries. Some of the most beautiful are to be found in Morocco in such cities as Meknes and Fez.

38. This is something like a cream doughnut, except filled usually with meat rather than cream.

39. One of the major mosque/*madrasah*s of Tehran that is still very active. It has one of the best collections of Islamic manuscripts in the world, especially in the fields of philosophy and theology.

40. If *gūl* is pronounced as *dūl*, it becomes a name for men's genital organ.

41. He was one of the most famous members of the Nasr family. He became governor of the northern province of Mazandaran during the war when this province was occupied by the Russian army, and later mayor of Tehran and minister in several cabinets. He died in 1981.

42. The *Shāh-nāmah* ("Book of Kings") is the greatest epic poem of the Persian language, composed by Abū'l-Qāsim Firdawsī in the 10th century. It deals with the history of Iran from prehistoric mythological dynasties to the Arab invasion in the seventh century. The hero of this great epic is Rustam, who is like Ulysses in Homer.

43. Suhrāb was the son of Rustam who was killed by the father in battle without Rustam at first realizing the identity of his foe.

44. 'Abbās Qulī Gulshā'iyān (d. 1990) was one of the leading political and administrative figures of the Pahlavi dynasty and minister in many cabinets. He died shortly after World War II.

45. Ghulām Ḥusayn Rahnimā (d. 1946) was a mathematician who knew both Islamic and modern mathematics and was, like my father, one of the bridges between traditional and modern learning in Iran. He also became minister of education.

46. A province south of the Caspian Sea known for its lush forests and beautiful beaches.

47. "If you extend the hand of greed to grab people's wealth, you create a bridge over which passes your honor and reputation."

48. "Vali Allah Khan, you punished us well!"

49. The son of Reza Shah, he ruled Iran for thirty-seven years until the Islamic Revolution of 1979, which ousted him from power. He died in exile in Egypt in 1980.

Part Two

1. A city in Western Iran and near the Iraqi border.

2. Muḥsin Ra'īs (d. 1962) was one of the leading members of the Iranian diplomatic corps and ambassador in many different countries.

3. Muḥsin Ḥakīm was president of the senate and one of the major political figures of Iraq.

4. The son of a minister and himself a high official of the Ministry of Foreign Affairs in later life, 'Īsā Mālik was the last ambassador of Iran in Sweden during the royal regime. He now resides in the suburbs of Washington.

5. Maḥmūd Jam (d. 1969), a prime minister dear to Reza Shah, became close to the royal family when his son General Firaydūn Jam married one of Reza Shah's daughters.

6. My maternal uncle Emad Kia (d. 1975) was then our consul in New York. He became my guardian and played a very important role in my education during the early years of my stay in America.

7. My paternal cousin Taqi Nasr (d. 1990), the brother of Mohsen Nasr, was then the head of the Iranian chamber of commerce in New York. Later he became deputy to Dag Hammarskjöld, the Secretary General of the U.N., and he also became minister back in Iran. He was also a fine writer and scholar.

8. Saint Thomas Aquinas (d. 1274), the greatest medieval Christian theologian in the West, provided an Aristotelianized version of Christian theology. His *Summa Theologica* has been the mainstay of Catholic theology for the past seven centuries.

9. These two colossal figures of Catholic theology, who both lived in the 13th century, represented respectively the Dominican and Franciscan schools of theology and spirituality.

10. Tillich (d. 1965) was a famous German Protestant theologian who migrated to America. When I met him he was professor at Harvard University. Among his most famous works is *The Courage to Be.*

11. John Hick, from the University of Birmingham, is one of the outstanding living Protestant theologians involved in the development of a Christian theology of religious pluralism. He is the author of numerous books, including *The Metaphor of God Incarnate* and *An Interpretation of Religion.*

12. The *Dīwān* of Ḥāfiz, one of the supreme works of Persian poetry, is replete with verses that refer to the universality of revelation and the inner unity of religions beyond the differences of their outward forms.

13. "The spiritual music of Venus will bring Christ into a state of dance."

14. The daily canonical Islamic prayer performed five times daily by all pious Muslims. While *namāz* is used in Persian and most other languages of the eastern part of the Islamic world such as Urdu, in Arabic it is known as *ṣalāh.*

15. Famous philosopher of the sixth century B.C., considered by many as the founder of Greek logic and, along with the Ionian philosophers, of natural philosophy.

16. Today *physicist* means someone who has mastered the modern science of physics, which is related to quantitative knowledge of the natural world and is not concerned with the nonempirical, philosophical, and spiritual dimensions of that world. In contrast, the Greek term *physicos* refers to a person who had knowledge of the cosmos in its ontological reality and not only its physical and quantitative dimension as this term is understood today.

17. Famous Italian philosopher and historian of science and the author of such major works as *Hamlet's Mill*, *The Crime of Galileo*, and *The Age of Adventure.*

18. Seyyed Hossein Nasr, *Science and Civilization in Islam* (Cambridge: Islamic Texts Society, 2003). This work first appeared in a series edited by him. He, in fact, commissioned me to write the book.

19. Galileo Galilei (d. 1642) is well known as one of the founders of modern physics and astronomy, and for his critique of Aristotelian physics. He wrote several very influential works and essays including *Dialogue Concerning the Two Chief World Systems*, which was disseminated despite the opposition of the Catholic Church.

20. Immanuel Kant (d. 1804) is perhaps the most influential Western philosopher after Descartes and author of such celebrated works as *The Critique of Pure Reason* and *The Critique of Practical Reason.*

21. The most famous German philosopher of the 19th century, Georg F. Hegel (d. 1831) was the founder of what came to be known as dialectical philosophy that he interpreted in an idealistic manner. His works include *Philosophy of Mind*, *Phenomenology of Spirit*, and *Introduction to Philosophy of History.* Karl Marx used Hegel's philosophy to develop his thesis of dialectical materialism.

22. Major French orientalist and philosopher (d. 1978) and author of numerous works such as *En Islam Iranien*, *Avicenna and the Visionary Recital* and *History of Islamic Philosophy*, written mostly in collaboration with myself and Osman Yahya. I shall turn to him later in this book.

23. See *The Philosophy of Seyyed Hossein Nasr* in *The Library of Living Philosophers*, vol. XXVIII (Chicago: Open Court Press, 2001), pp. 3–85.

24. One of the most famous English philosophers of the 20th century, Russell (d. 1970) wrote on the logic of science, especially mathematics, general philosophy, the history of Western philosophy, and matters of general public interest. His most notable and well-known works include *Principia Mathematica* and *A History of Western Philosophy.*

25. A major French mathematician and philosopher of science, Jules Henri Poincaré (d. 1912) was well known for the view that physics is not concerned with the nature of things but with mathematical structures that "save the phenomena." Among his most important works is *Science and Hypothesis.*

26. Émile Meyerson (d. 1933) was one of the major philosophers of science who opposed the views of Poincaré and his followers. The debate about the nature of physics dominated much of philosophy of science in Europe during the early part of the 20th century. Meyerson's seminal works are *Identité et réalité*, *De l'explication dans les sciences*, and *Du cheminement de la pensée.*

27. French metaphysician and founder of the school known as that of Tradition, Guénon (d. 1951) spent the first part of his life in France and from 1930 to his death in Cairo where he embraced Islam openly and where he died and is buried. His study of Oriental doctrines, especially those of Hinduism and Islam, presented those teachings in an authentic manner for the first time in Europe and "opened" a whole new and at the same time perennial vista in the West. His voluminous works include *Introduction to the Study of Hindu Doctrines*, *Man and His Becoming According to the Vedanta*, *The Crisis of the Modern World*, *Symbolism of the Cross*, *The Reign of Quantity* and *Fundamental Symbols—the Universal Language of Sacred Science.*

28. René Guénon, *Introduction to the Study of the Hindu Doctrines* (Ghent, NY: Sophia Perennis, 2004).

29. René Guénon, *Man and His Becoming According to the Vedanta* (Ghent, NY: Sophia Perennis, 2004).

30. Of Greek origin, but educated in England, Marco Pallis (d. 1990) was himself a traditionalist. He traveled to Tibet and wrote *Peaks and Lamas*, which introduced the Tibetan tradition from the traditional point of view for the first time to the West.

31. The greatest authority on Indian art in the West during the 20th century, Ananda K. Coomaraswamy (d. 1947), who was half Sri Lankan and half English, was, like Guénon, also a metaphysician, defender of tradition and critic of the modern world, while being at the same time like Guénon a staunch defender of the traditional West. With the mastery of some twenty languages, he was also a formidable scholar as much at home in the Latin works of Saint Thomas as Sanskrit texts. Among his numerous writings one can mention *The Transformation of Nature in Art*, *Hinduism and Buddhism*, *The Bugbear of Literacy*, and *Time and Eternity*.

32. Considered by many as the greatest master of the *philosophia perennis* in his day, Frithjof Schuon (d. 1998) was a Teutonic philosopher and metaphysician and also Sufi master who spent most of his life in France and Switzerland and the last two decades in America, where he died. At once poet, painter, scholar of religions, and metaphysician, and a pillar of the traditionalist school, Schuon, like Guénon and Coomaraswamy, was very prolific. Some of his most important books are *The Transcendent Unity of Religions*, *Stations of Wisdom*, *Understanding Islam*, and *Esoterism—As Principle and as Way*.

33. One of the outstanding American authorities on Oriental art, Rowland (d. 1972) was deeply influenced by Coomaraswamy, whom he knew well personally. Rowland's numerous works include *The Art and Architecture of India* and *Art in East and West*.

34. D. T. Suzuki (d. 1946) was a major Japanese scholar of Zen and Shin Buddhism who first introduced Zen in a serious manner to the West. His many works include *Essays in Zen Buddhism*, *Japanese Buddhism*, and *Shin Buddhism*.

35. Ralph Waldo Emerson (d. 1882) was the most famous of the New England Transcendentalists and perhaps the greatest philosopher America has produced. At once essayist and poet, he was much interested in Sufism and Hinduism. His essays remain widely read to this day.

36. Like Emerson, William James (d. 1910) was a philosophy professor at Harvard. His *Varieties of Religious Experience* remains pertinent even today. Also like Emerson, but from another philosophical perspective, he was interested in religion and mysticism.

37. Alfred North Whitehead (d. 1947) was of English origin but taught at Harvard. He was one of the foremost Western philosophers of the 20th century, known especially for what has come to be known as process

philosophy. His major works include *Principia Mathematica* (with Russell), *Process and Reality*, and *Adventure in Ideas.*

38. William Ernest Hocking (d. 1966) became the leading philosopher after Whitehead in the school of process philosophy. His works include *The Meaning of God* and *Nature and Its Remaking.*

39. Willard V. O. Quine (d. 2002) was the most famous and influential analytical philosopher in America. His well-known works include *Word and Object* and *Philosophy of Logic.*

40. Howard Aiken (d. 1973) was a mathematician who had also become interested in logic. He played a major role in the development of computers.

41. Harry Wolfson (d. 1974) is perhaps the most learned authority in medieval philosophy that America has produced. At once at home in Greek, Islamic, Jewish, and Christian philosophy, his most important books include *Philo, Spinoza, Crescas' Critique of Aristotle,* and *Philosophy of the Kalam.*

42. George Sarton (d. 1956) was the founder of the discipline of the history of science in America and author of many works, including the multivolume *An Introduction to the History of Science.*

43. Holder of Sarton's chair after his death, I. Bernard Cohen had a good general knowledge of the history of science, but his field of specialty was the Scientific Revolution. His works include *Isaac Newton's Natural Philosophy* and *Revolution in Science.*

44. Ernst Mach (d. 1916), a famous Austrian philosopher, was one of the founders of the discipline of the history of science and a major figure in the school of logical positivism, as can be seen in *Ernst Mach: Studien und Dokumente zu Leben und Werk.*

45. In contrast to Sarton and Mach, Pierre Duhem (d. 1916), who was French, was strongly against positivism. His field of specialization was medieval and Renaissance Western science, and his many works include the monumental *Le Systeme du monde* and *Essays in the History and Philosophy of Science.*

46. *Science and Civilization in Islam* was published for the first time by Harvard University Press in 1966, republished in many later editions, and translated into numerous languages. It is still a text in courses on Islamic science in many countries.

47. Perhaps the greatest Islamicist that the English-speaking world has ever produced, Gibbs (d. 1971) was a master in Arabic and Islamic history, as well as a leading authority in the Islamic religion. Among his most famous books are *Muhammadanism* and *Islam and the West.*

48. Seyyed Hossein Nasr, *An Introduction to Islamic Cosmological Doctrines: Conceptions of Nature and Methods Used for Its Study by the Ikhwan Al-Safa, Al-Biruni, and Ibn Sina* (Albany: State University of New York Press, 1993). It was originally published by the Harvard University Press.

49. Arthur Darby Nock was a major scholar of Greek and especially Hermeticism and late Greek religion.

50. Paris, J. Vrin, 4 vols., 1949–1954.

51. Seyyed Hossein Nasr, *Knowledge and the Sacred* (Albany: State University of New York Press, 1989).

52. Much of the interest in the domain of traditional art in general, and the little knowledge I have of Oriental art in particular, has come from Coomaraswamy, Burckhardt, and Rowland.

53. Francis Birch (d. 1992) was a world-renowned authority in geophysics.

54. Marland Billings (d. 1996) was the premier authority on the structural geology and stratigraphy of New England.

55. World-famous authority on Greek culture, Werner Jaeger (d. 1961) had migrated from Germany to America. He is especially remembered for his *Paedeia—The Ideal of Greek Culture.*

56. One of the foremost Catholic historians of the 20th century, the Englishman Christopher Dawson (d. 1970) wrote numerous works on Christian and European history, including *The Making of Europe* and *The Formation of Christendom.*

57. Author of many essays on medieval institutions, Charles Holt Taylor was a leading medievalist of his day.

58. One of the most influential Catholic thinkers of the late 20th century, Jacques Maritain (d. 1973), who was French, taught in both France and America. His numerous works include *Integral Humanism*, *Existence and the Existent*, and *Art and Poetry.*

59. A French scholar and philosopher, Etienne Gilson (d. 1978) is considered by many to be the greatest authority of the 20th century in medieval European philosophy. His works practically defined the field and include *The History of the Christian Philosophy of the Middle Ages*, *Philosophers and Being*, and *The Christian Philosophy of St. Thomas.*

60. Aga Khan Professor of Iranian Studies, Richard N. Frye is still active in this field in which he has produced many works, including *The Heritage of Central Asia*, *The Heritage of Persia*, and *The History of Ancient Iran.*

61. One of the foremost Protestant theologians of the 20th century, Paul Tillich, the famous German theologian (d. 1965), came to Harvard to spend the last part of his life. His influential corpus includes *Heidegger and Jaspers*, *Christianity and the Encounter of World Religions*, and *Theological Writings.*

62. One of the most famous scholars of comparative religion, or what he preferred to call the history of religion, this very gifted Romanian scholar taught first in Paris and later at the University of Chicago, where his work influenced a whole generation of American scholars of religion. He died in 1986. His large corpus includes *The Myth of the Eternal Return*, *Images and Symbols*, and *The History of Religions.*

63. Friedrich Wilhelm Schelling (d. 1854) is one of the foremost philosophical figures of the German Romantic movement.

64. Another major Protestant theologian of the 20th century, Karl Barth (d. 1968) had a profound influence on American Protestant thought. Perhaps his most widespread work is *Church Dogmatics.*

65. One of the greatest of German mystics, Eckhart (d. 1327) left behind sermons which have become very influential in the past few decades. He spoke of the Godhead, and from his understanding of this subject to Tillich's "Ground of Being" one can draw a direct line.

66. Among the greatest of German mystical poets, Silesius (d. 1677) is best known for his *Cherubic Wanderer.*

67. Louis Gardet (d. 1986) was one of France's greatest Islamicists and at the same time Catholic thinkers. His many notable works include the masterly *La Cité musulmane.*

68. An Egyptian who had become a Catholic priest, Anawati (d. 1994) wrote numerous works on Islamic studies in Arabic and French, including the translation into French of the *Metaphysics* of Ibn Sīnā's *Kitāb al-shifā'.*

69. A well-known German Catholic, Rahner (d. 1984) was a theologian with modernistic tendencies.

70. Hans Urs von Balthasar, another German Catholic theologian (d. 1988), known for a more conservative theology in the post-Conciliar Church.

71. An Italian philosopher, Michele Federico Sciacca (d. 1975) was much interested in traditional philosophy. His works include *Filosofia e metafisica.*

72. Antonio Rosmini (d. 1855) is a major Italian philosopher and author of *Theosophia*, which is well known in Italy. He stood against the main currents of modern European philosophy.

73. Major philosopher and historian of science of Russian origin, Alexandre Koyré (d. 1964) lived and taught in both France and America. His many works include *Galilean Studies* and *From the Closed World to the Infinite Universe.*

74. The Indian philosopher Surendranath Dasgupta (d. 1952) is the author of the extensive *History of Indian Philosophy.*

75. Satchidanada Murty is one of the gifted contemporary Indian philosophers. His books include *Philosophy in India.*

76. Sarvapalli Radhakrishnan (d. 1975), Indian philosopher, diplomat, and statesman (he became president of India), was one of the main popularizers of Indian thought in the West. Among his many works one can name *Indian Philosophy.*

77. Famous Sinologist (d. 1940), his most popular work is *La Pensée chinoise*, but he is also the author of numerous other works including *Chinese Civilization.*

78. Joseph Needham, *Science and Civilization in China* (Cambridge: Cambridge University Press, 2006). Needham (d. 1995) also wrote several other works in Chinese science.

79. It is now available in America in the following edition—Chicago: ABC International, 2001.

80. Fung Yu-lan, *A History of Chinese Philosophy*, trans. Derk Bodde, 2 vols. (Princeton, NJ: Princeton University Press, 1983).

81. Martin Heidegger (d. 1976) is one of the foremost Western philosophers of the 20th century and the leading figure in the German school of *Existenz Philosophie.* His most widely known works are *Being and Time* and *Introduction to Metaphysics.*

82. Perhaps the most famous Byzantine philosopher, Gemistus Plethon (d. 1452) was a Platonist who was also seriously interested in Zoroaster and the philosophy of ancient Persia.

83. See Samuel Sambursky, *Physics of the Stoics* (Princeton, NJ: Princeton University Press, 1988).

84. Seyyed Hossein Nasr, *Religion and the Order of Nature* (New York: Oxford University Press, 1996).

85. Stephen MacKenna (trans.), *Plotinus: The Enneads* (London: Faber and Faber, 1966).

86. Fabre D'Olivet, *Golden Verses of Pythagoras* (London: Kessinger Publishing, 1977).

87. Saint Augustine, *Saint Augustine: Christian Instruction, Admonition and Grace, the Christian Combat, Faith, Hope, and Charity* (Washington, DC: Catholic University of America Press, 2002).

88. Saint Augustine, *The Confessions of Saint Augustine* (Oxford: Oxford University Press, 1998).

89. Saint Augustine, *The City of God against the Pagans* (Cambridge: Cambridge University Press, 1998).

90. Boethius, *The Consolation of Philosophy* (New York: Penguin Classics, 2000).

91. Erigena (or Eriugena; d. circa 877) is perhaps the foremost Christian philosopher of the early Middle Ages, who was deeply influenced by the Dionysian writings and in turn wielded a great deal of influence, especially his *De Divisione Naturae* or *Periphyseon*, ed. and trans. P. Sheldon-Williams (Dublin: Dublin Institute of Advanced Studies, 1978).

92. The most famous of all Islamic philosophers, Ibn Sīnā (d. 1037) wrote more than 200 works. His major philosophical text *Kitāb al-shifā'* (*The Book of Healing*) was partly translated into Latin and had a deep influence upon Latin Scholasticism.

93. Marcilio Ficino (d. 1499) was a major Italian Platonist and very instrumental in making Greek philosophical works available to the West, as for example in his *Platonic Theology*.

94. Heinrich Agrippa von Nettesheim (d. 1535) is known especially for his occultist works such as *Three Books of Occult Philosophy*.

95. Paracelsus (d. 1541) was one of the major alchemists and physicians of the Renaissance and a propagator of Hermetic philosophy, some of which is collected in his *Hermetic and Alchemical Writings*.

96. The French philosopher Michel de Montaigne (d. 1592) is especially known for his *Essays*, which propagate a form of philosophical skepticism.

97. Giordano Bruno (d. 1600), the Italian scientist, philosopher, and mystic, believed in the infinite universe and was finally burned at the stake.

98. The English alchemist John Dee (d. 1608) was famous in his day as an alchemist and natural philosopher.

99. Frances Yates, *The Rosicrucian Enlightenment* (London: Routledge, 1999).

100. Gottfried Wilhelm Leibniz (d. 1716), the German philosopher and scientist, is known especially for his monadology, that is, the idea that the universe is composed of independent units called *monads.* His basic opus is *The Theodicy.*

101. Philosopher of Jewish origin who was expelled from the Jewish community, Benedict Spinoza (d. 1677) sought to express philosophy in the form of geometric propositions and espoused a view that has been considered as being pantheistic. His best-known work, entitled *Ethics*, is a major text of 17th-century philosophy.

102. David Hume (d. 1776), a Scottish philosopher, is famous for casting doubt upon rationalism, especially in his most famous work, *An Enquiry Concerning Human Understanding.*

103. As I have already stated, Immanuel Kant (d. 1804) is perhaps the most influential modern German philosopher, known especially for his *Critique of Pure Reason.*

104. My interest in Friedrich Schelling (d. 1854) and German philosophers like him was that they were opposed to the mechanistic natural philosophy of the day.

105. Franz von Baader (d. 1841) is an important German philosopher who was a critic of Descartes and many other modern philosophers, but is not well known outside Germany. His works include *Über den Begriff der Zeit.* He introduced the works of Böhme to Schelling.

106. Gerhard Tersteegen (d. 1769) was at once mystic and theologian and lived in the margins of the Reformed Church. His major work is *Auserlesene Lebensbeschreibingen heiliger Seelen.*

107. Johann Georg Hamann (d. 1788), called the Magus of the North, was one of the leading German Lutheran theosophers and author of a large opus including *Socratic Memorabilia.*

108. See the articles of Corbin in the journal *Hic et Nunc.*

109. Jean-Jacques Rousseau (d. 1778) is one of the best-known French philosophers of the 18th century, who was deeply influenced by the French Revolution. He influenced the fields of both philosophy and education. His *Émile* is especially well known. He was also a musician and composed and wrote on music.

110. François-Marie Voltaire (d. 1778), a French philosopher who is known particularly as a free-thinker, wrote against both established religion and philosophy. His best-known work is *Candide*, which is also considered a literary masterpiece.

111. Denis Didérot (d. 1784) is the most famous of the French encyclopedists, who edited the famous *Encyclopédie.* This is one of the main philosophical works of the Age of Enlightenment. As for Marie Jean Condorcet (d. 1794), he was at once mathematician and philosopher who exercised great influence to the extent that he has been called the father of the French Revolution.

112. Ludwig Wittgenstein (d. 1951) was an Austrian philosopher who spent his later years at Oxford, where he developed his analytic philosophy. One of

the major philosophers of the 20th century, his works include the celebrated *Tractatus.*

113. Edmund Husserl (d. 1938) was a major 20th-century German philosopher who is founder of phenomenology as a philosophical system. His ideas on phenomenology, which became popular in both Europe and America, are expounded in his *Logical Investigations* and *Ideas: General Introduction to Phenomenology.*

114. Max Scheler (d. 1928) was a major German phenomenologist whose works such as *On the Eternal in Man* and *The Nature of Sympathy* have been rendered into English.

115. Contemporary American philosopher who denies that the goal of philosophy is the discovery of the truth and sees philosophy as a conversation.

116. Contemporary Iranian philosopher who was a student and friend of Corbin and the author of the most important work on him. See his *Henry Corbin—La topographie spirituelle de l'Islam iranien* (Paris: La Différence, 1990).

117. These are four of the greatest figures of the Islamic intellectual tradition. Ibn Sīnā (d. 1037) marks the peak of Islamic Peripatetic philosophy. His most extensive work is the *Kitāb al-shifā'.* The Persian philosopher Suhrawardī (d. 1191) is the founder of the School of Illumination (*ishrāq*) and author of *Ḥikmat al-ishrāq*. Ibn 'Arabī (d. 1240) was of Arab origin, but born in Andalusia. He is the primary founder of the School of Gnosis or Doctrinal Sufism. His most influential works are the *Fuṣūṣ al-ḥikam* and *al-Futūḥāt al-makkiyyah.* Mullā Ṣadrā (d. 1640), who hailed from Shiraz, is the main figure of the School of Isfahan. He synthesized the earlier schools of Islamic thought. His main work is *al-Asfār al-arba'ah.*

Part Three

1. I have dealt with this issue in several of my works. See Seyyed Hossein Nasr, *Islamic Art and Spirituality* (Albany: State University of New York Press, 1987).

2. Auguste Compte (d. 1857) was the leading positivistic philosopher of the 19th century who was completely opposed to metaphysics, theology, and spirituality. He tried to establish sociology on a positivistic foundation. His works on positivism include *Discours sur l'ensemble du positivisme* and *Leçons sur la sociologie—cours de philosophie positive.*

3. "Whoever has become separated from his roots, seeks the days of his union."

4. Known especially for his study of Ibn Sīnā's *al-Ishārāt wa'l-tanbīhāt,* Pūrḥusaynī became himself a professor at Tehran University.

5. One of Iran's leading contemporary thinkers and president of the Iranian Academy of Science, as well as professor at Tehran University, Dāwarī is known for his study of Fārābī and also critique of modern Western philosophy.

6. Dāwūdī (d. 1979?) was a professor at Tehran University when he disappeared mysteriously at the beginning of the Iranian Revolution. He translated several works on the history of philosophy and also Western philosophy itself into Persian.

7. Sayyid Jalāl al-Dīn Mujtabawī (d. 2005) was professor of philosophy at Tehran University, and after the Iranian Revolution became a well-known scholar.

8. Jahāngīrī is a professor at Tehran University, a leading authority on theoretical Sufism, and the author of one of the best-known works in Persian on Ibn 'Arabī.

9. Sa'dānī later became professor of Persian at the Muhammad V University in Rabat, Morocco. He died at the young age of 42 from a stroke.

10. He was a Christian Arab who later became a well-known intellectual figure in Lebanon.

11. Al-Sīsī was especially interested in Mīr Dāmād and completed his Ph.D. thesis on him under my guidance.

12. Īraj Afshār is perhaps the foremost authority on Iranian manuscripts today. I brought him as professor of Iranian history, and later on we made him director of the Central Library of Tehran University. He is a very prolific writer, the author and editor of over a hundred books as well as numerous articles.

13. Ikrām Shāh is now one of the most famous authorities in Persian and Persian literature in the Indian Subcontinent.

14. For many years professor at the University of Strasbourg, he is now in Central Asia studying the music of the region. His *Musique et mystique*, *The Art of Persian Music* and other titles have established him as a leading authority on the relation between Sufism and Persian music, which he also performs with mastery.

15. Chittick is my most famous student in America. He is professor at the State University of New York in Stony Brook and the leading authority on Ibn 'Arabī in the West. His more than twenty books include *The Sufi Path of Knowledge* (Albany: State University of New York Press, 1989) and *The Self-Disclosure of God* (Albany: State University of New York Press, 1998).

16. Murata is also at the State University of New York and the author of the well-known work *The Tao of Islam* (Albany: State University of New York Press, 1992) and with Chittick of *The Vision of Islam* (Albany: State University of New York Press, 1994). She is now working on the interaction between Islamic and Chinese thought.

17. Pūrjawādī, a professor at Tehran University, is one of Iran's leading authorities on the history of Sufism and on Aḥmad Ghazzālī and his school.

18. A'wānī is now the head of the Academy of Philosophy that I had founded and professor of Shahid Beheshti (formerly National) University. He is the author of many works including a well-known book on spiritual aesthetics.

19. After writing a number of works on philosophy, including one on Kant, Ḥaddād-i ʿĀdil entered politics fulltime and became the speaker of the parliament of the Islamic Republic of Iran.

20. Bakhtiyār was a gifted student of Persian literature but also interested in philosophy. He helped me on many projects, including the publication of the well-known journal *Maʿārif-e eslāmī*, which was the leading journal of Islamic studies in Iran in the 1970s.

21. Roloff Beny, *Persia, Bridge of Turquoise* (Norwalk, CT: New York Graphic Society Publishing Group, 1975).

22. A specialist in Persian religious and political history, he is now professor at The George Washington University. He is the editor of *Beacon of Knowledge* (Louisville, KY: Fons Vitae, 2003), consisting of essays presented in my honor.

23. Famous Palestinian scholar of Islamic studies and also activist, he and his wife were brutally murdered in their home in 1986. Fārūqī is the author and editor of many books including *The Atlas of Islamic History.*

24. Former professor and pro-vice-chancellor of the University of Malaya and the leading Malay scholar in the Islamic philosophy of science, he is the author of a number of important works in this field, including *Tawhid and Science*, republished in 1999 under the title *The History and Philosophy of Islamic Science* (Cambridge: Islamic Texts Society, 1999).

25. Aḥmad Jalālī is primarily a philosopher who spent years at Oxford teaching philosophy. When Seyyed Mohammad Khatami became president of Iran, he asked Jalali to become the Iranian ambassador to UNESCO. Jalali accepted and remained in this post until 2006.

26. The first woman to do her doctoral thesis on Islamic philosophy under my direction, she spent years studying in Canada and later the United States and is now professor at the National University in Penang, Malaysia. She is also the author of a recent book on Mullā Ṣadrā.

27. He is now professor at the International Institute of Islamic Thought and Culture in Kuala Lumpur and has translated several of my books into Malay.

28. While Yaapar was primarily interested in Islamic literature, the main interest of Fatimah was in education, in which she is very active in Malaysia.

29. Under Anwar Ibrahim, he became one of the most important functionaries in the government, and with the imprisonment of Anwar, Dr. ʿAlī ʿAbd al-'Aziz also fell from grace and has since met many difficulties.

30. Ḥāfiẓ Khān wrote a very significant thesis on the metaphysics of Shāh Walī Allāh of Delhi, which has unfortunately not been published. He remained in America and now heads an Islamic school in Atlanta.

31. She continues to work on comparative mysticism and Islamic thought.

32. One of the few scholars dealing with the relation of Islam and Sikhism, she is now professor at Colby College.

33. She is a famous preacher and lecturer on Christian mysticism and did her Ph.D. thesis on mysticism under my direction.

34. Now professor of religion at La Salle.

35. Professor at the Mary Washington University, he is the author of *The Wine of Wisdom* and *Suhrawardi and the School of Illumination.*

36. He also remained in America and is now teaching at Rutgers University.

37. Sayyid Muḥammad Riḍā Ḥijāzī had studied for many years in the traditional *madrasahs* of Qom in Iran and is now an *imām* of an Islamic mosque in New York. Sayyid Ḥasan Ḥusaynī returned to Iran and is now professor at Sharif University. He is the editor of my collected essays in Persian entitled *Ma'rifat-i jāwīdān* (*Perennial Wisdom*), in three volumes.

38. Those among them who have completed their doctoral work have all become professors: Kalin at Georgetown University, Lumbard at Brandeis, Dagli at Holy Cross, al-Ansari at the University of South Carolina, and Ahmed in Nigeria.

39. For example, "The Teaching of Philosophy" and "Islamic Education and Science: A Summary Appraisal."

40. For example in *Islamic Science—An Illustrated Study* (Chicago: Kazi Publications, 1998).

41. John Dewey (d. 1952) was a famous American philosopher who exercised great influence on educational philosophy in America. His works on this subject include *Democracy and Education* and *Experience and Education.*

42. His educational philosophy is based on a pragmatism deprived of a metaphysical vision.

43. 'Allāmah Sayyid Muḥammad Ḥusayn Ṭabāṭabā'ī (d. 1983) was one of Iran's greatest philosophers and also the author of the monumental 27-volume Quranic commentary *al-Mīzān* (*The Balance*).

44. Sayyid Muḥammad Kāẓim 'Aṣṣār (d. 1975) was also an outstanding master of traditional philosophy and gnosis and author of a collection of *Rasā'il* (*Treatises*) that treat some of the most difficult issues of philosophy and gnosis.

45. Maurice DeWulf (d. 1947) was a French scholar and one of the major revivers of medieval Latin philosophy in the 20th century. His many works on this subject include *Philosophy and Civilization in the Middle Ages* and *History of Medieval Philosophy.*

46. Henry Corbin, *Avicenna and the Visionary Recital* (Putnam, CT: Spring Publications, 1980).

47. Dhū'l-Majd Ṭabāṭabā'ī was a learned lawyer and lover of Islamic philosophy and gnosis. His house and garden were meeting places of many important teachers and intellectual gatherings, including the meetings between 'Allāmah Ṭabāṭabā'ī and Corbin.

48. Ḥājjī Mullā Hādī Sabziwarī (d. 1872) was one of the major philosophers in the 19th century in Persia. His many works include the *Sharḥ-i manẓūmah*, which is a commentary by himself upon his own poem containing the principles of Islamic philosophy. It remains to this day one of the most popular texts for the teaching of Islamic philosophy in traditional circles in Persia.

49. One of the last great classical poets of the Persian language and a commentator of Ibn 'Arabī, 'Abd al-Raḥmān Jāmī (d. 1492) wrote a number of gnostic works devoted to doctrinal Sufism in beautiful Persian including the *Ash''āt al-lama'āt.*

50. 'Irāqī, also known as 'Arāqī (d. 1289), is considered one of the greatest of Persian Sufi poets. He was also associated with the circle of Ibn 'Arabī and his student Ṣadr al-Dīn Qūnawī.

51. Murtaḍā Muṭahharī (d. 1979) was assassinated in the spring of 1979 after joining the Islamic Revolution. He was a very serious intellectual and perhaps 'Allāmah Ṭabāṭabā'ī's best student in Islamic philosophy in its confrontation with modern schools of thought. Muṭahharī is considered one of the heroes of the Revolution in Iran today. The Sepahsalar Mosque and *madrasah* have been renamed after him. Some of his works have even been translated into English. See his *Understanding Islamic Sciences* (London: Saqi, 2002); and *Divine Justice*, trans. Sulaymān Ḥasan 'Ābidī (Qom: International Center for Islamic Studies, 2004).

52. 'Īsā Sipahbudī, who died shortly after the Iranian Revolution, was professor of French at the Faculty of Letters of Tehran University and also taught aesthetics in the philosophy department. He loved Islamic philosophy and was closely associated with Corbin.

53. Dariush Shayegan is today one of Iran's leading thinkers and the author of numerous books in Persian and French, including *Qu'est-ce qu'une révolution religeuse?* (Paris: Presses d'Aujourd'hui, 1982) and *Henry Corbin—La Topographie spirituelle de l'Islam iranien* (Paris: Éditions de la Différence, 1990).

54. Badī' al-Zamān Furūzānfar (d. 1970) was one of Iran's leading authorities on Rūmī whose *Grand Dīwān* he edited critically for the first time among numerous other works edited and written by him on Rūmī and other Persian literary and Sufi figures.

55. Sayyid Jalāl al-Dīn Āshtiyānī was professor of philosophy at Mashhad University and one of the most prolific philosophers and scholars of Iran. He edited numerous texts, for which I usually wrote forewords. He also composed independent philosophical works. Later he collaborated with Corbin in the monumental *Anthologie des philosophes iraniens* of which four of seven planned volumes appeared before Corbin's death in 1978.

56. The supreme masterpiece of Mullā Ṣadrā, the *Asfār al-arba'ah* (*The Four Journeys*) is considered to be the most advanced book of Islamic philosophy in Persia.

57. *Sirr-i akbar* (*The Great Secret*) is a Persian translation of a number of Upanishads by the Mogul prince and Sufi Dārī Shukūh (d. 1659).

58. This is *Tafsīr al-mīzān* in some twenty volumes, the longest Quranic commentary of the 20th century, which exists in both Arabic and Persian, and has been published many times not only in Iran but also in Beirut.

59. A well-known mosque and religious center in the north of Tehran where many of the students of various universities and professors would assemble.

60. It was published later as Chapter 14 (pp. 215–240) of my *Maʿārif-i islāmī dar jahān-i muʿāṣir* (Tehran: ʿIlmī wa Farhangī Press, 1383 (A. H. Solar)).

61. These two works, *Bidāyat al-ḥikmah* and *Nihāyat al-ḥikmah*, one for beginners and one for advanced students of Islamic philosophy, are in Arabic, and they soon became a most popular text for the teaching of Islamic philosophy. They have gone through many editions and are also translated into Persian.

62. Meaning literally, "O Master who have made the pilgrimage to Makkah"; it is a polite form of address that we used for ʿAllāmah Ṭabāṭabāʾī.

63. Meaning "O master doctor." This is how I and people like me who have a doctorate degree are usually addressed in public in Iran.

64. *Qurʾān dar islām* meaning *The Quran in Islam* and dealing simply with how the Quran is understood and studied by Muslims and how its message directs their lives.

65. *Shīʿah dar islām*, or *Shiʿism in Islam*, is probably the most authoritative work written by a Shiʿite master scholar in the 20th century on Twelve-Imam Shiʿism.

66. Kenneth Cragg was one of the major voices for advancing the cause of comparative religious studies in America in the 1960s. He founded the famous center at Colgate University for comparative religious studies and edited the well-known book *Islam: The Straight Path.*

67. As *Shiʿite Islam* (Albany: State University of New York Press, 1975).

68. ʿAllāmah Ṭabāṭabāʾī, Sayyid Muḥammd, *Qurʾān in Islam: Its Impact and Influence on the Life of Muslims* (London: Kegan Paul International, 1998).

69. ʿAllāmah Ṭabāṭabāʾī and William C. Chittick, *A Shiʿite Anthology* (London: Muhammadi Trust of Great Britain and Northern Ireland, and Albany: State University of New York Press, 1981).

70. *Uṣūl-i falsafa-yi riʾālism* (*Principles of the Philosophy of Realism*) in five volumes is perhaps Ṭabāṭabāʾī's philosophical masterpiece. It has been published numerous times in the original Persian with commentaries by M. Muṭahharī on the first three volumes.

71. Ayatollah Burūjirdī (d. 1961) was the supreme source of emulation (*marjaʿ-i taqlīd*) and leader of Twelve-Imam Shiʿism at that time and resided in Qom.

72. Taqī Irānī, an ideologue of the Tudeh Party during the rule of Reza Shah, was tried, imprisoned, and executed in 1940.

73. Jamāl al-Dīn Asadābādī, known as al-Afghānī, was a Persian "reformist" figure of the 19th century who espoused the cause of pan-Islamism and traveled widely in the Islamic world. He settled in Cairo where he taught at al-Azhar University until he was expelled from Egypt as he had been from so many other countries including Iran. His most famous work is *The Refutation of the Materialists*, written against Western materialism. He died in Istanbul in 1897.

74. Famous Egyptian student of al-Afghānī, ʿAbduh (d. 1905) was one of the first among Egyptian *ʿulamāʾ* to travel to the West. He was for a while

Shaykh al-Azhar and sought to revive rational elements in Islamic theology. His most famous works are *The Treatise on Unity* and the Quranic commentary *al-Manār*, both of which reveal his rationalistic and modernistic tendencies. He and his teacher al-Afghānī are the most influential Muslim "reformers" of the late 19th and early 20th centuries.

75. "Matters have fallen into the hands of the young." Soon thereafter, Ayatollah Qazwīnī died in Qazvin.

76. Naṣīr al-Dīn Ṭūsī (d. 1274) is considered not only as one of the major Islamic philosophers, but also as the founder of Twelve-Imam Shi'ite theology, while being one of the greatest astronomers and mathematicians in history.

77. Singular of '*ulamā*' and meaning usually a religious scholar. But it can also mean any scholar, savant, or, these days, scientist.

78. According to Twelve-Imam Shi'ism, every Shi'ite must follow the rulings of a *mujtahid* (authority in Islamic Law who has reached such a level that he can provide his own views concerning the Law). The person who is thus emulated is called *marja'-i taqlīd*, or "source of emulation." At any given time, there are only a few who hold such a rank. Sometimes there is only one, as when Ayatollah Burūjirdī was alive.

79. Mahdī Ilāhī Qumsha'ī (d. 1973) was a well-known philosopher and translator into Persian of the Quran who taught at Tehran University. He was also an accomplished poet. His most famous work in the realm of philosophy is *Ḥikmat-i ilāhī khāṣṣ wa 'āmm*, which has been published many times in Iran.

80. Jīlī (d. circa 1428) was originally Persian but lived in the Yemen. He was one of the outstanding figures of the School of Ibn 'Arabī, and the author of *al-Insān al-kāmil* (*The Universal Man*), which is one of the main texts of this School.

81. Jawād Muṣliḥ, who migrated to America after the Revolution of 1979 and died shortly thereafter, came to Tehran from Shiraz to join the Faculty of Theology of Tehran University. He was a meticulous scholar and had a keen philosophical mind.

82. This work meaning *Divine Witnesses* is one of Mullā Ṣadrā's most important works.

83. *Sharḥ al-ishārāt*, the commentary upon the *Book of Directives and Remarks* of Ibn Sīnā, remains today one of the most popular texts for the teaching of Avicenna's philosophy. This work contains the text of Ibn Sīnā, its critical commentary by Fakhr al-Dīn Rāzī, and Ṭūsī's commentary defending Ibn Sīnā's philosophy.

84. Professor of the Faculty of Law at Tehran University, Maḥmūd Shahābī was an expert on Islamic jurisprudence (*fiqh*) as well as Islamic philosophy, especially of the School of Ibn Sīnā.

85. *Sharḥ-i gulshan-i rāz* is a long commentary in Persian by the 14th-century Sufi Muḥammad Lāhījī upon the famous poem of the seventh-century Maḥmud Shabistarī known as the *Gulshan-i rāz* (*The Secret Garden of Divine Mysteries*).

86. These two works, *al-Ḥikmat al-ʿarshiyyah* (*Wisdom of the Throne*) and *Kitāb al-mashāʿir* (*The Book of Metaphysical Penetrations*) are among Mullā Ṣadrā's most important shorter philosophical treatises. For the class, I translated the *Kitāb al-mashāʿir* into English myself. The translation with my long commentary in English are now being edited by Ibrahim Kalin, who was present in those sessions. We hope to publish it soon. This is the first time that commentary on such a text is made in the traditional manner but in English. For the *Ḥikmat al-ʿarshiyyah*, we used the fine translation of James Morris, which I altered here and there and then gave my own commentary.

87. Towards the end of his life, Ibn Sīnā spoke of a philosophy that he was going to expand for the elite and which he called *al-ḥikmat al-ma(u)shriqiyyah*. Since short vowels are not usually indicated in Arabic texts, this term could be read as either *mash* . . . or *mush* . . ., meaning either "oriental" or "illuminative." There has been much debate especially in the West on the meaning of his "oriental" or "illuminative philosophy." I accept Corbin's interpretation expounded in his *Avicenna and the Visionary Recital*, but both of us have been challenged and criticized by certain Western scholars for our views on this matter.

88. It was published in 1964 by the Harvard University Press as *An Introduction to Islamic Cosmological Doctrines.*

89. Swiss master of traditional doctrines and especially sacred art and Sufism who died in 1984. His main works, written originally in German or French, include *Sacred Art in East and West*, *The Art of Islam*, *Introduction to Sufism*, *Mirror of the Intellect*, and *Bezels of Wisdom* (translation of parts of Ibn ʿArabī's *Fuṣūṣ al-ḥikam*).

90. Famous modernistic Catholic theologian and scientist who tried to combine Christian doctrines with the Darwinian theory of evolution. Among his notable works are *The Phenomenon of Man*, trans. Bernard Wall (New York: Harper & Row, 1975); and *Christianity and Evolution*, trans. René Hague (New York: Harcourt and Brace Jovanovich, 1971). He died in 1955.

91. Frithjof Schuon, *Understanding Islam* (Bloomington, IN: World Wisdom, 1998).

92. I have already identified him earlier in this book, but it needed to be added here that this incomparable expositor of *sophia perennis* was at once Sufi master, metaphysician, poet, and painter, and has left behind numerous works of the greatest depth, including *The Transcendent Unity of Religions*, *Stations of Wisdom*, and *Esoterism as Principle and as Way.*

93. Translated into English as *Creative Imagination in the Sufism of Ibn ʿArabi* (Princeton, NJ: Princeton University Press, 1977). It has been republished more recently under the title of *Alone with the Alone* (Princeton, NJ: Princeton University Press, 1997).

94. The *Uṣūl al-kāfī* (*Sufficient Principles*) is the most important collection of Shiʿite traditions (*aḥādīth*). It was assembled by Kulaynī in the fourth/10th century and remains foundational to Shiʿite thought to this day.

95. This work constituted the third volume of Suhrawardī, *Opera Metaphysica et Mystica*, the first two edited by Corbin and the third by myself. The series has been reprinted several times, the last edition by the Iranian Institute of Philosophy in Tehran in 2002.

96. Translated by Corbin as the *Theosophy of the Orient of Light* and by some others as *The Philosophy of Illumination*. This is the major opus of Suhrawardī and one of the most important works in the history of Islamic philosophy.

97. Corbin also translated the whole of the third volume into French as *L'Archange empourpré* (Paris: Fayard, 1976).

98. The *Anthologie des philosophes iraniens* (Paris: Adrien Maisonneuve, 1971). In the four volumes that did appear there are selected texts in both Arabic and Persian, with introductions and analyses by Āshtiyānī in Persian and by Corbin in French.

99. He was prime minister of Iran for some thirteen years. Just before the Iranian Revolution he was imprisoned, and later upon the success of the Revolution he was executed in 1979.

100. Toshihiko Izutsu (d. 1986) is the greatest scholar of Islamic philosophy that Japan has ever produced. At home at once in Buddhist, Taoist, Islamic, and Western philosophy, he left behind a large number of works and essays in both Japanese and English, as well as books edited in Arabic.

101. *Ziyārat* means pilgrimage to a holy site. The supreme *ziyārat* for Muslims is the one to Makkah, but *ziyārat* can include visits to the tombs of prophets and saints as well as loci of sacred events.

102. *Ta'wīl* means spiritual hermeneutics, that is, being able to go from the outward meaning to the inner reality of things, which is also their source. It applies especially to revelation as well as to God's creation in the form of the natural world that surrounds us. *Ta'wīl* is essential to both Shi'ite and Sufi thought.

103. One of the greatest Indologists of his day who was deeply influenced by A. K. Coomaraswamy, Zimmer (d. 1943) migrated from Germany to America where he taught for some years at Columbia University.

104. Horten (d. 1945) was a professor of Islamic thought and seriously interested in Islamic philosophy and theology, on which he wrote a number of important works in German.

105. The greatest French Islamicist in the field of Sufism, Massignon (d. 1962) was a major spiritual bridge between Islam and the West, and his influence is still alive. His *magnum opus*, *The Passion of al-Ḥallāj*, is a classic that is still widely read.

As for Louis Gardet, he was a notable theologian deeply steeped in the Thomistic tradition. He studied different aspects of Islam, including philosophy and theology, but perhaps his most notable works were devoted to the social aspects of Islam in relation to theological teachings, as can be seen in his classical work, *La Cité musulmane*.

106. Meaning literally "unveiling the veiled," this term is often used in both Sufism and Shi'ism.

107. These two terms mean outward and inward, or exoteric and esoteric. They are also two of the Divine Names mentioned in the Quran.

108. Quṭb al-Dīn Shīrāzī (d. 1311) was a major philosopher, astronomer, mathematician, and physician who wrote the most popular commentary on Suhrawardī's *Ḥikmat al-ishrāq*. In the field of philosophy Quṭb al-Dīn is credited with many other works including the voluminous *Durrat al-tāj*, which, in contrast to his commentary written in Arabic, was written in Persian.

109. Mahdī Ḥā'irī was a notable philosopher (d. 1999) and author of *Principles of Epistemology in Islamic Philosophy: Knowledge by Presence* (Albany: State University of New York Press, 1992).

110. *Al-'ilm al-ḥuḍūrī* means literally "presential knowledge" or "knowledge by presence."

111. Jawād Āmulī and Ḥasan-zādah Āmulī, both students of 'Allāmah Ṭabāṭabā'ī, who are now perhaps the leading teachers of Islamic philosophy in Qom.

112. These are various names for a Sufi master.

113. Mīr Dāmād (d. 1631) is the founder of the School of Isfahan, teacher of Mullā Ṣadrā, and author of numerous philosophical works, chief among them the *Qabasāt*.

114. Raymond Klibansky (d. 2005) was a major Canadian philosopher with numerous works on Renaissance and modern philosophers.

115. 'Abd Allāh Intiẓām (d. 1983) was a statesman and former foreign minister of Iran, but he was also deeply interested in philosophy and personally immersed in Sufism.

116. Mahdī Muḥaqqiq, former professor and vice-dean of our Faculty of Letters, is a major scholar who has published numerous philosophical as well as literary works. His philosophical writings include *Fīlsūf-i rayy* (*The Philosopher of Rayy*), in reference to Muḥammad ibn Zakariyyā' Rāzī, the famous ninth-century Persian physician and philosopher.

117. One of Iran's leading literary figures and former professor and chairman of the Arabic department at our Faculty of Letters. He is known for many works, but especially his masterly translation of the *Nahj al-balāghah* of 'Alī ibn Abī Ṭālib into Persian. He was also for many years the chief editor of the *Dehkhoda Encyclopedia*.

118. A well-known physician, Luqmān al-Mulk (d. 1973) was also minister in several cabinets and senator.

119. One of the leading American authorities on Islamic philosophy and Sufism, he is now professor at Boston College. He is a translator and commentator of works of both Ibn 'Arabī and Mullā Ṣadrā.

120. *Ṭullāb* means students, but refers usually more specifically to religious students.

121. In the sense of traditional Islamic school.

122. Toshihiko Izutsu, *Towards a Philosophy of Zen Buddhism* (Boulder, CO: Shambhala, 2001).

123. This journal was published from 1973 to 1978.

124. The foremost woman poet of England in recent times, Kathleen Raine (d. 2004) was a specialist in Blake, about whom she wrote extensively. She founded the Temenos Academy, of which I am a fellow, and sought to revive the importance of creative imagination in the literary circles of England.

125. One of the major poets of the Romantic movement, Blake (d. 1827) was a severe critic of the Newtonian worldview based on the mechanization of nature, and besides much inspired poetry based on many traditional themes, wrote poetic criticisms against materialistic philosophies.

126. Meaning centers of traditional religious education and modernized universities.

127. This was a royal university under the patronage of the Shah. It was established in the 1960s and soon became Iran's foremost scientific university. After the Revolution of 1979, its name was changed to Sharif University and it remains to this day Iran's leading scientific university.

128. 'Alī Naqī 'Ālīkhānī was minister of economy for many years before becoming president of Tehran University. As for Hūshang Nahāwandī, he had been minister and then president of Pahlavi University before becoming president of Tehran University.

129. See for example my "Islam, Muslims, and Modern Technology" In *Islam and Science*, vol. 3, Winter 2005, No. 2, pp. 109–126; also *Islam, Science, Muslims and Technology: S. H. Nasr in Conversation with Muzaffar Iqbal* (Kuala Lumpur: al-Qalam, 2007).

130. A fine mathematician who had studied in America, Mahdī Zarghāmī became a professor at Aryamehr University and as vice-chancellor played a major role in the building of the Isfahan campus. He succeeded me as the president of the university.

131. This was a political organization founded in Iran in the late sixties based on the ideology of combining certain tenets of Marxism and Islam. It participated in violence and assassinations and played an important role in the 1979 Revolution in Iran, after which it was defeated and destroyed within the country. It is still classified as a terrorist organization in most of the West.

132. Known usually by its acronym SAVAK, *Sāzimān-i amniyyat* was the secret security and police arm of the government.

133. *Kāshī* means "from the city of Kashan," whose population is the subject of jokes by other Persians for being excessively afraid and lacking courage.

134. Originally the word *darwīshī* meant humility and indifference to the joys and sorrows of the world and was identified with Sufism, but gradually it gained also a negative connotation. It came to mean laziness, lackadaisicalness, unruliness, lack of discipline, passivity, et cetera.

135. 'Alī Amīnī, the grandson of a Qajar king, was one of Iran's major political figures during the reign of Mohammad Reza Shah. Amīnī became prime minister in 1961, and after the Iranian Revolution went into exile in Paris where he died in 1992.
136. Ḥasan 'Alī Manṣūr became prime minister in 1964 and was assassinated in 1965.
137. *Inqilāb-i Farhangī*, meaning literally "cultural/educational revolution," was promulgated in 1968 by the Shah to revamp Iran's educational system, especially higher education.
138. A colloquial expression meaning literally "having one's place in paradise" but meaning metaphorically adopting a haughty attitude and looking with disdain upon those who enter the arena of action in the world, especially politics.
139. The *zūrkhānah* or "house of strength" is a place where traditional physical exercises take place in an atmosphere combined with chivalry. The action takes place in a circular pit whose ground is considered sacred. Spectators sit outside the circular pit and watch the exercises, which are combined with music and poetry. One of the activities is traditional wrestling. The spectators often address their favorite wrestler and say "*lingish kun*," that is, "pin him." The expression has come to mean not accepting responsibility for anything oneself, but ordering others to do this or that.
140. Zāyandah Rūd is the name of the river that runs through the middle of Isfahan and is the source of water for the city and the agricultural fields around it.
141. "What is your view about these commotions that are going on?"
142. "What is being done is below the dignity of a religious scholar."

Part Four

1. David Gardner, who later became president of the whole University of California system, had been my guest in Iran and knew me well. He was also a great supporter of Islamic studies.

2. One of the pioneers of Middle Eastern studies in the United States, Khosrow Mostofi (d. 1992) had developed the University of Utah Center for Middle Eastern Studies from its beginning. Being a Persian, he had traveled to Iran often and we knew each other well since I had also lectured and taught at the University of Utah before the 1979 Revolution.

3. Under the editorship of Ewert Cousins, this vast encyclopedia had been published in New York by Crossroad since the 1980s.

4. Seyyed Hossein Nasr (ed.), *The Essential Writings of Frithjof Schuon*, published originally by Element Books, 1991, and later as *The Essential Frithjof Schuon* (Bloomington, IN: World Wisdom, 2005).

5. Published as *Knowledge and the Sacred* (Albany: State University of New York Press, 1989).

6. Appeared as *Religion and the Order of Nature* (New York: Oxford University Press, 1996).

7. Seyyed Hossein Nasr and Mehdi Aminrazavi (eds.), *An Anthology of Philosophy in Persia (Vol. 1)* (New York: Oxford University Press, 1999; new edition, London: I. B. Taurus, 2007–).

8. Famous scholar of Iranian history and a world-renowned authority on Safavid history, he is an old friend and colleague.

9. *Ideals and Realities of Islam* (Chicago: ABC International, 1999).

10. A local Persian cheese.

11. Grace or sacred presence.

12. Roloff Beny with text by S. H. Nasr, *Persia, Bridge of Turquoise* (Norwalk, CT: New York Graphic Society, 1975). I have dealt with this issue elsewhere, as in *Sacred Art in Persian Culture* (Ipswich, U.K.: Golgonooza Press, 1976); and *Iran* (Tehran: Offset Press, 1973).

13. The *Shahnāmah* ("Book of Kings") by Firdawsī is the national Iranian epic.

14. *Insān-i kāmil* means Perfect or Universal Man, a being according to Sufism who has realized all the possibilities, both vertical and horizontal, of the human state.

15. A demonic figure mentioned in the *Shāh-nāmah* of Firdawsī on each of whose shoulders grew a snake.

16. This figure named Kāwah, who was a blacksmith, hence Āhangar, is a great Iranian hero who, in the *Shāh-nāmah*, was able to overcome Zahhāk.

17. This is another common Persian word for sorrow or sadness. In most situations *ḥuzn* and *ghamm* have the same meaning.

18. *Dastgāh-i shūr* is one of the modes in classical Persian music. This mode is especially notable for its *ḥuzn*.

19. This work, written in Persian, which can be translated as *Treatise on the Reality of Love*, is one of the masterpieces of the 12th-century Illuminationist philosopher Shihāb al-Dīn Suhrawardī. See S. H. Nasr (ed.), *Suhrawardī, Opera Metaphysica et Mystica*, vol. III (Tehran: Institut d'Etudes et des Recherches Culturelles, 2001), pp. 268–291. It has been translated with commentary by H. Corbin in his *L'Archange empoupré* (Paris: Faynard, 1976), pp. 289–337.

20. *The Story of the Occidental Exile* is also a very important "visionary recital" (to use the terminology of Corbin) by Suhrawardī. See Corbin (ed.), *Suhrawardī, Opera Metaphysica et Mystica*, vol. II, pp. 274–297; and Corbin, *L'Archange empoupré*, pp. 265–287.

21. When the second Umayyad caliph, Yazīd, came to power, Imam Ḥusayn, the grandson of the Prophet and the third Shi'ite Imam, refused to pay allegiance to him. The people of Kufa in Iraq promised him support and so he set out with his family and a number of companions from Madinah across the desert towards Iraq. He was met by the army of Yazīd in a place south of Kufa known as Karbalā'. Far outnumbered, he, his family, and companions fought valiantly, and he along with all adult males, save his son who was ill, were martyred in 680. The day of his martyrdom on the 10th of Muḥarram, the first

month of the Islamic lunar calendar, still marks the peak of the religious calendar for Shi'ites in Persia, Iraq, Lebanon, Pakistan, and elsewhere, and is still comemorated even in Hindu India and a land as far away as Trinidad.

22. The word *'īd*, also written as *eid* in English, refers to any celebration that is designated usually in the calendar. The most important *'īds* for Persians are the Norouz (New Year), *Fiṭr* (the end of Ramadan), *Aḍḥā* (the end of the pilgrimage to Makkah), the birthday of the Prophet, *Ghadīr* (according to Shi'ite belief, the day of the investiture of 'Alī by the Prophet to become Imam), and the birthdays of various Imams and Fāṭimah, the daughter of the Prophet. In modern times, *'īds* have been added in relation to various political events or births of important political personages.

23. Literally "table cloth," *sufrah* involves laying out a table full of food. Prayers are performed and most of the food is given to the poor.

24. *Rawḍahkhānī*, which developed especially from the Safavid period onward, involves the gathering of many people in mourning listening to a preacher who usually recounts in the most sorrowful language the tragedy of Karbalā'.

25. *Ta'ziyah*, or passion play, is the most elaborate form of theatre in the Islamic world and has been compared to the medieval passion plays in the West. The drama of Karbalā' and other dramatic religious events are enacted on a stage accompanied by poetry and music.

26. *Nawrūz* means literally "new day," and marks the beginning of the new year on the first day of spring. It is based on the solar calendar and is widely celebrated by Iranians, Afghans, Kurds, Azerbaijanis, and the people of Central Asia.

27. Dānishkada-yi Hunarhā-yi Zībā is the name of the Faculty of Fine Arts (at Tehran University).

28. *Khānqāhs*, called *zawāyā* in Arabic, are Sufi centers where followers of a particular Sufi order assemble regularly to perform their sacred rites.

29. The foremost Egyptian architect (d. 1989) who sought to revive traditional architecture using simple, local material and who wrote the influential work *Building for the Poor.*

30. In Iran, *ḥusayniyyahs* and *takkiyahs* refer to places where Shi'ite preachers usually speak about the tragedy of Karbalā' and where other religious gatherings take place. In Turkey the word *tekke* is used for a Sufi center.

31. The thirteenth day of the Persian new year (*sīzdah bidar*) when Iranians leave the city and spend the day in the countryside where the signs of spring and the rejuvenation of life have already appeared.

32. The *Gulistān* (*The Rose Garden*) by Muṣliḥ al-Dīn Sa'dī (d. 1292), which is one of the greatest masterpieces of Persian literature, read and partly memorized by every student in Iran.

33. Shaykh Maḥmūd Shabistarī (d. 1320) is the author of *Gulshan-i rāz* (*The Secret Garden of Divine Mysteries*), one of the most sublime among Sufi poetic works.

34. *The Būstān*, the other great masterpiece of Sa'dī, can also be translated as *The Garden.*

35. Manṣūr al-Ḥallāj (d. 922) was one of the greatest of the early Sufis, who was put to death under tragic circumstances. Ibn 'Arabī (d. 1240), the supreme master of doctrinal Sufism, was also one of the greatest of the Arab Sufi poets. He has thousands of verses of poetry scattered in his prose works. In addition, he is the author of *Tarjumān al-ashwāq*, (*Interpreter of Desires*), which is a poetic masterpiece as well as a *Dīwān*. 'Umar ibn al- Fāriḍ (d. 1235), the Cairene poet whom many consider as the greatest Arab Sufi poet, composed many remarkable poems of which perhaps *The Wine Song* (*al-Khamriyyah*) and *al-Tā'iyyah* are the most famous. Shaykh al-'Alawī (d. 1934) wrote may beautiful poems, which are among the most profound Sufi poems of the modern era.

36. Seyyed Hossein Nasr, *Poems of the Way* (Oakton, VA: Foundation for Traditional Studies, 1998). Translated by Luce López-Baralt as *Poemas de la vía mística* (Madrid: Madala, 2002). See also the second volume of my poetry, *The Pilgrimage of Life* (Oakton, VA: Foundation for Traditional Studies, 2006).

37. Kathleen Raine, *Blake and Tradition* (two volumes) (London: Routledge, 2001).

38. The German Islamicist and poet Annemarie Schimmel (d. 2003) translated a great deal of Rūmī into German and also wrote important works on him in English such as *The Triumphal Sun* (Albany: State University of New York Press, 1993). She was the leading scholar of Rūmī in the West in her day.

39. William C. Chittick (trans.), *The Sufi Path of Love: The Spiritual Teachings of Rūmī* (Albany: State University of New York Press, 1983).

40. Seyyed Hossein Nasr, *Rumi—the Lament of the Reed* (Asr Media, 2001).

41. This Japanese term means sudden illumination and enlightenment that spiritual practitioners of Zen try to achieve.

42. Thomas Merton (d. 1968), who was a very well-known Catholic contemplative, became seriously interested in Sufism toward the end of his life. This aspect of his life is recorded in R. Baker, G. Henry, and W. Chittick (eds.), *Merton and Sufism: The Untold Story* (Louisville, KY: Fons Vitae, 1999).

43. *Majālis* is the plural of *majlis*, which means "gathering" in general, but in Sufism it refers specifically to the Sufi gathering that is usually held at the Sufi center (*khānqāh* in Persian and *zāwiyah* in Arabic) of a particular Sufi order.

44. See S. H. Nasr (ed.), *Islamic Spirituality* (two volumes) (New York: Crossroad Publications, 1989–1991).

45. A planned twenty-seven-volume work edited by Ewert Cousins that began to appear in the 1980s, published in New York by Crossroads Publications, but the project has never been completed.

Part Five

1. *Rūḥaniyyah* obviously comes from the Arabic word *rūḥ*, meaning spirit, whereas *ma'nawiyyat* used in Persia comes from another Arabic word, *ma'nā*, that is, "meaning," but in this case implying inner meaning and essence, in contrast to external form.

2. The word *barakah* in Arabic and *barakat* in Persian is difficult to translate into English. The best translation is "grace," but in the Islamic view this grace

is not opposed to nature, as it is in much of Christian theology, but flows in the arteries of the universe.

3. *Ṣūrat* used in this context, especially by Rūmī, means external features or form, not to be confused with the Aristotelian *morphos*, or form, that is also used by Islamic philosophers.

4. *Ṭarīqah* in Arabic means "path," but it is identified more specifically with the spiritual path to God and is associated mostly with Sufism. A Sufi order is in fact called *ṭarīqah* in Arabic.

5. Śri Aurobindo (d. 1950) was a renowned Hindu thinker of the early 20th century who sought to interpret religion in an evolutionary manner.

6. Jamāl al-Dīn Asadābādī, known also as al-Afghānī (d. 1897), was of Persian origin but traveled widely in the Islamic world seeking to start a pan-Islamist movement against Western domination, while at the same time being influenced by many Western ideas.

7. A student of Afghānī, Muḥammad 'Abduh (d. 1920) was an Egyptian theologian and professor of al-Azhar University who tried to develop a more rationalistic theology and was deeply influenced by many tenets of modernism.

8. 'Alī Sharī'atī (d. 1978) was an Iranian sociologist who sought to present an "Islamic ideology" to revive society. He wielded much influence during the 1979 Islamic Revolution in Iran and its immediate aftermath.

9. The *Sīmurgh*, or griffin, is a mythical bird residing at the top of the cosmic mountain Qāf. The *Sīmurgh* symbolizes the Divine Intellect, and in some literary works such as 'Aṭṭār's *Manṭiq al-ṭayr* ("The Conference of the Birds") the Divine Self or the Divine Essence Itself.

10. For a definition of *tradition* as used here, see my *Knowledge and the Sacred.*

11. I have mentioned this in my works on Mullā Ṣadrā.

12. By positing trans-substantial motion (*al-ḥarakat al-jawhariyyah*) as the matrix for time rather than planetary motion, he freed his "transcending philosophy" from reliance upon Ptolemaic and Aristotelian astronomy.

13. Ḥājjī Mullā Hādī Sabziwārī (d. 1878), the author of *Sharḥ al-manẓūmah* ("Commentary upon the [poem] *manẓūmah*") was one of the most famous Persian philosophers of the 19th century.

14. Āqā 'Alī Mudarris (d. 1889) was the author of *Badāyi' al-ḥikam* ("Marvels of Wisdom") among many other works and is also one of the major Islamic philosophers of the 19th century in Persia.

15. See among many other of his works *Introduction to the Study of Hindu Doctrines*, trans. Marco Pallis (Ghent, NY: Sophia Perennis, 2001); and *Spiritual Authority and Temporal Power* (Ghent, NY: Sophia Perennis, 2004).

16. *Khalīfah* (caliph) means literally "vice-gerent." In the Quran, human beings themselves are called God's *khalīfah* on earth, but also there developed the political institution of the caliphate after the death of the Prophet, an institution that was both political and religious.

17. *Mabādi' ārā' ahl al-madīnat al-fāḍilah* ("Principles of the Views of the People of the Virtuous City") is the most famous work of Islamic political philosophy written by a follower of the school of *falsafah* (philosophy in its

specific Islamic sense). Although it uses the term *city* in its title, following Plato, its political point of reference experientially is the vast *dār al-islām* or "abode of Islam."

18. Al-Māwardī (d. 1058) was a major theologian in the field of political thought, his most famous work in this domain being *al-Aḥkām al-sulṭāniyyah* ("The Ordinances of Government").

19. Abū'l -Ḥasan al-'Āmirī (d. 992) is the author of several important works on Islamic Peripatetic (*mashshā'ī*) philosophy. His most important work concerned with political philosophy is *al-I'lām bi manāqib al-islām* ("An Exposition on the Merits of Islam").

20. See, for example, my *Religion and the Order of Nature, Man and Nature* and *The Need for a Sacred Science.*

21. Seyyed Hossein Nasr, *Man and Nature: The Spiritual Crisis in Modern Man* (Chicago: Kazi Publications, 1997).

22. See, for example, my *Knowledge and the Sacred* and (ed.) *In Quest of the Sacred.*

23. The root *qds* in Arabic is related to the idea of sacredness, and several Persian words derived from that root are prevalent in that language, for example *qidāsat*, meaning "sacredness," and *quddūs* (which is also a Name of God), meaning "sacred," and also *qudsī*, meaning likewise "sacred."

24. This term *amr-i qudsī* means something that is sacred and has been used by many Persian translators of my works. The present book has in fact been translated into Persian as *Dar justijū-yi amr-i qudsī.*

25. For example, in *Knowledge and the Sacred*, and more recently in Nasr, *Islamic Philosophy from Its Origin to the Present* (Albany: State University of New York Press, 2006).

Part Six

1. See Nasr, *Islam and the Plight of Modern Man*, *Traditional Islam in the Modern World* and *A Young Muslim's Guide to the Modern World.*

2. René Guénon, *The Crisis of the Modern World,* trans. M. Pallis et al. (Ghent, NY: Sophia Perennis, 2004).

3. René Guénon, *The Reign of Quantity and the Signs of the Times,* trans. Lord Northbourn (Ghent, NY: Sophia Perennis, 2004).

4. See Schuon, *Logic and Transcendence*, trans. P. Townsend (New York: Harper Torchbooks, 1975).

5. See Lindbom, *The Tares and the Good Grain*, trans. A. Moore (Macon, GA: Mercer University Press, 1983).

6. M. M. Sharif, *History of Muslim Philosophy: With Short Accounts of Other Disciplines and the Modern Renaissance in Muslim Lands* (2 volumes) (Wiesbanden: O. Harrassowitz, 1963–1966).

7. Henry Corbin, *The History of Islamic Philosophy* (London: Kegan Paul, 2001).

8. Seyyed Hossein Nasr and Oliver Leaman (eds.), *History of Islamic Philosophy* (London: Routledge, 2001).

9. There are no separate works of S. H. Nasr on this subject, but there are many references to it in several of his works as far as religious and spiritual diversity, which are the basis of cultural diversity, are concerned. See for example, Nasr, "The One in the Many," *Parabola*, Spring 1994, pp. 12–19; and *The Heart of Islam*, (New York: HarperCollins, 2002) ch. 1, pp. 3 ff.

10. Quran, V: 48.

11. See Nasr, *Islam and the Plight of Modern Man* (Cambridge: Islamic Texts Society, 2003); and *Islam and the West* (New York: Recorded Books, 2004).

12. Yuḥannā al-Dimashqī in Arabic, who died between 754 and 787, wrote *The Fountain of Wisdom* in whose second part he criticized severely what he considered to be heretical in the Quran and the life of the Prophet.

13. One of the most important Christian authorities of the 12th century, he died in Cluny in France in 1156.

14. Francesco Petrarch (d. 1374), who was a Franciscan, was one of the major literary figures at the end of the Middle Ages and beginning of the Renaissance. His influence on the Renaissance was extensive, and his hatred of matters Arabic and Islamic became widespread.

15. I have already identified these figures earlier.

16. This mysterious "meeting" took place when Massignon was imprisoned in Iraq. Ḥallāj, the great 11th/fifth century Sufi saint, played a major role in Massignon's life to the very end.

Part Seven

1. See S. H. Nasr, *Islamic Art and Spirituality* (Albany: State University of New York Press, 1987); and two volumes of poetry: *Poems of the Way* (Oakton, VA: Foundation for Traditional Studies, 1999); and *The Pilgrimage of Life and the Wisdom of Rumi* (Oakton, VA: Foundation for Traditional Studies, 2007).

2. Benedetto Croce (d. 1952) was a famous Italian philosopher known particularly for his works on the philosophy of art, especially *Estetica come scienza dell'espressione e linguistica generale: teoria e storia* (*Aesthetics as Science of Expression and General Linguistics*). English translation by Douglas Ainslie (London: Transaction Publishers, 1995).

3. Kamāl al-Dīn Bihzād (d. circa 1536) is considered by many to be the greatest of all Persian painters.

4. The leading master of the School of Isfahan, Āqā Riḍā 'Abbāsī died in 1635.

5. Hans Sedlmayr (d. 1984) was one of the most profound historians of Western art. His works that pertain to this discussion include, besides *Kunst und Wahrheit*, *Verlust der Mitte* (*Loss of the Center*), which pertains to the loss of spiritual center in nineteenth- and 20th-century Western art.

6. El Greco (d. 1614), who was named originally Domenico Theotokopoulos and of Greek origin, was one of the most famous Spanish painters. He was inspired by the Christian art of the icon, but did not remain faithful to the traditional principles of iconic painting.

7. A shaykh of the Suhrawardiyyah Order and a follower of the teachings of the School of Ibn ʿArabī, Awḥad al-Dīn Kirmānī (d. 1238) became well known for poems dealing with the significance of the beauty of forms in the spiritual life.

8. "Religious Art, Traditional Art, Sacred Art: Some Reflections and Definitions," in *The Essential Sophia*, ed. S. H. Nasr and K. O'Brien (Bloomington, IN: World Wisdom, 2006) pp. 175–185.

9. Titus Burckhardt, *Sacred Art in East and West: Its Principles and Methods*, Lord Northbourne (trans.) (Louisville, KY: Fons Vitae, 2002).

10. Mircea Eliade, *Images and Symbols*, trans. Philip Mairet (Princeton, NJ: Princeton University Press, 1991).

11. René Guénon, *Fundamental Symbols—the Universal Language of Sacred Science*, trans. Alvin Moore, ed. Martin Lings (Cambridge: Quinta Essentia, 1995).

12. Georges Rouault (d. 1958) began as a stained glass designer and later turned to painting. His religious paintings are among the most important in 20th-century European art.

13. The *mirʿāj*, mentioned in the Quran and *ḥadīth*, is the Nocturnal Ascent of the Prophet from Jerusalem where the Dome of the Rock is located through all the higher levels of existence to the Divine Presence.

14. Mircea Eliade, *The Sacred and the Profane: the Nature of Religion*, trans. W. Trask, (New York: Harcourt Brace, 1959).

15. The Vienna Circle (*Wiener Kreis*) refers to a number of philosophers who assembled around Moritz Schlick (d. 1936). Members of this circle were opposed to metaphysics, considered experience as the only source of authentic knowledge, and sought to solve philosophical problems with the help of symbolic logic. The only major exception was Kurt Gödel (d. 1978).

16. The city of Ise, located in the Mei Prefecture in Japan, is home to the most sacred temple of Shintoism and a major site of pilgrimage. The city has come to be known as "The Holy City" (capital of the Kami) because of the presence of the temple.

17. Ruskin (d. 1900) was one of England's major art critics with views on the preservation of the traditional arts that were highly influential in Victorian and Edwardian England. He also had a deep influence on Coomaraswamy.

18. The Persian translation of this work, *Hunar wa maʿnawiyyat-i islāmī,* trans. R. Qasimiyān, has become like a bible for many art students in Iran today.

19. *Ḥaqīqah* here means the truth or inner reality of the Quran.

20. *Nastaʿlīq* is a style of calligraphy characterized by rounded forms was developed in Persia and has remained especially popular to this day in Persia itself as well as Afghanistan, Pakistan, and Muslim India.

Part Eight

1. On Sufism see S. H. Nasr, *The Garden of Truth—The Promise and Vision of Sufism, Islam's Mystical Tradition* (San Francisco: Harper One, 2007); and S. H. Nasr, *Sufi Essays* (Chicago: ABC International, 1999); S. H. Nasr (ed.), *Islamic Spirituality* (2 vols.) (London: Routledge, 2007). See also Titus Burckhardt, *Introduction to Sufism* (Bloomington, IN: World Wisdom, 2008).

2. Martin Lings, *What Is Sufism?* (Cambridge: Islamic Texts Society, 1999).

3. This is in reference to the Islamic testimony of faith, *lā ilāha illa'Llāh*, "there is no god but God."

4. 'Alī ibn 'Uthmān Hujwīrī (d. circa 1071), also known as Dādājī Ganjbakhsh, who is buried in Lahore, is the patron saint of the Punjab and the author of the first manual of Sufism in Persian titled *Kashf al-mahjūb*.

5. Abū'l-Ḥasan 'Alī Kharaqānī (d. 1034) was one of the foremost Sufis of Khorasan in the 10th century.

6. Imam Abū'l-Qāsim Qushayrī (d. 1074), at once religious scholar, scientist and Sufi master, is another major authority on Sufism from Khorasan. His *al-Risālat al-qushayriyyah*, written in Arabic, is still widely read.

7. Founded by Shah Ni'mat Allāh Walī (d. 1431), with its center in Mahan near Kerman, the Ni'matullāhī Order is the most popular Sufi order in Iran today.

8. Sayyid Mahdī ibn Ḥasan ibn Muḥammad, known as Baḥr al-'ulūm (d. 1797) was one of the major Shi'ite *'ulamā'* and authorities in Islamic Law of his day, and was also a Sufi of a high order.

9. With its center in Shiraz, the Dhahabiyyah Order has centers all over Persia and traces its lineage to the Kubrawiyyah Order and ultimately to Imam 'Alī al-Riḍā (d. 817), the eighth Shi'ite Imam.

10. The Khāksār order is more popular, and most of its followers are from the class of craftsmen, manual workers, farmers, and the like.

11. Āqā Muḥammad Riḍā Qumsha'ī (d. 1888) was called the Ibn 'Arabī of his day, in reference to his mastery of the gnostic teachings of Muḥyī al-Dīn ibn 'Arabī (d. 1240), the supreme authority on *'irfān* who hailed from Andalusia and who died in Damascus. Āqā Muḥammad Riḍā was also very well versed in the transcendent theosophy (*al-ḥikmat al-muta'āliyah*) of Mullā Ṣadrā (d. 1640) and was a contemporary of the most famous Qajar philosopher Ḥājjī Mullā Hādī Sabziwārī (d. 1878).

12. Mīrzā Mahdī Āshtiyānī (d. 1952) was one of the leading teachers of *'irfān* and spiritual ethics of his day in Tehran.

13. At once a teacher in one of Tehran's leading *madrasahs* and professor of Islamic philosophy at Tehran University, Sayyid Muḥammad Kāẓim 'Aṣṣār (d. 1975) also taught Sufism as well as participated on the level of practice in its reality.

14. In Sufism *walāyah/wilāyah* refers to the power of initiation and spiritual guidance that emanated from the Prophet and has been and still is transmitted

through the initiatic chain in various Sufi orders going back in nearly all cases to 'Alī who was the major recipient of this power from the Prophet.

15. The Sanūsiyyah Order was established and spread in the 18th and 19th centuries in North Africa and became a major political force to the extent that with the independence of Libya, the head of the Order became the king of that land.

16. One of the greatest figures of Sufism and masters of the School of Ibn 'Arabī, 'Abd al-Qādir al-Jazā'irī led a long battle against French colonialism until he was captured and exiled to Damascus where he died in 1883 and was buried next to Ibn 'Arabī. Upon the independence of Algeria from French rule, his remains were brought back to Algiers and buried with the greatest honor as remains of the foremost hero of that country.

17. Najm al-Dīn Kubrā (d. 1221) not only founded the Kubrawiyyah Order, but also wrote a number of works such as *Fawā'iḥ al-jamāl wa fawātiḥ al-jalāl*, which are among the most important classical texts of Sufism.

18. Najm al-Dīn Rāzī (died 1256 or 1257) is best known for his Persian masterpiece *Mirṣād al-'ibād* that remains popular to this day and even influenced the intellectual life of Chinese Muslims after its translation into classical Chinese and the language of Neo-Confucianism in the 17th century.

19. The word *salafī* comes from *salaf*, which means those who came before, or ancestors. It became the name of a movement that spread in certain quarters of the Islamic world from the 19th century onward and continues today and that is based on a literalist interpretation of the teachings of Islam and opposition to Sufism.

20. A Persian who went to Arabia, met the Prophet, embraced Islam, and became considered as a member of the "Household of the Prophet" (*ahl al-bayt*), Salmān al-Fārsī joined 'Alī in Iraq where he died in battle in 656 and where he is buried.

21. Ḥasan al-Baṣrī (d. 728) was a student of 'Alī and one of the greatest patriarchs of early Sufism.

22. See S. H. Nasr, *Sufi Essays; Knowledge and the Sacred*; and "Living in a Multi-Religious World," in W. Chittick (ed.), *The Essential Seyyed Hossein Nasr* (Bloomington, IN: World Wisdom, 2007) pp. 3–20.

23. Abū Rayḥān Bīrūnī (d. circa 1051) is the author of the unique work *Taḥqīq mā li'l-hind* (*India*), which many consider as the first scholarly and scientific book in human history on comparative religion.

24. Śri Ramakrishna (d. 1886) was one of the greatest Hindu saints of modern times and spoke openly of the inner unity of religions. After him, a movement to spread Hindu teachings began in Bengal, from which he hailed, and spread all over the world.

25. The French author Romain Rolland (d. 1944) popularized Hinduism through his widely read works such as *The Life of Vivekananda and the Universal Gospel* and *The Life of Ramakrishna*.

26. The most famous disciple of Ramakrishna, Vivekananda (d. 1902) was responsible more than any other figure for spreading the teachings of the Vedanta in the West, albeit with a modernist slant.

27. One of the greatest of Christian mystics, Meister Eckhart (d. 1328), who was German, wrote in not only Latin but also in German, his sermons being among the earliest examples of German prose.

28. While Saint Thomas was a Dominican, Saint Bonaventure (d. 1274) was Franciscan and formulated a more Platonic and Augustinian version of Christian theology.

29. An Italian saint, widely admired in Italy, who died in 1968.

30. A Catholic missionary, Foucauld (d. 1916) lived among North African Muslims as a presence of Christian teachings and not necessarily to convert them. He displayed great respect for Islam and was reciprocally respected and admired by Muslims.

31. Known for well-known books on the Prophet and the Islamic tradition, Dermenghem (d. 1971) was one of the European scholars most sympathetic towards Islam.

32. Monteil (d. 2005) was a notable scholar and one of the most visible French intellectual figures who had openly espoused Islam.

33. Suzuki (d. 1966) was the most important exponent of Japanese Buddhism, especially Zen, in the West.

34. Alan Watts (d. 1973) became one of the most famous expositors of Oriental teachings, especially Zen, in the United States.

35. Originally English, Heard (d. 1971) moved to America where he became a popular expositor of the Vedanta.

36. The famous English novelist Huxley (d. 1963) also moved to America and was at the forefront of the wave of interest in Oriental spirituality, the perennial philosophy (as understood by him), and even drug-induced mysticism.

37. Idrīs Shah (d. 1996), although of Afghan origin, presented himself as a kind of Oriental guru who, instead of teaching a dismembered version of Hinduism, sought to propagate Sufism as a spiritual path, but without the framework of Islam. For a while he gained many disciples in America, Europe, and even Australia. What was positive about his works was that they drew the attention of many to serious Sufism.

38. *Zen Catholicism* by Graham (d. 1984) was one of the first works by a Catholic to seek to integrate certain teachings and practices of Zen into Catholicism.

39. Bede Griffith (d. 1993) attracted many Christians who wanted to remain Christian but who were also deeply interested in Hindu spirituality. He represents one of the many Europeans such as Père Le Saux who settled in India to live a Hindu-like Christian life.

40. A monk of the Abbey of Gethsemani in Kentucky, Merton (d. 1968) became the central figure in Catholic circles for an opening towards the great spiritual traditions of the East, many of which he studied in depth.

41. Mīr Findiriskī (d. 1640) was one of the central philosophical figures of the School of Isfahan, which came into being during the Safavid period, but he also traveled to India.

42. The remarkable linguist Anquétil-Duperron (d. 1805) presented his translation of the Upanishads from Persian to Latin to Napoleon. This translation is at the origin of Western interest in the Upanishads and was read by many people including possibly William Blake.

43. A famous family of administrators and ministers at the court of the Abbasid caliphs.

44. President of Iran from 1997–2005, Muḥammad Khātamī proposed that the dialogue of civilizations be made a central concern of all nations as well as the U.N. and especially UNESCO.

Part Nine

1. See S. H. Nasr, *Ideals and Realities of Islam* (Chicago: ABC International, 2000); and S. H. Nasr, *The Heart of Islam* (San Francisco: Harper One, 2002).

Index

Note: The names of those Persians and others from the Islamic world who are contemporary and have used their names in Latin letters in various ways have been kept in their common form, while in the index all Persian and Arabic names and terms have been translated according to the norms of Western scholarship.

About the Author

Seyyed Hossein Nasr, Ph.D., is a university professor of Islamic studies at The George Washington University, Washington, D.C. Dr. Nasr was born in Tehran, Iran, where he received his earliest education. He earned his B.S. at the Massachusetts Institute of Technology in physics and M.S. and Ph.D. degrees from Harvard University in the history of science and philosophy. For 20 years, he was a professor at Tehran University, where he was also dean and vice chancellor for several years. Dr. Nasr was president of Aryamehr University in Iran and founder and first president of the Iranian Academy of Philosophy. He has taught at Harvard University, The American University of Beirut, the University of Utah, and Temple University. A volume of the *Library of Living Philosophers* series has been devoted to his thought, and he is a Gifford lecturer. Dr. Nasr is the author or editor of some 50 books and hundreds of articles, many translated into several languages.